D1596374

A Virtue for Courageous Minds

A Virtue for Courageous Minds

Moderation in French Political Thought, 1748–1830

AURELIAN CRAIUTU

PRINCETON UNIVERSITY PRESS

PRINCETON AND OXFORD

Jacket art: Simon Vouet (1590–1649). *Allegory of Peace*, ca. 1640. Photo credit:
© Erich Lessing / Art Resource, NY.

Library of Congress Cataloging-in-Publication Data

Craiutu, Aurelian.
   A virtue for courageous minds : moderation in French political thought, 1748-
1830 / Aurelian Craiutu.
   p. cm.
   Includes index.
   ISBN 978-0-691-14676-8 (cloth : alk. paper)   1. Political science—France—
History—18th century.   2. Political science—France—History—19th century.
3. Moderation—Political aspects—France—History.   4. France—Politics and
government—Philosophy—History.   I. Title.
   JA84.F8C72 2012
   320.0944'09034—dc23   2011040355

British Library Cataloging-in-Publication Data is available
This book has been composed in Sabon LT Std
Printed on acid-free paper ∞
Printed in the United States of America
10 9 8 7 6 5 4 3 2 1

Il ne faut pas toujours tellement épuiser un sujet, qu'on ne laisse rien à faire au lecteur. Il ne s'agit pas de faire lire, mais de faire penser.

—Montesquieu

This virtue of moderation (which time and situations will clearly distinguish from the counterfeits of pusillanimity and indecision) is the virtue only of superior minds. It requires a deep courage, and full of reflection, to be temperate when the voice of multitudes (the specious mimic of fame and reputation) passes judgment against you.

—Burke

For Sophia Alexandra

Contents

Acknowledgments

This book has been a long time in the making. I started thinking about it some twelve years ago while finishing my dissertation on the French doctrinaires whose *juste milieu* was a good example of political moderation. The final chapter of my thesis contained a brief reflection on the moderation of Guizot, Royer-Collard, and their fellow doctrinaires. In 2000, I wrote a long review-essay on the virtues of political moderation, which was published in *Political Theory* a year later. In 2002, I taught a graduate course on moderation and radicalism at Indiana University, Bloomington, and three years later, I wrote an essay about Tocqueville's paradoxical moderation that came out in *The Review of Politics*. In 2006, I published a book in Romanian, *Elogiul moderației* (*In Praise of Moderation*), which set the stage for the present volume. While *A Virtue for Courageous Minds* is on some level the continuation and the refinement of my previous reflections on moderation, it has an entirely different focus, exploring several faces of political moderation in modern French political thought from 1748 to 1830.

The research for this volume has been made possible by the generous financial support of several institutions to which I would like to express my deepest gratitude: my home institution, Indiana University, Bloomington; the Earhart Foundation (which offered me two summer research grants in 2004 and 2005); the American Council of Learned Societies, the Institute for Advanced Study in Princeton (which awarded me fellowships at a key moment in the completion of this project in 2008–2009); and the Social Philosophy and Policy Center at Bowling Green University (which hosted me as a fellow during the Fall 2005 semester). Also, special thanks to the Liberty Fund, which invited me to direct two academic colloquia on the political thought of Mme de Staël and Benjamin Constant (in 2004 and 2006) and published the English edition of Mme de Staël's *Considerations on the Principle Events of the French Revolution* (2008).

Over the past decade, I have been invited to present parts of this book in various academic settings in the United States, France, and Romania, and I am grateful to all those who provided valuable suggestions and criticism. Vladimir Protopopescu read the entire manuscript with a sharp eye, encouraging me to reconsider many claims and arguments. As always, Jeremy Jennings and Daniel Mahoney have generously shared with me their knowledge of modern French thought and commented on previous drafts of this book. Over the past decade and a half, I have learned a great deal from Lucien Jaume's writings on modern French thought which have opened up new directions for my research. Costica Bradatan has been an invaluable intellectual companion and friend with whom I have been in constant dialogue over the past years. While spending a year as Fellow at the Institute of Advanced Study in Princeton, I had the opportunity to discuss the virtues and limitations of moderation with Jonathan Israel and Melvin Richter, who challenged me to explore new conceptual and methodological vistas. The same can be said of Joel Olson, who has been working to rescue from oblivion the positive aspects of fanaticism. I am also grateful to Philippe Raynaud, Denis Baranger, and the Institute Michel Villey for the invitation to spend a month as Visiting Professor at the University of Paris II, Panthéon-Assas (May 2010), where I gave two lectures on Mme de Staël and Constant. The Interlibrary Loan Department at Indiana University, Bloomington, the HS-SS Library at the Institute for Advanced Study in Princeton, and the Social Philosophy and Policy Center at Bowling Green provided me with all the sources needed to complete this book. To all of them, my most profound gratitude.

It is a pleasure to acknowledge the support received from my colleagues and students in Bloomington. Special thanks to Russell Hanson, Jeffrey Isaac, and William Scheuerman, as well as to Alin Fumurescu, Jacek Dalecki, Matthew Slaboch, Bogdan Popa, and Jooh-yung Kim for their comments and suggestions on previous drafts of some of the chapters of this book. In November 2010, Jan-Werner Müller organized a one-day workshop on moderation at Princeton, and I am grateful to him as well as to Maurizio Viroli and the other participants for their comments on my paper (a version of chapter one in this book). Many other friends and colleagues have generously shared with me their suggestions on various themes related to moderation. The list is long and includes (but is not limited to) Ruth Abbey, Barbara Allen, Danielle Allen, Ira Allen, Richard Boyd, David Carrithers, Henry Clark, Harry Clor, Patrick Deneen, Ioannis Evrigenis, Venelin Ganev, Zouhair Ghazzal, Cristian Ghinea, Madelyn Gutwirth, Will Hay, Christine Henderson, Matthew Holbreich, Stephen Holmes, John Isbell, Andrew Jainchill, Alan Kahan, George Kateb, Luigi Lacchè, Charles Macdonald, Miguel Morgado, Sam Moyn, Adrian Papahagi, Ed Parsons, Cristian Preda, Helena Rosenblatt, Filippo Sabetti, Andrew Sabl, Jerry Siegel, Steven Smith, Karol Soltan, Ioan Stanomir, Mihai Şora, Sandy Thatcher, Vladimir Tismaneanu, Tudorel Urian, Diego von Vacano, Lee Ward, Richard Wolin, Niza Yanay, and Mark Yellin. I deeply regret that the late Matei Calinescu, who was a model of moderation, cannot see this book in print. It is a late tribute to a close friend and outstanding scholar whom I miss a great deal.

Unless otherwise mentioned, all translations from French inserted in the main text or notes are mine. In translating many passages from French, I benefitted from the invaluable help of Jean-Bertrand Ribat, whom I would like to thank again for his time and generosity. Where possible, I cited from the existing English translations of the texts used in this book.

Rob Tempio, Julia Livingston, and Beth Clevenger at Princeton University Press have been ideal editors: courteous, competent, friendly, punctual, and open to dialogue. The comments provided by three anonymous referees for the press have helped clarify the focus of this book and improve its arguments. Eva Jaunzems has been the ideal copy editor for this book, and it would be difficult to find the right words to properly describe her outstanding work. To all, my sincere gratitude for making this book possible.

Some of the arguments made here have also been presented elsewhere, but in significantly different form. I wrote about the group of Coppet in "Moderation and the Group of Coppet," a chapter in *Germaine de Staël's Politics of Mediation: Challenges to History and Culture*, Karyna Szmurlo, ed. (Oxford: Voltaire Foundation, 2011). I discussed the political thought of Mme de Staël and Constant from 1795 to 1799 in "Faces of Moderation: Madame de Staël's Politics during the Directory," *Jus politicum* (Paris, 2011).

Finally, it is my pleasure to dedicate this book to our daughter, Sophia Alexandra Craiutu. May she live with moderation and come to appreciate this noble virtue for courageous minds!

A. C.

Bloomington, September 2011

Abbreviations

ABC	*Annales Benjamin Constant*
AP	*Archives Parlementaires*
ARCF	Clermont-Tonnere, *Analyse raisonnée de la constitution française* (Paris, 1791)
CDFR	*A Critical Dictionary of the French Revolution*, François Furet and Mona Ozouf, eds., trans. Arthur Goldhammer (Cambridge, MA: Harvard University Press, 1989)
CG	G. de Staël, *Correspondance générale*
CGIII:1	*Lettres de Mézery et de Coppet, 16 mai 1794–16 mai 1795*, Béatrice Jasinski, ed. (Paris: Jean-Jacques Pauvert, 1968)
CGIII:2	*Lettres d'une nouvelle républicaine, 17 mai 1795–fin novembre 1796*, Beatrice Jasinski, ed. (Paris: Jean-Jacques Pauvert, 1972)
CPE	G. de Staël, *Considerations on the Principal Events of the French Revolution*, Aurelian Craiutu, ed. (Indianapolis, IN: Liberty Fund, 2008)
CR	Montesquieu, *Considerations on the Causes of the Greatness of the Romans and Their Decline*, trans. David Lowenthal (New York: The Free Press, 1965)
CS	*Cahiers staëliens*
CSG	J.-J. Mounier, *Considérations sur les gouvernements* (Versailles,1789)
DCA	G. de Staël, *Des circonstances actuelles qui peuvent terminer la Révolution et des principes qui doivent fonder la république en France*, Lucia Omacini, ed. (Geneva: Slatkine, 1979)
DFGA, DRP, DET	B. Constant, *De la force du gouvernement actuel de la France et de la nécessité de s'y rallier; Des réactions politiques; Des effets de la Terreur*, Philippe Raynaud, ed. (Paris: Hachette, 1988)
DIAP	J.-J. Mounier, *De l'influence attribuée aux philosophes, aux francs-maçons, et aux illuminés sur la Révolution de France* (Tübingen, 1801)
ETPEP	J. Necker, *An Essay on the True Principles of the Executive Power in Great States* (London: G.G.J. and J. Robinson, 1792), 2 vols. (translation of *Du pouvoir exécutif dans les grands états* [OCN, VIII:1 and VIII: 2])
FR	J. Necker, *On the French Revolution* (London: T. Gadell, Jun. and W. Davies, 1797), 2 vols.

	(translation of *De la Révolution française* [OCN, IX and X])
MGGS	*Major Writings of Germaine de Staël*, Vivian Folkenflick, ed. and trans. (New York: Columbia University Press, 1987)
NO	J.-J. Mounier, *Nouvelles observations sur les États-Généraux de France* (Paris, 1789)
OCC	B. Constant, *Œuvres Complètes* (multiple volumes)
OCC I	*Œuvres Complètes* I: *Écrits de jeunesse (1774–1799)*, Mauro Barberis et al., eds. (Tübingen: Max Niemeyer Verlag, 1998)
OCM	Montesquieu, *Œuvres Complètes*, 2 vols.
OCM I	*Œuvres Complètes*, Roger Caillois, ed. (Paris: Gallimard, 1949)
OCM II	*Œuvres Complètes*, Roger Caillois, ed. (Paris: Gallimard, 1951)
OCN	J. Necker, *Œuvres Complètes de M. Necker*, Auguste de Staël, ed. (Paris: Treuttel & Würtz, 1820–21), 15 vols. (volume eight has two parts)
OCS	G. de Staël, *Œuvres Complètes de Madame la baronne de Staël publiées par son fils* (Paris: Treuttel and Würtz, 1821), 3 vols.
OCS(NS)	G. de Staël, *Œuvres Complètes,* new series (multiple volumes)
OCS(NS) III: 1	*Série III: Œuvres historiques, Tome I, Des circonstances actuelles et autres essais politiques sous la Révolution*, Lucia Omacini et al., eds. (Paris: Honoré Champion, 2009)
ORF	*Orateurs de la Révolution française*, I: *Les Constituants*, François Furet and Ran Halévi, eds. (Paris: Gallimard, 1989)
OSPG	B. Constant, *Observations on the Strength of the Present Government of France and upon the Necessity of Rallying Round It*, trans. James Losh (Bath: R. Crittwell, 1797) (translation of *De la force du gouvernement actuel de la France et de la nécessité de s'y rallier* [1796])
PL	Montesquieu, *Persian Letters,* trans. C. J. Betts (Harmondsworth: Penguin, 1973)
POP (1806–1810)	B. Constant, *Principles of Politics Applicable to All Governments*, trans. Dennis O'Keeffe (Indianapolis, IN: Liberty Fund, 2003)
POP (1815)	B. Constant, *Principles of Politics,* in Constant, *Political Writings*, Biancamaria Fontana, ed. and

trans. (Cambridge: Cambridge University Press, 1988)

RC   J.-J. Mounier, *Recherches sur les causes qui ont empêché les Français de devenir libres et sur les moyens qui leur restent pour acquérir la liberté*, 2 vols.

RP   G. de Staël, *Réflexions sur la paix addresées à M. Pitt et aux Français* (1794), reprinted in OCS(NS), III: 1

RPI   G. de Staël, *Réflexions sur la paix intérieure* (unpublished, 1795), reprinted in OCS(NS), III: 1

SL   Montesquieu, *The Spirit of the Laws*, trans. Anne M. Cohler, Basia Carolyn Miller, and Harold Samuel Stone (Cambridge: Cambridge University Press, 1989)

A Virtue for Courageous Minds

PROLOGUE
WHY MODERATION?

Les extrêmes sont dans la tête des hommes, mais point dans la nature des choses.
> —Mme de Staël

C'est moins la force des bras que la modération des cœurs, qui rend les hommes indépendants et libres.
> —Rousseau

Moderation in France?

There is no agreement about what is the supreme political virtue. Some think that the crown must be reserved to justice, while others believe that it should be given to fairness or moral integrity. In my opinion, the quintessential political virtue is *moderation*, and I have written this book to justify this claim. Moderation, I argue, resembles a lost archipelago that must be rediscovered by historians and political theorists. This volume does not pretend to offer a comprehensive theory of moderation, nor does it provide a single definition of this virtue. Instead, it analyzes different *faces* of political moderation and examines a wide range of political, historical, sociological, and philosophical writings related to the French Revolution. By concentrating on this major historical episode that reshaped the entire European political landscape, I shall explore various *uses* of political moderation and the ways in which moderates responded to challenges posed by their opponents.

It seemed appropriate to focus on this subject and period—1748 to 1830—for several reasons. The first author studied in this book, Montesquieu, published *De l'Esprit des lois* in 1748, while the last author examined, Benjamin Constant, passed away soon after the Revolution of 1830. During this period, French society witnessed a profound political, social, and institutional transformation that created the conditions for the emergence of a distinctive form of political moderation meant to "end" the revolution. It was a period when, to quote John Adams, "the greatest lawgivers of antiquity would have wished to live."[1] I have studied a chapter of this fascinating history in a previous book on the political thought of the French Doctrinaires (2003) and explored the emergence of moderation in modern political thought in a volume published in Romanian in 2006 that contained chapters on Machiavelli, Gracián, Montesquieu, *The Federalist*,

Burke, Macaulay, Guizot, and Tocqueville.[2] The present book grew organically out of those works by developing and revisiting some of their themes and claims. We continue to live today in a democratic world shaped by—and built upon—the ideals and principles of the French Revolution. The latter was a threshold period, a *Sattelzeit*,[3] which has become an indispensable reference for our reflections on liberty, equality, and democracy, as well as for the study of political moderation and radicalism.

At first sight, though, very few might be inclined to associate moderation with French thinkers and the "moment of rage" of 1789. The common perception is that many French thinkers and politicians followed in Rousseau's footsteps, shunning moderation and opting instead for various forms of radicalism. There is undeniable truth to this claim, and the enormous influence of Rousseau's ideas cannot be denied.[4] In France, liberal principles associated with moderation were often rejected as inadequate and liberalism was treated as an oxymoron or exotic eccentricity. Within the span of fifteen years, from 1789 to 1804, France transitioned from one absolute power to another one, passing through the dark episode of the Terror. Four constitutions were tried in the course of those years and all of them found faulty, and then the country threw itself into the arms of the man—Napoleon—who promised to save it from ruin and restore its former glory. Nonetheless, the tragic course of the French Revolution mobilized the post-revolutionary generation to build effective representative institutions meant to bring the revolution to an end. It sharpened the differences between moderate and extreme positions and delineated a broad domain of "reasonableness." The ten years separating the Old Regime from the 18th Brumaire were a period of great intellectual effervescence during which many important political writings were published. The level of political oratory in the Constituent Assembly reached a peak in the summer and fall of 1789, when gifted speakers such as Sieyès and Mirabeau sparred with Mounier and Lally-Tollendal.

Although this is a book about moderation in modern French thought, the image of England as a country of moderation and compromise looms large in its pages, which explains why I have also included, where appropriate, occasional references to relevant English authors. This is justified by the fact that Montesquieu, Mounier, Necker, Constant, and Mme de Staël looked at England as a political model and drew inspiration from its politics and successful blend of liberty and order. In particular, the similarities and differences between the so-called French *monarchiens* and Burke on the principles of 1789 and the Constituent Assembly (examined in chapter 3 below) invite us to reflect on the different political trajectories of France and England in the nineteenth century. Although moderate temperaments were to be found on both sides of the Channel, the structure of government and the electorate ended up being conceived in strikingly different terms that warrant close investigation.

The Main Questions

The main goal of this volume is to study the institutional and constitutional aspects of political moderation in the history of modern France. The book interweaves two main themes relating to political moderation. The first deals with moderation under the Old Regime, when moderate agendas were used as means of criticizing a rigid and inefficient hierarchical structure and proposing concrete blueprints for political reform. The second examines various attempts at institutionalizing moderation during the revolution and its aftermath, when it was primarily interpreted and used as a means of "ending" the revolution.

The reader will note a certain convergence of several overlapping themes and questions: What kind of virtue is political moderation, and how can we study it? Is moderation a sensibility or temperament rather than a strategy, doctrine, or party platform? Is moderation best defined as a "positional" virtue, and to what extent is it contingent upon the existence and flourishing of various forms of political radicalism? What does it mean to be a moderate voice in politics? What do moderates seek in politics, and how do they apply their moderate views? How many "faces" does moderation have, and how do they relate to each other? What are the institutional aspects of moderation?

All of these questions are variations on a central "melody": How, when, and to what extent can moderation be institutionalized in politics? The book focuses on four major *meta-narratives*. The *first* examines how moderation evolves from an individual, moral virtue or character trait into a set of institutional arrangements calculated to uphold and protect individual liberty. The authors and texts discussed in this book do, in fact, follow a trajectory away from an emphasis on moderation as a personal trait to a view of moderation as a virtue that inheres within political institutions and institutional arrangements. The *second* meta-narrative is the deep affinity between political moderation and institutional/constitutional complexity as illustrated by Montesquieu's discussion of "moderate" government, Necker's theory of complex sovereignty, Mme de Staël's endorsement of the "complex center," and Constant's theory of neutral power. The *third* meta-narrative emphasizes moderation as "trimming" between extremes, a way of keeping the ship of state on an even keel.[5] This topic may overlap to some extent with the issue of the *juste milieu* between extremes, but it is not identical with it. A *fourth* meta-narrative has to do with the "eclecticism" of moderation. In stressing this point, I seek to demonstrate that moderation cannot be analyzed exclusively within our conventional political vocabulary, because it has *both* radical and conservative connotations that vary with time and place. I return to these meta-narratives in the epilogue.

The next chapters, following a historical line of the argument, are not intended as a comprehensive study of the authors covered in this book, but rather of the ways in which they used the concept of political moderation in their works. I have sought to reconstruct their intellectual dialogue by pointing out how they addressed each other's claims about moderation and the political implications of the latter. As such, the concept of political moderation must be seen as a gateway to their larger vision of a free society based on the principles of constitutionalism. I devote special attention to the different *faces* of moderation that appeared in their writings, such as moderate government, moderation as antidote to zealotry and fanaticism, moderation as a disposition to compromise, moderation as "neutral power," and moderation as a *juste milieu* between extremes. The significance of these themes will come to light only gradually, and I must therefore ask the reader to follow them patiently throughout the entire book. In time a larger story will unfold, in which the many faces of moderation will appear with increasing clarity. It is my hope that the reader will in the end be led to reflect on moderation in light of the problems and experiences of our own day.

I chose the theme of moderation and its various faces because it was important to the thinkers studied in this book and because it gave them the conceptual lenses through which they interpreted the world in which they lived. They might have been wrong on some issues, and some of their political strategies might seem questionable today. Nonetheless, the task of the historian is not to correct, but to present and interpret, and this is what I have attempted to do here.

For reasons of balance, space, and relevance, the list of authors is limited to a select group; the method adopted in each individual case has been to examine how the author in question defined (political) moderation and related concepts (such as neutral power and the center), and how he or she applied them in practice. Due to space constraints, I was unable to include chapters on several important authors and texts, some more relevant than others to our analysis of moderation. The first author who might well have deserved special attention is Jean Charles Léonard Sismondi, a prominent member of the Coppet group whose constitutional vision was a perfect complement to the ideas of Jacques Necker, Mme de Staël, and Benjamin Constant. Sismondi's close engagement with Rousseau's *Du contrat social* led him to articulate during the Directory and the Consulate an original theory of sovereignty that provided the background for Constant's own critique of popular sovereignty in the first version of his *Principes de politique*. Where appropriate, I shall briefly comment on Sismondi's ideas on sovereignty, limited power, and the balance of powers, but much more remains to be said about the originality of this moderate and cosmopolitan thinker, at home in several cultures. He was a truly encyclopedic mind admired by many, including Marx, and his reflections on the relationship between liberalism and democracy remain relevant today.[6] The second author I have in mind is Abbé Sieyès, who in many ways represents, to quote one of his biographers, "*la clé de la Révolution française.*"[7] Although the thinker who authored the famous pamphlet *Qu'est-ce que le Tiers État* (1789) and proudly claimed that he had deciphered all the secrets of political science was not, properly speaking, a political moderate and had many radical moments, his reflections on the balance of powers and the constitutional jury are relevant for the story told in these pages, as is his contribution to the drafting of the *Declaration of the Rights of Man and of the Citizen* in 1789. I shall briefly comment on Sieyès' texts insofar as they help us understand better the milieu from which the ideas of the monarchiens and of the Coppet group emerged. A third possible case study would be the political philosophy of the *Encyclopédie*, an original mixture of political moderation and philosophical radicalism that would deserve an entire book.[8] A full treatment of political moderation would, moreover, have to pay more attention to social and economic factors than it has been possible here. In a sequel to the present book, I plan to continue the reflection on moderation in nineteenth-century French thought. Two other manuscripts will be devoted to examining the meanings of moderation in English political thought and in contemporary political theory, thus rounding up a multi-volume research agenda at the heart of which lies the elusive concept of political moderation.

One of the conclusions of the present book to which I return in the epilogue is that moderation *does* have intrinsic substantive political orientations and values of its own and stands in a close connection with constitutionalism, a politics of skepticism as opposed to a "politics of faith" and of absolute ends. While the book focuses on the relationship between moderation and the political architecture of free regimes, it also presents moderation as a superior form of "civility" and an antithesis to all forms of monist politics. The latter assume that political matters ought to (and can) be decided from the single viewpoint of a coherent and comprehensive set of beliefs and ideas that must override all other considerations.[9] Another conclusion of this book is that moderation is a virtue that demands a lot of courage and involves many risks. At the same time, it does *not* seem to be a virtue for everyone and for all seasons. In fact, as Seneca once observed, we must sometimes allow ourselves to be carried to extremes[10] for, without a certain degree of immoderation, even moderation might become counterproductive, a grain of immoderation being necessary to reach the desired golden mean.[11] That is why our mind must be at times stimulated "without restraint and austere soberness must be banished for a while."[12] Under certain circumstances, moderation might be ineffective and inappropriate and ought to give way to a certain form of "creative" extremism. Sometimes, even a small dose of fanaticism *sui generis* might be a good thing in pursuing worthy political causes. Hence, one of the key questions regarding moderation is not so much whether it is a reasonable political virtue in general, but *when* and *how* it can serve as a worthy and effective principle, given that the means used to promote moderate agendas must always be adjusted to shifting political contexts.

Finally, I am also interested in understanding why radical spirits, who use hyperbole and extreme means, often triumph over moderate individuals, who endorse prudence, gradualism, and self-restraint. The main players in this book remind us that moderation usually has a high political cost, and that the sober appeal of moderates can rarely match the fascination exercised by bolder dreamers and utopian minds. This, in turn, prompted me to speculate on the road not taken. What might have happened *if* the moderate thinkers studied in this book had been successful? Might history have followed a different course *if* their ideas had prevailed?

How Should We Study Moderation?

While those engaged in writing the history of complex concepts such as moderation are inevitably bound to appear old-fashioned given their focus on reading and interpreting texts, they must also go *beyond* studying the language in which these notions are expressed. Since moderation has always been used with various intents and meanings, one must carefully examine the contexts in which it has been employed and the various functions and purposes it has served. Such complex concepts are never used in isolation but always in ideological constellations that constitute entire belief systems. This is all the more true of a complex and elusive concept such as moderation, which, as one historian pointed out, is *unlike* other classical concepts such as general will, sovereignty, or reason of state.[13]

That is why the nature and complexity of moderation cannot be captured by using a purely philosophical or analytical approach; it requires, instead, concrete historical examples and extensive historical forays which, in turn, demand thorough knowledge of various political contexts and actions. There is neither an abstract theory of moderation outside of particular situations, nor a controlled experiment or falsification procedure for testing moderation in theory. We can only write a history of the various *uses* of moderation and of the varying *intentions* with which it was employed over time by actors placed in specific political, social, and cultural contexts.[14] To this effect, we must examine the embodiment of moderation in specific time-bound institutions, constitutions, and practices, in order to study how various political actors used both abstract principles and practical/strategic considerations in pursuing their moderate agendas. Since the latter often implies significant trade-offs, it is also important to examine how moderates justified the compromises they were forced to make. The mentality of our authors will remain obscure if we do not take into account how they interpreted the political events and controversies that shaped their careers and lives. By drawing on such concrete examples, we should be able to make our arguments about moderation more vivid and persuasive than if we tried to offer a purely theoretical account of this elusive virtue.

At the same time, we need to pay due attention to the *philosophical* and *legal-constitutional* ramifications of the idea of moderation, distinguishing between moderate means (sometimes) serving "radical" goals and moderate agendas that (sometimes) may be furthered even by "radical" means. This approach presupposes a combination of textual analysis and contextual interpretation that calls for a sound balance between intellectual and political history, between conceptual (re)construction and in-depth analysis of political institutions and constitutions. This eclectic methodology reflects the diversity of viewpoints expressed by the thinkers discussed in this book.[15]

Moreover, the richness of moderation can be grasped only if placed within a larger conceptual field that includes related concepts (temperance, prudence, *juste milieu*, *modérantisme*,[16] mixed government, *mitoyen*), and antonyms (fanaticism, extremism, radicalism). In order to gain insight into the worldview of moderates, we must also examine radical and conservative ideas and the doctrines to which they responded. It would not be possible to study moderation without mentioning its relationship with fanaticism, a concept that first referred to religious zealots (described as "enthusiasts") before it acquired a more political significance.[17] Nor would it be possible to understand the pre-political meanings of moderation if we were to gloss over the ideal of the *honnête homme* and the concept of *civilité* in the seventeenth and early eighteenth centuries.[18] A study of moderation also requires taking into account its relation to the middle class (highlighted for the first time by Aristotle).[19] Over time, moderation came to be regarded as a corollary of civility and a virtue of the middle class that stood in opposition to fanaticism, defined as a malady of spirit leading to excess and destruction. What is particularly interesting is that, during the French Revolution, the two terms (moderation and fanaticism), often seen as antonyms, were linked in a surprising way, as when radical members of the Assembly denounced moderate defenders of constitutional monarchy, together with the nobles and the priests opposing the revolution, as *"traîtres, fanatiques, factieux."*[20] Aristocratic fanaticism was regarded as the "bad" type to be distinguished from the "good" fanaticism in the service of liberty, equality, virtue, and the revolution, advocated by Mirabeau, Desmoulins, Robespierre, and their disciples.[21]

In treating such a complex subject as moderation, it is natural to turn to both canonical authors and primary texts and to lesser-known (but relevant) books. Retrieving such authors and texts from oblivion is not only an act of intellectual justice meant to get history right, or an antiquarian exercise aimed at a small and select audience. Rather, by reading both non-canonical and canonical authors, we might come to appreciate better the historical and theoretical importance of the former when they are placed alongside and in dialogue with the latter. My interest in all these thinkers reflects my preference for an ecumenical form of intellectual history that takes into account the creativity of the so-called "marginal" authors, whose works can shed fresh light on the richness of the tradition of political moderation.

Outline of the Book

The book consists of two parts. Part I (chapters 1 through 3) begins with a survey of different visions of moderation in the history of political thought, starting with Plato, Aristotle, and Cicero, followed by a brief treatment of the place of moderation in St. Thomas Aquinas' works. I then turn to the tradition of political moderation in France before Montesquieu, examining briefly the meanings of moderation in the writings of Montaigne, Hotman, Seyssel, Pascal, and the French moralists (La Bruyère, La Rochefoucauld). Since the works of these predecessors of Montesquieu are outside of the main temporal framework of my book, they will be referred to only in connection with those aspects of their thought that are particularly relevant to the topic of moderation.

Chapters 2 and 3 examine the concept of "moderate government" and the meanings of moderation during the Old Regime and the initial phase of the French Revolution. The focus is on the political writings of Montesquieu and the French monarchiens (Mounier, Clermont-Tonnerre, Lally-Tollendal, and Malouet), the "radical moderates" of 1789. In their writings, moderation was no longer dependent primarily upon the virtuous character of individuals, but was predicated upon the existence of a sound balance of powers, institutions, forces, and interests. Central to their conceptual framework was a fundamental distinction between *moderate* and *immoderate* governments, accompanied by the claim that political liberty exists only in moderate governments in which power is not abused. The case of the monarchiens is particularly interesting for students of political moderation because it shows the revolutionary spirit of the moderates. It displays both the virtues and limitations of their "lost center" at a key moment in French history—the brief interlude in the spring and fall of 1789— when the Old Regime came to an abrupt end and a new political order was in the making.

Part II (chapters 4 through 6) examines political moderation in the writings of three prominent members of the so-called Coppet group: Jacques Necker, Mme de Staël, and Benjamin Constant. As the cradle of liberalism in France, this fascinating circle represented the intellectual Elysium of an entire generation, an island of freedom and moderation in the middle of Europe. The ideas of these thinkers, in spite of their differences, form a common and consistent discourse on liberty, limited power, sovereignty, and political moderation, inspired by their common appreciation for the English constitution. I pay special attention to Necker's defense of "complex sovereignty" and the "intertwining of powers," Mme de Staël's attempt to create a center in the aftermath of the revolution, and Constant's search for a "neutral power" that would function as a moderating device, keeping the ship of the state on an even keel.

In the epilogue, I emphasize that the authors studied in this book demonstrate that political moderation is neither a lukewarm middle between extremes, nor a synonym for indecisiveness or lukewarmness, but rather a bold virtue for courageous minds. It has significant institutional implications and can play a crucial role in securing (where absent) and strengthening (where present) liberal democratic government. Moderation also implies the rejection of political Manichaeism and the recognition of limits, along with a strong commitment to preserve and nurture the pluralism of ideas, principles, and interests that undergirds liberty in modern society.

While I hope that the historical and textual evidence supports my conclusions and meta-narratives, I am also aware that others might interpret differently the authors studied in these pages. They might even conclude that political moderation is, after all, an uninteresting virtue, one that it would be best to eschew most of the time. For my part, I remain fascinated by the extraordinary range of meanings and instantiations of political moderation, which can be best studied during "threshold" periods when our ways of thinking about politics and society change. At the same time, I grant that the concept of moderation might suffer from "semantic bleaching,"[22] for the term "moderation" is apt to be used in a loose sense that can stretch it beyond its legitimate domain. Moderation can sometimes be developed into an ideology *sui generis*, but most of the time it resists attempts at transforming it into a full-fledged political doctrine. Even then, it remains in danger of various forms of politicization, some more subtle than others.

Since this book draws upon the works of many scholars, I am very pleased to acknowledge their contributions, without which my foray into the history of political moderation would not have been possible.[23] Paraphrasing a point once made by Montaigne, with regard to all these borrowed ideas, I take the liberty of inviting the reader to judge "whether I have been able to select something which improves my themes"[24] and whether sometimes I got others to say much better what I could not put so well myself. My main goal has only been to stimulate a debate on moderation and to invite the reader on an interesting intellectual journey. As Burke once said, "a man who works beyond the surface, though he may be wrong himself, yet he clears the way for others, and may chance to make even his errors subservient to the cause of truth."[25] Hence, I shall be content if others, upon reading this book, might be encouraged to further reflect on moderation in order to give it the place it deserves in political philosophy. Finally, I hope that my book is neither so brief that the reader could memorize it, nor so long that he or she could never finish it.

PART I
VISIONS OF MODERATE GOVERNMENT

ONE

In Search of a Lost Archipelago

> C'est sortir de l'humanité que de sortir du milieu; la grandeur de
> l'âme humaine consiste à savoir s'y tenir.
> —Pascal

The Many Faces of Moderation

Almost three centuries ago, Montesquieu claimed that human beings tend to accommodate themselves better to middles than to extremities.[1] Remembering the twentieth-century Gulag and the other concentration camps would be enough, however, to make us question the power and influence of moderation over human passions. If anything, the last century has confirmed John Adams' warning that, "without the great political virtues of humility, patience, and moderation . . . every man in power becomes a ravenous beast of prey."[2] Nonetheless, it is difficult to be passionate about moderation, a complex and difficult virtue, with a discreet and sometimes obsolete charm, which is unlikely to appeal to everyone. It is, moreover, equally hard to act like a moderate, for moderates are often marginalized, derided, ignored, or simply forgotten, while moderation itself is "stigmatized as the virtue of cowards and compromise as the prudence of traitors."[3]

As such, moderation is bound to be a contested concept reflecting the ambiguity of our moral and political vocabulary. "With a subject of this sort," Harry Clor has recently remarked, "one does not prove things, yet one can make arguments more or less rationally defensible in light of pervasive experiences. This is an arena in which moral absolutes are very hard to come by."[4] The difficulty of agreeing on a definition of moderation is reflected in the wide range of views on its ethical, institutional, and political dimensions, as well as in the fact that moderation may not be suitable to all circumstances. Beginning with Aristotle, philosophers have highlighted a few paradoxes surrounding the principle of the excluded middle, and have argued that in some cases, an appeal to moderation might, in fact, be a logical fallacy. Known as the *argumentum ad temperantia* or "false compromise," such an appeal implies that the positions being considered represent extremes on a continuum of opinions, and that such extremes are always wrong, while the middle ground between them is always correct. In reality, some positions and arguments do not admit of a coherent middle, and not every compromise between extremes is always legitimate. Under some circumstances, in fact, *tertium non datur*: only extreme positions are possible, though not necessarily desirable. In other words, the principled pursuit of balance can sometimes create severe imbalances, which should be avoided if at all possible.[5]

The paradoxes do not stop here. The concept of moderation has been understudied, even though the works of many writers viewed as moderates—Aristotle, Montesquieu, Burke, and Tocqueville—are well known. They employ various concepts related to moderation, but their writings are not commonly seen as belonging to a larger tradition of political moderation. This explains in part why moderates have rarely been regarded as constituting a coherent alternative tradition of thought and have instead been considered exotic voices in the wilderness, too different one from another, or too weak to form a coherent political tradition.[6]

Furthermore, the tradition of moderation as a mode of argument and a form of political action lacks well-defined boundaries. While moderation is often interpreted as a temperament, a state of mind (disposition), or a trait of character, this view does not give due consideration to its institutional facets. Moreover, when defined as a virtue, moderation most often refers to political leaders and is interpreted as being oriented toward others, when in fact it can also be regarded as a virtue regulating our conduct with respect to ourselves. Last but not least, while moderation might also be taken as a synonym of reasonableness, a desirable form of civility, or an antonym of fanaticism, it is important to remember that it is *not* always rational or possible to espouse moderate positions. This might lead us to conclude that moderation is only a circumstantial virtue with limited relevance and appeal.

Having already suggested that it is virtually impossible to offer a single definition of moderation, I am prepared to admit that sometimes it might be easier to define moderation by looking at what it opposes: extremism, radicalism, zealotry, fanaticism, "terrorism," or madness.[7] More specifically, moderation opposes absolute power, conflict, tension, polarization, violence, war, and revolution. It can also be interpreted as an antonym of rigidity, stubbornness, dogmatism, utopianism, perfectionism, or moral absolutism. Some might argue that moderation is more than a sensibility but less than a doctrine. The perspective adopted in this book departs from this view and argues that a moderate agenda *cannot* be reduced to a minimalist program justified exclusively by the fear of—and the mere opposition to—extremes.

The question remains: what do moderates stand for? It would seem to me that they affirm three basic attitudes. First, they defend pluralism—of ideas, interests, and social forces—and seek to achieve a balance between them in order to temper political and social conflicts. Second, moderates prefer gradual reforms to revolutionary breakthroughs, and they are temperamentally inclined to making compromises and concessions on both prudential and normative grounds. They acknowledge that the best course of action in politics is often to "rally around the part least bad among your adversaries, even when that party is still remote from your own views."[8] Third, moderation presupposes a tolerant approach which refuses to see the world in Manichean terms that divide it into forces of good (or light) and agents of evil (or darkness). It consists in a distinct political style that stands in stark contrast to the overconfident *modus operandi* of those whose world is dominated by black-and-white contrasts. Moderates refuse the posture of prophets, even if sometimes they, too, may be tempted to make grand historical generalizations and predictions. Anti-perfectionists and fearful of anarchy, they endorse fallibilism as a middle way between radical skepticism and epistemological absolutism, and acknowledge the limits of political action and the imperfection of the human condition.

In practice, the institutionalization of political moderation sometimes amounts to—but is *not* limited to—finding a center between (or a neutral power above) all parties; more generally, though, it implies building "moderate" government, which may take various institutional forms. While it may be tempting to equate centrism with moderation, an identification between the two must *not* be taken as a universal axiom, for we can find moderates on the left, at the center, and on the right of the political spectrum. When moderates advocate the virtues of the center, theirs is a morally, ideologically, and institutionally complex center, and it should not be identified with weakness or opportunism.

Moderates have worn many masks over time: the Stoic (Seneca); the prudent man (Aristotle, Cicero, Machiavelli, Guicciardini, Gracián); the trimmer (Halifax, Oakeshott, Necker); the skeptic (Hume, Kant, Montaigne); the pluralist (Madison, Berlin); the liberal in the middle or between two worlds (Tocqueville); the critic of zealotry, fanaticism, and enthusiasm (Burke, Hume); the eclectic (Cousin); and the "committed observer" (Aron, Walzer). Among the concrete examples of moderate agendas, one could mention: the *juste milieu* between revolution and reaction; Ordoliberalism (in post-war Germany); social-democracy in Sweden as a middle ground between pure free market capitalism and full state socialism; and the New Deal in the United States. There were also political movements that have claimed to follow the principles of moderation: the Prague Spring movement of 1968 ("a revolt of moderates," as Milan Kundera once claimed); the Solidarity movement and the "self-limiting" revolution in Poland; Charter 77 in former Czechoslovakia; and the doctrine of the "Third Way" (in the United Kingdom under Tony Blair).

The Skepticism toward Moderation

Moderation has all these faces and virtues, but it is nonetheless an inconspicuous virtue prone to understatement. How can one be enthusiastic about something that lacks charisma, carries the connotation of small-mindedness and philistine dullness, and promotes what Nietzsche once denounced as bland or soft moralism? "Moderation sees itself as beautiful," he wrote, but "it is unaware that in the eye of the immoderate it appears black and sober, and consequently ugly-looking."[9]

The social sciences and the humanities have surprisingly little to say about the place of moderation in the hierarchy of virtues and tend to dismiss it as an elusive concept that cannot be rigorously defined. Major works such as John Rawls' *A Theory of Justice*, Sheldon Wolin's *Politics and Vision*, Michael Walzer's *Spheres of Justice*, Quentin Skinner's *Foundations of Modern Political Thought*, and Leo Strauss' *Natural Right and History*, as well as classic accounts of American society such as Robert Bellah's *Habits of the Heart* (a book that celebrates America's moderate political culture) pay scant or no attention at all to moderation, although the latter is related to many topics addressed in their pages. Moderation is conspicuously absent from the index of these books and from other recent works such as Deirdre McCloskey's *Bourgeois Virtues* (which praises prudence and temperance), Nancy Rosenblum's *On The Side of Angels* (which devotes an entire chapter to centrism and extremism), Avishai Margalit's *The Decent Society* (which celebrates a virtue—decency—that has many things in common with moderation), or Cass Sunstein's *Going to Extremes* (which explores the reasons leading people to espouse extremist positions in politics).

This reluctance to theorize about moderation has several causes. One of them is that moderation has often been understood as a vague virtue, too imprecise to be rigorously analyzed. To the extent that it connotes a certain character trait, or a habit of mind that is liable to change over time, its universe appears uncertain and fuzzy, defying apodictic and universal statements. With such a topic, one is forced to deal only with nuances of gray, leaving stark colors to others. It is in fact impossible to discover or to formulate moral absolutes and universal laws that define moderation. Recognizing moderates in actions is far easier than describing in theory what they stand for.[10]

Second, in ordinary language, a moderate person carries the connotation of someone incapable of making firm decisions or having strong feelings. Thus, moderation has sometimes been equated with docility, indecision, pettiness, and submissiveness, traits of the weak or the meek, that those who prefer bolder and manlier ways eschew. Moderation has been equated with "petty" politics, based on compromise and small steps, as opposed to the immoderation that characterizes "grand" politics, based on war and conquest.[11] Thus defined, moderation appears a bland and incoherent virtue, the opposite of fortitude and decisiveness, and incompatible with firmness and clarity of purpose. The most developed and brilliant societies of the past, Fourrier once argued, were those that risked the most and displayed a great deal of immoderation in their pursuit of the good life. "Where has civilization made most progress?" he asked. "This happened in Athens, Paris, and London, where people have not been friends of moderation."[12] Similarly, echoing Proudhon's argument that radicalism and enthusiasm can also be seen as preconditions of greatness, Marx justified radicalism by claiming that "to be radical is to go to the root of the matter," adding that the root is man himself.[13] On this view, moderation (as opposed to radicalism) appears as a negative or weak virtue, one that does not leave a memorable impression, while boldness and assertiveness tend to produce elevated emotions, enlivening our sense of dignity. As a second-best virtue, moderation seems therefore unable to quench our thirst for greatness and glory, a virtue best left to the tepid, middling, shy, timorous, indecisive, and lukewarm individuals who are, allegedly, incapable of great "heroic" acts and stories.[14]

Third, on many occasions, moderates' ideas have been dismissed as a mere expression of political opportunism or egoism, and the adjective "moderate" has been applied to the person who is too willing to engage in whatever compromises and tactical maneuvers suit his or her temporary interests. Often times, we admire those who stand firmly on absolute principles and whose universe consists entirely of primary colors and sharp contrasts. Hence, an unchanging viewpoint is generally considered a great and necessary virtue in statesmen, while moderation, which implies a middling mind open to compromise, is not. As Isaiah Berlin once noted, we tend to be impressed by self-absorbed politicians who march with determination and sometimes even ruthlessness toward their goals and stubbornly pursue their own one-dimensional vision.[15] In turn, as Norberto Bobbio reminded us, the symbols used to describe successful politicians are the fox (shrewdness) and the lion (force) rather than the lamb (innocence).[16]

To radical spirits—from Rousseau and Marx to Schmitt, Sartre, and Foucault—whose flamboyant rhetoric fascinates us through its combination of romantic revolt and intransigence, we are willing to grant a privilege that, as Bobbio remarked, is commonly denied to the majority of mortals: that is, the right to be immoderate, even the right to condone the occasional use of violence for the sake of "nobler" ideals.[17] Not surprisingly, in the Pantheon of great heroes one will find few moderate spirits, earthly glory being more often granted to those who have *not* been moderate, who conquered states and built powerful empires. It pays to be immoderate, it seems. Radical or extreme gestures and flamboyant words can create bold and colorful narratives, and these are arguably much more attractive than moderation. This is why we tend to underestimate those thinkers and actors whose universe consists mostly of various nuances of gray, who believe that in politics we do not have to choose between good and evil, but between what is preferable and what is detestable. As for the moderates themselves, they distinguish themselves through their own blend of prudence, self-restraint, and skepticism, reminding us that politics is a messy and tangled business far from a romantic quest for ultimate truths and certainty.

The peculiar nature of moderation is further illustrated by the fact that the latter is *not* a virtue for all seasons and all people. As Tocqueville remarked, "in times when passions begin to gain control over the conduct of human affairs, it is less what people of experience and knowledge think that deserves attention than what fills dreamers' imagination."[18] Moderation is sometimes viewed as a positional or circumstantial virtue, much like Aristotle's *mesotes* (middle), the exact location of which ultimately depends on the position (and strength) of the extremes that it seeks to temper. As such, moderation designates a stance that is far from ideologically fixed and whose contours are surprisingly fluid. What is moderate today might not be so tomorrow, and what was moderate in the past would not be viewed in the same light today. Being a moderate in the context of the 1920s and 1930s, when the values of parliamentary democracy were under assault, was radically different from being a moderate today, when democracy is the uncontested dominant political ideology in the entire civilized world. All this suggests that there are times when moderation is a virtue and other periods when it might be a political liability. Aleksandr Solzhenitsyn would not have been successful in challenging the orthodoxy of the Soviet communist system had he adopted a more moderate approach. Sometimes, only immoderate voices like his or Antigone's can successfully oppose tyranny, which explains why moderation is a double-edged sword. Its universe is multi-dimensional and its relevance depends on particular circumstances, further complicating its status as a stand-alone political agenda.

Last but not least, another critique of political moderation calls into question its commitment to promoting democratic principles and values. Jonathan Israel has recently argued that a great deal of the achievement of the Enlightenment was made possible by the efforts of its radical representatives who endorsed many of the democratic ideals we take for granted today. Drawing its roots from Spinoza and Bayle, the radical Enlightenment (in Israel's view) could not have achieved its goal of transforming the political and social framework of modern society by relying upon a moderate agenda. Reshaping public opinion and doing away with obsolete privileges required a radical and bold approach that did not allow for compromise on key issues such as equality, toleration, and pluralism. Israel's radical Enlightenment endorsed a package of basic concepts and values including rationalism, equality of all mankind (racial and sexual), individual rights, secular universalism, justice, toleration, freedom of belief and of expression, and democratic republicanism.[19] As such, according to Jonathan Israel, the radical approach of Diderot, Helvétius, and Paine was in irreconcilable tension with the political moderation praised by Montesquieu, Ferguson, Hume, Smith, Voltaire, and Turgot, the main representatives of the moderate Enlightenment. In Israel's words, the latter "was inherently antidemocratic, anti-egalitarian, and reluctant to concede a full toleration,"[20] seeking to limit the scope of reason and the use of rationalism as a political tool of social criticism.

While there is some truth in all of these critiques, it is also important to remember that radical philosophical rhetoric was sometimes used as an original strategy for promoting moderate political reform. A cursory look at key entries in the *Encyclopédie* (including those signed by Diderot himself, such as the one on political authority) shows that a certain degree of moderation in one area made radicalism in another possible, while radicalism with regard to some issues was accompanied by moderation on others.[21] Several entries by Jaucourt (such as the one on legislative and executive power) put forward a strong case for two principles connected to political moderation: the balance of powers and bicameralism, while others regarded consent and public opinion as key principles of any legitimate political regime. Not surprisingly, as we shall see later, during the French Revolution, moderation was denounced as a weapon used by dangerous intriguers and "traitors" of the nation, singled out for their commitment to "radical" principles, or for their alleged lack of civic allegiance and dubious commitment to the values of the fatherland.[22]

What many critics of moderation forget is that there are circumstances in which even remembering or evoking the idea of moderation would be enough to brand someone as traitor or an enemy of the people, and that moderation and the mean are *not* the morality of the herd, as Nietzsche once said. Appearances notwithstanding, moderation is, in fact, a *difficult* virtue for courageous minds.[23] As Burke once argued, moderation must be clearly distinguished from "the counterfeits of pusillanimity and indecision" and requires "a deep courage" and resoluteness when one must stand up against the voice and wishes of the majority.[24] Searching for the mean is always a demanding task, arguably more difficult than making one's journey along paths that are more extreme, because the mean is multi-dimensional and acting like a moderate requires balancing and weighing various principles in every situation rather than relying on a single set of universal principles or values. It presupposes reasoning and deliberation, but it can never rely on reasoning alone, since it also demands intuition, foresight, and flexibility. Therefore, a politics of moderation requires a complex mix of vision, boldness, and self-control, along with courage, patience, and a knowledge of the circumstances. In order to survive, moderates must always be *en garde. They are* obliged to blend the innocence of the dove with the shrewdness of the serpent.[25]

Moderation in the Classical and Christian Traditions

The ancients did not share the moderns' skepticism toward moderation. On the contrary, they regarded the latter as a cardinal virtue, opposed to the "extremism" of barbarians whom they considered to be incapable of following a rational middle course. The classical concepts of mean, moderation, and the middle share the root "med" which evokes the idea of driving something back to its natural measure.

Aeschylus' claim (in the *Eumenides*) that God gives the victory to moderation in every form expressed the classical belief in the power of this virtue identified with reasonableness and just measure. A few centuries later, the idea of the "golden mean" (*aurea mediocritas*) played a key role in Horace's *Odes*,[26] where it was also associated with proportion, just measure, and balance. Equally important, the doctrine of the mean also appeared outside of ancient Greece and Rome, occupying an important place in Confucius' writings and the *Bhagavad Gita* in which the mean was exalted as a way to maintain inner balance and mental harmony. "Perfect is the virtue which is according to the Mean! Rare have they long been among the people, who could practice it!" wrote the author of one neo-Confucian treatise, *The Doctrine of the Mean*. The opening paragraph of the text quotes the following aphorism attributed to Chung-ni: "The superior man embodies the course of the Mean; the mean man acts contrary to the course of the Mean."[27]

To understand the ancients' uses of moderation we must pay special attention to their conventional linguistic assumptions and vocabulary, which point to the existence of a close relationship between moderation, the golden mean, mixed government, and temperance.[28] The best place to explore this connection is in Aristotle's works, most notably the *Nichomachean Ethics* and the *Politics*. But already a few decades before Aristotle linked moderation to prudence and practical wisdom (*phronesis*), Plato had famously defined it (in the *Republic*) as the virtue that allows us to control or temper our passions, emotions, and desires. In another Platonic dialogue, the *Charmides*, Plato reflected on the relationship between *sophrosyne* and self-knowledge.[29] One of Plato's recent commentators has suggested a possible parallel between the "dialectical moderation" in the *Charmides* and the treatment of *sophrosyne* in the *Republic*, arguing that "the moderation of the intellectual/philosophical types . . . is shown to result primarily as a function of their intellectual interests and the sublimation and symbolic reintegration of the lower energies into the pursuit of knowledge."[30] Although *sophrosyne* was primarily understood to be a virtue of the soul, it also had several important institutional implications in Plato's writings. As one scholar put it, Plato was arguably the first man to systematically reflect on nearly every aspect of a balanced government, and he proposed specific ways of preventing the decay of political institutions and maintaining social order.[31] In the *Laws*, he wrote favorably about the mixed constitution of Sparta, which wisely divided power among four groups whose conflicting ambitions were moderated by a state council composed of three hundred sixty Spartans.

More so than Plato's dialogues, Aristotle's books allow us to follow the transformation of moderation from a predominantly ethical concept, germane to prudence, practical wisdom, and temperance, into a prominent *political* virtue. Books 2 and 6 of the *Nicomachean Ethics* are the *locus classicus* for examining the connection between moderation, prudence, and practical wisdom, as well as for the definition of virtue as a mean between extremes. According to Aristotle, "excess and deficiency are characteristic of vice," while "the mean of virtue."[32] On this view, virtue is identified with choosing what is intermediate—that is, "the mean relative to us," defined by reference to reason—and the mean must be sought and followed because it preserves order and freedom in society.[33] "A master of any art," Aristotle argued, "avoids excess and defect, but seeks the intermediate and chooses this."[34] Note here the seminal distinction between the middle and the mean. The middle is defined in relation to the extremes, whereas the mean is always designated in relation to the person who makes the decision and must take into account the shifting configuration of external factors and circumstances. Right action amounts then to finding the mean relative to *us* in each particular case, and for this no theoretical or universal formula exists. The mean is not one-dimensional, but multi-dimensional, and we must always assess and evaluate the context of our choices in order to decide on the appropriate course of action at the "right" time, in the "right" place, and with regard to the "right" people.[35]

Aristotle's claim that moderation can be attained only through experience and practice and that it is to be understood only in the context of specific situations leads to the conclusion that there can be no "science" (or theory) of moderation, since the latter is a mean between art and science. In Aristotle's view, moderation is a difficult virtue not suitable to the young, and this for at least two reasons. First, it presupposes experience, which can be gained only through trial-and-error over time; second, it is never easy to find the mean and the middle, and some actions (theft, murder) or feelings (envy) admit of no mean. In such cases, we may never be "correct" and must rely only on our discernment and foresight, trying to be as reasonable as possible by using our intuition and common sense in order to adjust our actions to "particulars" rather than universal rules.[36] The solution proposed by Aristotle amounts to a form of trimming between extremes that requires careful thought and prudence: "We must also examine what we ourselves drift into more easily . . . we must drag ourselves off in the contrary direction; for if we pull far away from error, as they do in straightening bent wood, we shall reach the intermediate condition."[37]

Aristotle identified two extremes: being overly changeable and inconstant (opportunism), and being too inflexible and rigid (dogmatism). In choosing a mean between these two courses of action, Aristotle's moderate politician seeks a middle ground between strict adherence to principles and artistic improvisation.[38] This also requires the cultivation of individual character so as to create a moderate citizen body practicing self-restraint. Paraphrasing Aristotle, one might then say that no one can be moderate (and prudent) without also being good and virtuous. The extent to which a person may deviate from the middle path before becoming blameworthy is not easy to determine by abstract reasoning and is contingent upon context and circumstances. "Such things," Aristotle claimed, "depend on particular facts and the decision rests with perception. So much, then, is plain, that the intermediate state is in all things to be praised, but that we must incline sometimes towards the excess, sometimes towards the deficiency; for so shall we most easily hit the mean and what is right."[39] Sometimes, we may have to forgo moderation to find the proper course of action. The idea that moderates, in order to remain faithful to their principles, might sometimes have to incline toward extremes is arguably one of the most intriguing implications of Aristotle's argument.

The individual type of moderation described by Aristotle found its institutional home in the concept of *mixed government,* defined as a combination of several forms of government in which power is shared by various groups and is exercised according to a combination of rules and procedures.[40] A mixed constitution was seen from the very beginning as an effective remedy for the concentration of political power. Although not all of those who have defended mixed constitutions were political moderates, there is a significant affinity between this concept and the idea of political moderation.[41] A proponent of *juste milieu,* Aristotle favored a mixed constitution on logical, prudential, and normative grounds. First, since virtue presupposes finding the mean between extremes, it follows logically that the constitution that gives priority to the middling ranks in society would be the best. Second, Aristotle viewed mixed government as a prudential middle ground between the extremes of pure democracy and oligarchy. He defined it as a type of constitution that does not grant unlimited authority to any group and uses a combination of democratic, oligarchic, and aristocratic standards for assigning political rights. To this end, Aristotle proposed a mixture of institutional mechanisms and electoral practices (election by lot and ballot) meant to secure the stability of the constitution and prevent revolutions.

Third, Aristotle offered a normative justification for mixing democratic and oligarchic elements and principles. The existence of a mere balance between classes, he argued, is no guarantee of social peace and prosperity. "Revolutions also break out when opposite parties, e.g., the rich and the people are equally balanced, and there is little or no middle class."[42] Hence, what is really needed for the preservation of a constitutional regime is the existence of a third moderating class in the middle: the more elements a constitution brings together, the more stable and just a political regime is. Mixed constitutions, Aristotle believed, satisfy the requirements of justice and fairness and grant a special role to the citizens of the middle class, arguably the strongest supporters of moderate government. On this view, a polity with a large middle class is far more stable than one in which this class is weak. The middle class, Aristotle claimed, is law-abiding and easily submits to authority, being free from factions and dissentions. "In that condition of life men are most ready to follow rational principles,"[43] and are conscientious about fulfilling their political and social obligations.

At first sight, Aristotle's theory might appear as an ideology justifying the particular interests of a single class as beneficial to the entire society. His description of mixed government in *Politics* IV:11, for example, grants precedence to a middle class arguably endowed with all the qualities required for creating and maintaining constitutional government. Nothing is explicitly said here about the necessary blending between the interests of various classes, a theme that would loom large in Cicero's writings. Nonetheless, Aristotle addresses this important issue in IV:9, where he gives specific recommendations for combining oligarchic and democratic procedures and principles in setting property qualifications and in the daily administration of justice. Moreover, in books 5 and 6 of *Politics*, Aristotle examines the best ways of preventing civil wars and revolutions, highlighting the importance of combining the interests of the rich and the poor in the government of the city. Hence, the simultaneous emphasis on the virtues of the middle class and the need to create a genuine balance of power in the state should be seen not as a contradiction in Aristotle's writings, but as a proof of his thesis that mixed government comes in various forms and is compatible with a wide range of constitutional arrangements.

Aristotle's skepticism about the ability of simple forms of government to stave off corruption was shared by Polybius, Plutarch, and Cicero, who also praised the virtues of mixed constitutions in their political and historical writings.[44] Plutarch had words of praise for Lycurgus' statesmanship, which combined soulcraft and statecraft to create a viable political regime whose strength came from its judiciously balanced constitution.[45] While Polybius considered three forms of mixed constitutions—those of Sparta, Carthage, and Rome—he clearly preferred the latter, because it allowed for territorial expansion and the attainment of power, something that the constitution of Sparta made impossible. In book 6 of the *Histories*, Polybius ascribed the success of the Roman republic to its mixed constitution combining monarchical, aristocratic, and democratic elements in a judicious way.[46] Simple forms of government, he affirmed, are by nature subject to revolutions, periodic changes in social structure, mores, and lifestyle, which statesmen can learn to anticipate and the consequences of which they can effectively address by striving to maintain a balance between the rule by one, the few, and the many.[47] Polybius paid special attention to the separation of functions between the senate, the consuls, and the people. The first had complete control over expenditures and revenues, the second made decisions on military issues, and the *populus Romanus* had the right to award honors and punishments.

While Polybius' conception of mixed government granted each of the three elements (monarchy, oligarchy, democracy) an almost equal share in the exercise of political power, Cicero took a different route. He did not describe the Roman constitution as a simple mixture of diverse elements, but as a harmonious synthesis between democratic and oligarchic elements (as represented by the consuls, the senate, and the popular assemblies) creating "an equitable balance of rights and duties and responsibilities."[48] In Cicero's *On the Laws*, the senate plays a key role as a stabilizing and moderating institution. Senators, Cicero believed, should be chosen from those who have held office, and no one should be allowed to reach the highest position without the approval of the people. This requirement, he added, "is moderated by the fact that in our law the authority of the senate is strengthened. . . . For it works out that if the senate is in charge of public deliberation, and if the remaining orders are willing to have the commonwealth guided by the deliberation of the leading order, then it is possible through the blending of rights, since the people have power and the senate has authority, that that moderate and harmonious order of the state be maintained."[49]

In *On the Commonwealth*, Cicero referred to mixed government as a "blended and mixed" (I:45) form, "an alloy of all three" (I:54), providing for a proportionate combination of dissimilar elements. He insisted that the constitution of Rome was both "moderate and balanced" and praised its "moderately blended form of commonwealth"[50] which combined equality, fairness, and stability. In his view, a mixed constitution was similar to a choir in which the singers' voices blend harmoniously:

> In playing the lyre or the flute, and of course in choral singing, a degree of harmony must be maintained among the different sounds, and if it is altered or discordant a trained ear cannot endure it; and this harmony, through the regulation of very different voices, is made pleasing and concordant. So too the state, through the reasoned balance of the highest and the lowest and the intervening orders, is harmonious in the concord of very different people. What musicians call harmony with regard to song is concord in the state, the tightest and the best bond of safety in every republic; and that concord can never exist without justice.[51]

This elegant passage is remarkable for a couple of reasons. First, it draws attention to the relationship between musical harmony (*concentus*) and social concord (*consensus*) which, in turn, are produced by the proportionate blending of unlike tones, and the agreement among dissimilar elements, brought about by a fair and reasonable blending together of the upper, middle, and lower classes, just as if they were musical tones. Cicero had in mind a concrete example, the Roman constitution in its best days, long gone by the time he came to write these beautiful lines. Second, although the passage suggests that this harmonious blending of classes and interests is the best guarantee of liberty, order, and justice in a state, Cicero believed that the senators and the wealthy members of the landed class should play a larger political role than the rest of the citizens. This ought probably be taken as an indication of Cicero's fear of excess and his concern with restoring and preserving the balance of powers in the state rather than as an ideological endorsement of a narrow set of class interests.

Moderation as temperance and self-restraint also occupies a key place in the Christian tradition, being regarded, along with prudence, as a cardinal virtue and the mold and "mother" of all the other virtues. The Desert Fathers believed that "everything which is extreme is destructive,"[52] and Christian theologians argued that moderation is *not* incompatible with fortitude, courage, and wisdom. In fact, they claimed, no one can be wise and courageous without also being prudent (and moderate) at the same time. In a certain way, the whole structure of the Christian view of man affirms the pre-eminence of prudence and moderation under the guise of temperance, which explains why the Christian view of moderation does not carry the usual connotations of mediocrity, selfish utilitarianism, and small-mindedness, being instead associated with true nobility of spirit and human dignity.[53]

This ordering of the virtues that grants pride of place to prudence and, vicariously, to moderation, was not accidental. For Christian theologians have argued that justice, fortitude, and temperance achieve their "perfection" only when they are founded upon prudence (and moderation), which implies a superior ability to make right decisions and choices, and a corresponding ability to realize one's full potential. On this view, moderation and prudence, while they do not in themselves constitute the perfection of human beings, are nonetheless indispensable if the latter are to carry through their impulses and instincts for right acting, and if they are to transform their naturally good predispositions into real virtues.[54] As such, moderation and prudence are the "true" measure of justice and goodness: what is moderate and prudent coincides with what is good. As Josef Pieper has pointed out, this understanding of moderation had little to do with the common (emasculated) image of this virtue as the opposite of any form of exuberance. Not only do moderation and prudence imply the proper directing of volition and action toward objective reality; they also presuppose the ability to gain an objective perception and superior understanding of reality in such a way that our knowledge of ends and the appropriate means for reaching them derives to a great extent from moderation and prudence. On this view, the latter are necessary to the attainment of moral virtue as well as to the execution of justice for the common good. The complex relationship between prudence and moderation as temperance was examined in detail in St. Thomas Aquinas' *Summa Theologiae*, in which he offered a classical treatment of prudence (XXXVI, 2a2ae 47–56) and temperance (XLIII, 2a2ae 141–154 and XLIV, 2a2ae 155–170). Although Aquinas did not explicitly refer to moderation, his theory of prudence and defense of temperance, deeply embedded in the Christian tradition, are relevant for our discussion of the classical faces of moderation.[55] Appropriating Aristotle's equation of prudence with practical wisdom, he rejected the latter's claim that *phronesis* can ever operate without the aid of first principles. Nor did Aquinas believe that prudence is only about means. Instead, he emphasized that prudence is concerned with the attainment of the good and is always dependent on first principles. He then went on to distinguish prudence as "wisdom in human affairs" from "wisdom pure and simple,"[56] and insisted that prudence as practical wisdom comes in different forms that must be distinguished one from the other: sham prudence, genuine but incomplete prudence, and genuine and complete prudence. "He who contrives fitting means to a wrong end," Aquinas wrote, "has false prudence, for his adopted end is not a genuine end, but merely resembles one."[57] This false prudence, as St. Paul reminded us, is that of sinners (*prudentia carnis mors est*).[58] A prudent man who pursues the end appropriate to some specialized employment (i.e., the prudent sailor or trader) has incomplete prudence because his goal is not the universal end for human beings and represents only a sectional or particular interest. The person who fails to act after reaching a sound judgment on important matters in life has incomplete prudence as well. This type of prudence is common to the upright and the wicked alike. Referring to the highest form of prudence, Aquinas noted: "There is the genuine and complete prudence which, with a view to the final good for the whole of human life, rightly deliberates, decides, and commands. This alone is prudence pure and simple, and in sinners it just cannot be."[59] Since it requires time and experience, that is, the practice of making good and effective decisions, prudence does not come automatically from nature, although "the aptitude for prudence is from nature."[60] It is a particular skill, comprised of the ability to make fair assessments and pursue realistic goals, quickness of wit, and the capacity to shoot at a mark and hit the point.

Early Modern Faces of Moderation

Sixteenth-century political thinkers such as Machiavelli, Claude de Seyssel, Louis Le Roy, and Étienne Pasquier drew inspiration from Polybius' and Cicero's theories of mixed government. It is in their writings that the connection between the mixed constitution and moderate government came to the fore two centuries before Montesquieu.[61] Unlike Cicero, Machiavelli did not insist on the connection between mixed government and *concordia ordinum*. In book 1 of his *Discourses*, he emphasized that social tensions, if properly channeled through adequate institutions, could, in fact, be a source of progress and liberty rather than turmoil and anarchy. This, Machiavelli insisted, was demonstrated by the Roman constitution, which owed its excellence not only to the judicious blending of monarchic, aristocratic, and democratic elements, but also to the proper institutionalization of the disunion and quarrels between the senate and the people.[62]

Seyssel's *La Monarchie de France*, written in 1515 and published in 1519, took over from the tradition of mixed government several key themes from the ancient theory of *concordia ordinum*. He described an ordered monarchy as a regime characterized by harmony, consonance, union, and correspondence among all estates, adding that "the affairs of the kingdom prosper to the extent to which the kings . . . are attentive in upholding this union and correspondence."[63] Seyssel's argument in favor of a mixed constitution was, in fact, an indirect apology for a moderate form of monarchy based on the interdependence of mutually limiting powers and authorities. As Nannerl Keohane pointed out, "the notion of complex legal and institutional constraints against the exercise of a *volonté desordonée*, and the notion of power increased rather than diminished by such constraints,"[64] recur as key themes throughout Seyssel's work. The authority of the king was to be regulated by three "bridles" limiting the will of the monarch: religion, justice, and "*la police*" (the latter different from what we understand by this term today). Seyssel emphasized the role of good laws, ordinances, and intermediary bodies in tempering the power of the monarch, and maintained that they were supposed to act in concert with customs, past examples, and the multitude of offices and magistracies. He granted to *parlements* and courts of justice the important political role of setting procedural patterns for the government of the kingdom.

Seyssel's ideas were developed by another sixteenth-century proponent of moderate monarchy, Étienne Pasquier, in *Recherches de la France*,[65] in which he commented on the institutional architecture of what Montesquieu later called "Gothic" government. Like Seyssel, Pasquier stressed that, in a moderate monarchy, the potentially arbitrary power of the king must be held in check by a complex institutional framework and legal instruments. In this well-ordered ideal monarchy, the authority of the king could never be absolute, being restrained and moderated by multiple sources of power, privileges, and rights. Both Pasquier and Seyssel defended a system of balance of powers *sui generis* in which the nobles and the *parlements* were regarded as effective countervailing forces capable of limiting the authority of a monarch invested with divine right.

The image of moderation as antidote to (political and religious) zealotry, fanaticism, and extremism appeared in the writings of several other well-known sixteenth- and seventeenth century writers. Montaigne's *Essays*, for example, can be interpreted as a sophisticated defense of moderation and temperance, two indispensable virtues that can prevent us from losing measure and composure in our pursuit of goodness, virtue, and justice. After confessing that he liked natures that are temperate and moderate and that "there is no pleasure, however proper, which does not become a matter of reproach when excessive and intemperate,"[66] Montaigne claimed that moderation represents the true greatness of man, whose "most glorious achievement is to live . . . life fittingly,"[67] that is, with temperance and without eccentricity. Far from being equated with dullness, this type of moderation has its own excellence which derives from understanding that the real "greatness of soul," as Montaigne wrote, "consists not so much in striving upwards and forwards as in knowing how to find one's place and to draw the line."[68] Nonetheless, Montaigne added, it is much easier to make one's journey along the margins, "where the edges serve as a limit and a guide, rather than take the wide and unhedged Middle Way; but it is also less noble, less commendable."[69] La Bruyère closed his famous *Caractères* by reminding the reader (in a section entitled "*Des esprits forts*"!) that moderation is a divine virtue, whereas everything that partakes of the extremes is imperfect and shares in the shortcomings of all human beings.[70]

Taking up a distinctively Aristotelian trope and following in Montaigne's footsteps (to some extent), Pascal offered one of the most memorable accounts of moderation as the virtue appropriate to the human condition. In his view, our limited mental and physical powers are nothing but a reflection of our middling nature, equally incapable of absolute knowledge and complete ignorance. Pascal's restless man—*le roseau pensant*—stands in the middle between non-being and infinity, limited in his intellectual and physical faculties, unable to know the whole truth, but not entirely ignorant either. He wanders over a vast plane, always uncertain of his final destination, but always cautious to avoid the extremes. Nature, Pascal concluded, has placed us in this middle, and the greatness of the human condition consists in knowing how to remain there. Since we can never achieve absolute certainty or stability, we must try to accommodate ourselves to our middling human condition and make the best of it. Leaving this middle would amount then to abandoning humanity, since our frail reason is easily deceived by appearances and is ever incapable of seeing the "true" forms beyond the shadows of reality.[71]

Baltasar Gracián wrote extensively about the link between moderation, prudence, and temperance, three concepts that loomed large in his writings, especially in the *Oráculo manual y arte de prudencia* (1647).[72] Quoting the ancient dictum *Est modus in rebus*, he argued that moderate (and prudent) people always look for measure in everything. They avoid being overly moralizing and pedantic, even when they are sure to be right, and are reluctant to ever take their principles to extremes. "Push right to the extreme and it becomes wrong," Gracián wrote. "Press all the juice from an orange and it becomes bitter. Even in enjoyment never go to extremes. Thought too subtle is dull."[73] In his view, "keen observation, subtle insight, and judicious inference"[74] are the prerequisites of that "judicious moderation"[75] without which there can be no sound judgment. As such, moderation is related in Gracián's works to a concept with deep roots in medieval theology—*syndéresis*, a natural virtue of the soul that, as *scintilla conscientiae*, gives us the inner knowledge of moral truths that is needed in order to live well.[76]

Drawing on ancient authors, Fénelon remarked that the wisdom and excellence of all governments consist in finding the middle between two extreme forms of liberty "moderated only by the authority of the laws."[77] The ethical image of moderation as a form of self-restraint and control of one's passions appeared in Antoine Furetière's famous *Dictionnaire universel* (1690), which defined moderation as "a virtue regulating all passions,"[78] and in the *Dictionnaire de l'Académie,* where moderation was equated with *sang froid* and the sound judgment that enables us to find the just measure in everything.[79] All of these meanings reappeared half a century later in Jaucourt's entry on this topic in the *Encyclopédie.* Jaucourt defined moderation as a cardinal virtue capable of restraining human passions and insisted that it is always the outcome of prudence and temperance. As such, he argued (quoting Horace), moderation is inseparable from moral integrity and represents the source of true happiness on Earth.[80]

A few words about the connection between moderation and the ideal of *l'honnête homme* are also in order.[81] While the roots of the latter can be traced back to the sixteenth-century image of the courtier, the best place to examine it is in the writings of seventeenth-century French writers, where it designated the person who effortlessly combines sociability, gallantry, and propriety with liberty, civility, and a strong sense of individuality. *Honnêteté* was described as the quintessential art of excelling in everything that concerns the amenities and delights of life. By implication, its exercise required a sense of order and propriety, measure, and moderation.[82] The ideal of *l'honnête homme* was inseparable from the image of the person who shies away from exaggerations and extremes, who combines wisdom and gaiety, erudition and politeness, firmness and flexibility, reason and wit.[83] At the same time, in the moralists' writings, *honnêteté* retained its ethical image as a virtue capable of tempering human passions with a view to finding the *juste milieu* between excess and deficit. "The extremes are vicious," wrote François de Callières in 1695, and affectation of any kind destroys even the most beautiful souls.[84] Moderation was not only regarded as a virtue of *l'honnête homme*, but was more broadly seen as capable of tempering great vices such as concupiscence, *amour propre* (vanity), and avarice.

A more critical view of moderation can be found in the writings of La Rochefoucauld, who claimed that people make a virtue of moderation only in order to limit the ambitions of great men and console their mediocre souls for their limited fortune and merits.[85] In reality, he argued, moderation can bring about neither security nor glory. In one of his maxims, La Rochefoucauld admitted: "Moderation is like sobriety: one would love to eat more, but one fears hurting oneself."[86] He praised boldness as a countervailing element to the alleged mediocrity of moderation: "Moderation cannot have the merit of fighting ambition and of subduing it; they are never found together. While moderation is the languor and laziness of the soul, ambition is its activity and ardor."[87] Almost half a century later, Lord Kames disagreed precisely with this view when commending "moderation in our desires and appetites" because it "fits us for doing our duty" and contributes "the most to happiness." He added that "even social passions, when moderate, are more pleasant than when they swell beyond proper bounds."[88]

Another face of political moderation, *trimming,* appeared around the same time in the writings of George Saville, Marquis of Halifax (1633–1695), and half a century later in Hume's historical and political writings. Halifax penned the classical definition of the moderate politician as a mediator between contending parties in his essay, *"The Character of a Trimmer,"* written in 1684–85 and published in 1688 (under the name of Halifax's uncle, Sir William Coventry).[89] Halifax's trimmer resembled Plutarch's portrait of Pericles: "the pilot of a ship who, when a gale blows up at sea, makes everything tight, trims his sails, and exerts his seaman's arts to the utmost, disregarding the tears and entreaties of the seasick and terrified passengers."[90] Halifax associated moderation with the art of compromise needed for maintaining equipoise between different interests, groups, and powers in any commonwealth. "This innocent word *Trimmer*," he wrote, "signifieth no more than this, That if Men are together in a boat, and one part of the company would weigh it down on one side, another would make it lean as much to the contrary; it happeneth there is a third Opinion of those, who conceive it would do as well, if the Boat went even, without endangering the passengers."[91] During Halifax's time and shortly thereafter, the word "trimmer" had pejorative connotations derived from the strong religious controversies of that period. It meant not only a "man of moderation" and a "man of Latitude," but also a "neutral" and uncertain person, as well as a "traitor."

It is worth pausing for a moment to consider, for example, the portrait of Halifax drawn by Hume, who practiced an original form of (methodological) trimming in writing the *History of England*, a sophisticated attack on— and correction of—previous Whig and Tory interpretations of the development of liberties and rights in England. As Hume himself acknowledged in his essay "Of the Protestant Succession," the historian who belong to neither party (Whig nor Tory) must "put all the circumstances in the scale and assign to each of them its proper poise and influence," aware of the fact that "there scarcely ever occurs, in any deliberation, a choice, which is either purely good, or purely ill."[92] True to this moderate outlook, Hume also believed that there is no more effective method of promoting a socially and politically beneficial end than "to encourage moderate opinions, to find the proper medium in all disputes, to persuade each that its antagonist may possibly be sometime in the right, and to keep a balance in the praise and blame, which we bestow on either side."[93] One might expect that Hume would have endorsed Halifax's trimming, but in reality, his portrait of the latter was far more nuanced. For Hume, Halifax was "a man who possessed the finest genius and most extensive capacity," but who affected a specious form of neutrality between the parties that was "more natural to men of integrity than of ambition."[94] Be that as it may, the main merit of Halifax's essay is to have given the term "trimmer" a more positive connotation, while also reminding his readers that trimmers, due to their eclecticism, are notoriously difficult to place on the spectrum of modern political ideologies. They share a number of affinities with both the conservative and liberal traditions, but neither can fully claim the trimmer as their faithful representative.[95]

In the eighteenth-century, along with Voltaire and Smith, Hume put forward a trenchant critique of fanaticism as a dangerous form of immoderation, one that they all equated with intolerance, corruption of the mind, and ignorance. For Hume, fanaticism represented a "bad" type of enthusiasm, one that had degenerated into superstition. As an antonym of "moderation," this form of corrupted enthusiasm arises from a presumptuous pride and confidence in one's power and intellect that persuades the zealous leaders of fanatical sects to falsely bestow upon themselves a dangerously sacred character. This type of immoderation, Hume warned, often produces "the most cruel disorders in human society" and is an enemy to civil liberty, while "true" enthusiasm is "a friend to it."[96] In his article on fanaticism in the *Encyclopédie*, Deleyre insisted that, of all the corrupters of moral sentiments, fanaticism has always been among the greatest and most dangerous ones because it is a "blind and passionate zeal born of superstitious opinions, causing people to commit ridiculous, unjust, and cruel actions without any shame or remorse."[97] Among the several causes of (religious) fanaticism, Deleyre mentioned flawed dogmas ("Truth does not make any fanatics," he confidently remarked),[98] "atrocious morals," the misinterpretation of duties, and religious intolerance and persecution. The condemnation of religious fanaticism during the Enlightenment pitched those who opposed "enthusiasm" against the defenders of superstition, obscurantism, and prejudice. As Chicaneau de Neuville remarked in 1756, "fanaticism is contrary to wisdom, moderation, and the true spirit of Christianity."[99] Voltaire provided a trenchant critique of fanaticism as a form of immoderation in his *Dictionnaire philosophique* (1764).[100] As soon as fanaticism penetrates into someone's mind, he claimed, the malady is almost incurable. Worse, often times the laws themselves are ineffective in combating fanaticism and those touched by this illness end up being led by crooks (*"fripons"*) who give them arms and motivation to pursue their dangerous ideals.

Yet fanaticism proved to be a remarkably ambivalent passion, for in the works of some authors both its positive and negative connotations could coexist. Arguably, the most interesting case in point was Rousseau. On the one hand, in *Lettres sur la providence* (1756), he criticized the irrational nature of fanaticism as a "stupid and blind furor," and in *Émile*, he argued that "it is less the strength of arms than the moderation of hearts which makes men independent and free."[101] On the other hand, in the same book he also described fanaticism as a strong passion capable of inspiring people and making them despise death. Comparing fanaticism with philosophic indifference which "resembles the tranquility of the state under despotism," Rousseau argued that the first, "although more deadly in its immediate effects than what is today called the philosophic spirit, is much less so in its consequences."[102]

What conclusions can we draw from our brief historical foray?[103] First, over time, moderation came to designate, in addition to one of the main characteristics of statesmen and legislators, an important trait of political institutions and laws, or the outcome of a particular institutional structure. Second, it is important to note the strong connection between moderation and institutional complexity, an idea that would resonate later with Montesquieu, Mounier, Necker, Mme de Staël, and Constant. Third, classical authors praised the institutional framework of mixed government, not only because the latter blended various social interests and elements, allowing them to coexist harmoniously, but also because it made it extremely difficult for any group to impose its will over others and exercise arbitrary power.[104] Fourth, linked to the idea of mixed government was the image of *balance* as expressed in the constitutional "checks and balances" that regulate and restrain competition for power. Balance also signified a proportionate combination of diverse social elements, either as a blending or a fusion, as demonstrated by several articles in the *Encyclopédie*.[105] While in theory it is possible for a constitution to be moderate without relying on a mixture of social elements, in practice most moderate governments have been characterized by a certain mixture or balance between social, political, and economic interests. As d'Holbach argued, the progress of any state is impossible in the absence of a "just equilibrium" between all the groups and classes in society that prevents any one of them from encroaching on the others. "All authority beyond measure," he wrote, "placed in the hands of a few members of society, is established at the expense of the safety and well-being of all."[106] As we shall see later, the constitutional interpretation of balance loomed large in the works of Mounier and the Coppet group, and the image of *scale* eventually came to be regarded as an appropriate metaphor (though not the only one!) of political moderation.

TWO
THE ARCHITECTURE OF MODERATE GOVERNMENT
Montesquieu's Science of the Legislator

L'esprit de la modération doit être celui du législateur.
—Montesquieu

The Highest Virtue

"I have written this work only to prove it: the spirit of moderation should be that of the legislator," writes Montesquieu at the beginning of Book XXIX of *The Spirit of the Laws* (1748).[1] The fact that this claim is made toward the end of the work is surprising. Why did Montesquieu wait so long to argue that moderation is the key virtue of all legislators? Might this be the secret "chain" that links together all the major themes of his difficult masterpiece?

To be sure, as the defining characteristic of free governments, moderation is a seminal theme in Montesquieu's political works. All of his views on law, order, and liberty coalesce around the concept of political moderation.[2] The centrality of the latter to Montesquieu's thought has been underscored by many of his interpreters, but it is not clear what exactly he meant by this surprisingly elusive concept. In his initial discussion of the nature and principles of moderate governments, he was surprisingly "coy" and prudent in affirming the priority of moderation.[3] Moreover, while the issue of moderation undergirds his critique of despotism in the *Persian Letters*, it is only in *The Spirit of the Laws* (henceforth abbreviated *SL*) that Montesquieu's critique of despotic governments is developed into a full-fledged normative agenda in praise of political moderation and institutional complexity.[4] The epigraph of the latter—*Prolem sine matre creatum*—inspired by Ovid's *Metamorphoses*, reflects Montesquieu's bold ambition of writing an original and challenging work. Its thirty-one books comprised of six hundred five chapters describe, sometimes in painstaking detail, the institutional and constitutional architecture of moderate political regimes. Montesquieu drew a seminal relationship between moderation, limited power, the separation of powers, and the rule of law, and he made the concept of political moderation the keystone of his liberal political philosophy.

Published anonymously in Geneva in October 1748, Montesquieu's masterpiece enjoyed instant success. No less than fifteen editions, some in anonymous versions, had appeared by the end of 1749 in four countries.[5] Montesquieu's *SL* was described as "the code of reason and liberty,"[6] "the triumph of humanity, the masterpiece of genius, the Bible of all politicians."[7] Fully aware of the importance of style and taste, Montesquieu paid special attention to the literary aspect of his composition, whose complex structure points to the existence of a sophisticated plan (perhaps *ad usum delphini*) requiring special hermeneutical skills.[8] Montesquieu's esoteric tone and elliptical style make liberal use of mysterious hints, bold generalizations, learned references, and carefully chosen historical examples, and combines prudence with boldness in a most unusual and playful way. "I do not write to censure that which is established in any country whatsoever," he remarked in the preface of *SL*. "Each nation will find here the reasons for its maxims."[9] A few lines later, however, he announces that he intends to propose a new science of politics whose main aim is to cure others of their nefarious prejudices. At times, he spends entire pages discussing the intricacies of French feudal laws, at other times he presents his ideas in surprisingly short sentences, full of hidden meanings and erudite allusions.

The book displays an order that gracefully and gradually insinuates itself into the audience's mind; the sequence of themes is carefully chosen to keep readers interested in the development of Montesquieu's principles and to stir their imagination.[10] The incompleteness of some of his ideas is therefore deliberate, meant to constantly engage and stimulate the curiosity of his readers.[11] He directs their attention in a highly choreographed way, ever aware that "one must not always so exhaust a subject that one leaves nothing for the reader to do. It is not a question of making him read but of making him think."[12] At regular intervals, Montesquieu, a master of surprise and contrasts, addresses a reminder to his readers, urging them to remain curious and alert until the very end of the book, in spite of the plethora of ideas and historical details he presents. His sophisticated style, the complex organization of the book, and his own digressions are an invitation to patient and slow reading which leaves it up to the readers to supply the missing links between ideas and decipher the true message of the book.[13] He had to give voice to important truths whose direct enunciation might have offended influential persons in positions of authority, and so Montesquieu prudently "veiled" them from those to whom they would have been harmful, without however letting them be lost for the "wise."[14] This prudent consideration, along with Montesquieu's interest in style, explains the peculiar strategy and rhetoric whereby he encourages his audience to discover the principles of liberty "*as in a mirror*" and go beyond appearances in order to comprehend the "nuances of things"[15] and discover for themselves the underlying meanings.

Fully aware of the difficulty of his book, Montesquieu believed that only a "holistic" reading would enable his readers to follow the development and interdependence of its major themes. In the preface to *SL*, he wrote: "I ask a favor that I fear will not be granted; it is that one not judge by a moment's reading the work of twenty years, that one approve or condemn the book as a whole and not some few sentences. If one wants to seek the design of the author, one can find it only in the design of the work. . . . Many of the truths will make themselves felt here only when one sees the chain connecting them with others."[16] Much ink has flowed on this enigmatic metaphor which continues to fascinate Montesquieu's interpreters. Did he have in mind freedom or virtue, as some commentators claimed,[17] or something else? Without underplaying the significance of political liberty or virtue for Montesquieu, I believe that the mysterious "chain" to which Montesquieu referred on several occasions is related to the concept of political moderation which, in his works, completes the transition from character trait to a fundamental constitutional principle.

In addition to curing others of their prejudices, Montesquieu had at least two other main goals in mind when writing his masterpiece: to correct abuses and to teach and instill the spirit of moderation, the supreme virtue of any legislator. The ideas of his book were meant to teach rulers how to govern with moderation by avoiding excesses of cruelty and promoting free inquiry and *les lumières*.[18] This in itself was no minor task, given the political context in which Montesquieu wrote. That is why Montesquieu's writing style resembles more a complex lens than a clear window and why the apparent coolness of his dense prose often conceals the heat of a volcano within. Attentive readers must come equipped with adequate hermeneutical strategies in order to decipher his cryptic messages. It is important, therefore, that we begin our journey by examining the core principles from which he started, for they may help us to better understand Montesquieu's conceptual framework and political vision at the heart of which lies the concept of political moderation.[19]

The Complex Nature of Moderation

Montesquieu's belief in the power of moderation is demonstrated by various arguments strategically placed in different chapters of *SL*. As already mentioned, he does not explicitly acknowledge the fundamental role of moderation until near the end of the work (*SL*, XXIX: 1, 602). This seminal claim is foreshadowed, however, by a number of hints found earlier in the text. For example, in book VI, Montesquieu points out that "men must not be led to extremes, [but] should manage the means that nature gives us to guide them" (*SL*, VI: 12, 85) and in book XXII he affirms that "moderation governs men, not excesses" (*SL*, XXII: 22, 426). Yet at the same time, Montesquieu also thought that truly moderate spirits were surprisingly rare and hard to find: "By a misfortune attached to the human condition, great men who are moderate are rare; and, as it always easier to follow one's strength than to check it . . . it is easier to find extremely virtuous people than extremely wise men" (*SL*, XXVIII: 41, 595). We need to ask how these statements can be reconciled.

As with many other passages in Montesquieu's writings, it is difficult to ascertain if these were intended to be normative claims or factual statements, since the line that separates them is difficult to draw. Montesquieu's belief in the power of moderation—a difficult and rare virtue—must be related to his claim that moderation corresponds to the "nature" of things and has an ontological foundation reflecting the order of the world. His emphasis on nature must be taken with a grain of salt, for in his opinion building moderate government is *never* a mere work of nature, but is instead the outcome of a sophisticated constitutional design requiring great skills, prudence, and discernment. What makes Montesquieu's case interesting for us is that he no longer regarded moderation primarily as an exclusive virtue of well-ordered souls (a prominent theme in classical political philosophy, beginning with Plato), but as an essential feature of a certain type of government, that is, a *moderate government*. In his view, moderation depended to a great extent on the nature of the laws and the constitution of each country, and it played a key role in tempering the exercise of power, thus ensuring the harmonious coexistence of various interests and classes in society. As a result, moderation comprised a complex web of interrelated elements with constitutional, penal, fiscal, religious, and ethical dimensions, all closely linked to one another.

Although moderation was presented as the outcome of a complex institutional alchemy, its *ethical* dimension was not absent from Montesquieu's works. Describing moderation as a cardinal virtue, he distinguished between two types of moderation: one founded on genuine virtue and another "that comes from faintheartedness and from laziness of the soul" (*SL*, III: 4, 25).[20] At the same time, he remarked that moderation presupposes a certain social condition characterized by the existence of a particular set of mores, manners, values, customs, and traditions.[21] Thus, moderation appears as a feature of "gentle" (*doux*) regimes that avoid the extremes of cruelty and suffering. Furthermore, in the footsteps of Aristotle, Montesquieu drew a close connection between moderation, practical wisdom, and opposition to extremes, advising legislators and citizens: "Do not go too far to the right . . . do not go too far to the left: stay between the two" (*SL*, XXX: 10, 627). On this view, moderation becomes an expression of the discernment, prudence, and common sense which, Montesquieu insisted, should be the primary virtues of all legislators.

Moderation and Mixed Government

Montesquieu followed in the footsteps of his predecessors by drawing a close relationship between moderation and mixed government.[22] As Michael Sonenscher has remarked, this connection in Montesquieu's work has a complex and interesting genealogy. In particular, Montesquieu's interpretation of the "double majesty" of the Roman emperors and of the obscure origins of the ancient government of the Germans allowed him to account for the gradual emergence of moderate governments in which the king had the right to power but not the right to judge, that being reserved to intermediary bodies.[23]

Although Montesquieu was reluctant to refer to the "best" form of government in general, he made a rather surprising claim after discussing the constitution of England in XI: 6, praising in unusually glowing terms the so-called "Gothic government" as a mixture of aristocracy and monarchy. In spite of its drawbacks (the common people were slaves, Montesquieu remarked), this regime which had existed in some parts of Western Europe was a good government which had the capacity to change and improve over time:

> Giving letters of emancipation became the custom, and soon the civil liberty of the people, the prerogatives of the nobility and of the clergy, and the power of the kings, were in such concert that there has never been, I believe, a government on earth as well tempered as that of each part of Europe during the time that this government continued to exist; and it is remarkable that the corruption of the government of a conquering people should have formed the best kind of government men have been able to devise (SL, XI: 8, 167–68).

The use of the superlative here is striking because Montesquieu was notoriously reluctant to make bold generalizations of this kind. Since his enthusiasm for the "Gothic government" seems to be at odds with his previous cautious tone, it remains an open question whether or not it should be read as an expression of Montesquieu's admiration for mixed constitutions based on a sound balance between various groups and interests in society.

Along with the English constitution, "Gothic" government became the model for Montesquieu's theory of moderate government. As Lee Ward has argued, Montesquieu explored "the potentiality for moderate government in some combination of British and Gothic principles."[24] At the same time, his account of constitutionalism has many striking similarities with his description of the distribution of powers in ancient Rome and must be interpreted in light of Montesquieu's understanding of the main features of the so-called "Gothic" constitution. The latter held sway over a loosely connected feudal system, intermediate institutions, and territorially divided powers between the center and the periphery. Montesquieu admired the complex interdependence between the power of the monarch, the privileges of the nobles, the clergy, and regional assemblies with overlapping jurisdictions. This was not only the genius of the ancient constitution of France, he argued, but also of the Roman constitution. "The laws of Rome," Montesquieu wrote, "had wisely divided public power among a large number of magistracies, which supported, checked, and tempered each other."[25]

An attentive reader of Roman historians, Montesquieu traced the origins of the mixed constitution back to the Roman republic and recommended the study of Roman history to anyone interested in politics. "Study the Romans," he wrote; "their superiority will never be more evident than in the choice of the circumstances in which they did good and evil things."[26] Montesquieu attributed the rise of the Roman republic to its successful combination of well-designed institutions and civic virtue that allowed its citizens to live in peace and prosperity at home and wage successful wars abroad. In the early stages of the republic, Montesquieu remarked, the Romans were at the same time prudent and audacious, self-interested and committed to the common good; the most salient features of the early republic were its citizens' love of liberty, hatred of tyranny, and love of equality. As a mixture between monarchical, aristocratic, and popular elements, the Roman government eventually achieved a sound "harmony of power" (*SL*, XI: 12, 172) that tempered disputes between the classes. As a result, the government of Rome came to be based upon a judicious distribution of powers between the people, the senate, and other magistracies which, along with its sound constitution, made it possible to correct or prevent abuses of power.[27] The republic derived its force from the civic virtue of its citizens and from the existence of sound institutions. Every soldier was at the same time a citizen who had a stake in working for maintaining the prosperity of the republic.

In chapter IX of the *Considerations,* Montesquieu attributed the decline of the Roman republic to the corruption of mores and the disappearance of the balance of power that tipped alternatively in favor of the people, the patricians, or the consuls at the expense of rival classes. "The distracted city no longer formed a complete whole,"[28] Montesquieu noted, and he pointed to the growing propensity to abuse power on all sides in order to explain the progressive corruption of the Roman republic.[29] This argument was expanded in an important letter of Montesquieu to William Domville (included in the *Pensées*). Referring to the corruption of the people as a whole, Montesquieu pointed out that military tributes and the pillage of Rome's enemies had the long-term perverse effects of creating a large gap between rich and poor that ended up destroying the unity of the city and corrupting the civic spirit of its citizens.[30]

A cursory look at what Montesquieu wrote in chapters VIII, IX, and XI of the *Considerations* reveals an interesting relationship between the mixed constitution and the concept of the balance of powers. It is not a mere coincidence that he returned to Cicero's old metaphor of the *symphonia discors* and linked it to the metaphor of "scale" in order to describe a moderate form of government in which the monarch is in the center of the scale, and the intermediate powers (the nobles and the people) in the balances. On this view, what keeps a city together and constitutes its force is "a union in harmony" which does *not* exclude well-tempered social dissonances and political differences:

> That which we call union in a political body is a very equivocal
> thing: the true unity is a union in harmony, which operates in such
> a fashion that all the different parts, however opposed they may
> appear to us to be, concur in the general good of society, as disso-

nances in music agree in the concord of the whole. Thus there can be union in a state where one would expect only turbulence: that is to say, a harmony that gives birth to happiness, the only true peace. It is like the parts of the universe itself, eternally linked by the action of some and the reaction of others.[31]

In this wonderful passage reminiscent of Cicero, Montesquieu compares the harmony of moderate government to the cosmic order and the accord of celestial spheres. The underlying idea is that, just as the order of the universe derives from its diversity, so the order of moderate governments results from their internal balance and from a concord between their various components as well as from their plurality. The political balance in the state manifests the harmony of the world, and the intricate complexity of moderate government reflects *harmonia mundi*, being the outcome of the successful "tempering" of competing political powers and social interests.[32] As such, the essence of moderate government lies in its internal consonance and "discordant accord."

The use of Cicero's musical metaphor in the *Considerations* underscores Montesquieu's intention to stress the internal complexity of moderate governments, a major theme to which he returned again and again in *SL* and in the *Pensées*, where he contrasted it with the simplicity and uniformity of despotic regimes.[33] As Nannerl Keohane has argued, Montesquieu understood quite well that "creating a moderate government means deliberately lifting a polity out of simplicity, instituting a complexity of form where there would otherwise be pure domination."[34] While moderate governments are complex human artifices resulting from a sophisticated alchemy of passions, interests, and powers, despotic regimes spring up naturally from the common human instinct to dominate and oppress. Despotism is no longer seen as a corruption of monarchy, as it was portrayed in the older scheme of classifying governments; it appears now as a different type of political regime, one that demands special consideration.

One must resist the temptation of interpreting Montesquieu's account of moderate government as a mere endorsement of mixed (Gothic) government, or as an accurate description of the English political system, which he strongly admired. Almost none of Montesquieu's contemporaries believed that he accurately depicted the reality of English politics as it was practiced across the Channel during his time. Montesquieu was favorably disposed toward moderate monarchy à *l'anglaise*, because in this regime laws reign rather than the will of individuals (in the Aristotelian sense), and the authority of the sovereign is effectively limited by intermediary powers and fundamental laws. Yet, his admiration for England should not be interpreted as an unqualified approval of the country's limited monarchy, nor must it be seen as an endorsement of a strict version of the separation of powers.[35] As M.J.C. Vile remarked, it is no mere coincidence that, when enumerating the forms of government at the beginning of *SL*, Montesquieu made no mention of mixed government. He returned, however, to this theme later, in book XI, to praise mixed government for successfully protecting liberty and rights.[36]

Moderation and Political Liberty

At the core of Montesquieu's conceptual apparatus lies the fundamental distinction between moderate and immoderate governments, which underpins his constitutional theory based on the doctrine of the balance of powers. By distinguishing between moderate and immoderate governments, Montesquieu departed from previous classifications. For him, the fundamental question was no longer *who* exercised power—one, the few, or the many—but *how* power was exercised, that is, moderately or immoderately. Political liberty, he argued, exists only in moderate governments and only in those governments in which power is not chronically abused.

By identifying moderation as the cornerstone of free governments and drawing a fundamental dichotomy between moderate and immoderate governments—a distinction pregnant with important normative connotations—Montesquieu achieved two important things. First, he shifted the focus of inquiry from the ethical to the *institutional* aspects of moderation, paying special attention to the architecture of constitutional government in which political moderation is embedded.[37] Second, he extended the scope of the concept of *gouvernement modéré* by applying the label not only to republican regimes, whose main principle is political virtue defined as love of country and love of equality,[38] but also to monarchies, whose underlying principle is honor and in which intermediary bodies act as effective countervailing forces to the authority of the monarch. According to Montesquieu, moderation founded on virtue is "the soul" of aristocratic governments, and all moderate governments are, by nature, "gentle" regimes incompatible with arbitrary power.

The opposition between a gentle and cruel way of exercising power was a major theme of Montesquieu's "liberalism of fear," which sought to avoid all forms of cruelty and intolerance. "All felicity," he claimed, "lies in the people's opinion of the gentleness of the government" (*SL*, XII: 25, 209), and gentleness reigns only in moderate governments, that is, only in those regimes in which power is limited and exercised with moderation, the antonym of cruelty, harshness, and intolerance.[39] Such governments are most in conformity with reason, and their functioning is not disturbed by internal friction and turmoil; they tend to act with minimal political constraints, which allow them to relax their springs without peril. In such governments, citizens tend to be happy because they feel secure and their dignity is duly respected; the situation is different in democratic and despotic regimes, which are not by nature moderate and in which power is chronically abused.

Montesquieu's emphasis on *félicité* points to the existence of a seminal relationship between political happiness, liberty, and moderation. Liberty, he argues, exists and thrives only in moderate regimes, tempered by the separation of powers, the presence of intermediary bodies, and the rule of law; it accompanies moderation and ought to be seen as its natural complement or outcome.[40] Montesquieu's conception of political moderation is perhaps nowhere so salient as in books XI-XII of *SL* where he articulates his views of political liberty by using several overlapping narratives of liberty. These focus on different yet related concepts and themes, such as social liberty, constitutional liberty (in England), Gothic government, and also the absence of liberty (in despotic Asian regimes).

Montesquieu was as fully aware of the semantic richness of liberty as he was of the conceptual complexity of moderation. "No word has received more different interpretations and has struck minds in so many ways as has *liberty*," he wrote. "Some have taken it for the ease of removing the one to whom they had given tyrannical power; some, for the faculty of electing the one whom they were to obey; others for the right to be armed and to be able to use violence; yet others, for the privilege of being governed only by a man of their own nation; or by their own laws."[41] Montesquieu opposed the definition of liberty as freedom *from* the laws because, in his view, it offered a one-sided perspective on liberty, highlighting only one particular aspect of it, namely freedom from coercion or security. He was equally skeptical of the alternative republican approach, which defined liberty as freedom *through* the laws and emphasized political participation, a concept that does not loom large in Montesquieu's conceptual framework. Finally, he expressed reservations regarding the equation of liberty with natural rights, for he did not believe that the latter were valid universally without regard to the diversity of social and political contexts.[42]

Equally important is the distinction Montesquieu drew between *political* and *philosophical* liberty. True liberty, he argued, is identical neither with independence nor with caprice: "It is true that in democracies the people seem to do what they want, but political liberty in no way consists in doing what one wants. In a state, that is, in a society where there are laws, liberty can consist only in having the power to do what one should want to do and in no way being constrained to do what one should not want to do" (*SL*, XI: 3, 155). A few pages later he returns to this point, distinguishing between two types of political liberty. The first (philosophical) consists in "the exercise of one's will," while the second (political) consists in "security or, at least, in the opinion one has of one's security" (*SL*, XII: 2, 188). On this view, liberty is the right to do all that the laws permit or do not explicitly prohibit. Hence, liberty can mean many things: the absence of fear; personal security; the rule of law; free competition for power; the economic freedom to pursue one's interests unhindered; and the freedom of individual will.

Nonetheless, for Montesquieu none of these definitions and narratives of liberty taken alone was satisfactory because none of them captured the richness and multifaceted nature of liberty, which was not the exclusive preserve of any particular form of government (republic, monarchy, aristocracy, or democracy). He eschewed the customary practice of associating freedom with a particular form of government (constitutional monarchy for Locke, the democratic republic for Rousseau) and argued that, although political liberty can be found only in moderate governments, it is not always present in moderate states. Liberty must be defined in connection with the *manner* in which authority is exercised and depends on a complex alchemy of powers and a set of political institutions; it exists only when power is not abused and is properly limited by constitutional devices, customs, or religion. In other words, liberty is the complex outcome of the interaction of many factors and elements that vary from one form of government to another.[43] This is why liberty can be found in both moderate monarchies and republics and, as Montesquieu put it, it is no farther from the throne than from the senate.[44]

The close relationship between political liberty, moderation, and laws deserves additional scrutiny. While moderation cannot be identified with liberty, it is nonetheless one of the prerequisites of the latter.[45] Montesquieu insisted that political liberty and moderation depend to a great extent on the nature of the laws, adding that there can be no liberty and moderation when laws are disregarded or misinterpreted to suit the interests of rulers. Freedom is derived from the fixed, stable, and impersonal nature of the law, which, in free states, is everywhere known and respected by all citizens, regardless of their rank or wealth.[46] Worth noting here is the connection Montesquieu draws between liberty, moderation, balance of powers, and the rule of law. Correspondingly, political liberty and moderation are absent from those regimes in which fear and uncertainty dominate and where there is no trust, honor, or personal security.

It is worth noting that Montesquieu refused to embrace the language of rights, preferring instead "to put cruelty first."[47] At the same time, he devoted two major books of *SL* (XI and XII) to discussing *political* liberty in relation to the constitution (the distribution of powers in the state) and *civil* liberty in relation to the citizen. "It is not enough to treat political liberty in its relation to the constitution," he argued; "it must be shown in its relation to the citizen" (*SL*, XII: 1, 187). While liberty is promoted by a certain distribution of the three powers in the state that prevents those exercising the legislative and/or the executive power from having the power of judging, political freedom means much more than the separation (or distribution) of powers and the presence of intermediary bodies. Properly understood, liberty depends on extra-political factors such as mores, manners, education, customs, and religion which, by regulating the internal and external conduct of individuals, promote, directly or indirectly, the spirit of moderation.[48] As such, political liberty represents much more than the opposite of despotism: it designates a particular way of social life whose main trait is moderation.

Wary of carrying any principle—including the allegedly "good" ones—to extremes, Montesquieu stopped short of considering the distribution or separation of powers and the rule of law as absolute prerequisites of free regimes. He opposed taking the letter of the law too seriously, suggesting instead that moderation is needed to make the application of laws more humane and that circumstances must always be taken into account. "It could happen that the law, which is simultaneously clairvoyant and blind, might also be too rigorous in certain cases," he wrote. "It is for its supreme authority to moderate the law in favor of the law itself by pronouncing less rigorously than the law" (*SL*, XI: 6, 163).

Penal Moderation and Montesquieu's Theory of Jurisprudence

This important dimension of moderation in *SL* comes to the fore in Montesquieu's philosophy of jurisprudence.[49] The extended treatment of penalties in book VI and the corresponding discussion of jurisprudence in book XII, along with the analysis of the power of judging and other related topics, add important dimensions to Montesquieu's reflections on the art of legislation, political moderation, and the rule of law. Among the safeguards of individual security, he paid particular attention to the existence of an independent judiciary[50] and a certain manner of judging that follows precedents and the formalities of justice, with their complex and slow procedures meant to protect individuals against the loss of their life, liberty, and property.

Before examining in detail Montesquieu's ideas on penal laws, it is important to get a clear picture of what he had to say about laws in general. Books VI, XIX, XXVI, and XXIX of *SL*, in which Montesquieu examined civil and criminal laws as well as penalties, can be interpreted as a sophisticated critique of the idea of a uniform and simple jurisprudence which some of his contemporaries favored. Montesquieu went to great lengths to argue that laws must always be properly worded and should be supported by solid and clearly formulated rationales. Their style must be concise and simple and ought to avoid vague expressions that might lead to conflicting interpretations: "The laws should not be subtle; they are made for people of middling understanding" (*SL*, XXIX: 16, 614). Furthermore, the legislator should never lose sight of the fact that several laws must correct and support each other and that they ought to be in harmony with each other and should be judged collectively rather than individually.

The underlying assumption of Montesquieu's theory of jurisprudence is explicitly stated in *SL*, XII: 2 where, after defining political liberty as consisting "in security or, at least, in the opinion one has of one's security," Montesquieu goes on to add that "the citizen's liberty depends principally on the goodness of the criminal laws" (*SL*, XII: 2, 188). Since civil liberty is equated with freedom from arbitrariness, freedom is predicated upon a knowledge of the rules and their predictable application in criminal judgments: "Though tribunals should not be fixed, judgments should be fixed to such a degree that they are never anything but a precise text of the law"

(*SL*, XI: 6, 158).[51] Since criminal laws can be a major source of injustice and abuse, effective safeguards must be created in order to protect the security of individuals and shield them from the arbitrary application of the laws by those in power. Liberty itself, as the title of XII: 4 shows, can be affected by the nature and degree of penalties. The connection between moderate penalties and an absence of arbitrariness is evident in the opening paragraph of this chapter: "It is the triumph of liberty when criminal laws draw each penalty from the particular nature of the crime. All arbitrariness ends; the penalty does not come from the legislator's capriciousness but from the nature of the thing, and man does not do violence to man" (*SL*, XII: 4, 189).[52] To the question when the legislator should punish or pardon, Montesquieu answers that "this is something better felt than described" (*SL*, VI: 21, 95), admitting that a wise legislator must enact penalties that draw "from the nature" of each case and should act with prudence and moderation.

In spite of the liberal tone of his theory of jurisprudence, which unambiguously condemned torture, Montesquieu stopped short of challenging some of the most controversial articles of the Criminal Ordinance of 1670, a code that contained several strikingly illiberal provisions.[53] Montesquieu did not publicly object to the stipulation that trials were to be conducted in secrecy, nor did he think that the cross-examination of witnesses by defense counsel was essential to a fair trial. Furthermore, Montesquieu did not object to the practice of not granting a right to counsel in criminal cases. Instead, he insisted that wise legislators should use the means nature gives them and prescribe a just mixture of penalties and rewards, drawing upon the maxims of philosophy, morality, and religion, the rules of honor, the love of the homeland, and the fear of blame.[54] In moderate (gentle) regimes, Montesquieu argued, a good legislator "can form anything into penalties" and, as a result, will insist "less on punishing crimes than on preventing them; he will apply himself more to giving mores than to inflicting punishments" (*SL*, VI: 9, 82–83). That is why, Montesquieu argued, "a good legislator takes a middle way: he does not always order pecuniary penalties; he does not always inflict corporal penalties" (*SL*, VI: 18, 93). There are cases when legislators should apply the full extent of the law and cases when they should refrain from doing so: "An administration is sublime if it is well aware what part of power, great or small, should be used in various circumstances" (*SL*, XII: 25, 209).

A few concrete examples will be useful to illustrate these points. The importance of letters of pardon in moderate governments did not escape Montesquieu's attention. With regard to civil penalties for accusations of heresy, he recommended moderation, arguing that legislators must be "very wary" of punishing alleged heretics (*SL*, XII: 5, 193). In such cases, prudence is especially called for as proving that someone has heretical views always involves controversial and potentially arbitrary interpretations of other people's beliefs. Discourse and speech cannot form the *corpus delicti* because they can always be easily misinterpreted: "Nothing makes the crime of high treason more arbitrary than when indiscreet speech becomes its material. Discourse is so subject to interpretation, there is so much difference between indiscretion and malice and so little in the expressions they use, that the law can scarcely subject speech to a capital penalty" (*SL*, XII: 12, 198). Once again, applying moderate penalties would be preferable to an accusation of high treason.[55] Moreover, accusing someone of holding or propagating heretical views becomes dangerous in proportion to people's ignorance and fears. That is why Montesquieu insisted that laws should be charged only with punishing external actions and should never seek to guess and discipline inner thoughts or penalize secret intentions.[56] A regime in which people could be charged with crimes of high treason on the grounds of their thoughts would be a harsh tyranny, since many ideas seen as challenging the *status quo* could be interpreted as treason. The word "treason," Montesquieu noted, is ambiguous, and its vagueness represents a danger to individual liberty. "Vagueness in the crime of high treason is enough to make government degenerate into despotism," (*SL*, XII: 7, 194) because it is always possible to exaggerate or misrepresent the nature of the alleged crime.

Montesquieu also addressed crimes against religion, supporting the decriminalization of sacrilege and blasphemy. In so doing, he combined both prudential and normative reasons. "Penal laws," he wrote, "must be avoided in the matter of religion," (*SL*, XV: 12, 489) as they almost never have a positive effect and are often used as a means of stifling dissent and punishing rivals.[57] The promises made by religion are so great that, no matter what penalties the magistrates might impose, they will never be effective deterrents. Legislators must act as "political men and not theologians" (*SL*, XV: 9, 487) when judging these matters, striking a balance between giving religion its due and limiting its jurisdiction over people's private lives. Montesquieu prudently acknowledged that "the institutions of religion are always presumed to be the best," while also warning against trying to enact by divine laws "that which should be enacted by human laws" (*SL*, XVI: 2, 495). "Human laws," he argued, "enact about the good: religion, about the best. The good can have another object because there are several goods, but the best is one alone and can, therefore, never change" (*SL*, XVI: 2, 495).

Montesquieu's views on penal laws were inseparable from his belief that liberty is secure only in those regimes in which it is duly protected by the formalities of justice. In such governments, the forms and rules of justice protect the dignity and liberty of ordinary citizens, for justice is administered according to fixed, impersonal, and certain standards. "Tribunals of the judiciary," Montesquieu wrote, must always be "coolheaded and, in a way, neutral in all matters of business" (*SL*, VI: 6, 80). Impartial procedures along with unchanging rules and clear and known laws constitute the essence of moderate government: "Law is everywhere wise; it is known everywhere, and the lowest of the magistrates can follow it."[58] The administration of justice requires scrupulous inquiries and carefully weighed decisions according to the spirit of the law, while also taking into account the existence of "many rules, restrictions, and extensions, that multiply particular cases and seem to make an art of reasoning itself."[59] In free regimes, one always finds a multiplicity of such regulations and conventions reflecting the numerous distinctions in the nature of men's goods, ranks, and social conditions. As a rule, the "formalities [of justice] increase in proportion to the importance given to the honor, fortune, life, and liberty of the citizens" (*SL*, VI: 2, 75).

In moderate regimes, the manner of forming judgments is deeply imbued with a spirit of moderation, which requires that scrupulous inquiries be conducted according to that spirit. Neither the prince nor his council exercises judicial power; the laws are supposed to be "the prince's eyes; he sees with them what he could not see without them" (*SL*, VI: 5, 80), and he may never ignore or abuse them.[60] The judgments rendered by the prince would otherwise be an inexhaustible source of injustice and abuse, much like the judgments of a despot whose will meets with no effective obstacle and whose power is virtually unlimited. Not only is the monarch prevented from exercising judicial power in moderate regimes, but judges are prevented from making the rules, which they are expected to follow to the letter while also making sure that "no law can be interpreted to the detriment of a citizen when it is a question of his goods, his honor, or his life" (*SL*, VI: 3, 76). The existence of a genuine spirit of judicial compromise and of extensive judicial formalities temper the exercise of power and modify the ways in which authority is dispersed and exercised, promoting respect for the life, liberty, and property of ordinary citizens. Thus, "the head of even the lowest citizen is esteemed" (*SL*, VI: 2, 75),[61] and his honor and goods can be removed from him only after careful examination conducted according to clearly formulated procedures and laws.

By virtue of their complex structure, in moderate regimes power is mediated by an intricate hierarchical structure that counter-balances the authority of magistrates and the prince.[62] Unlike despotic regimes, moderate governments can, as much as they want and without peril, "relax" their springs from time to time. Social life under these regimes is not based on fear and intimidation.[63] They maintain themselves primarily by laws and mores that effectively limit power and foster a general beneficial spirit of moderation, accommodation, and compromise.

Fiscal Moderation

Given the importance of collecting and using the revenues of the state, it is not surprising that fiscal moderation[64] occupies a central place in Montesquieu's agenda. He turns to this subject in book XIII, in a discussion that complements his previous analysis of constitutional and penal moderation.

In the opening chapter, he introduces the importance of fiscal moderation by stating that "there is nothing that wisdom and prudence should regulate more than the portion taken away from the subjects and the portion left to them. . . . In order to fix these REVENUES well one must consider both the necessities of the state and the necessities of the citizens" (*SL*, XIII: 1, 213). He insists that it is the state that must adjust to society rather than vice versa, adding that "one must not take from the real needs of the people for the imaginary needs of the state" (*SL*, XIII: 1, 213). Among the imaginary needs of the state Montesquieu included "the ones sought by the passions and weaknesses of those who govern," needs that are often nothing more than a result of the "sick envy of vainglory, and a certain impotence of spirit in the face of their fancies" (*SL*, XIII: 1, 213). Public revenues may not be adjusted to suit the imaginary needs and fancies of those in power, but ought rather to reflect what people should and can give for the pursuit of common interests. By stressing this point, Montesquieu declared his opposition to those theories which argued that it is the richness of the state that constitutes the well-being of its subjects.

According to Montesquieu, the nature of any fiscal system is a corollary of—and reflects—the principles of each political regime, an observation that brings us back to the fundamental distinction between moderate and immoderate regimes. Under a moderate government people are more willing to contribute to the welfare of the state than in any other regimes, because taxation is based on a tacit contract that respects individual liberty and property. Taxes are easier to collect, and the majority of them are direct, mostly imposts on commodities. "Taxes can be increased because the moderation of the government can procure wealth there"; correspondingly, taxes will be seen by citizens as "a kind of reward to the prince for the respect of the laws" (*SL*, XIII: 13, 221). If taxes are wisely raised and spent, the people will be almost unaware of their existence and will not feel them as oppressive. What is more, not only are moderate governments able to raise higher tax revenues in the short-run, but liberty itself leads to higher taxes in the long run. Lower taxes are most often a mark of unfree states, for "extreme servitude cannot be increased" (*SL*, XIII: 13, 222), and despotic regimes have few means of increasing the burden upon their subjects. As a general rule, Montesquieu argued, "one can levy heavier taxes in proportion to the liberty of the subjects and one is forced to moderate them insofar as servitude increases. . . . In moderate states, there is a compensation for heavy taxes; it is liberty. In despotic states, there is an equivalent for liberty; it is modest taxes" (*SL*, XIII: 12, 220–21).[65]

What are the implications of Montesquieu's plea for fiscal moderation? As Catherine Larrère has pointed out, "one can find here in Montesquieu's thought the liberal idea that individual interest is the best guide for each person's conduct and that no repressive authority is needed, along with a special emphasis on the need for, and right of everyone, for ease and wealth."[66] In Montesquieu's view, the art of good government requires that rulers and legislators take advantage of the passions of the people—cupidity, a desire for gain, the ambition to rise, and vanity—in order to guide them with a "gentle" and moderate touch. That is why the best course of action is to follow nature and exercise constraint, while employing extreme measures only sparingly. "Nature is just toward men," Montesquieu wrote. "She rewards them for their pains; she makes them hard workers because she attaches greater rewards to greater work. But if an arbitrary power removes nature's rewards, the distaste for work recurs and inaction appears to be the only good" (*SL*, XIII: 2, 214). Fiscal moderation encourages people to work, fostering frugality and foresight: "In a nation that is in servitude, one works more to preserve than to acquire; in a free nation, one works more to acquire than to preserve."[67]

Montesquieu's call for fiscal moderation and his declared preference for a rationalization of fiscal policies are peculiar in at least one other important respect. In spite of his avowed economic liberalism, he did *not* follow the Lockean classical scheme of "no taxation without representation." In moderate governments, Montesquieu maintained, taxes are not based on an explicit contract of submission, but are seen as a way of "rewarding" the rulers for obeying the laws and treating their subjects with respect. As such, taxes are an expression of public trust in rulers and laws and an obligation arising from tacit consent.[68]

The Constitutional Framework of Moderate Government

Montesquieu's concept of moderation begins to come into sharper focus now as more light is shed on its ethical, constitutional, penal, and fiscal dimensions, all of which are connected to political moderation. The next step in our analysis will involve a close examination of his theory of political moderation as illustrated by several key chapters in *SL* (V: 14; XI: 6-8) and the *Considérations* (VIII, IX, XI). In these chapters, moderation is presented both as a constitutional principle and as a prerequisite of political and social pluralism essential to the preservation of liberty. Building moderate government, Montesquieu argued, requires no less a masterwork of legislation, combining both practical wisdom and vision. In order to form a moderate government, "one must combine powers, regulate them, temper them, make them act; one must give one power a ballast, so to speak, to put it in a position to resist another." As such, moderate government is a work of art, "a masterpiece of legislation that chance rarely produces and prudence is rarely allowed to produce" (*SL*, V:14, 63). The alchemy necessary for reaching this fragile equipoise is a true work of political art at the core of which are political moderation and limited power.

The previous discussion of Montesquieu's analysis of Rome's mixed constitution drew our attention to the existence of an important relationship between the concepts of mixture, equipoise, balance, and harmony. Much as musical harmony is the outcome of an interplay between dissonance and concord, so political order is the result of well-tempered and regulated conflict and tension mediated by sound laws and effective checks and balances. The moderation characterizing free governments is the result of the smooth flow of power through mediating channels, which transform discordant passions and interests into social harmony. In such governments, political liberty results from the "agitation" and friction that is produced when diverse social groups and interests collide. It is the upshot of *"une convention de plusieurs et une discussion d'intérêts"*[69] based on an intricate web of mutually controlling passions and interests, intermediary (corporate) bodies, local customs, and liberties. Two different yet related meanings of moderate government emerge from Montesquieu's use of the twin metaphors of scale and balance. The first refers to the harmonious interplay or cooperation between different political forces in the state, while the second connotes "a regulated conflict of opposing groups, from whose institutionally controlled struggles for power results the freedom of the state."[70] It is to this second meaning that we turn next in order to explore the constitutional architecture of moderate government.

Montesquieu paid particular attention to this topic, especially in *SL*, XI: 6, a chapter often viewed as a panegyric of the English constitution and its alleged "separation" of powers. A closer look reveals, however, that Montesquieu in fact favored a blending rather than a strict separation of powers and referred in his book to *pouvoirs distribués* and not to *pouvoirs séparés*.[71] Moreover, he had serious misgivings about what he feared were excesses of liberty in England and warned that the prodigious love of liberty among the English might run to regrettable extremes if not properly regulated by mores and channeled into adequate institutions.

A conceptual clarification is in order here. Montesquieu began his famous chapter XI: 6 (in *SL*) by defining the three main powers in the state as follows: "In each state there are three sorts of power: legislative power, executive power over the things depending on the right of nations, and executive power over the things depending on civil right" (*SL*, XI: 6, 156). He argued that "the masterwork of legislation is to know where properly to place the power of judging"; and he added that the latter "could not be placed worse than in the hands of the one who already has executive power" (*SL*, XI: 11, 169). Worth noting here is the definition of judicial power as "the executive power over the things depending on civil right" (Montesquieu used, in fact, the phrase la *puissance de juger* instead of *pouvoir judiciaire*). This reminds us that in Montesquieu's writings, the judiciary does not have yet the prominent position it would have a few decades later in the *Federalist Papers*.[72] Although Montesquieu considered independent judges an essential condition for the preservation of freedom, he did not grant the judiciary a status equal to that of the legislative and executive powers. Nonetheless, to the question whether the judiciary power can and should be entirely independent from the other two powers, Montesquieu responded in the affirmative, stressing the importance of the rule of law in securing political moderation.

What, then, is the relationship between these concepts and the famous "separation" of powers? The works of Michel Troper and M.J.C. Vile point to two different ways of thinking about constitutionalism, separation, and the balance of powers.[73] According to Troper, it is important to distinguish between doctrines proposing a *hierarchy* among powers and those seeking to create *equilibrium* between them, without assigning superiority to any one. The doctrine of the balance of powers has historically been grounded in the recognition of the supremacy of the *legislative* power,[74] a fact amply confirmed by the U.S. Constitution, among others. It does *not* imply a strict separation between the legislative and the executive powers and refers instead to the balance between the two main powers sharing in the exercise of the legislative *function*. The different authorities sharing in the legislative function may include the two chambers of parliament, the ministers as agents of the executive power, and the constitutional monarch or other head of the state. Hence, Troper concluded, we must distinguish between the separation of powers and the balance of powers, as the latter can be achieved either through separation or specialization.[75]

It was the doctrine of the balanced constitution rather than the theory of the strict separation of powers that became the basis of Montesquieu's account of the English constitution in *SL*. One will find in his writings neither a defense of a functional separation of powers nor an unambiguous case for the separation of the personnel of the legislative and executive powers.[76] His key point can be stated as follows: liberty and moderation cannot exist in a state in which power is chronically abused and which lacks proper checks and balances. In order to build moderate government and prevent abuses of power, one must create viable institutional mechanisms that can effectively block attempts at usurping power: "So that one cannot abuse power, power must check power by the arrangement of things" (*SL*, XI: 4, 155).

Hence, what is usually referred to as the "separation" of powers in Montesquieu's work can be summarized by the following two principles: (1) the legislative power may never be combined with the executive power in one single person or body of magistrates; (2) the power of judging must be separate from both the legislative and executive power so as to be able to tell the truth to those in power and effectively protect the rights of individuals. Hence, in moderate regimes no single person or body of magistrates can simultaneously exercise both the executive and the judiciary power. "All would be lost," Montesquieu acknowledged, "if the same man or the same body of principal men, either nobles, or of the people, exercised these three powers: that of making the laws, that of executing public resolutions, and that of judging the crimes or the disputes of individuals" (*SL*, XI: 6, 157).[77]

In many kingdoms of Europe, Montesquieu added, "the government is moderate because the prince, who has the first two powers, leaves the exercise of the third to his subjects" (*SL*, XI: 6, 157).

While distinguishing between the separation and distribution of powers, Montesquieu also redefined the boundary between the three powers in the state in such a way that they could exercise mutual oversight and keep each other in check at all times. To prevent the omnipotence of the legislative power, he stipulated that the legislative body should never convene itself and should not remain in permanent session. If the executive did not have the power to regulate the opening and duration of legislative sessions, the assembly could well become despotic. At the same time, to prevent the tyranny of the executive, Montesquieu insisted that the legislative power must also have the right "to examine the manner in which the laws it has made have been executed" (*SL*, XI: 6, 162). Montesquieu also highlighted the importance of the inviolability of the monarch. His person should be "sacred"[78] and placed above political groups and parties, as a guarantee of the stability of the social order. The constitutional monarch ought to be politically unaccountable in order to be able to properly exercise his political role. Because the monarch is ultimately bound by the fundamental laws of the kingdom, his power, Montesquieu insisted, is in fact limited and moderated by countless intermediary bodies, customs, and mores, all acting as tempering devices.

Montesquieu granted a share in the legislative and executive power to both parliament and the monarch in carefully calculated degrees so as to create a functional and flexible system of checks and balances and overlapping jurisdictions. Parliament, he argued, must have the right to examine how laws are executed and should retain the right to approve or reject the raising of public funds by the executive power. In turn, in a moderate monarchy, the sovereign authority must have the right to veto the laws voted by the two chambers: "Executive power should take part in legislation by its faculty of vetoing; otherwise it will be stripped of its prerogatives" (*SL*, XI: 6, 164). Nonetheless, the participation of the monarch in the exercise of the legislative power ought to be limited, and the monarch should never take part in legislation by enacting laws; if he were to do so, "there would no longer be liberty."[79]

Furthermore, Montesquieu did *not* explicitly advocate the political responsibility of the king's ministers in parliament[80] and stopped short of endorsing the more traditional doctrine of "the king-in-parliament."[81] In a seminal passage, he described the final outcome of these constitutional provisions as follows: "Here, therefore, is the fundamental constitution of the government of which we are speaking. As its legislative body is composed of two parts, the one will be *chained* to the other by their reciprocal faculty of vetoing. The two will be *bound* by the executive power, which will itself be *bound* by the legislative power. . . . As they are constrained to move by the necessary motion of things, they will be *forced to move in concert*" (*SL*, XI: 6).[82] What is remarkable in this passage is that Montesquieu refers to independent powers that are "chained" to each other, stressing that they are interdependent and always bound to act "in concert" for the sake of the common good.

We are now in a better position to understand how Montesquieu was able to reformulate in modern terms the old Ciceronian theory of *concordia ordinum* (discussed earlier) by giving it a modern constitutional twist. Although the two main powers in the state (the legislative and the executive) are in theory independent of each other, in reality they are often obliged to compromise and temper their political ambitions. The deputies' initiatives cannot become laws without the approval of the monarch, a royal veto forcing in each case parliament to return to the drawing board. At the same time, the monarch must carefully weigh the options for the formation of his cabinet, being expected to propose to the two Chambers only those ministers who would govern according to (and not against) the wishes of the majority in parliament. Thus, *de iure* independence of powers is not the same thing as *de facto* independence. Many interpretations of Montesquieu make the error of confounding the two by assuming that the first necessarily implies in practice a strict separation of powers and their functions.[83]

It might seem odd, then, that Montesquieu's alleged "separation" of powers becomes in the end a *balance* of mutually controlling powers that keep each other in equipoise and are bound to act in concert for promoting the common good.[84] This interpretation reflects Montesquieu's endorsement of a hybrid constitutional model combining the "separation" of powers with the decentralized framework of the older Gothic constitution, based on a complex vertical system of overlapping institutions and jurisdictions. As Lee Ward perceptively noted, "Montesquieu presents the federal principles embedded in the decentralized Gothic Constitution as a vital supplement to the separation of powers, and a corrective to the problem of concentrated power in modern England and France."[85] This seminal point becomes evident in the last (often neglected) books of *SL*, where Montesquieu offers a detailed examination of French feudal laws that is essential to an understanding of his political moderation. He examined the system of the justice of lords according to which justice was a right inherent in the fiefs,[86] insisting on the "infinity of charters prohibiting the judges or officers of the king from entering the territory to exercise any act of justice whatever or to require any judicial emolument whatever" (*SL*, XXX: 20, 652). This is important because it confirms that, under feudal government, the authority of the monarch was in fact a limited power, especially after the reign of Charlemagne. The king, Montesquieu wrote, "had almost no more direct authority: a power that had to pass through so many other powers and through such great powers was checked or lost before reaching its goal. Such great vassals no longer obeyed, and they even used their under-vassals in order not to obey any longer" (*SL*, XXXI: 32, 716).

Thus, Montesquieu's theory of the balance of powers achieved in the end something that a strict separation of powers would never have been able to accomplish on its own. For the principle of the separation of powers does not actually determine how powers ought to be composed; it merely separates their functions and spheres of competence and is common to several types of commonwealths. Montesquieu understood this point better than anyone else. In his eyes, moderation as a constitutional principle combined the horizontal separation of powers among various branches of government with the vertical diffusion of power among several layers of authority.[87] According to this view, it would be incorrect to simply call parliament the "legislative" power and government the "executive" power, since neither power is placed exclusively in the hands of either parliament or the government. They are, in fact, *blended* and *mixed* between the two in such a way that both powers are able to reciprocally control and temper each other's initiatives.

By refusing to give the direction of the commonwealth to a single body or person, Montesquieu challenged competing theories of sovereignty—those of Bodin, Hobbes, and Rousseau—which endorsed a unitary and undivided source of sovereignty. In this respect, one can detect an important affinity between Montesquieu's ideas on sovereignty and those of his contemporary Jean-Jacques Burlamaqui (1694–1748), whose *Principes du droit naturel et politique* was published in 1747, a year before Montesquieu's *magnum opus*. Burlamaqui's conception of the balance of powers, which resembled Montesquieu's constitutionalist agenda, exercised considerable influence on the Founding Fathers. There is, in fact, ample evidence that his work was widely known in mid-eighteenth-century American colleges.[88] In an important passage he explicitly referred to the balance of powers and checks and balances in a tone that reminds one of Montesquieu:

> This partition produces a balance of power, which places the different bodies of the state in such a mutual dependence, as retains every one, who has a share in the sovereign authority, within the bounds which the law prescribes to them; by which means the public liberty is secured. For example, the royal authority is balanced by the power of the people, and a third order serves as a counter-balance to the two former, to keep them always in an equilibrium, and hinder the one from subverting the other.[89]

Commenting on the relationship between divided sovereignty, mixed government, balance of powers, and political moderation, Burlamaqui reached a set of conclusions similar to Montesquieu's: "From what has been said on the nature of mixed or compound governments," Burlamaqui wrote referring to moderate governments, "it follows, that in all such states, the sovereignty is limited; for as the different branches are not committed to a single person, but lodged in different hands, the power of those, who have a share in the government, is thereby restrained; and as they are thus a check to each other, this produces such a balance of authority, as secures the public weal, and the liberty of individuals."[90]

At the same time, it must be pointed out that Montesquieu went *farther* than his Genevan contemporary in linking moderation to balance of powers and political pluralism as prerequisites of a free society. Liberty, Montesquieu argued, is best protected in a regime in which the power and the government of society are in the hands of various social groups and interests competing for supremacy. Thus, moderate governments can survive and thrive only if their institutions foster and successfully channel the genuine pluralism of interests and ideas without which there can never be any lasting freedom or security.[91]

The Good Legislator and the Spirit of Moderation

I have already referred to Montesquieu's claim that the good legislator should be imbued with the spirit of moderation. For all its brevity, this remains an ambiguous remark. Why should moderation be the supreme virtue of the legislator rather than fairness or justice? Montesquieu's answer to this question is worth examining in detail since it is central to the main themes of the present book. As Céline Spector has pointed out, Montesquieu's theory of moderation is, above all, "*une théorie de la mesure*,"[92] and in his writings, moderation is grounded in a larger vision of the "political good." He was aware that few concepts were likely to generate more controversy than the latter, and he preferred to say of the political good only that, "like the moral good, [it] is always found between two limits" (*SL*, XXIX: 1, 602) and does not lend itself to a more precise formulation. The difficulty in finding the right balance is compounded by the fact that, in the realm of politics, the right measure can never be discovered with the aid of apodictic formulas. Similar to the political good, any virtue or political principle—including liberty, equality, and justice—can easily be abused.[93] Hence, wise legislators must seek to carve out a middle ground between extremes, and the only resources they have at their disposal are prudence, discernment, and moderation.

Montesquieu devoted many pages to discussing the art of legislation in painstaking details. Drawing a fundamental distinction between laws and the "spirit" of the laws, he emphasized the dependence of political institutions and laws on social, economic, and cultural factors. Nevertheless, the political sphere retained a key role in his writings as the main stated purpose of *SL*—namely, the education of the legislator—suggests. Montesquieu believed that the nature of a society is primarily a derivative of the nature and principles of its government and claimed that principles always exercise a fundamental influence on the nature of the laws. Appearances notwithstanding, there is no *a priori* contradiction between stressing, on the one hand, the importance of non-political factors and, on the other hand, affirming the primacy of the political sphere.[94] Wise legislators always seek to work with—rather than against—the general spirit and the mores of a country, and the greatness of legislative genius consists "in knowing in which cases there must be uniformity and in which differences" (*SL*, XXIX: 18, 617).

This might help explain why Montesquieu, who rejected the idea of uniform legislation, refused to admit that political questions could ever be reduced to a few general and simple propositions or universally applicable recommendations, a position that would be shared by Condorcet a few decades later.[95] It is revealing that in the last chapter of book XXIX of *SL*, Montesquieu counted neither Locke nor More nor Harrington among mankind's greatest legislators. Instead, he invoked the names of Aristotle and Machiavelli, the two great masters of prudence, the contextual virtue *par excellence* and one that Montesquieu appreciated as well. More importantly, it was Montesquieu's endorsement of the fundamental *indeterminacy* of the political good that gave his political theory a moderate tone, preventing it from becoming deterministic or axiomatic.[96] As we have seen, Montesquieu argued that there is more than one good form of government, adding that wise legislators must try to moderate the shortcomings of each type, a task that is possible in all governments save despotism. This undertaking requires prudence and discernment and imposes upon legislators the duty to promote toleration and pluralism.

It is in this light that one must examine Montesquieu's ideas on climate and geography. Far from being deterministic, Montesquieu admitted in unambiguous terms that a multiplicity of factors govern human behavior: "Many things govern men: climate, religion, laws, the maxims of the government, examples of past things, mores, and manners; a general spirit is formed as a result" (*SL*, XIX: 4, 310). Worth noting here is Montesquieu's emphasis on the *plurality* of factors that influence and constrain the choices of legislators. At the same time, he argued that while it would be unwise to ignore the power of mores, customs, and manners, these factors never fully determine the range of the possible in politics. Accordingly, wise legislators always take into consideration the needs of different climates, which in turn foster different ways of living and demand corresponding kinds of laws.[97] While Montesquieu recognized that "there are climates in which the physical aspect has such strength that morality can do practically nothing" (*SL*, XVI: 8, 269), he stopped short of endorsing resignation or fatalism.[98] Instead, he argued that when the physical character of a climate goes against natural laws governing interaction between human beings, legislators can and must make civil laws that counteract the effects of the climate.[99] Bad legislators favor and encourage the vices caused by the climate of a country, while good ones try to enact measures that mitigate and limit their nefarious effects, such as laziness, indifference, and apathy.[100]

To better illustrate Montesquieu's moderation, it might be helpful to contrast his approach to legislation in book XXIX of *SL* with Condorcet's views included in Destutt de Tracy's work on Montesquieu. Condorcet found book XXIX to be "one the most curious chapters of the work . . . which obtained for Montesquieu the indulgence of all the prejudiced people, of all those who detest light, of all the protectors and participators in abuse."[101] In his commentary on Montesquieu, Destutt de Tracy echoed Condorcet's criticism: "There is nothing instructive here, except what arises out of the manner in which Condorcet has criticized this book, or rather new modeled it."[102] Unlike Montesquieu, Condorcet put *justice* above moderation, claiming that justice and reasonableness rather than moderation must be the guiding principles of any legislator: "I know that the spirit of a legislator should be justice. . . . The first duty of a legislator is to be just and reasonable."[103] This is why, in Condorcet's view, "it is not by the spirit of moderation, but by the spirit of justice, that criminal laws should be mild, that civil laws tend to equality, and the laws of the municipal administration to liberty and prosperity."[104]

Consequently, Condorcet criticized Montesquieu's moderation for its ambiguity and failure to give justice its due, referring to it as "that spirit of uncertainty which alters by a hundred little irrelevant motives, the principles of justice, which are in themselves invariable."[105] Condorcet also disagreed with Montesquieu on the nature of the laws and the relationship between the particular and the universal. Moreover, while Montesquieu favored complexity and particularity, Condorcet inclined toward simplicity and uniformity. Convinced that injustice is often caused by unnecessarily complicated formalities and rules, he argued that the diversity of laws is usually the outcome of prejudice and habit rather than reason. On this view, all reasonable individuals could (and should) ultimately agree on natural, uniform, and unchangeable standards in legislation such as would ensure that "truth, reason, justice, the rights of men, the interests of property, of liberty, of security are in all places the same."[106] Since laws are nothing but "a faithful regard to the laws of nature," they ought to be seen as universally valid, similar to mathematical laws: "A good law should be good for *all* men. A true proposition is true *everywhere*."[107] The upshot of Condorcet's view was that, for the sake of justice and fairness, uniform laws could be established without danger to liberty and security. Justice must trump moderation in *all* circumstances.

Montesquieu opposed this approach to legislation with a trenchant critique of uniformity. He argued:

> There are certain ideas of uniformity that sometimes seize great spirits (for they touched Charlemagne), but that infallibly strike small ones. They find in it a kind of perfection they recognize because it is impossible not to discover it: in the police the same

weights, in commerce the same measures, in the state the same laws and the same religion in every part of it. But is this always and without exception appropriate? . . . And does not the greatness of genius consist rather in knowing in which cases there must be uniformity and in which differences?[108]

This passage is interesting because it raises the question of Montesquieu's complex and ambiguous attitude toward natural law.[109] In *SL*, XXVI: 1, he acknowledged that natural law is only one of the many categories of laws by which men are governed. It takes its place alongside divine law, ecclesiastical law, the law of nations, the general political law, and the civil law of each society. While natural law may sometimes provide effective standards for judging political and civil matters, it cannot be applied uniformly, without giving due consideration to particular circumstances and contexts. In this respect, the cardinal virtues of all legislators are prudence and moderation, virtues that defenders of uniformity tend to overlook or underestimate. The centrality of prudence to (good) legislation looms large in the first chapter of book XXVI, in which Montesquieu admits that wise legislators must acknowledge the existence of different orders of laws and remarked that "the sublimity of human reason consists in knowing well to which of these orders principally relate the things on which one should enact and in not putting confusion into the principles that should govern men" (*SL*, XXVI: 1, 494). In the next chapter Montesquieu defined the art of legislation as using the right principles to suit various circumstances. Wise legislators, he claimed, know that laws have different effects varying with time and space, and that good legislation is the art of the particular and the possible rather than of the best.[110]

It is in this context that one must interpret and understand Montesquieu's advice in *SL*, XXIX: 16 about the many things that must be observed in the composition and reform of the laws. In order to avoid or limit arbitrariness, the style of the laws is often as important as their content, and laws must be "concise" and "simple." "It is essential for the words of the laws to awaken the same ideas in all men" (*SL*, XXIX: 16, 613) and vague formulations must be avoided at all costs. "The laws," Montesquieu insisted, "should not be subtle; they are made for people of middling understanding; they are not an art of logic but the simple reasoning of a father of the family" (*SL*, XXIX: 16, 614). Reasons for changing a law must be clearly formulated and communicated; it is preferable not to include limitations, modifications in a law, for such complicated details would require, in turn, new details and additional justification. Moreover, legislators must pay due consideration to the difference between a law and the means of implementing it. The most reliable principle they can use in this regard is moderation, which teaches legislators "what part of power, great or small, should be used in various circumstances" (*SL*, XII: 25, 209), or how and when to apply various orders of laws to particular circumstances and objects (the themes of books XXVI and XXIX of *SL*). With regard to the differences between civil and religious laws, Montesquieu argued that "one should not enact by divine laws that which should be enacted by human laws, or regulate by human laws that which should be regulated by divine laws" (*SL*, XXVI: 2, 495). Civil laws must seek to promote human justice rather than divine justice, which lies outside of their realm; "religious laws are more sublime; civil laws are more extensive" (*SL*, XXVI: 9, 502). Hence, "human laws enact about the good; religion, about the best" (*SL*, XXVI: 2, 495). Montesquieu warned that legislators should not decide by the precepts of religion when matters of natural law are in question, nor should they try to apply the laws of religion (whose main goal is to promote the moral goodness of individuals) to those things that ought to be governed by the principles of civil law, and whose guiding principle is the general good of society.

Similar relations obtain between civil and political laws. The first depend on the political laws of a country and cannot be separated from the context from which they have emerged. Montesquieu affirmed that things that depend on principles of civil law should not be ruled by principles of political law, as for example in questions of private property rights, where "It is a fallacy to say that the good of the individual should yield to the public good" (*SL*, XXIX: 15, 510). Some things, such as whether the domain of the state is alienable, should be decided by political laws and not by civil laws. Furthermore, Montesquieu denied that a particular society can make laws for another society, since there is *no* such thing as a universally good law, independent of various political and extra-political conditions.[111] When legislators seek to transfer civil laws from one nation to another, they must carefully examine and compare the similarities and differences between their systems of legislation, their institutions, and their mores. On this view, prudence is required even when dealing with laws which, at first sight, might appear to be universally just and fair, for their application may have unintended consequences that limit their general effectiveness.

Montesquieu believed that one of the greatest mistakes of legislators is to try to imprudently change the general spirit of their nation, and he insisted that they would be well advised to refrain from attempting to correct everything by means of laws. Instead, he opined, legislators must always follow "the spirit of a nation when doing so is not contrary to the principles of the government" (*SL*, XIX: 5, 310). Hence, he concluded, legislators must not confuse laws with mores and manners and should avoid introducing new laws aiming at changing the general spirit of a nation. Most often, it is laws that follow mores rather than vice versa, and it would be an unwise idea to try to change by laws what should be changed only by manners: "When one wants to change the mores and manners, one must not change them by the laws, as this would appear to be too tyrannical; it would be better to change them by other mores and other manners. . . . It is a very bad policy to change by laws what should be changed by manners" (*SL*, XIX: 14, 315). Wise legislators, Montesquieu believed, must not try to correct everything; instead, they should learn how to work with nature which "repairs everything" (*SL*, XIX: 6, 311), taking a little from here, and adding a bit there, always with moderation, and knowing that "moral qualities have different effects according to the other qualities united with them" (*SL*, XIX: 9, 313).

Since there can be no recipe for good legislation in general, legislators must be flexible in order to avoid the misfortune of becoming tyrannical. Montesquieu praised those legislators who attempted to instill civic virtue rather than merely inflicting punishment, and he admired as well eclectic legislators who drew on the lessons of philosophy, morality, and religion in order to make effective laws promoting freedom and sound mores. Legislators who want to change laws must model new mores and shape old ones in keeping with each country's traditions, mores, manners, and culture.[112] For example, "in moderate states, love of the homeland, shame, and fear of blame are motives that serve as restraints" (*SL*, VI: 9, 82) and support the laws, which is not the case in despotic regimes. Furthermore, it would be foolish to try to impart a pedantic spirit to a nation naturally full of gaiety, since such laws would unwisely disturb or curb the people's sociable humor. Montesquieu boldly called for a redefinition of political virtue and vice, arguing that "not all political vices are moral vices and not all moral vices are political vices" (*SL*, XIX: 11, 314). Aware that "the various characters of the nations are mixtures of virtues and vices, of good and bad qualities" (*SL*, XIX: 10, 313), prudent legislators will therefore seek to achieve an alchemy of passions *sui generis* by using the nation's virtues in order to limit its vices.

One final consideration is in order here. In Montesquieu's opinion, political moderation is not incompatible with firmness in extreme circumstances, when the authority of the laws is challenged and public order is threatened. Special provisions must be made for the emergency powers necessary for solving crises that are not entirely manageable under constitutional or statutory law. Such provisions presuppose the consolidation of powers normally divided between the executive and legislative, but they can also refer to the derogation of rights and liberties enshrined in the constitution. Montesquieu acknowledged that "if the legislative power believed itself endangered by some secret conspiracy against the state or by some correspondence with its enemies on the outside, it could, for a brief and limited time, permit the executive power to arrest suspected citizens who would lose their liberty for a time only so that it would be preserved forever" (*SL*, XI: 6, 159). A few pages later, he commented on the circumstances in which the usage of liberty may be legally suspended in a republic. "There are cases," he wrote, "where a veil has to be drawn, for a moment, over liberty, as one hides the statues of the gods" (*SL*, XII: 19, 204). The examples Montesquieu chose were taken from Athens and Rome, much like the ones to which Machiavelli referred in his *Discorsi*. One of the laws passed by the Romans provided for investing dictators with absolute powers such as would allow them to take swift and timely decisions in emergency situations, while at the same time special conditions were devised to prevent them from abusing their power and authority.[113] These derogatory powers were to be granted solely for a "brief and limited time" and for a single task: to enable the state to protect liberty.[114]

How Can Democratic and Aristocratic Regimes Be Moderated?

Montesquieu was particularly interested in the mechanisms whereby aristocratic and democratic regimes might be moderated, and he resorted to a subtle reconstruction of the architecture of aristocratic governments at the core of which he placed the concept of pluralism. Far from linking moderation to a single principle, group, or class (such as aristocracy), Montesquieu believed that moderation is the result of *many* combined factors creating a framework incompatible with social and political monism.

Acknowledging the diversity and pluralism of aristocratic regimes, Montesquieu highlighted the affinities between the spirit and institutional architecture of aristocratic and moderate governments, noting that moderation represents the "soul" of aristocratic regimes. "The spirit of moderation," he wrote, "is what is called virtue in aristocracy; there it takes the place of the spirit of equality in the popular state" (*SL*, V: 8, 51). In aristocratic governments, the nobles restrain their ambitions either by a "great virtue that makes [them] in some ways equal to their people," or by "a lesser virtue, a certain moderation that renders the nobles at least equal among themselves, which brings about their preservation" (*SL*, II: 4, 24). Nonetheless, the nobles' sense of honor must always be complemented by the existence of a sound balance of powers, which in order to be achieved, requires true political art, wise institutional crafting, and effective legislation capable of tempering the tendency of aristocratic regimes to extreme inequality.[115] In order to prevent the latter, laws should never sanction any caste privileges. Among the means of moderating aristocratic regimes, Montesquieu singled out laws aimed at equalizing families' fortunes, which at the same time contribute to maintaining their unity.[116] Montesquieu recommended that the laws "remove the right of primogeniture from the nobles so that fortunes are always restored to equality by the continual division of inheritance" (*SL*, V: 8, 54). Moreover, there should always be a higher tribunal to correct abuses of public administration, and magistrates should refrain from drawing stipends from their offices and should never be allowed to divide the revenues of the state among themselves with impunity.

Montesquieu granted a special role to intermediary powers—nobles, *parlements*, the clergy, local authorities—in preserving moderation and liberty in monarchical regimes. The importance of these *corps intermédiaires* derived mainly from their ability to successfully restrain and temper the momentary and potentially capricious will of the monarch. If you abolish the prerogatives of the nobles, Montesquieu warned, the political equipoise would disappear: "No monarch, no nobility: no nobility, no monarch."[117] Monarchies, he argued, are corrupted when the prerogatives of the established bodies and local liberties (the privileges of the towns) are gradually removed and destroyed.[118] In moderate regimes in which the monarch exercises power only in keeping with the fundamental laws and customs of the country,[119] the power of the sovereign is also tempered by the existence of many differences in rank, origin, and condition that carry with them significant distinctions in the nature of men's goods and laws. No monarch ever enjoys an absolute, unlimited power in modern society: "Just as the sea, which seems to want to cover the whole earth, is checked by the grasses and the smallest bits of gravel on the shore, so monarchs, whose power seems boundless, are checked by the slightest obstacles and submit their natural pride to supplication and prayer" (*SL*, II: 4, 18).

In addition to fixed and fundamental laws, various customs, social codes, religious norms, and political forms protect the honor, fortune, life, and liberty of citizens by moderating the ambitions of princes and ensuring that things are rarely carried to excess.[120] In these regimes "temperings are proposed, agreements are reached, corrections are made; the laws become vigorous again and make themselves heard."[121] Of special importance is the presence of a "depository of laws which can only be located in political bodies such as *parlements* and courts of justice, which announce the laws when they are made and recall them when they are forgotten" (*SL*, II: 4, 19). Montesquieu included among the intermediate, subordinate, and dependent powers and political bodies the *parlements*, whose task was to preserve, use, and interpret the laws.[122] Because these bodies were independent of the prince's council, they constituted an effective balance that, along with other limitations placed upon the monarch's will, was supposed to prevent the latter from becoming arbitrary.

Montesquieu's account of moderating democracy complements his discussion of moderating monarchies in *SL*. Good connoisseur of Greek and Roman history that he was, Montesquieu admired the discernment and political acumen of ancient legislators like Solon, whom he regarded as a genuine example of moderation. Commenting on Solon's prescriptions for electing and controlling magistrates, he noted that, in Athens, those positions which had significant political clout and involved significant expenses were granted by election, while others were decided by lot. Military officers belonged to the first category, senators and judges to the second. In order to limit the shortcomings of the lottery, Solon decided that one could elect only from the number of those who presented themselves, that judges would examine those who had been elected, and that magistrates ought to be required at the end of their mandate to give an account of their activities. The situation, Montesquieu added, was not very different in Rome, where the people had the right of making new laws, but the senate retained the right to pass and enact normative acts. The validity of these acts was, however, limited, usually to one year, and they could become permanent only after the people gave their explicit consent.[123]

There is another important facet of Montesquieu's argument about moderating democracy that can be explained in light of his views on equality. While Montesquieu was aware of the importance of this concept, he realized that it would be impossible to determine once and for all the desirable level of equality in democratic regimes. In *SL*, VIII: 3, he distinguished between tempered (regulated) and untempered (unregulated) democracy, noting that in the former people are equal only as citizens, while in the latter equality indiscriminately spreads to all areas of social life. Thus, one is equal not only as citizen, but also as magistrate, senator, judge, father, husband, or master. In the footsteps of Aristotle, Montesquieu suggested that proper equality is a mean between extreme forms of equality and inequality: "As far as the sky is from the earth, so far is the true spirit of equality from the spirit of extreme equality. The former consists neither in making everyone command nor in making no one command, but in obeying and commanding one's equals. It seeks not to have no master but to have only one's equals for masters" (*SL*, VIII: 3, 114). Moderating democracy amounts, then, to finding the right mix of equality and inequality that promotes the true spirit of citizenship and fosters proper social bonds. "The principle of democracy," Montesquieu affirmed, "is corrupted not only when the spirit of equality is lost but also when the spirit of extreme equality is taken up and each one wants to be equal of those chosen to command" (*SL*, VIII: 1, 112).

Given that the tendency to leveling and uniformity in democratic regimes inclines them toward despotism,[124] Montesquieu argued that laws must be devised with the goal of preventing extremes of both equality and inequality: "Although in a democracy real equality is the soul of the state, still this equality is so difficult to establish that an extreme precision in this regard would not always be suitable. It suffices to establish a census that reduces differences or fixes them at a certain point; after which, it is the task of particular laws to equalize inequalities, so to speak, by the burdens they impose on the rich and the relief they afford to the poor" (*SL*, V: 5, 46–47). At the same time, Montesquieu insisted that there will always be individuals who will be distinguished by birth, wealth, or honors and who will seek social recognition for their "superiority," forming a "body that has the right to check the enterprises of the people, as the people have the right to check theirs" (*SL*, XI: 6, 160). Wise legislators should therefore tolerate the existence of inequalities and try to moderate them, as long as they are drawn, as it were, "from the nature of democracy and from the very principle of equality" (*SL*, V: 5, 47).

Moderation, Pluralism, and Commerce

Finally, the relationship between moderation and pluralism can be examined in connection with Montesquieu's discussion of the moderating effects of commerce, as well as in light of his claim that one should speak of political "goods" (in the plural) rather than the political "good" (in the singular). The implication of the latter statement is that the political good can never be defined in an unambiguous and universal manner, independent of the particular social and political condition of each country. At the same time, Montesquieu admitted that there is one such supreme unchanging good which is the object of religion, whose realm is fundamentally *different* from that of politics.

Montesquieu's claim about the impossibility of giving an unambiguous definition of the political good needs further explanation. In light of his elusive references to "Gothic government" in book XI of *SL*, Montesquieu's refusal to view *any* political regime, including the English system, as the "best" is indicative of his moderate approach and stands in sharp contrast to the ideas of some of his predecessors or contemporaries such as Rousseau.[125] While both Montesquieu and Rousseau believed that the most important political problem is to find a form of government that places the law above the man, Rousseau also admitted that, if this form could not be found, it would be "necessary to move to the opposite extreme, and all of a sudden place the man as far above the law as possible, and thus establish the most arbitrary despotism." While Rousseau saw "no viable middle point between the most austere democracy and the most perfect Hobbism,"[126] Montesquieu was convinced that such a middle point did exist and could be achieved in practice if legislators were moderate and flexible.[127]

The contrast between Montesquieu and Rousseau is interesting for yet another reason. It suggests that the line between the moderns and the ancients should not be traced purely along chronological lines (as is commonly done by historians of political thought), but must be rethought in light of the monist-pluralist dichotomy mentioned above. This line separates, in fact, advocates of pluralist polities such as Aristotle, Machiavelli, Montesquieu, and Burke, who believed in the essential indeterminacy of the political good and endorsed moderation, from philosophers such as Plato, Hobbes, Rousseau, and Marx who advocated monist theories of the political good and embraced various forms of radicalism.[128] Montesquieu firmly belongs to the pluralist camp because his liberalism of fear, based on moderation and pluralism, rejected any unitary definition of sovereignty and the political good.

Moreover, Montesquieu also believed that the line between vice and virtue changes over time in such a way that what was previously considered a vice may later be seen as a virtue (or vice versa). In a famous passage that must have worried his Catholic critics, Montesquieu went so far as to propose a redefinition of the concept of political virtue, insisting that "moral qualities have different effects according to the other qualities united with them."[129] One such example is vanity. In unfree governments, vanity combined with arrogance can lead to laziness, poverty, and prostration. In free governments, the situation is different and vanity often has the beneficial effect of encouraging habits of work and serving as an effective spring of government. Among the innumerable goods resulting from vanity, Montesquieu listed luxury, industry, the arts, fashion, politeness, and taste.

For all of Montesquieu's skepticism toward monist theories of the political good,[130] he did not fall into the trap of relativism and did not espouse a postmodern form of "perspectivism." He unambiguously rejected cruel and intolerant regimes in which power was unlimited, insisting that in normal circumstances one must *always* govern with moderation and gentleness. The political good, he believed, exists between two boundaries that can and must be properly identified and rejected. It is within this middle ground that prudent legislators, mindful of the essential indeterminacy of the political good and the dependence of laws on the social condition in each country, must seek to reconcile different values and principles in order to preserve human dignity and uphold the ideal of moderate government. In this respect, Montesquieu's pluralist perspective followed, to some extent, in the footsteps of Hobbes, who also believed that in the political sphere there is always a *summum malum* on which people agree. In Montesquieu's political writings, this absolute evil was despotism, characterized by cruelty and arbitrary power, and the political good was defined by the absence of cruelty.[131]

Nonetheless, one might argue that Montesquieu made an equally important argument for the existence of a *positive* political good—moderate government—which represents much more than the opposite of a despotism based on fear and arbitrary power. In his view, the English constitutional monarchy and the French feudal monarchy were variations on the same form of government, moderate government. Montesquieu considered them pluralist regimes with intricate structures consisting of overlapping centers of powers and interests. Worth noting is not only Montesquieu's emphasis on pluralism as one of the most important sources of moderation, but also his claim that all regimes that fail to protect social diversity and political pluralism cannot—and should not—be called "moderate." Social diversity and political pluralism depend on a constant competition for power between various interests, principles, ideas, and groups, none of which is able to rise to a position of absolute supremacy. Reflecting the diversity of mores, manners, and customs of a nation, the competition between these various principles and social interests serves as an effective break on intolerance, fanaticism, and extremism. The moderation prevailing in England and France reflects their social pluralism and is, in turn, the outcome of a sound distribution and blending of powers.

Finally, as already mentioned, it is possible to relate the pluralism and gentleness of moderate governments to the beneficial influence of *commerce* on the political sphere. Because commerce is instrumental in promoting new forms of communication and opening up new channels and forms of exchange, it has a strong impact on the way in which power is exercised. As a rule, commerce promotes gentle governments and tempers excessive political passions, such as ambition and the desire for power and domination, by channeling them into peaceful and benign activities that aim at material gain and wealth rather than power and domination.[132] Commerce, Montesquieu pointed out, is "a kind of lottery" in which everyone loves to take part in the hope of getting rich. Considerable wealth can be amassed or lost within a short span of time, and as a result social life comes to resemble a Brownian movement *sui generis* in which people constantly rise and fall along with the fortunes of the stock market. Public life is not immune to this agitation, being inevitably affected by the chronic restlessness and dissipation induced by commerce and its accompanying passions (restlessness, frivolity, and vanity). Above all, Montesquieu argued, commerce helps cure destructive prejudices, promotes gentle mores and moderation, and spreads knowledge of the mores of all nations everywhere" (*SL*, XX: 1, 338). Where commerce is allowed to follow its course unhindered, people cooperate with each other more easily and acquaint themselves with new ways of life and values. "The natural effect of commerce," Montesquieu famously argued, "is to lead to peace. . . . The spirit of commerce produces in men a certain feeling for exact justice" (*SL*, XX: 2, 339) encouraging people to take into consideration one another's interests and adjust their interests. Moreover, the moderating spirit of commerce brings with it not only new social distinctions, but also fosters "the spirit of frugality, economy, moderation, work, wisdom, tranquility, order, and rule" (*SL*, V: 6, 48).

All of these ideas can be found in the portrait of England's moderate government drawn by Montesquieu in *SL*, as well as in his *Pensées* and *Notes sur l'Angleterre*.[133] For all his appreciation of the unwritten English constitution and his sometimes-elegiac tone, Montesquieu's account of England was, to use Michael Sonenscher's phrase, "strikingly Janus-faced."[134] Montesquieu stopped short of affirming that the English political system was the "best" existing political regime and noted (not without concern) that "in order to favor liberty, the English have removed all the intermediary powers that formed their monarchy."[135] In reality, as several commentators have remarked, Montesquieu inserted a critical note in his descriptions of each of the regimes he deemed to be good (including that of England).[136] While he believed that the English constitution protected political and individual freedom better than any other existing regime, he was nonetheless ambivalent toward several aspects of English politics and the English way of life. In his view, in order to understand the English political system one must not limit oneself to examining its constitutional architecture, but must also study the ways in which liberty is connected to and affected by commerce and the invisible hand of the market.[137]

Montesquieu's depiction of English social life and mores in *SL*, XIX: 27 sheds additional light on his conception of moderate government and should be read in conjunction with his famous analysis of the English unwritten constitution in *SL*, XI: 6. It reveals his mixed feelings about the extreme consequences of the sovereignty of individual will, which leads each citizen to consider him a "monarch" and a monad at the same time. Montesquieu perceptively grasped that the commercial way of life in England made every individual value his independence according to his own tastes and inclinations. English society, he noted, is a highly individualistic society in which "all the passions are free . . . hatred, envy, jealousy, and the ardor for enriching and distinguishing oneself . . . appear to their full extent" (*SL*, XIX: 27, 335). Voicing concern about the spirit of "extreme liberty" in England (*SL*, XI: 6, 166) that ensued from its commercial way of life, Montesquieu questioned how secure political liberty was there. Although his reference to the existence of a "delirium of liberty" might strike us as hyperbolic, it cannot be denied that Montesquieu was deeply concerned about this aspect of English society, especially in light of his claim about the absence of intermediary bodies in that country. In his *Notes sur l'Angleterre*, Montesquieu noted (with a hint of sadness) that the English had not always been worthy of their liberty, which they sometimes preferred to "sell" to their kings.[138] In a rather enigmatic passage from *SL*, Montesquieu affirmed that people are not as free as they think even under moderate governments such as England's, for liberty is constantly under the pressure of the highly individualistic and competitive ethos of society. He praised the love of liberty prevailing across the Channel, but also remarked that the English tended to love their liberty "prodigiously," that is, immoderately and excessively. As a recent commentator argued, "the prodigious love of liberty among the English is in some measure alarming to Montesquieu, even potentially monstrous, because it implies a possible violation of the order of nature, which points to moderation rather than extremes. . . . Without resorting to 'political moralism,' Montesquieu suggests that a constitution of liberty, in order to endure over time, needs motives beyond fear and interest."[139]

Montesquieu's reader should not be surprised then by his warning that the English have the potential to become one of the most enslaved peoples on earth if they take liberty to extremes. The political system of England, Montesquieu claimed, "will perish when legislative power is more corrupt than executive power" (*SL*, XI: 6, 166). His reservations were meant to sound a cautionary note about the dangers facing a regime that combines the "separation" of powers with a spirit of unbridled self-interest and extreme individualism and liberty. It is no mere coincidence that Montesquieu also criticized the "frenzy of liberty" (*SL*, XI: 16, 176) that characterized political life at a certain stage of the Roman republic, and he believed that the spirit of extreme liberty was one of the most important causes of the decline of the Roman republic.

Helvétius' Warning

Helvétius is credited with having once said that the best way to recognize a fool is to meet someone who claims to understand Montesquieu well. His witty words remain as valid today as in his time. Not surprisingly, after finishing *SL*, the reader can hardly avoid the impression that moderation remains an elusive concept in Montesquieu's writings, in which it is related to a theory of prudence, *juste mesure*, and political judgment. With ideas and truths of a certain kind, Montesquieu once said, "it is not enough to make them appear convincing: one must also make them felt."[140] One such idea is political moderation.

In praising the latter, Montesquieu put forward a complex, normative agenda that gained him many prominent admirers in Europe and America, from Catherine the Great of Russia and Frederick the Great of Prussia to James Madison and Alexander Hamilton in the New World.[141] The prescriptive side of Montesquieu's ideas comes to the fore, for example, in his analysis of the relationship between moderation and pluralism when describing the benefits of commerce. Montesquieu constantly moved from what "is" to what "should be," using moderation as an important rhetorical weapon in his critique of despotic regimes. In so doing, he followed a normative route in a remarkably prudent way, avoiding the sometimes-radical tone of his English forerunners, such as Hobbes and Locke.[142] Far from being a relativist, Montesquieu believed in the existence of a few "fundamental" principles, but he insisted that the latter, valuable as they may be, cannot and should not be applied uniformly and everywhere, without paying due consideration to the social and political condition of each country. It is revealing that Montesquieu even refused to view the principles of moderate government—in particular the separation and the balance of powers—as universally applicable. These principles, he insisted, must not be treated as apodictic axioms even though they are important conditions of liberty.[143]

Montesquieu's ambition did not limit itself to contributing to the education of modern legislators and citizens. Comparing himself to a painter *sui generis*, he wanted to offer a new science of politics that combined the old with the new in an original synthesis.[144] This helps explain his emphasis on history and precedent as well as his warning against all forms of political anachronism.[145] He sought a *via media* between the political thought of Aristotle and Cicero, centered on the notions of civic virtue and political participation, and on modern theories of power, sovereignty, and rights. His search for a middle ground between these competing conceptions of politics was informed and motivated by his skepticism toward strong foundational principles in politics such as natural right. Not surprisingly, the political sphere retained pride of place in Montesquieu's system even if he spent a lot of time discussing the influence of non-political factors upon the spirit of the laws.

Thus, in his works, moderate government becomes a synonym for a well-ordered and balanced pluralist system whose equipoise results from the interaction between various groups, powers, and interests in society. Equally important, Montesquieu's writings demonstrate how classical preoccupations with the moral virtue of moderation become institutionalized and operationalized in a particular system of government, the carefully harmonized soul of the individual being mirrored by a finely tuned and carefully balanced equilibrium of institutional powers and forces. That is why to argue that for Montesquieu, moderation was "a matter of luck rather than good judgment," as one of his recent interpreters claims, does not render full justice to his outlook.[146] One of Montesquieu's most important lessons is that, if properly channeled into adequate institutions and laws, the dissonances and divisions for a free society may, in fact, contribute to its strength and increase rather than diminish its internal capacity for self-correction. Yet, to achieve this subtle alchemy of powers and interests, much more is needed than mere luck. Moderate government is a real political masterpiece that requires limiting, separating, balancing, and combining powers, and adjusting the laws and the institutions to suit the customs and mores of each country.

Montesquieu's theory of political moderation and pluralism had a major influence on Madison and Hamilton and became a central tenet of all subsequent theories of moderate government. A few decades later, the French monarchiens tried to create a new constitution for France incorporating many of Montesquieu's ideas. Their fascinating story will be the subject of the next chapter.

THREE
THE RADICAL MODERATES OF 1789
The Tragic Middle of the French Monarchiens

> Il n'est pas d'autre moyen de salut pour un état en convulsion que
> celui de la modération au milieu de tous les parties extrêmes.
> —Malouet

Who Were the Monarchiens?

On September 14, 1791, Louis XVI swore his oath to the new constitution
that had just been adopted by the Constituent Assembly after two years of
intense debates. The king's unsuccessful attempt to flee France and his arrest
at Varennes on June 21, 1791 had weakened the authority and prestige of
the monarch, who subsequently became powerless in the face of an ever
stronger and bolder legislative power. Although the atmosphere in the room
was grave on that September day, it lacked the genuine solemnity appropriate to such a momentous event. Louis XVI stood bareheaded in front of a
seated and defiant assembly and took his oath in an impersonal voice. Only
one member of the audience had the courage to stand with the king, paying
due homage to the person who was still the legitimate monarch of France.
That deputy was Pierre Victor Malouet, the last remaining active member of
the group of French monarchiens in the Constituent Assembly, and a man
who believed that moderation was the only solution for bringing about social and political peace in revolutionary France.[1]

The solitary and defiant example of Malouet in September 1791 epito-
mizes the courageous position adopted by this moderate group from the
outset of the revolution. Although they were not the revolution's last genuine moderates (a title that, according to Ran Halévi, should go to the Feuillants),[2] the monarchiens constituted the most important moderate group to
emerge during the initial phases of the uprising. It is worth mentioning that
the term "monarchiens"[3] did not exist in 1789 but was coined a year later
by their opponents, the Jacobins. In addition to Malouet (1740–1814), the
monarchiens' group also included Jean-Joseph Mounier (1758–1806), Tro-
phimé Gerard de Lally-Tollendal (1751–1830), and Stanislas de Clermont-
Tonnerre (1757–1792). There was also, on the fringes of the monarchiens'
group, Jacques Mallet du Pan, a Geneva-born journalist and political
thinker who championed the groups' ideas in the *Mercure de France* before
eventually turning to the right.[4] As defenders of moderation in dark times,
Mounier and Lally-Tollendal had relatively short political careers; they
withdrew from the Assembly soon after the events of October 5–6, 1789
and went into exile. Clermont-Tonnerre paid with his own life for his cour-

age in standing for moderate ideas and principles. He was murdered in his own house in August 1792.

The case of Mounier is particularly insightful for our study of political moderation in revolutionary times.[5] As R. R. Palmer once remarked, despite all the prominent positions he occupied during the early months of the revolution, Mounier was one the least known revolutionary leaders outside France.[6] Benefiting from the prestige gained in his native region of Dauphiné, where he had been instrumental in the peaceful reunion of the three orders in 1788–89, he was hailed as the man who resurrected liberty and as the restorer of the rights of his province. One of the most prominent French legislators, a prolific writer, and a remarkable political thinker in the orbit of Montesquieu, Mounier emerged as one of the most important defenders of representative government on the eve (and during the first years) of the revolution, along with Sieyès and Mirabeau. His intellectual output was prodigious. In less than a year, from January to October 1789, he wrote three major books, chaired the constitutional committee, and became for a brief period the president of the Constituent Assembly. This took a high toll on Mounier, who withdrew from the latter in early October, exhausted and discouraged by the turn of events.

Unlike Mounier, Malouet remained in the Constituent Assembly after his colleague's departure and gave numerous speeches addressing key issues such as constitutionalism and the rights of man.[7] He was instrumental in the formation of the *Club des Impartiaux* in January 1790, which brought together moderate deputies who, as defenders of constitutional monarchy, declared themselves to be "enemies of all violent and exaggerated measures"[8] and to be led only by true patriotism, reason, justice, and truth. The *Impartiaux* insisted that, while they had not initially wanted a revolution, their mission was to bring the latter to an end, by placing the rights of the nation and the Crown on a new and stable foundation. "In general," they claimed, "we do not love at all rashness, haste, and rage in the legislative functions. We are more inclined to forgive than to condemn, more disposed to reconcile than to divide."[9]

With several exceptions, interpreters of the French Revolution (beginning with Burke) have been reluctant to give the monarchiens their due for their important role during the initial stages of the revolution. This reluctance can be explained in part by the fact that the monarchiens never constituted a unified group with a homogeneous political philosophy and did not attempt to offer a systematic account of their political philosophy, many of their publications being written in response to fluctuating political circumstances. Second, although the monarchiens were regarded as defenders of a strong royal power, the doctrinal identity of Mounier and his colleagues remained fuzzy in the eyes of their interpreters and critics. Some considered them mere followers of Montesquieu, given their common admiration for the English constitution and constitutional monarchy, while others regarded them as critics of Montesquieu, pointing out the disagreements between them, for example with regard to their views on the role of intermediary bodies in constitutional monarchies. Furthermore, although the monarchiens' allegiance to the principles of 1789 could not be called into question, they eventually came to be denounced as opponents of the Revolution on account of their endorsement of the absolute royal veto and bicameralism.

What makes the monarchiens a fascinating case study for students of moderation is that they were "revolutionary"[10] spirits attempting to build a moderate government on the ruins of the Old Regime. In this regard, they shared important affinities with the Feuillants, though there were as well significant differences between the two groups.[11] The moderate political agenda of the monarchiens met with both the distrust of their fellow revolutionaries, such as Sieyès (a long-time rival of Mounier), and the hatred of ultraconservatives who—all things considered—should have been on their side. The aristocrats and the clergy distrusted the monarchiens, however, as much as the radicals on the left, and their odd alliance of hatred finally brought about the political defeat of the monarchiens by the end of 1789. On several key issues, such as the veto and bicameralism, the monarchiens' ideas were defeated by *la politique du pire* practiced by the right side of the Constituent Assembly that endorsed monocameralism "in the hope of obtaining good by the excess of evil."[12]

Many of the monarchiens' writings and legislative initiatives challenge the conventional wisdom that defines moderation as a conservative defense of the *status quo*. Tocqueville, in fact, remarked that their actions on occasion displayed what he called "the revolutionary spirit of the moderates."[13] It is interesting that the monarchiens considered themselves pragmatic political actors and often invoked the lessons of experience, while some of their contemporaries took them to task for their alleged lack of political realism. A closer look at their writings shows that they combined progressive ideas with conservative institutional proposals in ways that were not always effective. Mounier and his colleagues, for example, simultaneously endorsed the initial demands of the Third Estate and defended the principles of constitutional monarchy by seeking to reconcile the rights of the nation and the rights of man with the prerogatives of the monarch. They believed that the king was supposed to play an essential political role in the economy of the new regime and viewed his limited authority as essential to the preservation of the balance of powers in the state. Critics of the nobiliary vision of politics, most of the monarchiens feared the ascendancy of local interests which, in their view, threatened the unity of the French monarchy.[14] Mounier was one of the leading voices in the drafting of the *Declaration of the Rights of Man and of the Citizen* and, together with Lally-Tollendal and Malouet, he played a key role in the debates on the royal veto and the relationship between the executive and the legislative power.

Although the monarchiens' political agenda overlapped with that of Necker, the leading theorist of executive power in modern society, their political philosophy was different in several important respects from that of

Louis XVI's famous minister.[15] The most important difference had to do with their divergent positions on the royal veto and on the preeminence of the executive or the legislative power. The monarchiens defended the absolute veto, while Necker reluctantly ended up supporting the suspensive one; and they emphasized the importance of the legislative power, while Necker thought the executive the most important power in modern society. Eventually, Necker abandoned bicameralism—by 1789 a lost cause in his eyes—to endorse monocameralism, much to the dismay of the monarchiens. The relationship between Sieyès and Mounier was equally complicated. Their rivalry intensified in the summer of 1789, when the two leaders of the Third Estate vied unsuccessfully for the confidence of their fellow deputies. Asked to choose between their respective drafts of the declaration of the rights of man, the representatives disapproved of both. A few weeks later, Sieyès and Mounier advanced different interpretations of the royal sanction, and again both of their proposals were rejected by the majority of the assembly.

Mounier, Montesquieu, Rousseau, and Sieyès

Before we go any further, it may be helpful to explain in more detail the relationship between the monarchiens and the two towering figures of eighteenth-century French political thought, Montesquieu and Rousseau. While it may be tempting to argue that the key principles of the monarchiens' political philosophy were derived directly from the *Spirit of the Laws*, their attitude toward Montesquieu has not yet been fully explored. I will focus here for the moment on Mounier, because he devoted special attention to clarifying his debt toward Montesquieu.[16]

In *Considérations sur les gouvernements* (1789) as well as in *Recherches sur les causes qui ont empêché les Français de devenir libres* (1792), Mounier explicitly referred to Montesquieu in favorable terms, pointing to their common commitment to moderation and tempered monarchy, the latter defined as that form of government in which "the sovereign is free to do good and prevented from doing evil."[17] Reminiscent of Montesquieu were Mounier's praise of complexity in politics and his corresponding rejection of all simple systems, which, he claimed, could easily be misinterpreted and distorted to further despotism or anarchy. The knowledge of the "true" principles of liberty, Mounier maintained, could only be achieved through a detailed examination of the advantages and limitations of various forms of government.[18] Furthermore, Montesquieu's claim that political liberty is to be found only in moderate governments was reiterated almost word by word in Mounier's *Considérations*.[19] He defined liberty as that condition in which citizens "cannot be constrained or hindered in their actions or in the enjoyment of their property or of their industry except by laws in force at the time and established in the public interest, and never by the arbitrary authority of any man, whatever his rank or power."[20] On this view, as long as there is a single unlimited power in the state, there can be no true political liberty. A good constitution, Mounier claimed, "should prevent the concentration of all power in the hands of the representatives and maintain the independence of the king."[21] In particular, any confusion must be avoided between the power that makes the laws and that which executes them. But, Mounier added in a Montesquieuan vein, this should not be narrowly interpreted as an endorsement of a strict separation of powers: "In order for different powers to be able to remain divided forever, they should not be entirely separated."[22] Only a sound division of powers and a system of checks and balances could provide effective guarantees against possible encroachments upon civil liberties: "This is therefore the final goal to which the efforts of all those involved in government must tend: the division of powers; but in order for them to remain divided, they must be guaranteed against their reciprocal attacks or usurpations."[23]

At the same time, Mounier disagreed with Montesquieu's assessment of the role played by the nobles in a moderate monarchy. Mounier's critique can be found in chapter XXII of his *Nouvelles observations sur les États-Généraux de France* (1789), in which he criticized the corporatist spirit under the Old Regime that had led the nobles and the clergy to separate themselves from the whole of the nation. Montesquieu, Mounier claimed, was wrong to place such great emphasis on the power and capacity of intermediary bodies to act as pillars of liberty: "Montesquieu should have recognized that it often happens that a nation is oppressed by many despots, with different degrees of power."[24] Montesquieu's monarchy, Mounier argued, was "a detestable government" which had "almost no relationship to the one that the French want to maintain today."[25] Mounier was particularly suspicious of the hereditary and feudal privileges that Montesquieu granted to the nobles, and regretted that his predecessor did not recognize the right of the people not to be taxed without their consent.[26] A decade later, in a work examining the alleged influence of the *philosophes* and freemasons on the French Revolution, Mounier returned to the themes he had addressed in *Nouvelles observations*, maintaining again that in *SL*, "one of the most beautiful works that this century produced,"[27] Montesquieu was wrong to gloss over the abuses of the French nobles, who did not form a viable intermediary body between the monarch and the nation.

Hence, while Mounier's constitutionalism owed a great deal to Montesquieu's theory of the division of powers, there were also important differences between their views on the institutional architecture of moderate government. Paraphrasing a point made by Jules Michelet in his history of the French Revolution (without endorsing his bias against Montesquieu), I would argue that Montesquieu may be seen as the "interpreter of Right,"[28] while Mounier was both the witness of Right and the theoretician of Justice, because the latter insisted that the legitimacy and soundness of any constitution depend not only on the existence of checks and balances but also on the constitution reflecting the will and the sovereignty of the nation (a concept that is not emphasized by Montesquieu).

Mounier's eclectic stance on this issue is worth examining in further detail. His views on the separation of powers were compatible with the spirit of the emerging anti-absolutist doctrine that emphasized the sovereignty of the nation and the idea of the constituent power of the people. Yet, Mounier ultimately remained skeptical toward the concept of the unitary will of the nation, which was at the core of the most radical version of the new doctrine. "Let us protect ourselves against the inclination of our nation to rush toward the extremes,"[29] he warned his fellow deputies in the summer of 1789. He opposed both Rabaut Saint-Étienne's claim that the legislative power must be as indivisible and simple as the sovereign[30] and Sieyès' argument that "a nation should not and cannot subject itself to constitutional forms."[31] The position espoused by Mounier contained, however, a potential tension illustrated by his simultaneous endorsement of the Rousseauian idea that the source of all sovereignty resides in the general will of the nation,[32] and his belief that the sovereignty of the nation must be limited in practice.

Overall, Mounier's eclectic approach, which distinguished between two types of sovereignty (actual and potential), made a strong case for constitutionalism as he believed that no unlimited power may ever be allowed to exist unchallenged in society. In Mounier's opinion, no liberty was possible in France as long as an all-powerful assembly existed, having the capacity to act unhindered and encountering no effective limits to its authority. "In a state where all sovereign power rested without restriction with the people," Mounier wrote, "there would be neither political liberty nor personal liberty.... A judge who is the slave of a princely court is a hundred times preferable to a judge who is the slave of the multitude.... The word of a single tyrant is much less to be feared than the clubs and daggers of a populace in frenzy."[33] Mounier foresaw the emergence of a new form of parliamentary absolutism as the result of the assembly's attempt to legitimate its rule in the name of the sovereignty of the nation, by first putting the people in place of the king and then replacing the people with their representatives. This double substitution, Mounier argued, was the extreme consequence of the popular argument according to which a one-chamber legislature was the sole logical expression of the will of the sovereign and the unitary nation.

While endorsing the sovereignty of the nation, Mounier called upon his fellow deputies to promote the latter's claims with prudence and moderation and distanced himself from the radical spirit of Rousseau's theory of popular sovereignty which advocated an absolute form of democracy incompatible with political representation. In *Nouvelles Observations*, a work written as a rejoinder to Sieyès' *Qu'est-ce que le Tiers État*, Mounier rejected "the tumultuous democracy, under which there is neither rest, nor security, nor genuine liberty, and where the law is powerless."[34] The government, he argued, must be instituted for the happiness of all citizens and should never be entirely subordinated to the decisions and whims of the multitude. "Let us not be afraid of setting some obstacles to the decisions of people's representatives," Mounier wrote. "The people, for whom and by whom all power exists, may not retain the right to indiscriminately follow their will. They must prescribe themselves limits and ought to subject the use of their power to constant rules"[35] without, however, becoming so weak as not to have any resources against oppression. To this effect, Mounier drew a seminal distinction between actual and potential sovereignty. "Being the principle of sovereignty and exercising sovereignty are two very different things," he claimed. "I confidently maintain that a nation would be very unwise and unfortunate if it retained the exercise of sovereignty. One must understand by this last word an indefinite and absolute power."[36] While the source of sovereignty resides in the nation and all authority emanates from it, this does not automatically mean that the nation can govern itself directly at all times, nor does it imply that its sovereignty resides in the general will. Mounier was skeptical toward theories claiming that the people have unlimited constituent power and that the constitution of a country is primarily the act "of the people constituting a government."[37] On this view, there would be no limits on what the people may do.

This point was precisely what, in Mounier's view, Rousseau, Paine, and their disciples[38]—all of them critics of mixed and balanced constitutions—failed to acknowledge. Opponents of the English constitution, they believed that a mixed government based on the balance of powers was an artificial and defective system, made of many discordant and poorly connected parts. In such a system, Paine argued, corruption would prevail and political responsibility would be impossible. This form of government "hath all the distinctions of an house divided against itself" and is dominated by the will of the monarch that represents the "overbearing part in the English constitution."[39] Referring to *Du Contrat Social* as "the worst work ever written on government,"[40] Mounier took Rousseau to task for having entertained an "absurd dream of democracy" and having wrongly presented the representation of the people as a proof of servitude. This made Rousseau promote a false doctrine of the general will that declared impossible its delegation and representation. In order to believe that a people can be sovereign in the absolute sense of the word, Mounier argued, one must confound sovereignty and the right to force: "To affirm that sovereignty belongs to the people is as absurd as claiming that a general must be subordinated to his soldiers, a magistrate to his inferiors, a father to this children."[41] Because no nation as a whole can retain the exercise of sovereignty, it must delegate its sovereignty in order to create a functioning government. This does not necessarily imply the alienation of sovereignty; it only means the temporary delegation of its exercise, for the nation can reclaim sovereignty whenever its representatives abuse their authority.[42]

To Rousseau's allegedly "absurd" dream of democracy, Mounier opposed his version of "mixed" government (*sui generis*) based on Montesquieu's doctrine of balance of powers. "The democratic part of mixed governments," he wrote, "must be limited to what is absolutely indispensable. The secret of political liberty consists in achieving a more or less perfect mixture between popular influence, the aristocracy of the councils, and the power of the magistrates charged with the task of executing the laws."[43] While Mounier claimed that there had never been any government that had not granted a certain role to "aristocracy" (broadly defined), his statement did not amount to a defense of aristocratic privileges, being in accord with Sieyès' views on this topic. Yet, the two thinkers drew widely different conclusions from their critique of social and political privileges. While Mounier insisted on the importance of securing a proper balance between the popular, royal, and aristocratic elements in a free government, Sieyès dismissed the concept of balance as a nefarious Gothic superstition that plays no significant part in securing political liberty. Mounier regarded the existence of an (open) aristocratic body as essential to maintaining political balance in the state, and insisted that this "third" power ought to be independent from the Crown and the people in order to effectively protect the throne and offer the people an effective refuge against the errors of its deputies and the potentially arbitrary power of the monarch.[44] Referring to the conditions that must obtain in order for such a "third" power to create a sound equipoise between the authority of the king and the power of the people, Mounier asserted that its interests should never conflict with the rights of the citizens and the prerogatives of the monarch. To that effect, this moderating power must represent no class of citizens in particular and should have sufficient authority and distinction to counterbalance the influence of the lower chamber and the monarch.[45]

The importance of this concept in the political thought of the monarchiens is evidenced by the fact that the notion of a "third" power also loomed large in Lally-Tollendal's important speech on the organization of the legislative power and the royal sanction (August 31, 1789). Pointing to the limitations of bicameralism, he argued that a "third" moderating power, in addition to the representatives of the nation and the monarch, was needed to reconcile their interests in such a way as to make them act in concert.[46] The establishment of such a power, he concluded, was the quintessential condition for securing lasting political liberty in France.

"Le marasme du modérantisme"

Within the span of a few months in 1789, the concept of moderation descended from abstract heights into the political arena. There it would become a powerful rhetorical and political tool used by its proponents to position themselves in the political field, condemned by its opponents on account of what they saw as its "pernicious" nature. Moderation and *modérantisme* were, its enemies alleged, masks worn by hypocrites or radicals seeking to advance their own agendas and interests, or shrewd and insidious strategies for promoting the spirit of faction under the guise of false impartiality.

Jacobin leaders such as Saint-Just and Robespierre attacked moderates as dangerous intriguers and traitors to the nation, "abominable people" whose actions were nothing but covert ploys to destroy the work of the people and further the cause of tyranny. "When the courage of the people had swept all away," Saint-Just claimed in a famous speech delivered during the king's trial in December 1792, "Louis [XVI] armed himself with moderation."[47] Robespierre showed equal contempt for moderation which, in his view, was the mask worn by those who formed *le parti mitoyen*, a "hypocrite faction" of bad citizens that, according to him, included the Girondists, the aristocrats, and the supporters of the king.[48] The moderates, Robespierre argued, were the most dangerous enemies of the people and the constitution, in spite of their deceiving rhetoric meant only to hide from people's view their real intentions and dark plans.[49] He denounced the "middlingness" of all those tainted by "*modérantisme*," a large group that included apathetic or ill-intentioned citizens (*intrigants*) plotting to thwart the power of the people.[50] In turn, Brissot, who echoed Robespierre's warning against the hypocrisy of the moderates, asked his fellow citizens to distrust all those preaching moderation because it was only a mask hiding their nefarious plans. "The moderates," Brissot claimed in December 1791, "are the aristocrats of the new regime."[51] He focused his ire on the so-called *impartiaux* whom he accused of falsely pretending to be the friends of the people. He contrasted them with the "real" friends of the people who, Brissot argued, ought to reject this pernicious form of moderation in unambiguous terms.[52] At the same time, the *Catéchisme révolutionnaire* of 1793–94 denounced moderation as "a crime against humanity"[53] and branded moderates as the main enemies of the revolution seeking to arrest its inevitable progress. The author of an article published in *Révolutions de Paris* in December 1790 also condemned moderates for their hypocrisy, noting that, in spite of their meek appearance as harmless lambs, they were in reality ferocious "devouring wolves."[54] While some argued that the moderates were selfish sophists, others criticized them for being indifferent and hostile to the public good and, at the same time, acting against the "true" interests of the nation. An alleged complicity between moderates and aristocrats was often invoked to justify this claim.

Even more moderate representatives of the democratic left such as Sieyès denounced "those cowards who adopt the title of the sage and play the man of moderation."[55] The immediate target of Sieyès' critique was the strategy of those moderates who put the goal of maintaining the tranquility of the state above everything else. Such "degenerate nullities," he argued, "are no more than corpses," souls enfeebled by their age, who "only know how to preach moderation, when what matters is to be active and able."[56] Sieyès'

Qu'est-ce que le Tiers État was written, in fact, as a direct challenge to "those disposed toward moderation who are always inclined to be afraid that the truth will come out at the wrong moment."[57] Instead, Sieyès enjoined political philosophers to be daring and radical in their attempt to reform political institutions and eliminate past abuses. Philosophers, he wrote, should not proceed like cautious administrators; they must instead be radical because it is their task to clear the path that future administrators will follow. They ought to denounce error wherever they encounter it, and in so doing they must go "to the very end," for otherwise they cannot be sure that they are truly following "the right path."[58] Philosophers should not accept any restraints on their imagination and must not let their practical reason be disturbed by the sight of possible obstacles. Their task, Sieyès insisted, is to refuse compromise with the shortcomings of political life, for the inclination to compromise is, like moderation, most often a sign of weakness and weariness.

It must be added that the condemnation of *modérantisme* was not the exclusive privilege of the radical left. On the right, one could find similar words of disdain for moderates, denounced time and again for their pretentiousness and lack of sincerity.[59] Conservative deputies criticized the moderates' *"vernis de modération,"*[60] along with their alleged chameleonism and opportunism. Abbé de Fonnea compared moderates to serpents hiding in the grass, adding that their shrewdness made them even more dangerous than tigers and lions which hunt openly for their prey.[61] After claiming that the sect of moderates belonged to the "coterie" of Louis XVI, he condemned the monarchiens for the alleged affinities between their theories and the ideas of the *philosophes* and freemasons, anathema to the right. Vaudreuil regarded the monarchiens as "a thousand times more dangerous than the Jacobins"[62] and spared no words in denouncing their alleged hypocrisy and perverse character. Others took the monarchiens to task for being too revolutionary, or endorsing a centralized form of reformism at odds with local aristocratic privileges. "The monarchien is a being who always adjusts himself to his environment," we read in an article denouncing Mounier and his colleagues. "He is a true chameleon. Moreover, he is like a snake that finds a way to escape when you think you have caught him. He is not at all what he says and thinks he is. . . . He can give you the most devastating blows when proposing a compromise."[63]

Even those who were not in principle entirely opposed to the monarchiens' agenda felt compelled to draw a distinction between *modérantisme* and genuine political moderation. The first, they argued, is a synonym for weakness and powerlessness, while the second is a salutary conservative principle, indispensable to the preservation of the social order.[64] Others distinguished between "true" and "false" moderation, endorsing the former and rejecting the latter. Such a distinction appeared, for example, in Montlosier's *Des effets de la violence et de la modération dans les affaires de France* (1796), in which the author made a case for a "bold" form of moderation and acknowledged his dislike of the moderation displayed by many who called themselves by that name. "I need something which has strong and energetic traits, and which presupposes efforts and sacrifices," Montlosier wrote.[65] "Violence tempered by moderation," he went on, constitutes the "true force" in politics; "he who has too much moderation achieves less because he lacks sufficient energy; he who comes too close to pure violence achieves less because he lacks measure."[66]

"Fixing" the French Constitution

The progressive and rapid radicalization of the French political scene in the long summer of 1789 is a key episode in the unfolding of the drama inaugurated by the opening of the Estates-General on May 5, 1789. Might moderation have won at a point in time when the country lacked genuine political experience of parliamentary government and the representatives of the three orders were convened for the first time in more than a century and a half to discuss in common the affairs of the nation? Were moderates within all three orders well positioned to make their voices heard and respected by their peers?

Historians still disagree on the answers to these questions. While the standard approach has been to admit that the deputies showed increasing signs of radicalism from the very outset, a closer look at the French political scene shows a much more complex picture. Many of the leadings names among the nobles—the Lameth brothers, Clermont-Tonnerre, La Rochefoucauld, and Lafayette, among others—were, in fact, open to making significant concessions, such as renouncing their fiscal privileges.[67] Within the ranks of the Third Estate, too, moderates such as Mounier, Malouet, and Dupont de Nemours were highly respected by their peers, and the majority of them seemed willing to endorse moderation and to make reasonable compromises. The moderate principles of the Dauphiné caucus, stressing the importance of conciliation between the three estates, enjoyed especially high prestige.[68] Furthermore, in the days preceding and following the opening of the Estates-General in early May 1789, many deputies lavished praise on the king in the belief that the will of the nation and that of the monarch were easily reconcilable. This initial optimism quickly gave way to a darker mood, however, and calls to moderation remained unheeded, while several attempts at mediation between the three orders and the king failed in June 1789. Why so great a change in such a short period of time?

Although the chief stumbling blocks proved to be the verification of powers and the question of voting by head or order, the growth of intransigence and the increasing rigidity on all sides cannot be ascribed to these factors alone. To be sure, there were significant differences of background and wealth between the members of the three orders, magnified by the existence of obsolete rules of order for presiding over the meetings of the Estates-

General.[69] These rules and the differences between its members did much to erode the trust of the deputies of the Third Estate in the fairness of deliberations within the assembly and further deepened existing or latent social antagonisms. But there were as well deeper reasons for the radicalization of the assembly: fear, vanity, personal rivalries, anti-clericalism, and the lack of (or limited) parliamentary experience of many deputies of the Third Estate.

The sum of these factors in the end gave radicals in all of the camps significant leverage, even if, as Patrice Gueniffey has reminded us, on numerous occasions, the assembly, which could have done almost everything in principle, displayed a surprising willingness to limit its power and will.[70] Internal divisions within the orders further contributed to the rise of radicalism. Of the three estates, the most divided was the clergy, and the size of the liberal group within its ranks was very small.[71] The failure of leadership on the part of the monarch also played a key role. Overall, the nobles and the clergy feared the numerical superiority of the Third Estate, while the members of the latter, espousing strong anti-clerical views and swayed by powerful orators such as Mirabeau and Sieyès, gradually became convinced that any negotiations with the privileged orders on the verification of powers were futile. The fact that there were two parties among the deputies of the Third Estate—one led by Mounier and Malouet, the other by Sieyès and Mirabeau—pursuing at times different (or conflicting) agendas on key issues such as bicameralism and the royal veto further contributed to the erosion of the moderates' influence.[72]

Thus, partly by calculation and enthusiasm, partly under the force of circumstances and the galleries,[73] and also due to a complex collective psychology fueled by the condescension of the privileged orders toward the Third Estate and the antipathy of the latter toward the former,[74] many deputies came to enthusiastically endorse or strongly oppose radical claims, making the task of the moderates increasingly difficult. Although the will of the nation supported the claims of the Third Estate—for freedom of religion, liberty of the press, and free elections—the representatives of the *tiers état* were confused about the purpose and goals of the assembly (beyond fiscal and legal equality) and did not agree on the best strategy for pursuing them. Until the beginning of June 1789, they remained convinced that these goals could be achieved only under the auspices of a reformed monarchy. At the same time, the intransigence and the rigidity displayed by the first two privileged orders helped develop cohesion within the Third Estate and a sense of common purpose. And, as a further example of the importance of the unintended consequences of human action, it was some of the most prominent moderates within the Third Estate who, through their own choices and strategies, strengthened the power and influence of radicals within their ranks. By mid-June, however, it became clear that the moderation of some of the leading members of the Third Estate was out of tune with the actual disposition and interests of all parties. The time for concessions and compromise was quickly running out.

The most radical representatives of the Third Estate demanded that the issue of voting in common or separately be decided immediately rather than submitted to further negotiations among the delegates of the three orders. They indicated that they would not compromise on the principle of voting by head and would oppose any attempt to enforce voting by order. Some went so far as to claim that the Third Estate was the only true representative of the nation. Their determination was fueled by the most inflexible members of the first two privileged orders, who rejected voting on issues of national interest in a common assembly with the members of the Third Estate. For the majority of the latter, there were by now no matters that could be discussed by each order in separate assembly. All political issues—from feudal rights and fiscal privileges to the organization of the clergy and the future meetings of the Estates-General—now concerned the entire nation and had to be determined by its self-proclaimed representatives deliberating together according to newly agreed rules.

On June 17, under the spell of Sieyès' proposal, the National Assembly boldly declared itself the sole body capable of interpreting and representing the general will of the entire sovereign nation. Sieyès argued that, "since it pertains only to the representatives who have been verified to form the national will, and all the verified representatives are in this assembly, we must conclude that it is in the power of this assembly, and this assembly alone, to represent the general will."[75] In voting for Sieyès' proposal (491 to 90), the Third Estate sent an ultimatum to the two other orders: they had to join them without delay to begin deliberations on a new constitution. The decision of the assembly to declare itself a Constituent Assembly at the Tennis Court in Versailles signaled that the time for compromise had finally run out. The deputies took a collective oath not to separate until the constitution of the kingdom was fully established and affirmed on new foundations. The assembly decreed that it was called to establish this constitution and to bring about the regeneration of the public order, while also maintaining the true principles of monarchy.[76]

This declaration represented more than a symbolic affirmation of the will of the assembly: it was the first decisive step toward the destruction of the Old Regime, a process that would be completed in early August. As Lord Acton pointed out, "the real event of the Tennis Court was to unite all parties against the Crown and to make them adopt the new policy of radical and indefinite change."[77] For once, moderates and revolutionaries were united in their opposition to a form of absolute power which they unanimously rejected as illegitimate. The nation appeared for the first time like a sovereign, feeling that nothing could any longer limit its power.

Several moderate deputies, however, opposed the adoption of the title "Constituent Assembly." One of them was Malouet, who disagreed with both Sieyès' proposal ("*Assemblée des représentants connus et vérifiés de la nation française*") and Mounier's ("*Assemblée légitime des représentants de la majeure partie de la nation, agissant en l'absence de la mineure partie*").

Malouet claimed that the deputies had not been sent to Versailles to constitute a new form of government, but to regulate the exercise of powers in keeping with the instructions received from their constituencies. In the end, Malouet reluctantly endorsed the title of "National Assembly" proposed by Legrand,[78] opting for a middling position offering a much-needed conciliatory tone. At the same time, Malouet insisted that deputies should not compromise on the principle of the indivisibility of the Estates-General, and maintained that they did not have the right to declare themselves the *sole* representatives of the nation, excluding from the assembly the representatives of the clergy and the nobles. Such a radical approach, he argued, could compromise their rights, being contrary to the dictates of reason and the public interest.[79] The deputies, Malouet insisted, were bound to respect the royal authority and the principles of monarchical government. They were called to discuss only the means of *reforming* them and to signal abuses of power that needed to be corrected. According to Malouet, the greatest error of the assembly, born out of its *hubris* in pretending to represent the new government of the country, was to have misunderstood its original mission by proceeding to annul the mandates (at the recommendation of Talleyrand) and to declare itself free from the instructions given by its mandataries. In taking this radical course of action, Malouet argued, the assembly had usurped power and abandoned the only effective barrier against risky innovations and extremism—the mandates—which stipulated that they preserve the stability of monarchical government, protect the king, the property, and religion, and reform old abuses in a gradual and peaceful way. The mandates also called upon deputies to acknowledge that the monarch, too, was a representative of national sovereignty, and as such he was expected to play an important role in the new constitutional framework.[80]

At the core of the debates in the new Constitutional Assembly was the urgent task of "fixing" the French constitution, a complex and highly controversial topic involving major institutional questions, political challenges, hermeneutical ambiguities, and legal hurdles. The Tennis Court Oath had left open the question whether the assembly was called and entitled to restore the constitution (in spite of its obvious flaws), or to create an entirely new one. This ambiguity paved the way for the emergence of major controversies between the two camps holding opposing views on this issue. The controversies in the assembly centered on arcane conceptual distinctions between "establishing," "reestablishing," "maintaining," "giving," "laying the foundations of," and "making" an entirely new constitution, all of which are relevant to our study of moderation in revolutionary times.

They show above all that "fixing" the French constitution represented a highly controversial subject, which had in fact been debated prior to the meeting of the Estates General.[81] As Élie Carcassonne demonstrated, the author who arguably did the most to demonstrate the existence of an old French constitution had been a woman, Mlle de Lézardière. Born in 1754, she wrote two important works under the influence of Montesquieu: *Tab-*

*leau des droits réels et respectifs du Monarque et des sujets depuis le fonde-
ment de la monarchie française jusqu'à nos jours* (1774) and *Essai sur le
rétablissement possible de quelques points de la Constitution* (1778). The
second text acknowledged the imprescriptible rights of assemblies, including the Estates-General, and the sharing of the legislative power between the
people and the monarch as the most important principles of the existing
French "constitution." An important countervailing power was constituted
by the authority of the thirteen *parlements*, consisting of independent judges
enjoying life tenure. Hence, while everything was possible in theory to the
king of France, not everything was permitted in reality to the monarch.

Reactions to this interpretation were quick to appear. Pierre L. Claude
Gin's *Les vrais principes du gouvernement français* (1777, 1782, 1787) and
Jacob-Nicolas Moreau's *Exposition et défense de notre constitution monarchique française* (published in two volumes in 1789) forcefully restated the
traditionalist position on this issue (Moreau's book was officially endorsed
by the Court).[82] Without resorting to the doctrine of divine right, Moreau
claimed that the National Assembly did not have the right to propose a new
constitutional text. The ancient constitution, he argued, was anterior to all
laws and human artifices (including a hypothetical social contract) and
sanctioned absolute monarchy. Although it did provide for a limited representation of the nation through legislative councils whose role was "to give
advice" to the monarch, it also demanded the separate meeting and deliberation of the three orders.[83]

There was something paradoxical and unsettling about claiming, on the
one hand, that an old constitution existed whose traces could be found in
the liberties of Germanic tribes and medieval assemblies and, on the other
hand, affirming that this forgotten but still "living" constitution had to be
defended against those who denied its reality. And it was equally surprising
that even the faintest traces of a supposedly ancient constitution seem to
have vanished as soon as the representatives of the Third Estate put forward
their new constitutional proposals.[84] The intensity of the debate on these
issues revealed not only the fragility and untenability of the traditionalist
position, but also the difficulties encountered by those who argued that
such a constitution did not exist and had to be established *ab novo*.

What was the monarchiens' position in this debate? Did they speak with
one voice, or did they hold different views on this topic? Mounier articulated his position in *Nouvelles observations,* published in February 1789,
and in his *Rapport du comité chargé du travail sur la constitution*, presented
on July 9, 1789. (He was to reaffirm the same ideas three years later in *Recherches*).[85] In these works, he espoused an eclectic approach that illustrates
his commitment to moderation. On the one hand, he emphasized the existence of several fundamental principles of the French monarchy to which
the king himself was bound: the indivisibility of the throne, the rule of the
primogeniture, consent to taxation, and the Salic law. As Mounier argued in
his report of July 9, it was not possible to deny the existence of these funda-

mental laws that expressed the will of the nation, albeit in an imperfect and inconstant manner. At the same time, he was aware that this acknowledgment could have been interpreted as implying two things: first, that in spite of its many imperfections, France did have a more or less "legitimate" government before the revolution; second, that the sovereignty invoked by the king was *anterior* (and superior) to that of the nation.[86] For this reason, Mounier went on to add that the mere survival of these fundamental principles and laws was insufficient to ensure the existence of a stable and fixed form of government in which powers were clearly separated and limited. If the authority of the monarch had no clearly defined limits, he opined, it could easily become arbitrary. Moreover, Mounier added, France needed a new set of written rules to govern the meetings of the Estates-General and a new division of powers reorienting the relationship between the executive and the legislative power. "We do not have a constitution," he concluded, "because all the powers are confounded, and because no limit is set to them. We have not even separated the judiciary from the legislative power. The authority is scattered; the diverse parts are always in contradiction with each other; and in their perpetual collision, the rights of citizens are betrayed."[87] Mounier's report ended with a memorable call to "fix" the constitution of France: "Let us place in the body of the constitution all the true principles as fundamental laws. Let us repeat them once more to give them renewed force . . . let us destroy that which is obviously vicious. Let us finally fix the constitution of France."[88]

All these ideas had previously loomed large in Mounier's *Nouvelles observations* whose chapter XXII explained why France lacked a proper constitution in which powers were clearly divided and distributed. Mounier defined the constitution simultaneously as *"un ordre fixe et établi dans la manière de gouverner,"* based on fundamental principles created by the free and formal consent of the nation, and *"une forme précise et constante de gouvernement, ou, l'expression des droits et des obligations des différents pouvoirs qui le composent."*[89] In France, Mounier maintained, liberty was constantly threatened because no serious attempt had been made to limit the existing powers, beginning with the royal power.[90] Mounier reiterated many of these points a few years later in *Recherches*, one of the most powerful and coherent critiques of the Constituent Assembly, coming from the pen of a political moderate reflecting on the causes that had prevented the French from becoming free in 1789. Mounier noted that nothing regulated in a precise manner the rights of the Crown and the people, and remarked that the nobles had an exceedingly strong influence on government prior to 1789. He argued again that political liberty did not have a solid foundation in France under the Old Regime whose "Gothic ruins" did not offer sufficient guarantees for the protection of individual liberties and the security of the throne.[91] The kingdom of France, Mounier wrote, only had customs and maxims consecrated by tradition and prescription and incompatible with the rule of law. The absence of the latter meant that the laws were "only means for oppressing the weak"[92] rather than promoting the public interest. Mounier also criticized the proliferation of edicts, ordinances, declarations, orders, and rulings of sovereign courts—in his words, "*décisions passagères*"[93]—which had often made the implementation of laws inefficient, chaotic, and arbitrary, and fostered the development of a pernicious corporatist spirit deepening the separation between classes.[94] Furthermore, the power of ministers was in practice unlimited and their political responsibility poorly defined and enforced.[95] Mounier was particularly critical of the *parlements* which, in his view, had displayed a strong spirit of partiality in their fight for strengthening local privileges. In so doing, they furthered the growth of absolute power and failed to serve as effective counterweights to the authority of the monarch.[96]

Nevertheless, Mounier stopped short of arguing that France had no government, or that it lacked any legitimate authority, as some of the more radical members of the assembly claimed. He invited his fellow deputies to choose a middle way, by displaying moderation, proceeding with prudence in reforming the country's old institutions, and refraining from making exaggerated claims in the name of liberty. "We shall never give up our rights, but we shall be careful not to exaggerate them either," he wrote. "We shall not forget that the French are not a new people that has recently emerged from the wilderness in order to form an association, but rather a great society of twenty-four million people who want to tighten the links that unite all the parts of that society and to regenerate the kingdom, and for whom the principles of true monarchy will always be sacred."[97]

The *Declaration of the Rights of Man and of the Citizen*

As the members of the Constituent Assembly, organized in thirty *bureaux*, began discussing the articles of the new constitution in early July, they were confronted with a challenge. They would have to decide whether the constitution had to be preceded by a declaration of the abstract rights of man, or whether the codification of these rights ought to be made after drafting the constitution. Some of the *cahiers des doléances* had touched upon this issue, but it was only now that the rights of the nation came to be discussed within the larger framework of drafting a new constitution for the kingdom of France. This question would occupy the attention of the Assembly in July and August of 1789.

The monarchiens all agreed that any version of such a declaration should be concise and clear and must not be presented before the completion of the constitutional text, but there were some differences of opinion among them on the actual drafting of such a declaration. Both Mounier and Clermont-Tonnerre offered elaborate accounts of the nature and timeliness of the *Declaration*, and Lally-Tollendal made an important intervention on this topic in the assembly on July 11, followed by a second statement on August

19. Clermont-Tonnerre provided a detailed analysis of the strengths and limitations of the *Declaration* in an important book, *Analyse raisonnée de la constitution française* (1791). The rivalry between Mounier's, Mirabeau's, and Sieyes' drafts of the *Declaration* was one of the high moments of the parliamentary debates in the summer of 1789. Although in the end the assembly chose the draft of the sixth bureau led by the Archbishop of Bordeaux, Champion de Cicé, the influence of Mounier's version is demonstrated by the fact that the first three articles of the *Declaration's* final text retained his original formulations.

The elaboration of this important document and the intense controversies triggered by it constitute a fascinating chapter in the history of ideas.[98] Without seeking to retrace all the important moments of this process, a few details are worth recalling because they allow us to understand how moderates like the monarchiens sought to carve out a middle ground among radical factions. The first important decision was taken on July 6, when the majority of the Constitutional Assembly decided that its members would devote their energy and time to drafting a declaration of rights *before* the completion of the constitution. The deputies agreed that the latter must guarantee the natural and fundamental rights of men, which amounted to declaring that rights precede laws, and that legislators ought therefore to be bound by general theories and abstract maxims in drafting laws. The deputies who held this opinion seemed unconcerned about the potentially radical implications of an abstract declaration of rights likely to be interpreted differently by various groups in keeping with their political agendas.

Three days later, on July 9, speaking on behalf of the constitutional committee, Mounier reaffirmed this point, claiming that in order for a constitution to be good, it must be grounded in—and should protect—the rights of man. Mounier then went on to address the issue of natural rights as a prolegomena to any constitutional work. In order to prepare a new constitution, he maintained, legislators must know and apply "the rights which natural justice grants to all individuals," and ought also to be familiar with the "principles which must form the basis of all types of society."[99] Every article of the constitution, he claimed, must be the consequence of an abstract fundamental principle, and the *summa* of these principles ought to form a declaration of rights. He recommended that, after drafting the latter, the deputies should proceed to discuss the principles undergirding a "true" monarchy, followed by the rights of the French nation, the rights of the monarch, the rights of citizens, and the organization and functions of the National Assembly and of provincial and municipal assemblies. Lastly, the deputies were expected to tackle the principles and duties of the judiciary and the military.

The final recommendations of the committee reflected Mounier's moderate approach. The report warned that drafting a declaration of rights before examining all the articles of the constitution would have significant inconveniences, resulting from separating abstract ideas from their consequences and blurring the line between fundamental and secondary principles. The members of the committee recommended that the declaration be "short, simple, and precise" and be presented as a preamble to the constitution, which could then be finalized only *after* the discussion of all the constitutional articles.[100]

Although Mounier's report, accompanied by a detailed plan of action, was coherent and well drafted, it did not take long for him to realize that his plea for moderation and prudence in drafting the *Declaration* was destined to be ineffective. Lafayette, who shared Mounier's moderate approach on this issue, presented his first draft of the *Declaration* two days later, on July 11. Echoing the points made by Mounier in his report, he declared that the document ought to contain "the first principles of every constitution, the first elements of all legislation." Such a text, Lafayette insisted, should be precise and concise, and "should say what everyone knows and what everyone feels," reaffirming "the sentiments which nature has engraved in the heart of each individual" and expressing "those eternal truths from which must derive all institutions."[101] Only under those circumstances could the *Declaration* become an effective guide. To his credit, Lafayette presented the Constituent Assembly with a short draft containing only nine articles, which included several formulations and concepts (such as the sovereignty of the nation, civil equality, and consent) that would also appear in the final document adopted a month and a half later.

In this context, Lally-Tollendal was among the first to sound a warning signal, intervening in the debate soon after Lafayette. Not convinced that the constitution must begin with a statement of abstract rights, he challenged the assembly to rethink the necessity for such a declaration of rights, insisting on the inconveniences and dangers of an abstract document that distinguished natural from positive rights. Lally predicted that, unlike the American Bill of Rights, the French declaration would embolden radicals to ignore the lessons of experience and tradition and could, in fact, further their attempts to subvert legitimate authority. In particular, Lally-Tollendal feared that an abstract declaration of the rights of man would prove a needlessly sophisticated system of abstract metaphysical ideas, more apt to create turmoil than to give society a solid legal foundation. He worried that the elaboration of a declaration of rights before the completion of the constitution would trigger long and sterile debates on abstract concepts and theories, always subject to controversial and conflicting interpretations.[102]

The soundness and prescience of Lally-Tollendal's warning became evident nine days later, when Sieyès presented his own draft of the *Declaration*, a very long text consisting of thirty-two articles and preceded by a substantive theoretical preamble, entitled *Reconnaissance et exposition raisonnée des droits de l'homme et du citoyen*. Seeking to achieve, in his own words, a "superior" form of clarity on such a difficult and important subject as the rights of man, Sieyès drew inspiration from Rousseau in affirming the superiority of civil over natural liberty, while at the same time parting company with him on the issue of the guarantees necessary for the protection of individual liberty. Sieyès famously distinguished between *pouvoir constituant* and *pouvoirs constitués* and identified two forms of citizenship, passive and active.[103] For all of its conceptual sophistication, his long text failed to impress his audience, which regarded it as "enigmatic and perfidious" (Lally-Tollendal) or, in Landon's words, as "an entirely useless catechism of metaphysics"[104] unsuitable to the great work which the deputies were called to undertake.

Finding Sieyès' draft to be "too metaphysical and obscure," Mounier presented his own declaration on July 27, 1789. A rivalry ensued between the two projects, and more generally between those who, like Duquesnoy,[105] believed that it was desirable to print the *Social Contract* as a preamble to the new constitution, and those who sought to achieve a balance of powers after the model of the unwritten English constitution and the American constitution. Comprising only sixteen articles and drawing inspiration from Lafayette's declaration, Mounier's version was significantly shorter than Sieyès'. He did not seem to be entirely convinced of the necessity of a separate declaration, fearing that abstract ideas and theories, if not linked to practice, might have perverse effects. In the end, Mounier proposed a short, simple, and precise *Declaration,* arguing that it should not be published before—and independent from—the completed text of the new constitution.

That is why in his intervention on July 27, Mounier proceeded to present the constitutional principles of the French government, thirty-five articles in total, beginning with an unambiguous endorsement of the monarchy and the rule of law.[106] The main points of his draft restated the conventional wisdom, while remaining true to the call for moderation voiced in his report of July 9. The goal of the government, Mounier argued, must be the general felicity of the governed (Art. II); only those laws to which people have consented are legitimate (Art. VI). The idea of the sovereignty of the nation was proclaimed in Art. III, while the separation of powers was the object of Art. IX, which presented it as the most important means of preventing despotism and securing the rule of law. Mounier's text made, however, no reference to the need for a national convention to be called to periodically revise the constitution, an issue raised by Art. XXXII of Sieyès' draft of the *Declaration.* While Mounier acknowledged the equality of rights (Art. I), the tone of his version was different from the more aggressive accent of Sieyès' text, as illustrated, for example, by the latter's vituperation against all kinds of privileges.[107] Among the fundamental rights and freedoms (Art. IV), Mounier listed liberty, property, security, freedom of thought and expression, freedom of the press (with some restrictions), freedom of religion (with the exception of non-Catholics), and the right to resist oppression. What Mounier did not include was precisely the right to social assistance and the right to work demanded by Sieyès.

In the end, confronted with a proliferation of projects, the deputies retained neither Mounier's nor Sieyès' versions, but the more modest and cautious draft prepared by the sixth *bureau*.[108] A brief remark made by Adrien Duquesnoy in his memoirs conveys an idea of the general impression produced by Mounier's text presented on July 27. "I would not want to judge him based on this reading," Duquesnoy wrote about it, "but, in general, the principles are true, the views are sound, and yet the text is too long, it has several false ideas, some of them dangerous, and many of them useless."[109] Duquesnoy was not alone in criticizing Mounier's approach. Two other critiques came from within the monarchiens' camp, from the pen of Malouet and Clermont-Tonnerre. Malouet would have preferred the declaration to be not of natural rights, but of positive rights; moreover, he believed that a declaration of rights should have been drafted only after the completion of the constitutional text in order to avoid long and futile debates on controversial issues.[110] The formulation of a set of abstract rights, he warned, would be like bringing people onto the top of a high mountain where they would be shown a limitless perspective hiding from their view the numerous obstacles they would encounter at every step when descending the mountain. The drafting of an abstract declaration, Malouet feared, might give people unrealistic expectations about liberty and rights, and was likely to foster endless controversies on abstruse topics of law and philosophy, while obscuring from sight positive rights and obligations and delaying the finalization of the constitutional text.[111]

Clermont-Tonnerre fully shared Malouet's apprehensions. Pointing to the differences between the American and the French understanding of rights, he argued that the former sought only to reclaim old and legitimate rights that had been violated prior to 1776. In defending several rights such as those endorsed by the famous Virginia *Declaration of Rights*, the Americans had avoided metaphysical abstractions, keeping their feet firmly on the ground. Theirs was the powerful and genuine cry of a people long oppressed, and it carried a profound awareness of past wrongs and of the possibility of future injustices. The French took a different route. In Clermont-Tonnerre's view, their *Declaration of the Rights of Man* suffered from metaphysical dogmatism. By sanctioning a right to individual resistance and giving it a rigid interpretation, it risked promoting anarchy and license; an inflexible interpretation of such a right could, in fact, be used to subvert social order rather than render it legitimate.[112] Referring to Art. III of the *Declaration* ("The source of all sovereignty resides essentially in the nation") inspired from Mounier's text, Clermont-Tonnerre argued that this article was marred by its flawed definition of sovereignty and failure to state that a nation may *not* use its right to sovereignty as it pleases.[113] In large societies where people are too numerous to deliberate in common, they cannot exercise sovereignty in the proper sense of the term. The nation is sovereign only in a *limited* way, in the same sense that the principle of individual liberty resides in each person, but is restrained and limited by the conventions and the social pact to which each individual tacitly or explicitly consents when living in society.[114]

As such, Clermont-Tonnerre maintained, the seminal Article III of the *Declaration* had a twofold vice. It was silent about the need for the nation to partly give up or temporarily renounce the use of its sovereignty, and it did not acknowledge the necessity of delegating sovereignty to the nation's representatives. This article should have recognized instead "the absolute necessity to defend this sovereignty from the usurpation of individuals and bodies," which was no small matter, since "liberty is destroyed when sovereignty entirely resides in one single individual or a single group."[115] Moreover, the rights enshrined in the *Declaration* had an ambiguous relationship with positive laws. The latter were an illusory guarantee of rights so long as the declaration of rights did not clearly define the laws to ensure that the latter were just and protected freedom.[116] The *Declaration* was presented as a barrier that no law might transgress, but at the same time the authors of the text gave to positive laws the authority to decide in exceptional circumstances when the temporary curtailment of the rights of man was acceptable.[117] Clermont-Tonnerre claimed that an abstract declaration could not prevent the despotism of the many, in spite of liberal provisions such as Art. XVI regarding the separation of powers, for that article seemed somehow disconnected from the other articles of the *Declaration*. The spirit in which the latter was conceived made it a powerful weapon against the constitution and risked diminishing the respect due to it. Thus, Clermont-Tonnerre concluded, the *Declaration* was a circumstantial work which could not serve as a useful guide to future legislators. It was marred by the vagueness of its definitions, the falseness of its maxims, and the incoherence of its ideas.[118]

In the second volume of *Recherches*, Mounier acknowledged the pertinence of these critiques while attempting to justify his middling position. He pointed out that his own version of the *Declaration* sought to minimize the inconveniences of an abstract declaration of rights, which the majority of his colleagues on the left were determined to adopt, regardless of any objections that might be made against it. Mounier recognized, however, that he should have insisted more adamantly that all abstract ideas and speculations on the rights of man could be easily misinterpreted, leading to perverse consequences.[119] Although Mounier's integrity cannot be questioned, his statement must be taken with a grain of salt. His eclectic position on the *Declaration* is not easy to evaluate since as a moderate, he attempted to straddle two different political and conceptual traditions in tension with each other. On the one hand, Mounier believed in the existence of natural rights and did not seem to be concerned about the difficulties surrounding their codification into positive rights. On the other hand, unlike many deputies on the left, he did not want to do away with tradition and experience. To his more radical colleagues, Mounier recommended caution, calling upon them to affirm the rights of the nation with due moderation.

In the end, it was deeply ironical that, of all the deputies, it was Mounier who, as president of the Assembly on the eve of the tragic events of October

5-6, 1789, was sent by the deputies to the king's court at Versailles to ask for the monarch's endorsement of the *Declaration*. Those two days turned out to be an omen of future violent episodes. A few days later, exhausted and discouraged, Mounier left Versailles and withdrew from political life.

The Elusive Balance of Powers: The Debates on Bicameralism and the Royal Veto

What happened during the three weeks between the passing of the *Declaration of the Rights of Man and of the Citizen* in late August of 1789 and the rejection of bicameralism and adoption of the suspensive veto in September, represents one of the most intensive and important phases of the French Revolution. And it has much to teach us about political moderation. The attempt to institutionalize a third power between the monarch and the people proved to be a stumbling block for the monarchiens, ultimately contributing to their early political defeat.

While the political scene had become increasingly radicalized from the beginning of August, when the Constituent Assembly voted to abolish the privileges of the first two orders, the deputies did agree on several important points. They admitted that parliament must meet regularly and that its members would be elected indirectly, by equal districts, on the basis of moderate property qualifications. There was also wide agreement that the constitution was not going to be subject to royal veto, that the king's ministers should not be members of the legislative assembly, and that the initiative of drafting laws should rest exclusively with the deputies. Nonetheless, disagreements soon arose over whether or not the laws passed by parliament could be vetoed by the king, and if so, what kind of veto should be granted to the monarch. Even greater controversies were triggered by the question of whether the initiatives of the representatives of the people might be checked by the members of an upper chamber, modeled either upon the American Senate or the English House of Lords, or whether the deputies ought to adopt the model of a single chamber representing the unitary will of the nation.

Although, as Lord Acton noted,[120] in August 1789, the "constitutional" party was still powerful in the assembly, whose newly elected president, the Bishop of Langres, was an advocate of an upper house, the support for the twin principles of balance of powers and bicameralism quickly waned. In defending these two principles, the monarchiens swam against the tide. They emphasized the connection between legal and institutional complexity and political liberty, insisting that despotic systems naturally tend toward uniformity, while free regimes are never uniform and simple. The latter nurture complexity and thrive on it, combining a sound balance of powers and a rigorous administration of justice with a myriad of legal formalities that provide for the security of property and persons.

Mounier's defense of bicameralism and an absolute royal veto represented the high moment of his political career, and the speech he gave on September 5, 1789—"*le chant du cygne d'un parti en perdition*" according to Furet and Halévi[121]—was one of the most important discourses in the Constituent Assembly, echoing the ideas presented a week earlier (on August 31) by Lally-Tollendal in another important discourse. These two long speeches are among the most coherent and important statements of the monarchiens' moderate political philosophy.[122] Lally-Tollendal's discourse in favor of bicameralism restated the classical case for prudence. "A single assembly," he claimed, "perpetually runs the danger of being carried along by eloquence, of being seduced by sophisms, led astray by intrigues, enflamed by passions that one wants to share, carried away by sudden movements that are communicated to it, and stopped by the terror that one inspires in it by a sort of public cry."[123] A monocameral parliament cannot be properly bound by its deliberations and, in an instant of imprudent exuberance, might easily break with the laws and norms to which it had previously consented. Such an assembly would be capable of abruptly revoking its most solemn decisions and rigorous decrees. All this was incompatible with the slow and prudent deliberation that must usually take place in parliament (the situation was different with regard to the executive power, whose most distinctive traits are swiftness and unity).

Mounier echoed Lally's argument, claiming that a monocameral assembly would be much more dangerous than a bicameral one, since it would always be able to invent new ways and means of ignoring, defeating, or circumventing any limits and challenges to its power. Only two chambers deliberating separately could successfully offset the dangers and limitations of a unitary assembly claiming to represent the general will of the nation. The two chambers would complement each other and would bring into legislation a much-needed "second thought" and an element of prudence, preventing the adoption of hastily conceived projects that could undermine liberty and order. Underlying these precautions was the idea that the ship of the state must not be entrusted to inexperienced hands and reckless minds that could bring about its shipwreck and provoke anarchy.[124] Mounier's speech restated a few points he had previously made in *Nouvelles observations,* where he outlined the composition of an upper (pseudo-aristocratic) chamber with power and prerogatives so limited as to render it incapable of blocking legitimate attempts to eliminate or reform old abuses. In his view, even an assembly composed of arguably the best and most skilled individuals should never be allowed to enjoy unlimited power in one single chamber. Mounier also emphasized that the upper chamber must not represent only the first privileged orders, nor should it resemble the old *Cour plenière* instituted in May 1787, which triggered the indignation of the Third Estate. Such an upper chamber, he insisted, should have neither the right of legislative initiative nor veto power over the laws drafted by the representatives of the nation assembled in the lower chamber. Furthermore, Mounier maintained, the main mission of the upper chamber should be to defend the rights of the Crown and maintain the constitution.[125]

A few months later, in *Considérations sur les gouvernements*, Mounier warned once more against the dangers of a monocameral assembly endowed with powerful prerogatives and dominated by power-hungry demagogues seeking to replace the will of the nation with their own will. France, he maintained, would benefit from the creation of a body, not unlike the English House of Lords, interposed between the king and the representatives of the nation, and charged to maintain an effective balance of power between them. Nonetheless, he added, the members of the House of Lords were different from the French nobility, for unlike the latter, they did not form a class entirely separated from the rest of the citizens.[126] Unlike Mallet du Pan,[127] the monarchiens did not insist that a French upper house ought to be of aristocratic extraction, because they were skeptical that hereditary peerage could be created in France following the English model. Life magistratures, they believed, were preferable to a second aristocratic chamber. In his writings from the summer of 1789, Mounier proposed a Senate consisting of 300 members, serving six-year terms, eligible by provincial assemblies, and satisfying the minimal conditions of political capacity (being at least 35 years of age, and having a minimum income of 10,000 livres). This Senate, he argued, ought to protect the constitution and defend the Crown by making sure that the smallest political changes would be in conformity with the rules agreed upon by the representatives of the nation.[128] Such an upper house, composed of distinguished individuals worthy of their fellow citizens' trust, could serve as an effective break upon the initiatives of the representatives of the nation by ensuring that the deputies protect public liberties and the prerogatives of the monarch. The task of this chamber would be to make it impossible for deputies to destroy or usurp royal authority, and to prevent the king from encroaching upon the rights of his subjects. To this end, the two chambers must not be led by the same passions and interests and should have different forms of election.

The issue of bicameralism cannot be separated from the controversies over the royal sanction and the related question of whether the king should be given the power of dissolving the elected assembly. At the heart of these debates lay the twin issues of the balance and separation of powers. It will be recalled that Article XVI of the *Declaration of the Rights of Man* stipulated that political liberty does not exist in the absence of a strict separation of powers. Mounier and Lally-Tollendal worried about the radical implications of this article, especially the ensuing demotion of the executive to the rank of an ancillary power created by the constitution rather than preceding it. "Just as the complete union of these two powers [the executive and the legislative] would lead to tyranny," Lally-Tollendal argued, "their complete separation would lead to the same result."[129] Hence, the necessity of establishing a constant point of contact between the legislative and the executive powers. As Montesquieu had demonstrated, such a point of contact presupposed the existence of a sound balance between two powers with clearly delineated and overlapping spheres of authority and influence. It mattered a great deal whether the king had the right to absolutely veto the legislative initiatives of the deputies, or whether he had only a suspensive veto power for two consecutive legislatures. Not only was the monarch's independence *vis-à-vis* the assembly at stake in these debates, but those who regarded the king only as *primus inter pares* called the very nature and survival of monarchy into question. There were two key questions. Did the king, who claimed the right of veto, also have a share in the exercise of the legislative function broadly construed, and if so, to what extent? Wasn't the monarch granted only a form of "negative" power, a mere *faculté d'empêcher*? And, could the king also have been considered the "coauthor" of legislative acts, in spite of the fact that he had neither *la faculté de statuer* nor the right to initiate laws?

Opposing the attempt to downgrade the executive power in the name of the sovereignty of the nation, the monarchiens warned against creating an emasculated form of monarchy misrepresented as "royal democracy."[130] The solution they proposed—an absolute veto for the king—had a lot in common with the English doctrine of "the-king-in-Parliament" (discussed by De Lolme in *La Constitution de l'Angleterre*) and implied that the monarch should be seen as "an integral part of the legislative power,"[131] or, as Mirabeau (another defender of the absolute veto) put it, "the perpetual representative of the people."[132] This was an unacceptable thesis in the eyes of those, like Sieyès, who believed that the nation as a homogeneous whole was the only real sovereign, and viewed the king as a mere organ of the nation.[133] They wanted to give legislative power exclusively to the representatives of the nation and regarded the executive power (composed of the monarch and his ministers) with great distrust. Not surprisingly, Sieyès opposed any form of veto, maintaining that the nation must speak with one single voice—that of the national legislative power—and arguing that the monarch should not have any say in the exercise of the latter. The monarchiens stood firm in their defense of a strong royal power, insisting that the king was to be considered as one of the representatives of the nation (along with the deputies in the lower chamber), and was expected to play an important role in maintaining the equipoise of the political system. At the same time, the participation (the "concert") of the Estates and the monarch in the exercise of the *legislative* function was seen by them as one of the pillars of the Constitution.[134]

The few principles on which the deputies agreed did little to temper the intensity of debates on the balance of powers, a complex constitutional issue that soon became a highly contested political one as well. The monarchiens had hoped that the creation of a sound balance of powers, according to which the legislative and executive functions were shared in different degrees by the king and the assembly, would provide the foundation of an ordered liberty within the framework of constitutional monarchy. In the footsteps of Montesquieu, Mounier emphasized that, while making the agents of the executive power participate in the legislative power, great attention had to be paid to ensure that these two powers would remain both distinct and balanced.[135] The monarch was to have only a limited share in the exercise of the legislative function (through his veto); he was not granted the right to initiate new laws, but only to approve or reject the laws passed by the lower chamber. "Initiative, that is to say, the right to propose, discuss, and draft laws belongs exclusively to the National Assembly," Lally-Tollendal argued. "The royal authority acquires in this way the right only to prevent evil, and not to do it."[136]

Malouet proposed a slightly different interpretation of the royal sanction in another important discourse given on September 1, 1789. After examining the historical evolution of the rights of the Crown, he went on to define royal sanction as "a right and a national prerogative, granted to the chief of the nation by the nation itself, in order to declare and guarantee that any resolution of its representatives is or is not the expression of the general will."[137] The link between the general will and the royal sanction must be duly underscored in Malouet's intervention because it brings into the equation a third important element, the rising power of public opinion, universally acknowledged by the deputies as a force to be reckoned with. Malouet also argued that, while the monarch had the right to veto the legislative initiatives of the representatives of the nation, he could not oppose or ignore the nation's right to draft and adopt a new constitution (a similar point had been made by Mirabeau). In the end, on September 11, the deputies accepted a compromise on the veto proposed by Barnave, voting for a suspensive veto (673 against 235) and rejecting Mounier's proposal for bicameralism (849 against 89). The next day, Mounier, Lally-Tollendal, and Clermont-Tonnerre resigned from the constitutional committee.

The monarchiens' defense of an absolute royal veto was the upshot of their theory of the balance of powers, reflecting the complex ways in which they attempted to reconcile the sovereignty of the nation with the rights of the monarch. Liberty, they believed, could exist only in a political system in which individuals, institutions, and powers have different interests, motives, and passions and are free to pursue them. On this view, the statesman's task is to maintain the orderly balance of powers and interests that makes such a pursuit possible, and to prevent the union of powers in the same hands that would lead to despotism. "Place insuperable obstacles to the union of powers," Mounier recommended.

> To achieve this goal, it is necessary to organize the different powers in such a way that they will never be united in the same hands. Whenever one finds union or overlapping of powers, there is bound to be despotism. Liberty does not exist if the public force and judg-

ments are arbitrary and inspired by circumstances or diverse passions. Previous laws, elaborated during peaceful times and after long deliberations, must always serve as a guide to them.[138]

In practice, creating a proper division of powers proved to be an immensely difficult task. "Nothing is simpler," Mounier acknowledged, "than leaving the task of correcting, abolishing, and creating new laws in the hands of various powers and orders which moderate or balance each other. . . . But when we have been quite imprudent in allowing an assembly to enjoy unlimited power, there can be no limit to further innovations."[139] The difficulty arose not only from the unique configuration of the French political scene in 1789, but also from the monarchiens' preference for a classical conception of politics, one that sought to preserve a complex polity based on mixed and balanced government.

Unlike Necker, the monarchiens did not propose a theory of "intertwined" powers, nor did they elaborate a full-fledged theory of "neutral power," similar to Constant's.[140] For the most part, their conceptual vocabulary remained in the orbit of Montesquieu and De Lolme. Thus, referring to the interaction between the legislative and the executive power, Lally-Tollendal resorted to a Montesquieuan language that signaled clearly the affinities between their political outlooks. (He also invoked the name of John Adams).[141] He argued that it was necessary to oppose an active force with another active force without creating a conflict between them; the entire society would suffer if these powers were perpetually at war with each other. From this, Lally-Tollendal argued, follows the necessity of creating a balance of powers by dividing the legislative power "not in two, but in three parts."[142] Lally-Tollendal warned:

A single power would inevitably end by devouring everything standing in its way. Two powers would fight among themselves until one of them would destroy the other one. But *three* powers would maintain themselves in a *perfect equilibrium*, if combined in such a way that, when two of them fight with each other, the *third* power— equally interested in maintaining the other two—would join with the one that is oppressed against the one that oppresses, and would restore peace among them.[143]

The upshot of this complex alchemy of powers was *un triple pouvoir*, with each of the three powers—the two chambers and the king—having a particular interest, independent of the general interest, and a different composition.[144]

In turn, Clermont-Tonnerre advocated the balance of powers in a discourse given on September 4, 1789. A defender of bicameralism, which he regarded as an indispensable moderating device in tempered monarchies, Clermont-Tonnerre believed that the constitution itself was nothing but the result of a sound balance of powers. He justified the creation of a second chamber by invoking the need for *moyens modérateurs*[145] capable of protecting civil liberties and securing social order. In his analysis of the Constitution of 1791, Clermont-Tonnerre highlighted the importance of the balance and separation of powers—two terms that he sometimes used interchangeably—but refrained from offering any clear advice on how the two main powers (the legislative and the executive) ought to be combined in order to be able to cooperate effectively.[146]

The balance of powers envisioned by the monarchiens could be interpreted as a form of mixed government *sui generis* capable of making the exercise of political power more effective and regular by limiting or preventing abuses of power. Nonetheless, what the monarchiens advocated was different from the classical understanding of mixed government as a combination of the rule by one, few, and the many, reflecting the mixture of social orders. In other respects, however, they followed the conventional wisdom, as when arguing that in such a mixed regime, "the three forms of government, finding themselves thrown together and mixed up, would produce one that offers the advantages of all of them without having the inconveniences of any of them."[147] The monarchiens' conception of the balance of powers was only indirectly related to the Aristotelian, Polybian, and Ciceronian theories of mixed government, which called for a proper mixture of social forces, classes, and interests. In the monarchiens' view, the balance of powers amounted to prudently distributing all the powers in such a way that each component of government has sufficient means to carry out its tasks, and is thus led to respect the other powers and maintain the constitution which guarantees them all.[148] Although this view implies to some extent a sharing of power between different social classes and groups, its ultimate meaning lies elsewhere. It reminds us that power is created through the interaction of the various institutions and individuals sharing in the exercise of *both* the legislative and executive functions.

Unfortunately, the monarchiens advocated the creation of a pluralistic system of powers and social interests at the very moment when France, subject to a strong passion for equality, was seduced more and more by the charms of the latter. During the summer of 1789, arguing for a balance of powers and a tempered (constitutional) monarchy resembled, in fact, the Sisyphean attempt to square a circle. The monarchiens' moderate agenda advocating social and political pluralism, bicameralism, an absolute royal veto, and a balance of powers had little chance of swaying a public opinion decidedly against what some dismissed as "Gothic superstitions," and at a time, moreover, when distrust of Louis XVI and his ministers was on the rise, fueled by speculations about their alleged secret agreements with the most radical elements of the nobility and the clergy. The assembly preferred social and political unity and constitutional simplicity to pluralism and complexity. The majority of deputies repudiated the English model, voting instead for the suspensive veto and monocameralism.

The final result of their deliberations—the Constitution of 1791 adopted in early September 1791—was nothing more than a *trompe-l'œil* in the opinion of the monarchiens and their like-minded colleagues.[149] It had a monarchical façade, but its foundation was anti-monarchic and democratic, insofar as it refused to grant Louis XVI, now transformed into the first public functionary of the kingdom, *primus inter pares*, the authority needed for the proper exercise of his royal functions. Moreover, as Malouet insisted in an important text on August 8, 1791 (which he was not allowed to read in the assembly), the new constitution had created an abstract sovereignty that did not offer sufficient guarantees for the effective protection of individual rights and private property. Its monocameral legislative power could not guarantee the natural and civil rights that the Constituent Assembly granted on paper to all citizens. All in all, Malouet concluded, the new constitutional text contradicted the major principles to which he and the other monarchiens had been faithful and, as such, it could not receive their endorsement.

The Dialogue between the Monarchiens and Burke

A perceptive interpreter of the revolutionary mind, Edmund Burke foresaw these developments early on and became convinced that nothing good could emerge from the principles of 1789. Burke remained unpersuaded, however, by the ideas of the monarchiens, whom he perceived as sharing a significant part of responsibility for the revolutionary turmoil that set France ablaze in 1789. Burke criticized the monarchiens for their propensity to build "imaginary constitutions" and their "wild spirit of adventure."[150] A closer look at their dialogue suggests, though, that the author of *Reflections* did not fully understand the nature of the monarchiens' moderate political agenda and the tragic role played by moderates in the summer of 1789, and that he underestimated their achievements.

It is important to pause for a moment to examine why Burke, whose Whiggism was ultimately not so different from the monarchiens' moderation, came to be critical of the latter. There are several references to the monarchiens in Burke's writings (including a few words in *Reflections*), and not all of them are negative; the most substantive can be found in *A Letter to a Member of the National Assembly* (1791). On the one hand, Burke acknowledged "the eloquence and general purity" of the monarchiens' motives, along with their good intentions.[151] On the other hand, he believed that their talents were not enough to compensate for their inexperience, their alleged lack of moderation and pragmatism, and their unsound political judgment. Burke described them as imprudent and overconfident in their power to reform the constitution of France and criticized them for letting themselves be intoxicated by the revolutionary fervor that swept the country in 1789. Being "busy in the confections of the dirt-pies of their imaginary constitutions,"[152] the monarchiens forgot that the theoretical schemes with which they wanted to reform the country were (according to Burke) more or less utopian. "I saw very well from the beginning, the mischiefs which, with all these talents and good intentions, they would do to their country, through their confidence in systems," Burke wrote. "But their distemper was an epidemic malady. They were young and inexperienced; and when will young and inexperienced men learn caution and distrust of themselves? And when will men, young or old, if suddenly raised to far higher power than that which absolute kings and emperors commonly enjoy, learn any thing like moderation?"[153]

Thus, according to Burke, it was the monarchiens' hubris and inexperience that finally led to their political defeat:

> These gentlemen conceived that they were chosen to new model the state, and even the whole order of civil society itself. No wonder that they entertained dangerous visions, when the King's ministers, trustees for the sacred deposit of the monarchy, were so infected with the contagion of project and system (I can hardly think it black premeditated treachery) that they publicly advertised for plans and schemes of government, as if they were to provide for the rebuilding of an hospital that had been burned down.[154]

Guided by their heated imagination and "reckless" spirit of adventure, these revolutionary moderates, Burke believed, failed to notice that France did have, in fact, an ancient constitution which could and should have been reformed rather than torn apart and rebuilt from the scratch. That is why, he argued, "the fault of Mr. Mounier and Mr. Lally was very great."[155]

Yet, on the other hand, this fault "was very general" and the monarchiens were far from being the only ones who committed this error. According to Burke, Mounier and his colleagues did have at least one great merit, that of repenting on time of their political sins, "when they came to the brink of the gulf of guilt and public misery, that yawned before them in the abyss of these dark and bottomless speculations."[156] Guilty as they may have been of entertaining utopian ideas at the outset of the revolution, the monarchiens courageously parted company with their colleagues when it became obvious that the original course of the revolution had been abandoned. "They who consider Mounier and Lally as deserters, must regard themselves as murderers and as traitors: for from what else than murder and treason did they desert? For my part, I honour them for not having carried mistake into crime."[157] The monarchiens, Burke pointed out, understood that it was a necessary preliminary to liberty in France to reestablish order and property rights and strengthen the monarchy.

In two long letters published in 1791 and 1792, Lally-Tollendal responded to Burke's accusations, which he found unfair and inaccurate. He took Burke to task for having failed to listen to the members of the moderate party whose contribution to the preservation of liberty in France was far from being insignificant, in spite of their political setbacks. "The citizens of the moderate party," Lally-Tollendal wrote, "saved the state, established the foundation of liberty, the rights of the Crown, and the principles of a government which, by holding to a middle ground between two factions, eventually succeeded in bringing them closer to each other."[158] Lally argued that only the moderates could provide the anchor essential to the stability of the state[159] and identified the monarchiens' agenda with that of the moderate party broadly construed: "This is the goal toward which the moderate party has constantly tended in the chamber of the nobility. To become one with the public opinion; above all, to bring to life the Estates-General; then to serve the cause of the people and freedom, and, in order to promote it, to conserve, honor, and remind the nobles of their true *raison d'être*—this is what our project has always been."[160] Like Burke, Lally-Tollendal insisted on the similarities between England and France, arguing that France could have followed a path that would have led her to adopt English institutions, if circumstances beyond her control had not pushed the country in a different direction. At the same time, Lally claimed that the support for doubling the number of deputies of the Third Estate in 1789 was not an expression of radicalism, as Burke suggested. In reality, the measure was necessary to eliminate a major flaw in the constitution of the country, and it was to the monarchiens' credit that they tried to correct it in due course.[161] Referring to the challenges faced by the monarchiens, Lally-Tollendal remarked that their appeal to moderation was all the more timely and their defense of property all the more courageous.

A closer look at the monarchiens' moderate agenda shows that it was not far from the plan recommended by Burke, even if the latter underestimated the extent to which a new form of organization of the Estates-General was needed in 1789. In the second volume of *Recherches*, Mounier gave a highly critical account of the Constituent Assembly that overlapped in some particulars with the description offered by Burke. The assembly, Mounier noted (confirming Burke's initial fears and predictions), demanded absolute submission to its will, violated its own laws or ignored existing laws when it suited its plans. It multiplied retroactive laws, obstructed the freedom of the judiciary, and sanctioned arbitrary arrests along with blatant violations of privacy. It also professed disrespect for individual security, disregarded freedom of expression, and introduced prosecution for the crime of *lèse-nation*, which was never clearly defined. In so doing, the deputies encouraged moblike behavior in the galleries and ignored the mandates of their own electors while demagogically invoking the doctrine of popular sovereignty. Moreover, the assembly adopted an unwise and unfair policy toward the clergy by imposing an illegitimate oath, and behaved hypocritically by promoting fiscal irresponsibility. Thus, it fostered the corruption of mores and condoned anarchy.[162]

The most significant difference between Burke and the monarchiens lay, however, in their views on what could have been done to avoid a revolution in 1789. Unlike Mounier, Malouet, and Lally-Tollendal, who believed that moderation did have a real chance to prevail in the summer of 1789, Burke remained unconvinced of its prospects and displayed little empathy for the agenda of the moderates who sought to carve out a middle course between extremes. In spite of the above-mentioned similarities, the thrust of Burke's account of the Constituent Assembly differed from that of the monarchiens, who believed that the majority of the deputies were motivated by pure intentions, wanting to avoid social turmoil and promote liberty and the rule of law.[163] As Malouet remarked, all things considered, the majority of deputies were honest and patriotic, even if some of them had only modest political experience. Although there were also radicals within their ranks, many of them had "just ideas" with which they sought to remedy both real and imaginary problems and dangers.[164]

Burke instead saw the majority of deputies as a mass of inexperienced and imprudent legislators, unprepared for their historical task of reforming the constitution of France. It was this divergence of opinions that led Malouet to describe Burke as having the mindset of a French aristocrat, criticizing him for his ideological intransigence and rigidity.[165] In turn, Burke dismissed Lally-Tollendal's second letter as "not being worthy of an answer," and accused him of shallowness. "This worthy Gentleman," Burke wrote, "is the very surface of superficiality,"[166] an immoderate and unfair claim that, sadly, drew the curtain over what could have been an interesting dialogue between two genuine friends of liberty. Lally-Tollendal was not the only one among the monarchiens (or their close associates) who became critical of Burke's outlook, being joined by Mallet du Pan, who also found some of Burke's ideas extravagant.[167]

It is a pity that the dialogue between Burke and the monarchiens ended here. What should have brought them closer together was precisely their common commitment to political moderation. In an important letter to Depont from November 1789, Burke made a moving *éloge* of moderation, which he opposed to weakness and opportunism:

> In all changes in the state, moderation is a virtue, not only amiable but powerful. It is a disposing, arranging, conciliating, cementing virtue. In the formation of new constitutions, it is in its province. . . . This virtue of moderation (which time and situations will clearly distinguish from the counterfeits of pusillanimity and indecision) is the virtue only of superior minds. It requires a deep courage, and full of reflection, to be temperate when the voice of multitudes (the specious mimic of fame and reputation) passes judgment against you.[168]

There was little in Burke's words that the monarchiens would not have wholeheartedly endorsed, beginning with the description of moderation as a difficult virtue, suitable only to noble and courageous souls. This latter point was, in fact, made by Mounier in a book published in 1801, in which he described moderation in terms strongly reminiscent of Burke:

> A great philosopher has remarked that truth is always to be found between the two extremes. This axiom is continually repeated, but its just application is always forgotten. Because it has sometimes happened that timid or selfish men have wished to honour with the name of moderation their cowardice or their indifference, it is very commonly believed that moderate principles are the marks of weakness; whereas, in fact, it is impossible to avoid error, without adopting such principles, and as it requires a great portion of firmness to remain faithful to them, the weak, who are violently attached to exaggerated opinions, pass successively from one to another.[169]

A critic of the Constitution of 1791, Mounier insisted that constitutional revisions and the elimination of past abuses ought to have been carried out without haste and with great caution in order to avoid turmoil and convulsion.[170] Liberty itself, he believed, should be pursued with moderation, prudence, and self-restraint. "If one tried to undertake too much, one would risk being unsuccessful," he argued. "The most important duty is to guarantee public freedom, and in order to do so, it is enough to organize the legislative body and establish the limits required to prevent various powers from attacking each other and being placed in the same hands."[171] A few lines later, Mounier renewed his appeal to caution by calling upon his fellow deputies to refrain from attempting to reform at once all past abuses. Their elimination, he insisted, must be done "justly and slowly," so that individuals are never sacrificed for the sake of abstract theories.[172]

Mounier was not the only monarchien to espouse a Burkean reformist tone. Referring to the political situation in the summer of 1789, Malouet also remarked that only a spirit of compromise, self-restraint, and conciliation could have saved the country from ruin in such a time of crisis.[173] To those who criticized the monarchiens for being advocates of radical change, he answered with a moving plea for prudence that could have also been written by Burke. "In my view," he wrote in his memoirs, "recreating all the powers was an act of usurpation; to destroy them was a breach of trust; to regulate their exercise and set limits to them was our duty. Thus, I have never entertained the goal of scattering and dissolving all the elements of a vast monarchy in order to recompose them later. Do not disrupt anything, I was crying; try to reform and steer, without breaking all the springs at the same time."[174] It was an admirable profession of faith, and it demonstrates that the monarchiens did not advocate a *tabula rasa*, but remained true to the very end to a policy of compromise and moderation, the two virtues that Burke also constantly praised in his writings.

The Limits of Moderation in Revolutionary Times

It is not easy to assess the monarchiens' political agenda, an unconventional mixture of moderation and radicalism which at times might have seemed (and might have been) out of touch with reality.[175] Mounier and his colleagues advocated a strong executive power at a time when trust in royal power had reached a historical low; their constitutionalism did not grant a prominent role to parliament at the very moment when public opinion wanted a stronger legislative power.[176] While the monarchiens emphasized the importance of consent, their theories of national sovereignty and the separation of powers should not be seen as a diluted French version of Lockeanism. In their writings, one cannot find the strong emphasis on negative freedom—freedom from interference—that had been dominant in the Anglo-American political tradition, beginning with Hobbes and Locke. Instead, one finds a constant concern with creating a new balance of powers, a preoccupation that attests to the liberal aspirations of their political agenda as it struggled to make headway in an essentially illiberal culture and a conflict-ridden context.

At first sight, the tragic destiny of Mounier and his colleagues might suggest that in politics, the success of ideas depends a great deal on contingency and factors beyond human control, and that complex doctrines such as the balance of powers and bicameralism are unlikely to prevail over simple ideas and principles of the sort that appeal to human passions.[177] Yet, the monarchiens' ideas won praise from some of the most important interpreters of the French Revolution, even if their accounts of the monarchiens' agenda were mixed. That was the tone taken by their one-time close associate, Mallet du Pan, who praised the moderation of the monarchiens in forming a necessary middling party between Jacobins, pure royalists, and les constitutionnels. The monarchiens, he argued, remained true to the wishes of the nation in 1789 by defending liberty, constitutional monarchy, and the balance of powers and opposing unlimited power and anarchy. The "middle" that the monarchiens' sought was, in Mallet du Pan's view, the reasonable position from which the revolution should never have strayed. At the same time, there was something tragic about the monarchiens' moderation insofar as it condemned them to being "an intermediary sect rather than an active party exercising significant influence on the affairs of the kingdom."[178]

In her *Considérations sur les principaux événements de la Révolution française*, Mme de Staël referred to Malouet, Lally-Tollendal, and Mounier as "the most conscientious men in the assembly" who courageously tried to establish a wise, free, and durable constitution in France. She praised Lally-Tollendal's "impressive" eloquence, Mounier's theoretical insight ("a political writer of the greatest judgment"), and Malouet's political realism ("a practical man of first-rate energy").[179] In the unfinished volume 2 of his *L'Ancien Régime et la Révolution*, Tocqueville also commented on the monarchiens' agenda, having carefully read and annotated Mounier's works. He applauded Mounier's political moderation, pointing to the continuity between his ideas and the principles undergirding the liberal Charter of 1814. What Mounier wanted as the final government of France was "very close to what was established in 1814 and continued from 1830 to 1848."[180] At the same time, Tocqueville was intrigued by the coexistence of "revolutionary passions and ideas" along with moderate sentiments and opinions in the works of Mounier, who allegedly believed that the new Constituent Assembly ought to have unlimited power to change everything.[181] Ultimately, Tocqueville argued, the moderation of the monarchiens was marred by their overly optimistic assessment of the chances for reforming the constitution of France, and they were tragically led to espouse contradictory ideas and causes that went far beyond their initial goals.[182] What Mounier and his colleagues wanted to make happen (such as introducing bicameralism and royal veto) was in tension with some of the very things they desired to destroy, such as hereditary privileges.

Tocqueville's assessment of Mounier was not entirely accurate. In particular, he was wrong to claim that Mounier and the monarchiens did not believe that there existed a past with its own unwritten norms, habits, and customs, which one should seek to alter only cautiously. Contrary to what Tocqueville argued, the monarchiens did not want a single assembly and realized that change must come gradually, with no abrupt break between the past and present.[183] This is precisely what Lord Acton emphasized in his lectures on the French Revolution, in which he put the monarchiens in the camp of moderate liberals and defenders of constitutional liberty in France. The words of praise he lavished upon them are in stark contrast with the critical views of Burke and the more reserved opinion of Tocqueville. For Acton, "Mounier, with some of his friends, deserves to be remembered among the men, not so common as they say, who loved liberty sincerely."[184] Acton praised Malouet's policy of moderation and described him as "a man of practical insight and experience . . . a man of great good sense, as free from ancient prejudice as from modern theory, [who] never lost sight of the public interest in favour of a class."[185] Acton reserved even higher praise for Mounier, "one of the deepest minds of that day, and the most popular of the deputies," who believed that "principles are not subject to the law of change."[186] Mounier, Acton claimed, belonged to a superior and rare class of statesmen whose bold form of moderation enabled them to defend revolutionary doctrines in a "conservative" temper. Unfortunately, the success of Mounier's plan depended on a real conciliation that other deputies were unwilling to endorse in the summer of 1789.

At the same time, Acton remarked, Mounier's austere and rigid character sometimes went against his natural propensity to moderation. The English historian was equally surprised by his attitude toward Montesquieu. Although Mounier desired to adopt the English model—which meant representation of property, an upper house founded upon merit and not descent, and a royal veto and the right of dissolution of the elected chamber—and endorsed the division of powers without isolating them, he considered Montesquieu to be "radically illiberal."[187] This was all the more surprising since, at the core of the monarchiens' political project, lay the concept of a balance of powers with a distinctive Montesquieuan ring. The idea that power must be moderated through various constitutional means was shared by Montesquieu and the monarchiens, in spite of their disagreement on the role of the nobility as an intermediary body in a limited monarchy. The monarchiens followed a coherent constitutionalist agenda and regarded the constitution as a means of regulating and moderating the national will rather than an instrument for accomplishing the popular will. While Mounier was critical toward the *parlements* as intermediary bodies and viewed with skepticism Montesquieu's praise of the nobles as indispensable to the survival of liberty in a tempered monarchy, he never went as far as Sieyès and Rabaut Saint-Étienne in their critique of intermediary powers. In *Essai sur les privilèges* (1789), Sieyès affirmed that all intermediary bodies that are formed in society on bases other than equality and individual will cannot serve as a proper link between the government and the people. Such bodies, he warned, are nothing other than "a pernicious excrescence" that becomes an additional burden upon the community, for it has no connection whatsoever to the preservation of political liberty.[188]

These accounts of the monarchiens prompt us to revisit the limits of moderation in revolutionary times. Although the agenda pursued by Mounier and his colleagues addressed the long-term interests of the country, it failed to gain the confidence of their fellow citizens. The monarchiens were forced to quit the battleground early on, after being defeated by their more radical opponents. In this respect, they shared the fate of other moderates who were accused of giving the people "a poisonous bread," in the famous words of Barnave.[189] The tragic destiny of all moderates in the Constituent Assembly became evident as early as July 31, 1789, when Adrien Duquesnoy noted in his journal: "Wise and moderate people are beginning to lose courage; they are being carried away by the stream; passionate individuals are rising every day, the most violent language, the most extreme expressions, and the most extreme parties are applauded and celebrated; people speak indifferently about spilled blood, executions, punishments, etc., and when the words generosity, humanity, kindness are pronounced, either they do not listen or these words are pure makeshift."[190]

These challenges notwithstanding, the monarchiens pursued their middling project with firmness, convinced that "there is no other means of salvation for a country in turmoil than moderation in the middle of all extremist parties."[191] And yet, by acting as moderates, they never managed to become the masters of the political game that was being played in Paris.[192] Of all the revolutionary parties of 1789, the monarchiens were the first to take the stage and the first to exit the scene. By the end of October, their political fate was sealed, although some of them (Malouet for one) continued to be active in the *Club des Impartiaux*. The monarchiens shared the fate of moderates who came to be branded either as shrewd politicians unfaithful to the true interests of the French nation, or as secret agents of the Court. Aristocrats refused to endorse the monarchiens' reformist plans for constitutional monarchy, while members of the popular party viewed them as indecisive and weak, and hence incapable of leading in times of crisis.[193] Even those who should have been their close allies, like Necker, who also defended a strong executive power, were not entirely convinced by their ideas.[194] The monarchiens failed to persuade the assembly not to endorse a radical conception of the constitution as a document to be created anew by an act of the sovereign national will. The absolute veto supported by Mounier, Clermont-Tonnerre, and Lally-Tollendal was rejected in favor of a suspensive veto. The monarchiens' plan for creating constitutional monarchy in France, moreover, could not close the gap between constitutionalism and the unlimited sovereignty of the nation. The ideas of Mounier's greatest rival, Sieyès, fared only slightly better, but his unrelenting critique of the royal veto (both absolute and suspensive) contributed a great deal to the defeat of Mounier and the other monarchiens.

Since the monarchiens' early defeat was an omen of darker times to come, it is tempting to ask if France might have avoided the tragic Terror of 1793 had the ideas of Mounier and his colleagues carried the day early on. It is perhaps possible to argue that, after all, it was not the monarchiens who espoused unrealistic plans, but their opponents on both the left and the right, who refused to address the real long-term interests and needs of the French nation, and defended anachronistic agendas.[195] The monarchiens' political project resembled the one that triumphed in 1814 and was consolidated during the July Monarchy. Unfortunately, in 1789, France was not prepared for the constitutional monarchy that would later give the country thirty years of relative peace and prosperity—the obvious shortcomings of the reign of Louis-Philippe notwithstanding. Yet, one can only be impressed by the firmness with which the monarchiens defended their ideas under the relentless crossfire of the extremes. Some of their critics even accused them of doctrinal rigidity and inflexibility, while others condemned them for having abandoned their liberal views, after being co-opted by Napoleon to serve in the administration of the First Empire. Does the historical record support this view?

Again, Mounier's example is revealing. Nominated in 1805 to the *Conseil d'État*, his principles did not change after the revolution, and especially not after the events of the 18th Brumaire. In a reported conversation with the emperor, Mounier insisted that his principles remained thoroughly liberal. To Napoleon's remark that he continued to be "the man of 1789," Mounier responded: "Undoubtedly, Your Majesty. Times change, but principles do not."[196] He remained faithful to the principles outlined in the summer of

1789: "I am the enemy of authority only when it seeks to oppress the people; I loathe the abuses of power and the tyranny or the license of the multitude as much as the arbitrary power of a single individual. I have attempted to express my love of justice and moderation; I have professed my profound attachment to monarchy. I have never separated the freedom of the people from the legitimate power of the monarch."[197] Denounced by some as a zealous innovator, by others as traitor to the people, detested simultaneously by the aristocratic and democratic parties, Mounier consciously placed himself in the middle, where he could best defend his political principles, confident that truth always lies between the extremes. Much the same can be said of Malouet, who also championed a politics of compromise and believed that the only means to salvation in times of crisis was moderation.[198] In the letter he sent to his electors on May 13, 1790, Malouet expressed his belief that moderation was essential in revolutionary times, and endorsed a reformist approach open to conciliation and compromise, based on self-restraint and opposed to perfectionism.[199]

Nonetheless, in spite of the soundness of the monarchiens' political vision advocating a compromise between tradition and innovation, between the sovereignty of the nation and royal power, there was also something unsettling and tragic about the way in which they defended key principles such as bicameralism and the absolute royal veto. According to one of his commentators, Mounier's political doctrine was too rigid and, hence, unable to adjust to shifting circumstances.[200] Sometimes their timing was poor. The monarchiens' endorsement of a two-chamber legislature as a means of securing political liberty came only a couple of months after heated debates on the vote by head and the composition of the Third Estate, debates that revealed a growing hostility toward the two privileged orders. One of monarchiens' contemporaries, Périsse de Luc, remarked that such a proposal was both necessary (for creating a sound balance of forces) and utopian (in light of the prevailing aversion to aristocracy).[201] At a moment when the deputies and public opinion preferred a *régime d'assemblée* that recognized virtually no limits to their authority, the monarchiens defended a strong royal power. They wanted to give a role to the nobles in the government of the country when the popular cry was for "careers open to talents, not birth." They invoked the force and authority of the rule of law when the power of words and the will of the multitude rather than reason and dispassionate argument were carrying the day. Had Mounier and his colleagues been more flexible, willing to compromise on controversial issues such as the royal veto and bicameralism, they might have been able to pursue other principles of their political agenda. Instead they occupied an awkward middle that opposed both those who sought the regeneration of France through the absolute destruction of its old regime, and the émigrés who lacked a coherent plan for reforming the country.[202]

Finally, it remains an open question whether the monarchiens fully understood the rules of the parliamentary game that they wanted to introduce in France. Little in their writings shows a clear appreciation for opposition and alternance in power; but again, they were not unique in this respect, at least in France.[203] Furthermore, as Roberto Moro argued, if Mounier's doctrine of representation outlined in *Nouvelles observations* was designed to suit the political milieu prior to the convocation of the Estates-General, his vision of representation quickly became outdated within a few months, out of sync with what the other influential members of the Constituent Assembly desired for France after July 14.[204] Mounier and his friends, Barnave claimed, failed to realize the extent to which their original ideas had triggered a genuine revolution, and they wanted to reform the structure of the Old Regime by using materials that had already become obsolete by the time they sat down to write a new constitution for the country. The monarchiens' agenda was thus an ill-timed attempt at mediation between a power (the nation) that was now everything and a power that had become almost null (the monarch).[205]

Through the monarchiens' political odyssey we can follow the transformation of moderation from a theoretical weapon against absolute power into a contested political tool in the service of constitutionalism. This evolution was not only a consequence of the internal logic of the agenda of these revolutionary moderates who failed to realize their political dreams, but also a response to some of the tensions and contradictions inherent in the very concept of political moderation. The question remains: were the monarchiens ultimately defeated because they failed to foresee the magnitude of the changes they were instrumental in bringing about, or because they adopted several untimely and excessively legalistic strategies? Were their ideas bound to fail because they misread the political situation in the summer of 1789 and resorted to moderation when they should have been more radical? Might it be the case that the revolution, once started, was simply unstoppable with the instruments of moderation? And finally, what if the monarchiens were not moderate enough?

The latter hypothesis was put forward by Boissy d'Anglas, a liberal-minded thinker who affirmed that an "inflexible constancy" in the middle of revolution could in fact be a serious political liability rather than a moral virtue.[206] Was Boissy d'Anglas right in suggesting that such a rigid attitude condemned the monarchiens to failure? Malouet, for one, disagreed with this view and believed that it was above all the combination of interests and passions dominating the political scene in the summer of 1789 that contributed to discrediting moderation, which he equated with "sound reason."[207] If Malouet was right, then the political defeat of the monarchiens was the inevitable outcome of the highly unstable political and social situation in which they lived and acted, polarized contexts being favorable to the appearance of various forms of radicalism and extremism. In such an environment, no moderate voice could have triumphed in the long-run. At the same time, one might argue that many of the monarchiens' ideas ultimately prevailed in the works and initiatives of like-minded liberals such as Boissy d'Anglas, whose liberalism, while socially and economically conservative, stood for a strong but limited state.[208]

In *Considérations sur les gouvernements*, Mounier explained why those who prefer simple ideas and principles and overlook the lessons of experience and human nature are always more likely to seduce the masses than moderates who ground their theories on experience and prudence.[209] He equated moderation with equanimity, *sang-froid*, discernment, and realism, and drew a corresponding parallel between radicalism, imprudence, rashness, and lack of realism. Moderation, he concluded, is a difficult virtue that should not be equated with indecision or weakness. In reality, only weak minds tend to extremes. Strong characters gravitate toward moderation.

And indeed, for all its eclecticism, the political philosophy of the monarchiens and their tragic destiny do not prove so much the weakness of the idea of political moderation as, paradoxically, its enduring strength and appeal even in dark times. Few other political thinkers who proclaimed their commitment to moderation ever found themselves in a more challenging situation than the monarchiens in 1789. By using a Montesquieuan vocabulary with a Rousseau-esque touch, Mounier and his colleagues tried to break free of the grip of absolutism and carve out a middle ground between revolution and reaction. In so doing, they paved the way for those who, a few years later, would try to "end" the revolution by building representative institutions on the ruins of the Terror. The next three chapters will focus on their equally heroic saga, as illustrated by the political writings of three leading members of the Coppet group.

PART II
MODERATION AND THE LEGACY OF THE REVOLUTION

FOUR
Moderation and the "Intertwining of Powers"
Jacques Necker's Constitutionalism

Il n'est point de liberté réelle . . . s'il existe au milieu de l'état une
autorité sans balance.
　—Necker

A Modern Cato?

Looking back at his distinguished political career, Joseph Necker, the former minister of Louis XVI, described himself as a pragmatic moderate who
had managed to preserve his independence, realism, and integrity in dark
times. Referring to his "attachment to wise and moderate principles,"
Necker claimed:

> I have never run after systematic novelties. I have been partial only
> to approved maxims; though even these I have not constantly de-
> fended, like a servile enthusiast; for, from time to time, I think I
> have shown the power of seizing ideas at their first origin. The only
> difference is that, in raising myself to this level, I have not remained
> suspended in the clouds as some of the metaphysical politicians of
> our time.[1]

For all his commitment to moderation, morality, and reason, this honorable politician suffered from what one of his commentators called "the fatal
handicap of moderation."[2] His writings have constantly been neglected in
both his native France and abroad, and his image has been that of a failed
or second-rate thinker and politician who is not worth studying. In 1821,
deploring Necker's unfair proscription, Boissy d'Anglas wrote the following
note: "Of all statesmen, Necker has been treated with the greatest injustice.
Many have spoken about him; few have known him, and even fewer have
wanted to know him."[3] Boissy d'Anglas' words remain as valid today as
they were two centuries ago. One of the most respected ministers under the
Old Regime, Necker never received from historians the consideration he
deserved, most especially for his seminal contribution to the development of
constitutionalism in France and for his reflections on the role of the executive power in modern society.[4] As Necker himself acknowledged in 1791, he
was the unfortunate victim of a series of injustices the likes of which are
rare in the annals of history.[5] When not neglected, Necker has been portrayed either as a petty bourgeois and ambitious banker excessively obsessed with his reputation and personal fortune, or as a hesitant and inefficient politician. Why has posterity been so unfair toward someone whose

political choices proved in hindsight so effortlessly sensible and reasonable? And why did Necker, who was by nature a moderate, elicit virulent attacks from so many quarters?

In answering these questions, we should not forget that Necker was also hailed by others as the only technocrat whose expertise and moral integrity might have saved France from ruin in late 1780s. He was arguably "the most important name in French history from 1776 to 1789,"[6] and some of his contemporaries, Rivarol for one, considered him the true "father" of the French Revolution.[7] Others, however, remained unconvinced of Necker's political skills. Among them was Thomas Jefferson, who in a letter to the U.S. Secretary of State written on June 17, 1789, referred to Necker in unflattering terms: "It is a tremendous cloud which hovers over this nation, and he at the helm has neither the courage nor the skill necessary to weather it. . . . His judgment is not of the first order, scarcely even of the second, his resolution frail, and upon the whole it is rare to meet an instance of a person so much below the reputation he has obtained."[8] Condorcet mockingly referred to Necker as "*l'homme aux envelopes*," while Mirabeau described him as an individual devoid of talent.[9] Prominent historians of the French Revolution like Tocqueville and Michelet were not attracted to Necker's ideas either.[10]

Biographical reasons may have played a significant role in Necker's *oublieuse proscription*. Born a citizen of the Republic of Geneva, he was a devout Protestant who lived in a predominantly Catholic country (France). He was also a very rich man, having been a successful banker (in Geneva and Paris) for almost twenty years prior to his appointment as director of the Royal Treasury in October 1776 and, later, as director general of finances of the kingdom of France in June 1777. The physiocrats, Turgot, Condorcet, and Mirabeau, shared a common dislike for their rival whom they dismissed as a *parvenu*. Another explanation for the hostility toward Necker can be found in the libels against him written by those who felt threatened by his administrative and economic reforms.

If Necker is remembered at all today, he is recognized mostly as a skilled banker and economist rather than an original political thinker. While in charge of the finances of the country, his most famous decision in February 1781 was to make public for the first time the budget of the kingdom of France, a novelty in an absolute monarchy where the practice had always been to make a mystery of the state of its finances.[11] The publication of Necker's *Compte rendu* brought him instant fame. Over three thousand copies were sold the very first day. But at the same time, Necker was accused of trying to subvert the foundations of the kingdom by revealing state secrets, and three months later he was forced to submit his resignation.[12] Seven years later, he regained his position. Necker advocated a broad program of administrative, political, and economic reforms aiming at modernizing the Old Regime and calling for the meeting of the Estates-General. Most of his proposals were, however, disregarded by the king, who also rejected the legitimate demands of the Third Estate for a fair representation in the new assembly. Such was Necker's reputation that, when Louis XVI dismissed him on July 11, public dismay over the king's decision was truly stupendous in the French capital. A contemporary of Necker recalled, "One would have thought there was a public calamity . . . people looked at each other in silent dismay and sadly pressed each other's hand as they passed."[13] Foreign powers also regarded with concern the dismissal of Necker who represented a guarantee of the trustworthiness of France and its fiscal solvency. The Emperor of Austria immediately inquired if he was available to take a position in Vienna.

Recalled again a week later by Louis XVI, Necker returned to a capital that had been completely transformed by the events of July 14, 1789. Subsequent developments only confirmed the reasonableness of Necker's trimming agenda, which aimed at keeping the ship of the state on an even keel. As the new legislative body became all-powerful in the aftermath of the fall of the Bastille, Necker made it his mission to defend the executive power and authority of the monarch against the radical proposals of the nation's representatives. In the end, his moderate agenda proved a losing card. Necker's withdrawal from public affairs was regarded by some as a tacit acknowledgment of his political defeat at the hands of the more radical members of the Assembly. During the last fourteen years of his life, from the fall of 1790 until April 1804, Necker lived in retirement at Coppet, in Switzerland. Unlike his daughter who thrived in—and longed for—the vibrant atmosphere of the capital, Necker never returned to Paris, though he had lent the Royal Treasury two million livres, a huge "stimulus package" *avant la lettre*, which he never managed to recover during his lifetime.[14] The glamorous life of Parisian salons did not suit his austere nature, and he felt comfortably at home in the sober and solitary atmosphere of Coppet.[15]

Nonetheless, Necker did not cease to follow events in France, devoting a lot of time to writing and reflecting on political matters. He outlined his political philosophy in three important books reflecting his commitment to moderation, freedom, limited power, and representative government: *Du pouvoir exécutif dans les grands états* (1792), *De la Révolution française* (1796), and *Dernières vues de politique et de finance* (1802). In the first book, which consolidated his reputation as a major theorist of executive power, Necker endorsed a tempered monarchy similar to the one existing in England.[16] In his reflections on the French Revolution, an unduly ignored masterpiece that has been out of print for more than two centuries, Necker gave a detailed account of his conduct during the turbulent events of 1788 and 1789.[17] He consciously placed himself at the distance of posterity by writing from the perspective of a later century in order to judge the ideas and actions of those who took part in the revolution. The publication of Necker's last book in 1802 was a courageous and bold statement of independence made by a man who had always pursued his goals with prudence and moderation. Although he called Napoleon a "necessary man"[18] who had been successful in preventing the return of anarchy in France, Necker went on to criticize the First Consul's ambition to establish a new form of monarchy with a fake nobility of his own creation. After having defended in his previous books the cause of constitutional monarchy, Necker examined what kind of republican regime might be possible in post-revolutionary France, reiterating that the dignity of republican institutions stems mainly from—and reposes upon—the consent of the nation. Necker's book was virulently attacked in the official press, and Napoleon was particularly vexed by Necker's courage in drawing attention to his secret ambitions and plans for becoming the absolute ruler of France. The First Consul subsequently forced Necker's daughter into exile and refused to consider any requests for the return of his loan to the Treasury.

Necker's admirers applauded his steadiness in defending freedom and moderation, along with his unflinching commitment to morality and religion. "He was the only individual," Mme de Staël wrote, "who had shown himself profoundly skilled in the art of governing a great country without ever deviating from the most scrupulous morality. . . . Eloquence had not hurried him away beyond the limits of reason, nor had reason ever deprived him of a single emotion of true eloquence."[19] Necker defended the principles of constitutional (limited) monarchy successively against the king, the nobility, and the representatives of the people. As a "trimmer" politician, he lent his support at every juncture to the authority that was the weakest, and as a writer he held to the same course, exposing in turn the errors of the Constituent Assembly, the Convention, the Directory, and Bonaparte, each when they were at the height of their power and influence. For all of these reasons, he occupies a special place in the history of political moderation.

The Impossible Reform of the Old Regime

Although Necker commented on reforming the Old Regime in several of his works, his most important theoretical statements on this issue can be found in *De la Révolution française* (1796). In his view, *l'ancien régime* was the opposite of moderate government because it lacked effective barriers against despotism.[20] France, Necker argued, did not have a regular constitution, and its tax system was unjust and obsolete, placing undue burdens on the Third Estate which did not enjoy proper political representation. The whole regime resembled "a changeable assemblage of customs and exceptions, whose demarcation had never been traced by any agreement or any charter."[21] Legislative power was vested and exercised in an uncertain manner and changed according to times and circumstances. Both the legislative and the executive power belonged to the monarch, and no other magistrate or political body, including the *parlements*, was effective in limiting the king's prerogatives. The interests of the French nation were not properly represented, nor were its rights duly protected, as long as their sanction depended solely on the will of the monarch. That is why the status of the Estates-General was uncertain and demanded urgent reform. Because they had not met since 1614, they could not serve as a reliable guarantee of the liberties and rights of the nation, and were not to be considered an integral part of the French constitution.

Necker's skepticism toward the *parlements*' ability to serve as effective checks on royal power deserves further comment. In his view, they were neither genuine representatives of the nation nor reliable defenders of civil liberties and the rule of law. In particular, Necker refused to admit that the right to exercise the most august of all prerogatives under the Old Regime—the exercise of legislative power—should have been placed in the hands of magistrates who could buy their office with money. Moreover, the narrow legal training of the members of *parlements*, focusing on civil or criminal jurisprudence, rendered many of them unprepared to properly deal with public affairs. Necker added that the *parlements* often acted upon narrow and selfish interests, thus making possible the maintenance of obsolete and costly privileges. They were sometimes indifferent to the arbitrary acts of the government and never took into their hands the cause of private individuals in order to defend them against oppression.[22]

Necker had initially pinned his hopes of reforming the Old Regime on provincial assemblies and their administration. He proceeded cautiously by setting up two such assemblies in the provinces of Berry and Haute-Guyenne.[23] He conceived of these provincial assemblies as genuine deliberative bodies (consisting of landed proprietors) whose task it would be to enlighten the will of the king. They would not be passive instruments of the centralized administration in Paris. Deliberation within the assemblies was to be conducted in common, and the Third Estate was to have as many members as the other two orders combined. Thus configured, Necker hoped that the provincial assemblies could serve as effective means of reforming *l'ancien régime* by introducing significant changes at the local level of administration, in the areas of finances, the tax system, economic growth, and public works. Reform of the tax system was arguably the most urgent task, as the preamble of the decree announcing the creation of the provincial assembly of Berry shows. It promised to bring to an end "arbitrary assessment and to assure justice in the partition of the tax burden."[24] Provincial assemblies were also expected to wrest some power from the hands of the *intendants*, who were not supposed to take part in the regular deliberations (although they could request to be present) and were to have some of their attributions curtailed or even eliminated.

Necker's hopes were dashed after he was forced to resign in May 1781, three months after the publication of his famous *Compte rendu* that made public for the first time the finances of the kingdom of France. The significance of his initial proposals for administrative reform lies precisely in the fact that the creation of provincial assemblies was to be the beginning of a liberal reform plan in stark contrast to other plans for reform that bore the imprint of enlightened despotism. Six years later, Necker welcomed the meeting of the Assembly of the Notables in 1787,[25] composed of princes of blood, clergy, former ministers and counselors of state, deputies of *pays d'états*,[26] and municipal heads of cities, many of them ennobled. Yet, he was aware that the opinion of the notables was far from impartial and could not compete with—or obstruct—public opinion. Eventually Necker came to believe that the only effective countervailing force was public opinion, which had slowly acquired the status of a universal tribunal before which all citizens, magistrates, and governments were called to appear and be held politically accountable.[27] Public opinion, depicted in the epoch as a judge sitting on a throne in a court of last resort, was supposed to redress offenses and offer comfort to the injured, but the term *opinion publique* remained a fluid concept, being sometimes used indistinguishably from related concepts such as *esprit public* or *voix publique*. The rise of public opinion reflected, however, the steady progress of knowledge and information. Necker grasped this point and insisted upon the link between public opinion and reason. "A new power, public opinion, had mingled with all others, and had surpassed them all,"[28] he claimed, and went on to describe it as "an invisible power, which, without any treasury, guards, or army, rules over the city, the court, and even within the palace of kings."[29]

The rise of public opinion had important consequences for the exercise of power and institutional design. In an important speech delivered in May 1789, Necker described it as "large in its views and thoughtful in its advance; it refines our personal opinions and interests by placing them at a certain distance from us, in order to better assemble them later and combine them with the common good."[30] The authority of public opinion was called to mediate between the other powers in the state in order to create a proper balance between them. In Necker's view, the real balance of power in France did not exist in the organization of the government but lay entirely in the authority of public opinion, "an authority whose force increased with the progress of information and the spirit of sociability."[31] The importance of public opinion, Necker argued, derived from the fact that, without relying upon any written laws, it served in reality as a "moderator of every kind of excess."[32]

Nonetheless, Necker's argument should not be construed as an implicit endorsement of a politics of open and unregulated contestation, with public opinion hovering impartially above the contending parties. He distinguished between "real" public opinion and the fluctuating whims of the people, and used the term "public" to mean not the people at large, but only the enlightened and educated strata of society that, in his view, were alone capable of properly judging the interests of society. Furthermore, while Necker emphasized the role of *publicité* (publicity) as an instrument of reform, he did not view it as a substitute for royal power and representative institutions. While publicity was supposed to play a more prominent political role in reforming the institutions of the Old Regime, it was expected to serve only as a complement to royal power and existing representative institutions rather than as a substitute for them.

Necker's Trimming Agenda

The two months separating the first meeting of the Estates-General at Versailles from the fall of the Bastille represented a crucial episode in Necker's political life. It was on the occasion of the opening session on May 5, 1789 that Necker reaffirmed his political moderation in front of the three orders brought together for the first time since 1614. The location, la Salle des Menus Plaisirs, an older store which had previously hosted the Assembly of Notables in 1787, was redesigned to accommodate the representatives of the three orders. For Necker, the meeting represented the endpoint of a long process that was supposed to give legal sanction to the participation of the Third Estate in the most important deliberations in the state. Few realized at the time the far-reaching consequences of bringing the three orders together in order to deliberate on the common affairs of the country after such a long hiatus.

On that solemn occasion, Necker gave a three-hour speech that elicited a wide range of reactions from the audience. Suffering from a cold, he began reading the text, but after fifteen minutes asked a clerk to read the remainder (he managed, however, to regain energy and delivered himself the final part). The sheer length of the discourse—one hundred dense pages—seemed excessive, especially to those who found it difficult to follow Necker's obscure financial technicalities and who may had been put off as well by his austere presence and solemn tone. Even his daughter expressed reservations about the speech, which, she argued, excelled at offering technical recommendations for improving taxation and the management of public debt but "hardly touched on constitutional matters."[33] Some members of the Third Estate complained that Necker had treated them as mere provincial administrators rather than political representatives of the majority of the nation. Others, however, appreciated the professional tenor of Necker's speech, the honesty, and the accuracy with which he addressed the fundamental problems of the kingdom.

The claim that Necker's discourse did not touch on constitutional matters must be taken with a grain of salt. In fact, his speech offered an in-depth diagnosis of the financial health of the country and proposed concrete measures for reforming its institutional and political framework. The last thirty pages outlined a clear agenda for creating a true constitutional monarchy in France and securing cooperation between the three orders and the king. Central to Necker's moderate agenda as outlined in the speech was a modern theory of representative government, based on the division of the legislative power into two chambers, the sharing of sovereignty between the king and the nation, regular elections, fiscal equality, and administrative decentralization.

By examining Necker's discourse we can better grasp and appreciate how a moderate thinker and politician navigated between the Scylla of revolution and the Charybdis of reaction in addressing three urgent and contested topics: the constitution of France; the issue of constituent power; and the reform of voting procedures. On all of these controversial topics, Necker sought a middle ground and proposed sensible compromises.[34] He began by inviting the deputies to exercise wisdom and prudence in their deliberations and decisions and ended his discourse by laying out specific steps for reforming the political system. Necker had long believed that the meeting of the Estates-General was rendered necessary and urgent by the country's deep financial crisis; now he insisted that it was also demanded by public opinion, which considered the preservation of vast fiscal inequalities as inefficient and unjustified. The Third Estate was already contributing significantly to the growth of the national wealth and had been admitted into provincial assemblies, while the two privileged orders were beginning to see their authority decline. The decay of the nobility, illustrated by the fact that, on the eve of the revolution nearly half of the aristocracy came from families ennobled within the previous two centuries, was a particular threat to both the monarch and the country.[35] At the same time, Necker was concerned about the impatience with which the planned meeting of the Estates General was being hurried on. The deputies of the nation, Necker remarked, assembled before many of them had had the opportunity to reflect on the significance of this major event and prepare themselves for the political role they were now called to play. Some had not had time to rethink and discard their old prejudices, while others were full of confidence in "those light wings with which they thought they could rise into air, and soar at pleasure above all political activities."[36]

As we have already seen, one such controversial issue was whether or not France had a constitution in the proper sense of the word. If the question was answered in the negative, the revolution might have been justified as a way of replacing the unjust institutional and legal framework of *l'ancien régime* with a new and fair one. If answered in the affirmative, the logical inference was that the Old Regime might be reformed by peaceful and gradual means. Was there a third option that could reconcile these two apparently incompatible positions?

Necker was aware that the proliferation of historical views on this thorny issue threatened to undermine the authority of the past, deepening the distrust between the three orders and making their cooperation extremely difficult. He chose a middle ground that combined respect for the independence of the assembly with a firm call to moderation and self-restraint. Starting from the assumption that the preservation of a strict separation of orders enjoying particular privileges was untenable,[37] Necker pointed to the significant changes that had taken place in social mores and public opinion. He argued that a legislative assembly divided into three political orders, poorly linked to each other, could not properly address the real problems and needs of the country. Moreover, he remarked that, before any talk of reform could become meaningful, the deputies would need to study the organization of the previous assemblies of the three orders in order to propose new and fair voting procedures and rules.

At the same time, Necker referred to "the remnants of the old and respected Constitution," an adroit rhetorical stance meant to conjure up the danger of reckless innovation ever present when men thought themselves invested with unlimited constituent power. Reforming political institutions, he claimed, was a difficult and complex task requiring not only caution and moderation, but also a bold vision for the future that should take into account both the demands of justice and stability. In order for a constitution to be effective, he continued, it ought to be in harmony with the manners, opinions, customs, and habits of a nation and must be transmitted, "from age to age, not by scattered traces consecrated in its archives, but by a continuity of existence."[38] Necker warned that it was not possible to resume "a constitution incessantly interrupted, and even completely forgotten, during two centuries," and added that "it was a failure of respect for antiquity to reject every kind of modification of the three orders deliberating and voting separately, when not one of them was what it had been."[39] He reminded those who invoked the existence of an ancient constitution in order to justify their opposition to any political change that the object of their dogmatic respect was an "imagined" constitution, "effaced from all memory [and] dragged suddenly from the bottom of obscure archives, where it had so long remained unknown."[40] Therefore, it was not possible to view it as a real constitution, one that had been respected and followed without interruption or alteration.

With regard to the claim that the assembly possessed constituent power, Necker also sought a middle way. At the beginning of his speech, he insisted that the new affairs of the nation could be properly addressed only by a government cooperating with the nation's representatives. He went on to invite the representatives of the three orders to leave aside for a moment their factional interests and take into consideration the general, long-term interests of the nation. Necker admitted that the assembly's role should not be a passive one and insisted that its members were free to choose their own agenda and rules of procedure for the meeting of the Estates-General. If he refrained from referring to the "constituent power" of the assembly, he did not deny it explicitly.[41] Instead he called upon the deputies to show proper respect toward the authority of the monarch and exercise their new power with a heightened sense of responsibility so as to form "a great alliance" and "union" with the throne. To this effect, he argued, personal rivalries and radical claims had to give way to a pragmatic spirit of moderation and conciliation.[42]

Necker's call to deputies to form a better union for the sake of reforming the country's institutions and constitution was built around the idea of moderation and had a clear Burkean tone. He appealed to modesty, self-restraint, and caution and warned the assembly not only against rejecting plans for reform due to "imaginary evils," but also against entertaining excessively bold ideas that called for a complete break with the past in the name of an ideal world disconnected from reality:

> In order to succeed you will avoid exaggerations; you will not entertain imaginary evils and will be suspicious of opinions which are too innovative. You will not think that the future has no connection with the past, you will not listen to speeches or endorse projects that transport you into an ideal world; you will rather choose those thoughts and counsels which, less spectacular but more practical, give rise to fewer controversies and bring greater stability and permanence. Finally, gentlemen, you will not be envious of what only time can achieve, and you will leave something for it to do. For if you attempt to reform everything that seems imperfect, your work will lead to poor results.[43]

Necker was aware that the three orders contained within their ranks moderates who were ready to make concessions, but whose position was unstable and fragile. He realized that the success of political reform depended on the creation of a sound balance between the Third Estate, the privileged orders, and the throne, without allowing any one of them to gain superiority over the others. This, Necker admitted, would be possible only if all orders displayed moderation and self-restraint: "For obtaining so perfect a concert among political antagonists, it is necessary, either that foresight should aid the weakest, or moderation check the strongest; otherwise the parties will resemble plenipotentiaries negotiating peace in the midst of battles, and raising or lowering their demands, according to successes or defeats."[44]

Necker's call for moderation and concessions addressed to all the members of the assembly gained him the reputation of a trimmer who believed that the greatest skill of statesmen consists in the art of knowing when to follow public opinion and when to guide it tactfully, and in the ability to distinguish between what is ideal and what is practicable in any given context. Necker compared himself to Michel de l'Hôpital who, as chancellor of France at the outset of the wars of religion in the sixteenth century, had attempted to mediate between contending Catholics and Protestants.[45] That Necker in fact considered himself a trimmer is further illustrated by the following passage, an important account of his political role in the summer of 1789:

> It was therefore proper to speak to some of the sacrifices that circumstances advised, and to others of the moderation that belonged

to every season. It was also proper continually to represent the importance of public order to those who beheld every thing in liberty, and the importance of executive power to those who beheld every thing in law. It was proper also, in these times of system, to defend with confidence the present against the future, the certain against the possible, and all real ideas against the daily invasions of the metaphysical spirit. In fine, it was especially a rigorous duty on a public man to show himself constantly the respectful friend of justice and good faith, and to remain invariably faithful to the protecting principles of society; to those eternal principles, consecrated among all nations by the laws of morality, and the precepts of religion.[46]

This passage deserves close attention. Let us consider a few concrete examples of Necker's trimming agenda, beginning with the compromise he proposed on the issue of voting procedures in the new assembly. The Royal Session of December 27, 1788 had failed to give a clear answer to the question of whether the voting should be by head or order, leaving open the issue of how the three orders should deliberate (in common or in separate assemblies).[47] Aware of the deficit of trust among the orders, Necker proposed the following compromise. He advised the nobles and the clergy to voluntarily renounce their tax privileges in the hope that this generous sacrifice would encourage the members of the Third Estate to display greater openness toward the deputies of the first two orders. At the same time, he asked the deputies of the Third Estate to give to the representatives of the nobles and the clergy "the entire honor of such a noble sacrifice,"[48] and he warned them against the nefarious consequences that would likely follow on their unwillingness to compromise. Necker called upon the three orders to designate representatives to discuss in common, in a calm atmosphere of mutual confidence, which issues ought to be submitted to common deliberation and which reserved to separate assemblies. The three orders, he recommended, should vote by head on national common affairs and then proceed to discuss matters pertaining to each order's affairs in separate assemblies. Necker did not believe that the government was entitled to specify what constituted "national" matters apart from voting procedures, which explains why he wanted to leave it to each order to decide which issues needed to be discussed in common and which separately. In his opinion, this dual system of deliberation enjoyed the advantage of combining innovation with due respect for tradition and was unlikely to trigger revolutionary turmoil.

Two weeks after the opening of the Estates-General, Necker met with the king and submitted a new declaration to his consideration. The text has not been preserved—oddly enough, Necker himself did not mention it in *De la Révolution française*—and all the information we have about it comes from his daughter.[49] Necker, she claimed, sought to persuade the king to adopt a constitution similar to that of England and advised him in the strongest possible terms to make the necessary concessions before it was too late. The main priority of the moment, he had insisted, was "to accede to the reasonable wishes of France" as expressed by the Third Estate. Seeking to diminish the monarch's skepticism toward the English constitution, Necker is reported to have advised Louis XVI to endorse the main principles undergirding the English constitutional monarchy.[50] In addition to the proposed declaration, Necker also submitted a plan outlining a few priorities regarding voting procedures, the creation of a bicameral legislature, the future meetings of the Estates-General, and urgent financial matters. The deputies were to be invited to vote by head regarding taxes (this would have satisfied the demands of the Third Estate) and to deliberate separately concerning the privileges, interests, or other matters peculiar to each order, until they could agree on the main principles of a new constitution. The king was also advised to sanction the Estates-General as a legislative body composed of two chambers and to endorse a few popular proposals in regard to legislation and finance. Necker made a renewed attempt at reconciliation and a new plea for moderation on June 4, 1789, when he presented to the assembly the king's proposal for a solution to the vexing question of the verification of the credentials of the deputies. The conciliatory spirit of the new proposal mirrored the moderation of Necker's speech of May 5, to which it added a few concrete and pragmatic recommendations. Necker proposed that the contested delegations be discussed in common by a commission consisting of representatives of all orders, which would then refer its recommendations back to each order for a final vote.

Alas, once again, Necker's call for moderation went unheeded. The fact that he spoke in the name of the king's government triggered skepticism among the members of the Third Estate for whom Necker's plan evoked unpleasant memories of past *lits de justice* when the monarch forced the *parlements*' obedience to royal edicts. Others saw Necker's new attempt at mediation as infringing upon one of the principles stated in his previous speech of May 5, according to which the Estates-General should be absolutely free to decide on their new mode of organization, without any outside interference or pressure. Since it was in the monarch's interest to sow the seeds of discord in order to strengthen his power, Bailly and Mirabeau warned, it was dangerous to allow him to decide contested cases. Worse, Necker's latest proposal was denounced by Camus, a radical member of the Third Estate, as containing "principles that were a violation of public rights [and] destructive of liberty."[51]

If Louis XVI had published the declaration proposed by Necker, and if Necker's mediating plan had been adopted, the country might well have avoided the turmoil that followed. It is of course impossible to rewrite the course of history, but one thing is certain. Such a step on the part of the king would have preempted the decision of the members of the Third Estate to declare themselves the sole representatives of the nation on June 17. As a moderate, Necker had legitimate reasons to be concerned about the implications of this unprecedented decision. Both the events of June 17 and June

20 suggested the idea of a new sovereign power residing not in the king, but in the National Assembly, with the corollary that, since it represented the nation's will, the authority of this new sovereign did not have to be limited. It was deeply symbolic, as Robert Harris pointed out, that "the National Assembly now considered itself endowed with a majesty hitherto reserved for the king."[52] The June events clearly showed the power of public opinion and the futility and danger inherent in opposing it. Necker was convinced that recourse to force would have been counterproductive, that moderate sacrifices and concessions by all orders were absolutely necessary, and that "a prudent flexibility might better serve them and the king than an obstinate resistance."[53] There were, he believed, only two possible courses of action: to try to defeat public opinion, or to act according to it. The first option was unrealistic while the second posed countless challenges, given the general climate of uncertainty and distrust.

Referring to her father's impossible mission in the summer of 1789, Mme de Staël noted that, while Necker the trimmer was contending with the Court for the cause of liberty, he had at the same time to defend the royal authority and the nobility against the most radical claims of the Third Estate. "All his hours, and all his faculties," she noted, "were employed to guard the king against the courtiers, and the deputies against the factious."[54] He reproached both camps for their excessive claims and rigidity, calling upon them to admit the power of circumstances and try to find common ground before it was too late. If only the national representatives of the Third Estate had made a moderate use of their triumph, he opined, that victory would have been consecrated as one of most memorable in the annals of liberty.

Necker's plea for moderation met not only with the opposition of many members of the privileged orders, who were reluctant to make the compromises and concessions he demanded, but also with skepticism and opposition from prominent defenders of the Third Estate (Sieyès and Mirabeau, for example), who also believed that the new institutions and laws must reflect the will of the nation. Under normal circumstances, Sieyès and Mirabeau should have been Necker's natural allies, but they ended up opposing his plan of moderate reform. (Mounier was more open toward the latter.) On many issues, Necker's thought overlapped with the agenda of the moderates within the Third Estate. Mounier and Necker might have been on different sides in May and June 1789, but they both praised the virtues of the English constitution (although they interpreted them differently) and fought for bicameralism, royal veto, and a strong executive power. They understood that all powers, including the authority of the majority, had to be properly checked and limited.[55] And yet, a rift remained between the monarchiens and Necker until he withdrew from public life in 1790.

Noting the growing tendency to immoderation within the ranks of the Third Estate, Mme de Staël remarked that, although the national wish strongly supported many of the claims of the Third Estate—freedom of reli-

gion, liberty of the press, and free elections—the majority of the representatives of the nation, partly by calculation, partly by enthusiasm, partly under
the force of circumstances, perceived early on which way the wind was
blowing and endorsed radical claims. There were, as already noted, additional reasons for the radicalization of the assembly, all of which gave radicals early leverage over moderates. It was under these circumstances that
the most radical representatives of the Third Estate demanded that the issue
of voting in common or separately be decided immediately rather than be
submitted to negotiation among the delegates of the three orders. Some
went so far as to claim that the Third Estate was the only true representative
of the nation. This was the opposite of what Necker asked the orders to do
in his plea for moderation on May 5. Reaching an agreement on Necker's
proposals would have required concerted action, moderation, and self-
restraint from all parties. Unfortunately, none of them was disposed to espouse moderation or prudence in the summer of 1789.

The Consequences of Immoderation

The events of June 17–20, 1789 would not be Necker's only political defeat.
Three more setbacks followed soon after: the first on June 23, when the
king refused to make the concessions recommended by his minister; the
second on July 11, when Louis XVI dismissed Necker; and the third in September 1789, when the assembly rejected the absolute veto and bicameralism. Yet a fourth blow would come in the wake of the events of February 4,
1790, when the deputies decided not to give the executive power the authority it needed to properly discharge its role.

Necker gave an account of the June 23, 1789 Royal Council in the first
volume of De la Révolution française.[56] Although subjective, his side of the
story is valuable because it shows how a moderate thinker and politician
perceived and explained the growing polarization of the political scene, the
intransigence of many groups, and the general drive to extremes fostered by
centrifugal forces. Necker noted the following paradox. As "all opinions
were fluctuating, [and] men were irresolute which they should finally
adopt,"[57] the issues on which compromises could be reached became fewer
and fewer, and all parties grew increasingly immoderate. Necker had hoped
that the king would not lose a single second in attempting to arbitrate between the three orders, but the monarch refused to assume this mediating
role. Necker emphasized as well the errors committed by Louis XVI's advis-
ers, who convinced him to reject the compromises demanded by the new
political context, such as granting the right of individual voting in regard to
taxes. Although the final declaration acknowledged some of the claims of
the Third Estate, such as the abolition of fiscal privileges and the admission
of all citizens to civil and military employments, the king refused to accept
the union of the three orders and demanded that they continue their delib-

erations separately. His decision to maintain the ancient distinction of the three orders ran counter to public opinion and the new balance of forces on the ground (the Third Estate was becoming the strongest party in the assembly), further irritating the nation's representatives.[58]

In Necker's view, this course of action was unwise in the extreme, signaling a poverty of judgment on the king's part that was matched only by his feeble sense of opportunity. Louis XVI did not understand that a decision of the first two orders to join the Third Estate would have helped moderate the views of the latter and might have, in fact, strengthened the royal authority by giving it an opportunity to steer the Estates-General. The king's advisors wrongly imagined that, with a stroke of the pen, they could irrevocably fix the rights of the nation and the privileges of the monarch and the nobles. It was this illusion and their lack of moderation and prudence that ended up compromising the royal authority "with unpardonable want of skill."[59] The price of their immoderation was going to be paid within a fortnight, when the king was compelled to make the same concessions under the ever-growing threat of general public discontent.

The difference between the two moments could not have been greater. What Louis XVI could have done with prudence and dignity, he was obliged to do ignominiously and under the pressure of circumstances. The legitimate demands of the Third Estate, backed by public opinion, were accepted a few days later by a monarch whose authority, reputation, and power had been severely diminished by his inability or unwillingness to compromise. Thus, the king imprudently lost the popularity that he had won by granting a double number of deputies to the Third Estate in the Estates-General and acquired instead the image of an unreliable monarch unwilling to defend the nation against the first two privileged orders. Pressed between opposite parties, Louis XVI did not possess an accurate estimate of his own strength and failed to properly appreciate the full extent of the opposition from both aisles. One of the two parties, Necker pointed out, harbored absolute distrust of royal authority, while the other, which wanted the monarch to make no concessions, rejected the idea of creating a constitutional monarchy in France. Because none of these groups could have served as a reliable rampart for the throne, Necker believed, it was indispensable that the king pay due regard to the empire of circumstances and adopt a language of prudence and moderation.[60]

Louis XVI's decision not to do so contributed to the defeat of moderates like Necker. Yet the latter's failure to mediate between the three orders after the opening of the Estates-General must not be attributed exclusively to the actions of a hesitant and confused monarch. The impatience of many members of the Third Estate and the general climate of tension, distrust, and fear among the orders also worked against Necker's trimming agenda. Was Necker's plan simply ill-suited to the particular circumstances of the summer of 1789? How are we to explain that, although his main ideas were sound, they failed to bring about the much-needed compromises between rival groups? Is it possible that, under certain circumstances, moderation is a self-defeating strategy?

As for Necker himself, he admitted that he could have been bolder and more determined in his demands, especially in his private conversations with Louis XVI before and after the Royal Council of June 23, 1789. "It was a moment when I could have exacted everything from the king, and I found myself powerless to demand anything," he confessed. "A surge of generous feeling dictated my conduct, which certainly could be criticized but at the same time comprehended. I was not long in repenting it, and I understood once again that a sentiment of virtue in a private person can become a fault, and a very grave one in a statesman."[61] It is interesting to compare Necker's acknowledgment of the shortcomings of his moderation with his image sketched by Adrien Duquesnoy, a deputy who was by and large sympathetic to Necker's initiatives. Referring to his plans for mediation, Duquesnoy noted that Necker had excessive confidence in the virtues of men and would have needed a deeper understanding of the characters of other politicians in order to succeed in 1789. Although he guided himself according to a set of sound principles to which he was fully committed, he was forced to leave the scene early because he did not know how to get them accepted. "A too-honest soul sometimes is very dangerous for a minister," Duquesnoy maintained. "If M. Necker judges other men after himself, he surely does them too much honor."[62]

It might be argued, however, that Necker's self-restraint was not so much a fault as a consequence of his belief that one must resort to moderation *precisely* when one is in a position of strength and command. Although it was generally perceived that he supported the political claims of the Third Estate, Necker decided to keep himself equidistant from the throne and the nation, refusing to use his authority to obtain any secret deals.[63] At the same time, it cannot be denied that, by proceeding to write a new constitution for France, the deputies took a bold step in an unknown direction that was likely to favor radical or extremist rather than moderate views. "The Third Estate," Necker wrote, "by declaring itself alone a National Assembly, by affecting to dispense with the concurrence of the two first orders, by overlooking the utility of a counterbalance in a monarchical constitution, had, from the commencement of the Estates-General, laid itself open to that species of blame which belongs to an usurping power."[64] Since it was commonly argued that the country had no proper constitution, such an ambitious and radical endeavor had to start from scratch. Tradition and moderation were to be among the first casualties, soon followed by the monarchy.

After the Constituent Assembly began its deliberations on the text of the new constitution, Necker continued to act like a trimmer, even as his agenda underwent important transformations. The balance of forces had already shifted in favor of the Third Estate, which became the most important political force in the country after July 14, 1789. Necker was convinced that the Court and the nobles could have avoided the ensuing political debacle if they had chosen prudence and moderation over rigidity and inflexibility. Because they always fixed their attention on the past, and never on the present or the future, the two privileged orders bore a great share of the responsibility for subsequent political events: "By confounding, in the imprudence of their conduct, harshness with firmness, and obstinacy with courage, [they] became the promoters of a revolution which was effected by the authority of public opinion."[65] History, Necker believed, would condemn the privileged orders for their political anachronism and resistance to much-needed conciliatory measures. And yet he saw faults on all sides. All of the groups within the assembly made mistakes, he claimed, and they all stemmed from the same source. None of these parties—neither the Court, nor the nobles, nor the Third Estate—chose moderation when they had the upper hand and could easily have conducted themselves prudently rather than remaining inflexible in their demands.[66]

The balance of power shifted radically between July 11 and July 14, 1789, signaling a significant transformation of royal authority. "If the monarch, thus suddenly deprived of military means and pecuniary resources, appeared still seated on the throne, the royal authority had no longer any existence," Necker wrote.[67] He understood that he was now called to defend the authority of the monarch against the representatives of the nation, after having previously been the supporter of the latter in their negotiations with the king. This was not going to be an easy task since "the general discontent had armed with new power the national representatives without giving them the degree of wisdom and generosity to induce them not to abuse this advantage."[68] It was therefore critical, now more than ever, for Necker to preach moderation to those who, in light of their sudden rise to positions of authority, developed an exaggerated sense of their newly acquired power. It was moreover necessary to wean the king from his unwise and imprudent advisors and restore to the person of the monarch the respect and esteem that royal power required. To obtain these ends and to inspire a common wish for peace and reconciliation, power had to be used with extreme caution, regardless in whose hands it was placed.

Necker's trimming agenda met again with the fierce opposition of those who, being demagogues from self-interest, resolved to build their political fortunes by fostering divisions, distrust, and hatred. In his opinion, by making unfounded promises and rousing people's minds to ideas of severity, rigidity, and vengeance, leaders like Mirabeau cultivated a pernicious form of "proud enthusiasm"[69] culminating in the illusion that everything was up for change, an attitude which, in turn, fueled arrogance and vanity. Among the flawed laws hastily passed under the pressure of these circumstances, Necker pointed to the laws on inheritance and marriage, the new regulations concerning the clergy, and the economic measures put in place to raise new revenues. In the realm of policy, the assembly's irresponsibility was most clearly illustrated by the *assignats*, which reflected both the inexperience and the cupidity of the new political elites. Necker condemned the numerous confiscations that showed disregard for inheritance rights and induced a general sense of powerlessness.[70]

If the hypocrisy and irresponsibility of the deputies were responsible for many of their errors and abuses, there was another, equally important, cause. It had to do with the abstract style of politics that was in vogue, a style characterized by vanity and a metaphysical spirit rather than sound pragmatism.[71] Like Burke, Necker argued that the work of the Constituent Assembly was composed of "many abstractions chained together in an artful or unartful manner." As such, it lacked, "that auspicious union of judgment and feeling in which the strong and the weak man, the sentimentalist and the logician, the friend of order and the partisan of liberty might equally agree."[72] Benefitting from the charm of novelty, this passion for abstractions made the deputies bolder in advancing their claims. Liberty and equality, the two values with which they believed they could govern the world entire, became susceptible of every kind of elaboration and misinterpretation, and were "so loosely defined as to offer an inexhaustible resource to legislators ambitious of popular favour, as well as to political philosophers."[73] Being a simple principle, easily understood by all, equality seduced many people and made them overlook or underestimate the complexity of the social order and political institutions. It became a synonym for a general leveling that would in the end bring down even "the greatest and most disgustful of all supremacies, that of boldness and insolence."[74]

By pandering to popular passions, the deputies clung to what Necker considered a fictitious form of equality; they suppressed all ideas of decency and converted the moral world "into a vast plain, where every man will cross and elbow his neighbour, and all the advantage will fall to the most rustic and robust."[75] While shutting up the temples, they also "made a goddess of Reason. She had her ministers, and particularly her sacrificing priests, and, as the consummation of extravagance and impiety, prostitutes led along in triumph, were made the types or the idol of this new idolatry."[76] Within a few months, Necker wryly remarked, France became a "vast political Lyceum, where they dispute upon the different manners of commanding, without perceiving that the whole people have entered the hall, and that no one is left without it to obey."[77] The political scene came to be dominated by "clamorous spectators, passionate judges, and ungovernable agitators,"[78] all led by an insatiable passion for more equality which, in Necker's view, signaled an inexorable process. Once started, it could no longer be reversed or controlled, and would lead back eventually to a state of nature *sui generis*, incompatible with law-abidingness, public order, and liberty: "All separations have been destroyed, all the boundaries of imagination removed, all pretentions placed in action; it is no longer time to check any one; every one wishes to influence the government, everyone wishes to partake the pleasure of commanding, everyone one wishes to place himself in the avenues to power and authority."[79] In reality, Necker argued, absolute equality had never existed in the past, neither in Rome, nor in Athens or Sparta. Suddenly transformed into "a society of political Quackers"[80] enamored with equality, France became the first country to make political equality the pillar of its new government.

The deputies were soon to discover, however, that while dismantling the Old Regime required only favorable circumstances, building a new government demanded "the deepest reflections and all the sagacity of genius."[81] The members of the Constituent Assembly, Necker averred, "have fancied that they were enlightened more than others, by science and meditation, and yet they have conducted themselves like the chief of a horde of barbarians, by destroying all the solemnities of the moral world, and making uniformity by an universal debasement."[82] Exceedingly confident in their theories, they disregarded the wisdom of their predecessors and attempted to begin everything anew, relying for the most part on abstract principles with only a tenuous link to reality. In the eyes of moderates like Necker, the desire for novelty and originality at all costs, the uncritical attachment to abstractions, and the imprudent disregard for experience were serious political sins reflected in the final text of the Constitution of 1791, which consummated the two-year work of the Constituent Assembly.

A Missed Opportunity: The Constitution of 1791

In the summer of 1789, with the privileges of the nobles and the clergy abolished and the authority of the king severely damaged, the members of the Constituent Assembly found themselves in an especially favorable situation. With all things working to their favor, Necker argued, they ought to have used their new power with moderation and their political triumph should have prepared them "to think with calmness and to act with circumspection"[83] in order to consolidate their gains. They were called to establish a new form of government and give the country a regular and fair constitution, guaranteeing public order, justice, and liberty. This required "an immense work, composed of an infinite number of parts, the union of which ought to be considered in all its harmonious proportions, if we would form a right judgment of it."[84] The greatest challenge, in Necker's view, was not so much to discuss and examine the ideas of each article, as "to regard them as a whole, and to estimate them by one and the same spirit, one and the same interest, one and the same rule."[85] Everything would have favored the success of "wise and moderate proceedings," if only the deputies did not abuse their power.

If the task of dismantling the political framework of the Old Regime was completed by the end of August 1789, that of rebuilding the institutional structure of government had only begun. According to Necker, two courses of action were open to the deputies: "the one pointed out by wisdom and moderation, the other by those extravagant ideas which had so constantly misled the Constituent Assembly."[86] The latter chose the second path and showed, from an early stage, a strong passion for praise and applause, failing to appreciate "the aid that might be derived from moderation and prudence."[87] The deliberations of the Constituent Assembly were often chaotic and tumultuous, and were not sheltered from the pressure of public opinion and demagoguery. The sheer size of the assembly and the fact that it was open to spectators made it prone to disunity, intrigue, and factions, and encouraged a spirit of partisanship among the many jarring interests and passions. As many deputies found it necessary constantly to enhance their reputations with the people, declamations against the executive power and royal authority dominated the daily agenda. Skillfully manipulating the minds of the people with simple ideas and persuasive slogans, crafty rhetoricians excited in them new desires and dreams, but without providing them the knowledge they would need to pursue those dreams with prudence and reason.

Referring to the assembly's lack of pragmatism, Necker alleged that it had underestimated the difficulties of administration and converted the government into a mere *jeu d'esprit*, making France "like a chess-board, a scene in which, without obstacles, you can move the men wherever you please."[88] The deputies decided to treat all public affairs indiscriminately in the general assembly, abandoning the more reasonable original plan of dividing themselves into different committees, each to focus on a specific issue. Unlike American legislators, the French deputies examined, destroyed, and remodeled anew almost everything that came under their scrutiny: political, civil, and criminal laws, public administration, the ecclesiastical system, the maritime and military system, the rural code, statutes of mines and miners, statutes of commerce and high roads, taxation, coinage, and finance. Their original plan of working in committees would have much better suited the task of drafting a new constitution, which required expertise and diverse skills and should not have been left to the ever-changing dispositions of the legislative body as a whole. Furthermore, after weakening the executive power, the assembly was obliged to take the functions of the executive into its own hands, so that from that moment on, the drafting of the constitution became only one of the many items on the deputies' busy agenda.

Equally important, from an early stage, the assembly was under a grave delusion with regard to the real merit of its own accomplishments. "Nothing [is] more difficult than to stop oneself," Necker remarked, "when we are smitten with the love of admiration; nor does any thing hint to us the necessity of doing so, when we have established the field of our experiments in the land of abstractions."[89] The deputies exaggerated the obstacles they faced and rhetoricians skilled in the art of flattery and insinuation took turns encouraging rumors and fostering a general obsession with alleged conspiracies against the people and their representatives. By directing the attention of the public to obstacles and dangers—both real and imaginary—

they sought to diminish their responsibility for their own errors. Thus, "all moderation soon ceased to be observed, both in language and conduct, for rivalry in the search after applause and a desire to surpass others in popularity, allow of none."[90] The Jacobins distinguished themselves in this regard. Masters in the art of flattery, they understood early on that "the favour of the people became every day more and more the pledge of success in the new roads which ambition had offered."[91] They constrained the assembly "to be more democratic than it was by inclination, or than its knowledge and reflection would have suggested."[92] Seeking to pander to the passions of the people, Jacobin deputies felt entitled and encouraged to freely meddle with the new constitution in order to make it even more lax and democratic. They encouraged denunciations and calumny as proof of patriotism, took compassion and clemency as signs of weakness, and ingratitude to the living as evidence of courage.

In this climate of demagoguery, fear, and uncertainty, the deputies did not pay sufficient attention to the composition and establishment of the executive power, ignoring that "its creation and vital energy ought to be the first object of their deliberation."[93] Their professed allegiance to the principles of monarchical government was inconsistent with their actions, as the majority of the deputies continued to perceive the monarch as an alien and rival power and sought to transform Louis XVI into a public bureaucrat, divesting him of the quality of a representative of the nation, and refusing to grant the king the prerogatives and attributes essentially to his dignity. This offensive attitude toward the monarch betrayed the deputies' bellicose attitude toward the executive power, and epitomized their distrust of hierarchy and all gradations of rank. After July 14, the figure that remained on the throne of France was no longer a true monarch, but only a pale shadow of the former king. In the course of the following months, Louis XVI was deprived of many of the prerogatives and attributes necessary to the proper exercise of royal power. "It is an ever memorable fault on the part of an assembly of legislators to have wished to maintain in France a monarchical government," Necker wrote; "and yet, at the same time, to have imagined that this idea was carried into execution by placing a king at the head of a democratic constitution."[94]

According to Necker, the Constitution of 1791 suffered from a serious "want of proportions,"[95] as evidenced by the existence of an authority without counterpoise in the state—the omnipotent legislative. This "incomprehensible constitution," Necker argued, "has placed, on one side, a single permanent assembly . . . and, on the other side, an executive power, without prerogatives, without the means of effecting either good or ill, while it is stripped of all exterior splendor, by changes of every kind, which have deprived the throne of majesty and its ministers of respect."[96] An omnipotent assembly, he warned, would always be led by its nature to arm itself "with the exterminating sword"[97] in order to realize its intentions. The constitution failed to create a proper balance of powers and provided no effective links between powers such as would have ensured their smooth cooperation. By neglecting to grant to each power the necessary degree of strength to preserve it from the incursions of its rivals, the deputies were led to embrace a rigid version of the separation of *powers*, which they wrongly equated with the separation of *persons*.

In Necker's view, the most significant shortcoming of the Constitution of 1791 was its failure to understand the importance and complexity of the executive power. "It is an ever memorable fault on the part of an assembly of legislators," he wrote, ". . . to have omitted to treat of the most difficult question in the formation of a government, the institution of the executive power, a power which, by its easy combination, by its wise structure, might be able to secure public order, without endangering or giving offence to liberty."[98] Necker believed that "the constitution of the executive power forms the essential and perhaps sole difficulty of every system of government."[99] A properly constituted executive power "derives its perfection from the most exact combinations, where all is *proportion* and everything is *equipoise*."[100] The members of the Constituent Assembly viewed the defeat of the king and the weakening of the executive power as a triumph of liberty and imagined that a throne with reduced prerogatives could subsist "exposed to the fury of all the waves of equality."[101] What they did not foresee was that a diminished executive power might be the first step toward an eventual absorption of all powers into the assembly, and would finally allow the legislative to acquire absolute authority.

As we have already seen, the debates on the royal veto represented a major moment in the offensive against the executive power that began in the summer of 1789. Like other moderates who defended the principles of constitutional monarchy, Necker thought that king ought to have the right to veto the legislative initiatives of the nation's representatives; in his view, the veto was, in fact, compatible with the existence of a sound balance of powers.

Yet, unlike the monarchiens, he was not inflexible on this topic and, much to their chagrin, he ended up endorsing the suspensive veto, which, in his view, allowed the monarch still to play a much-needed moderating role in the legislative process. Necker's endorsement of the suspensive veto was to some extent the result of political calculation, as he came to realize that the absolute veto was a lost card given the representatives' extreme distrust of the executive power. But Necker also had a deeper theoretical consideration in mind when settling for the suspensive veto. He considered the royal veto a necessary complement to the sharing of the legislative function between the two main powers in the state. On this view, a genuine balance of powers could be achieved only if the king's ministers were allowed to participate in legislative debates. A good connoisseur of the English political system, Necker was aware that the participation of the executive power in the exercise of the legislative function could be assured not only by the royal veto, but also by granting the ministers the right to be members of the lower Chamber, as was the custom in England. This, however, was seen by many French deputies as an infringement of the principle of the separation of powers. Accordingly, the nation's representatives refused to accept that ministers might also be members of the lower Chamber and denied members of the executive the right to intervene in legislative debates. Necker regarded this as a grave political error pregnant with significant consequences. If the deputies had accepted the participation of the king's ministers in legislative deliberations, the monarch might have been encouraged *not* to use his right of veto, or to use it sparingly and only in extreme circumstances.

The course of events not only forced Necker to settle for a suspensive veto, which he equated with an indirect appeal to the people, but also led him to modify his position on bicameralism, which marked a further departure from the position of the monarchiens. Necker eventually endorsed a single Chamber when it became obvious that bicameralism, too, had become a lost cause, associated with aristocracy and hereditary privileges. For him, the priority was to salvage what was possible from the endangered authority of the executive power. He did not give up his belief that France needed a strong and limited power, but he was forced to adjust his ideas to shifting circumstances.[102] The unwritten constitution of England remained Necker's model, and he continued to believe that the French deputies would have done well to borrow their principles from across the Channel and then adapt them creatively to conditions in France. "The English government," Necker argued,

> Might well have served as an example to the Constituent Assembly, had it not been possessed by the spirit of reckless innovation. It wished to surpass Solon, Numa, and Lycurgus, and to overwhelm with its own glory all legislators, past, present, and to come; and great mischiefs have been the result of so unreasonable an ambition. How great would have been the difference . . . if instead of suffering so many praters on politics, so many mere novices, to wander and confuse themselves without end, they had ordered a simple secretary to mount the tribune, and there read, with the voice of a Stentor, the British constitution! . . . Vanity is the grant agent in the moral universe, and reason, with all its engines, can neither put any thing in motion or stop it in its progress.[103]

A closer look at the internal structure of the constitutional text reveals that it was not a work of "apparent symmetry and ideal beauty," as its defenders claimed. Its composite and incoherent structure did not offer a viable foundation on which to build a viable constitutional monarchy.[104] Necker attributed the failure of the constitution to its highly eclectic nature which ultimately made it impracticable: "The French constitution, monarchical in its title, republican in its forms, despotic in the means of execution, confused also in its principles, variable in its march, uncertain in its end, presents to our view an imperfect medley of every political idea and institution."[105]

The Constitution of 1791 was not going to be, however, the only failed post-revolutionary constitution of France. The text that was supposed to replace it two years later was a stillborn document that was never implemented. After the 9th Thermidor, the French legislators proceeded to write a new constitution seeking to "end" the revolution. In spite of their good intentions, the Constitution of 1795 lasted only four years, being replaced in turn by the Constitution of 1799. The challenges faced by the framers of the Constitution of 1795 constitute a fascinating subject for any student of political moderation. Necker's reflections on this important moment in the history of post-revolutionary France, as well as on the Constitution of 1799, can help us grasp better the challenges which French moderates faced in building representative government on the ruins of the Terror.

Necker's Critique of the Constitutions of 1795 and 1799

The period following the fall of Robespierre on the 9th Thermidor marked the beginning of a long, agitated, and painful apprenticeship of liberty.[106] Old political concepts such as the right of veto and bicameralism were taken up again, while others such as citizenship, property, balance of powers, equality, freedom, and representation were redefined in keeping with the new political circumstances. At the same time, new priorities emerged for moderates, such as redefining the scope and authority of the executive power, and carving out a much-needed center between extremes.

The drafting of the Constitution of 1795 reflected the moderates' desire to come to terms with the complex legacy of the Terror by building a system of ordered liberty. The new constitution represented an ambitious attempt to stabilize the republican institutions in France in a highly volatile political context. It was supposed to create a new balance of powers by dividing the legislative body into two chambers and limiting the authority of the legislature. The constitutional text was voted by the National Convention on August 22, 1795 and ratified in early September by a popular referendum in which less than a million French citizens participated.[107]

Historians and constitutional scholars have not rendered full justice to this interesting text which was peculiar in several respects. Adopted a year after the 9th Thermidor and firmly situated within the republican tradition, the Constitution of 1795 was a direct response to the previous Jacobin Constitution of 1793, which had been neither applied nor officially annulled. Often presented as the work of tired legislators desiring to close a long revolutionary chapter, the 1795 constitution was, in fact, a surprisingly ambitious and detailed document, the longest constitution France ever had, comprising 377 articles, most of them virtually impossible to revise in light of the numerous conditions set for the revision process. The fathers of the new constitutional text drew not only on documents in the republican tradition (such as the U.S. Constitution), but also borrowed from the conceptual framework of the limited monarchy in the Constitution of 1791. In so doing, they created an eclectic text that relied upon an idealized conception of citizenship and duties and spoke in highly moralizing overtones.[108]

The drafting of the text fell into the hands of the Commission of Eleven which included, among others, moderates such as Boissy d'Anglas, Creuzé-Latouche, Durand-Maillane, Lanjuinais, Thibaudeau, and La Réveillière-Lépeaux. The Commission was originally entrusted only with the task of revising the organic laws of the Constitution of 1793. The radical decision to propose a new constitutional text was taken sometimes after Cambacérès' important discourse of April 18, 1795, in which he spoke at length about the urgent need for new organic laws. It is still unclear when the members of the Commission actually made the bold step of proceeding to draft, in La Réveillière-Lépeaux's words, "the plan of a reasonable constitution."[109] The radicals on the left would have preferred the Commission to simply reactivate the Constitution of 1793, while the majority of the Convention was opposed to this solution. On June 23, Boissy d'Anglas presented a constitutional draft which became the object of intense debates that took place over the entire summer, focusing on key issues such as the nature of political representation, the separation of powers, veto power, and decentralization. The pragmatic (and eclectic) spirit of the new constitution was evinced by Boissy d'Anglas' appeal to moderation, calling upon his colleagues to cease acting like "gladiators of liberty" and behave instead as "its true founders."[110]

Born out of the fear of the twin dangers of Jacobin democracy and ultraconservative reaction, the new constitution aimed at officially ending the revolutionary state by anchoring republican institutions in a new set of principles, such as republicanism and the balance of powers. Drawing on the American example, often cited in the debates, the new constitution endorsed the principle of bicameralism which had previously been rejected by both the constitutions of 1791 and 1793. References to the example of England were also made during the debates. Some praised the division of parliament into two chambers, while others insisted on the moderation of the English constitution, made possible by the role of the monarch as a moderating force capable of containing all powers within their legitimate spheres of competence and authority.[111] At same time, the French deputies agreed on the necessity for bicameralism, now considered "one of those political axioms which it would be useless to try to demonstrate."[112] As a pillar of representative government, bicameralism was regarded as a key condition for what Eschassériaux called "*la pondération du pouvoir qui fait les lois*."[113] Accordingly, the new constitution provided for the establishment of an upper chamber—the Council of the Ancients—composed of experienced men whose knowledge and experience was supposed to temper the excessive fervor and passions of the lower chamber, the Council of the Five Hundred. The upper chamber was expected to serve as a moderating power, although, unlike the English House of Lords, it represented the same set of social interests as the lower chamber. Some, like Thibaudeau, believed that bicameralism alone could provide an effective barrier against absolute power, and deemed unnecessary the participation of the executive power in the exercise of the legislative function. Others like Delahaye expressed their concern that the differences between the two chambers in the new constitutional text were insignificant, and claimed that the new constitution did not provide an adequate framework for reconciling competing and diverse social and political interests. Between the existing powers in the state, Delahaye argued, there must be a "strong opposition of interests" which cannot result only from differences of age, but should be based on "*la contrariété des intérêts*" among powers which must be granted a proportionate force so as to be capable of resisting their mutual encroachments. Their reciprocal dependence and connection form "the equilibrium of authority necessary for moderating the authority of the government, securing the authority of the legislative power, and preserving social order and public liberty."[114]

It might seem surprising that the veto issue was taken up rather late in the constitutional debates of 1795. On August 17, Ehrmann introduced it on the agenda and argued that granting the right of veto to the executive power was absolutely necessary in order to give the constitution the solid foundation that it had previously lacked.[115] Such a provision, Ehrmann remarked, had been used with great success in America, where it had served as a pillar of representative government and the balance of powers. Lanjuinais agreed with Ehrmann, insisting that the veto ought to be regarded as the right of bringing to the attention of the legislative power its potential or actual errors. As such, Lanjuinais argued, "it is the right to invite to further reflect upon them, in one word, it is only a right of remonstrance"[116] compatible with political liberty. The close connection between the right of veto and the balance of powers must be duly underscored here. Not only was the latter used to justify the veto, but the veto itself was also seen a prerequisite of the balance of powers. In *Réflexions sur le plan de la constitution presenté par la commission des Onze* from July 1795, Vaublanc, a former member of the Legislative Assembly, defended the right of veto by arguing that no balance of powers could exist as long as the executive did not have the power to examine and raise objections to the initiatives of the legislative body. Endorsing the project proposed by Boissy d'Anglas, Vaublanc claimed that the executive power ought to have been equal (in power and dignity) to the legislative power, and argued that no genuine balance of the two could exist as long as the government remained weak and lacked the necessary authority required to properly discharge its role.[117]

While some regarded the executive's right to veto laws passed by the legislature as a fundamental condition and guarantee of the balance of powers, others saw in it an infringement of the separation of powers and vehemently opposed it. The final version of the constitutional text denied veto power to the executive; neither the proposals for a *veto suspensif* nor those for a *veto réviseur* could gather sufficient support among the members of the Convention. This decision effectively denied to the executive any possibility of sharing in the exercise of the legislative function.[118] Nor did the constitution give the executive the power and authority that would have made it respected at home and feared abroad. The directors had no control over the Treasury, which remained entirely under the influence of the legislative power (cf. Articles 315–320 and 325). The text made clear that the veritable power would reside in the legislative body, while the executive power, placed in the hands of five directors, became weakened, divided, and fragmented.

The Constitution of 1795 thus stopped short of creating a genuine balance of powers in spite of its authors' liberal intentions in drawing inspiration from the American constitution.[119] While invoking the principle of the balance of powers, the French legislators failed to create such a balance in reality. Critics of the Constitution of 1795 also condemned the eclecticism of the constitutional text evinced by the fact that, on the one hand, it included a declaration of the rights and duties of man while, on the other hand, it proposed an elitist form of republicanism, which acknowledged the importance of property as a criterion for citizenship and contained provisions for two-degree elections. Other critics mentioned the lack of any form of control over the constitutionality of the laws. Choosing to reject Sieyès' proposals for a *jury constitutionnaire*,[120] the authors of the Constitution ignored the need for an agency entrusted with control over the constitutionality of the laws, believing that this role could be fulfilled by the newly created upper chamber.

Finally, many critics (including Necker) alleged that the constitutional text misunderstood the complex nature and role of the executive power and provided for a rigid separation of powers that made smooth collaboration between the executive and legislative power nearly impossible. This last point was made, in fact, by Daunou, one of the framers of the constitution, who in an intervention of July 23, 1795, criticized the persistent skepticism toward the executive power displayed by members of the Convention, who continued to fear that a strong executive power would usurp liberty and bring about the ruin of the republic.[121] The very idea of the executive power as an *a priori* enemy of liberty was also criticized by the author of the previously cited article from *La Gazette française*,[122] who condemned hostility toward the veto as a nefarious legacy of the revolution. The interdependence of powers could be achieved, he believed, only by giving them proportionate authority so that they could reconcile their differences in a peaceful way.[123]

Did the Constitution of 1795 provide for a rigid separation of powers? According to Adhémar Esmein and Joseph Barthélemy, the tendency to isolate the two main powers from each other was illustrated by the affirmation (cf. Article 136) that the title of "minister" was incompatible with being a member of the legislative body.[124] And yet, a closer look at the constitution of 1795 invites us to reconsider the thesis of the "strict" separation of powers. The five directors were appointed by the legislative body and, according to Article 112, had penal responsibility for the proper execution of the laws (they were also responsible for blocking any attempts to subvert the constitution). Furthermore, the two chambers of the legislative body exercised a certain influence over the exercise of the executive power. According to Article 150, the legislature determined the number and attributions of ministers, and according to Article 161, the directors were supposed to submit in writing the information requested by the two chambers, which also had the Treasury under their jurisdiction.[125]

Necker was fully aware of these ambiguities, which he highlighted at length in *De la Révolution française*. The root of the evil, he argued, went deeper than the flawed organization of powers in the new constitution:

> The evil is in that real equality, in the public opinion, between the chiefs and the inferiors of government; an equality which renders inadmissible the ingenious system of responsibility introduced in England; and the evil is, moreover, in the total separation established between the two supreme authorities. This has placed the executive power completely independent of the legislature, and the legislature can only reach it by a menacing vigilance.[126]

The defects of the constitution mirrored the climate of uncertainty and chaos after the 9th Thermidor. The general laxity of mores gave the nation the appearance of being "on a holiday."[127] Moreover, the political foundations of the republic seemed shaky, resting upon a simultaneous allegiance to liberty, equality, and the indivisibility of government, three principles in tension with each other. In Necker's view, the indivisibility of government was dangerous to liberty and favorable to despotism because it made all legislation and administration proceed from the same center. It multiplied the potential means of tyranny and rendered them more dangerous in proportion as the circumference of the authority was enlarged.[128] Necker believed that the framers of the constitution ought to have paid particular attention to establishing a proper alliance or "union" between the executive and legislative power instead of trying to strictly separate them, ignoring the lessons of experience and prudence. "Their prudent association, their artful intertwining," he wrote in a memorable passage, could and should have been "the best security for mutual circumspection and efficacious vigilance."[129] As matters stood, the spirit of the constitution of 1795 simultaneously betrayed a disquieting fear of liberty and an impatience to break with the past at all costs. Describing the essential disposition of the constitutional text, Necker wrote:

> The capital disposition, and which may endanger its order or its liberty, is the complete and absolute separation of the two supreme

authorities; the one which makes the laws, and the other which directs and watches over their execution. They had united, confounded all powers in the monstrous organization of the national convention; and now, by another extreme, undoubtedly less dangerous, they preserve between them none of the affinities which the good of the state demands. They have suddenly laid hold of written maxims, and, upon the faith of a small number of political institutors, believed that they could place too strong a barrier between the executive and legislative powers.[130]

That a rigid separation of powers was possible was, Necker insisted, a dangerous illusion, and the attempt to put it into practice was bound to have dangerous consequences. He invoked the examples of England and America where powers were wisely intertwined and the head of the state—the monarch or the president—shared in the exercise of the legislative function, either through his veto power or through the participation of his ministers in the debates of the lower chamber (the case of England). Invoking the American constitution, Necker praised American legislators for having established close and permanent links between the executive authority and the two houses of the legislative body.[131] "Sometimes a Senate, the depositary of the executive authority, proposed laws to a more comprehensive council, or to the whole mass of the citizens," he wrote; and "sometimes the Senate, exercising in an inverse sense its right of association with the legislative power, suspends or revises the decrees of the greater number."[132] The French did not follow the American example and refused to allow the members of the executive power to participate in parliamentary deliberations. Such an organization of powers, Necker argued, was both inconvenient and imprudent: "These two powers will have no political tie, but exhortative addresses, and will only communicate together by means of messengers ordinary and extraordinary."[133] In Necker's opinion, what the French legislators failed to understand was that "of all the methods of establishing the executive authority in a republic, the most simple and least dangerous is to assign it a share, directly or indirectly, in the formation of the laws."[134] Little attention was paid to the question whether the power of the directors was to be exercised collectively or divided, whether the five directors were to have a separate authority or a joint one, and whether a joint authority was compatible with the multiplicity of affairs and the diversity of events to which the directors were supposed to respond. Necker feared that the five directors, when deliberating in common, would be obliged to divide their authority and enter into secret or tacit agreements in order to secure the majority of votes among them. This, he predicted, would make any uniform exercise of executive power impossible and would lead to internal frictions and a diversity of interests that might prove harmful to liberty.[135]

In Necker's opinion, another major flaw of the Constitution of 1795 was the improper distribution of power and authority between the two chambers ("councils") of the new legislative power.[136] Necker was particularly concerned by the limited authority and prestige of the Council of the Ancients, whose members were only entitled to say "yes" or "no" to the proposals of the lower chamber, and were not allowed to explain their position or approve some parts of a law while rejecting others that they deemed flawed. The right to initiate laws was expressly denied to the members of the upper chamber and was entrusted only to the Council of the Five Hundred. Divested of necessary authority, the Council of the Ancients lacked the power to moderate the initiatives of the lower chamber and, consequently, risked falling into discredit, because it would never be able to take the lead and was not able to repair injustices, protect the weak, or make proposals for increasing the prosperity of the state.[137] As such, the Council of the Ancients was condemned to be "a silent spectator of all existing circumstances"[138] and was, Necker feared, destined to become irrelevant by virtue of its being unconnected with the whole of the laws which were removed from its direct influence. This situation was precisely the opposite of the state of affairs in England and America, where close connections between the two chambers had been established and were maintained "by mutual propositions" and "an equality of rights."[139]

In Necker's view, a smaller body such as the Council of the Ancients (resembling a Senate or a House of Lords) should have had the right to initiate laws because its members were better prepared for engaging in indepth deliberations and capable of moderating the initiatives of the lower chamber:

> The small number is more fitly appointed than the larger one to meditate laws, to prepare them, to correct the details, and to examine all the parts with attention, and it can more easily repair a first error. . . . And it is a violation of all the laws of equilibrium, in the distribution of powers, to unite together the force of number, the force of age, the force of proposing laws, and the force of the right of accusation.[140]

There was, furthermore, another disposition in the text of the Constitution of 1795 that had been left vague and uncertain by its framers: the political responsibility of the directors and the responsibility of the ministers serving under them. The English, Necker remarked, had succeeded in combining the responsibility of the executive power with the inviolability of the monarch by simultaneously laying all responsibility upon the ministers and holding the person of the monarch inviolable. This ingenious strategy secured the monarch due respect in the name of order and the tranquility of the state, while holding his ministers politically accountable, should they betray the trust placed in them. Nonetheless, Necker added, this method was suitable only to constitutional monarchies and could not be applied to republics, where the head of state does not enjoy the majesty of a throne and is not strictly speaking inviolable, and where the authority of the leader depends to a great extent on the conduct of his ministers.

The Constitution of 1795 contained obvious shortcomings in this regard. With the exception of egregious cases of treason, it was practically impossible to hold the directors politically responsible or to correct their mistakes by resorting to legal means.[141] Because the five directors were expected to go out of office one by one, each director, upon giving up his position, could still count (for his security) on the support and complicity of the four others remaining at the helm of political affairs. These complicated rules made it practically impossible to accuse past directors without implicating the ones still in power. Moreover, Necker pointed out, the Directory was placed under no effective censure. While in many other countries the power of censure was confided to a Senate whose members had life tenure, the Constitution of 1795 renewed the power of inspecting and censuring authorities every three years, that is, more frequently than the regular five-year term of a director. Thus, when the directors returned to public life, there would be no witnesses of their public conduct left to pass judgment on them in the legislature.[142]

Necker also commented on the legislators' misinterpretation of the concept of "representation" in the new constitution. "The true representation of the will of a people," he wrote, "must be sought for in the immutable principles of justice and of reason; there it will be better found than in a constitutional article, united to three hundred and seventy-six others, and approved all together at the first reading, amidst the tumult of the primary assemblies."[143] In particular, Necker claimed that the system of absolute equality favored by some Thermidorians was incompatible with the aristocracy of property and political capacity demanded by the new social condition. He denounced the pernicious effects of the French legislators' indifference to the quality of landholder and argued that the criteria for granting full citizenship established by the Constitution of 1795 were poorly conceived and its stipulations ineffective.

In criticizing the provisions of the new constitution, Necker also reaffirmed the importance of protecting individual liberty, a leitmotif of the whole group of Coppet. In seeking to offer a new foundation for representative government, he believed that the constitution granted the legislative power excessive scope and authority, such as would likely jeopardize individual liberty and rights. Among other things, the legislative power had the right to curtail civil liberties—freedom of the press and the right to travel, for example—and could send individuals into exile if any suspicion arose that their actions might threaten the security of the state. That the constitution offered insufficient protection to individuals against encroachment upon their rights was further demonstrated by the fact that there was no independent public magistracy mandated to hear the complaints of citizens injured by an unconstitutional act of authority. Necker was concerned that in France, it was only administrators who served as judges of the abuses of the agents of administration, and citizens were subject to decisions made by administrators removable at the will of the government or the legislative power, against which they had no recourse.[144]

These shortcomings were particularly evident in the articles of the Constitution of 1795 concerning the status of the judges. "I see with pain, in the French constitution," Necker wrote, "the removal of the judges, and their election by the people, every five years. Sentiments of fear and of hope are incompatible with the august functions of magistrates called upon to decide the fortunes of citizens, and to direct the jury in criminal questions."[145] Tribunals, he argued, should not be composed of men elected at regular intervals and thus subject to the whims of the popular will, for such individuals would not have the required independence of mind and would not command the respect of other citizens.[146] In Necker's view, the uncritical extension of the principle of elections to all spheres of political life was a great error, and the French would have done better had they followed the examples set by the English and the Americans who opted for granting life tenure to judges.

Necker also objected to the articles pertaining to the revision of the constitution, which made this process far too cumbersome and impractical. It was absurd to write a constitution consisting of as many as 377 articles and then expect them to be semi-permanent.[147] But in order to be amended, the constitutional text would require three examinations to be held at three-year intervals, and then could not be revised without the assent of the French people represented in primary assemblies. "To serious and reflecting men," Necker wrote, "this consultation held with all the people upon a constitutional act composed of so many articles, is almost a kind of comedy."[148] Such provisions, he opined, were only capable of creating more confusion and disorder. They would allow of neither major nor minor corrections since any legislature would be reluctant to initiate the complex and time-consuming revision procedures in order to correct matters of small interest. In Necker's view, a proper constitution ought to be in two parts. The first, laying down the fundamental conditions of the new social order, should consist of a few—thirty to forty—general, simple, and clear articles, easily understood by all citizens. This section should not be revised frequently. The second part, longer and more detailed, might, depending upon circumstances, be modified by the deputies.

Warning that the text of the Constitution of 1795 laid open the possibility of a new form of absolute power, Necker opined that it prescribed many things useless to liberty and indifferent to the public order, while neglecting to take the most necessary precautions for the public good. "A kind of perpetual carnival will favour the enterprises of the supreme authority," Necker wrote; "it will give fetes, it will leave the people to laugh and enjoy themselves, provided the people will leave it to govern, and the policy of Venice will, perhaps, be adopted by the French government."[149] Religion, he predicted, would not be an effective countervailing force, since the framers of the new constitution had neglected its role as a pillar of social order, forgetting that it is not possible to separate morality from religion.[150] When the latter is attacked, other principles essential to social order come under siege as well: manners and education, honor, chivalry, and above all, the sense of duty. The French legislators had sought instead to promote an ambitious program of civic education and, in so doing, had rejected the authority of older moral principles: "No more manners, no more religion, no more paternal authority, no more habits of respect, no more prejudices favorable to the sentiment of respect, and claims all equal among twenty-five millions of men. What preparations for a durable order!" Necker exclaimed.[151]

His warning could not have been more prescient. Necker had indeed good reason to fear that France might succumb to a new form of military power that would bring down its representative government. Subsequent events and the Constitution of Year VIII (1799) vindicated his worst fears. His last book published in 1802 was an ambitious attempt to leave the realm of abstract speculation—"*le mieux abstrait*"—in order to examine "*les choses faites, et les choses possibles.*"[152] Necker's analysis of the constitution of Year VIII is particularly relevant to the topic of moderation because it sheds fresh light on his role as a trimmer. In *Dernières vues*, he emphasizes that the soundness of institutions must be judged according to the time or the civilization that engenders them.[153] Although he had never been a republican before, toward the end of his life, he engaged seriously with the project of creating and consolidating a republic "one and indivisible" in France. This topic forms the object of the long second section of the book, amounting to slightly over one hundred pages, to which Necker added a few additional reflections on the possibility of a federative republic in France.

In 1799, he had no reason to be worried any longer about the weakness of the executive power. On the contrary, signs of Napoleon's political ambitions were already quite obvious, even if Bonaparte, whom Necker called "*l'homme nécessaire,*"[154] had not yet become the absolute ruler who would reign despotically over France a few years later. It was now the excessive strength of the executive power that preoccupied Necker, in spite of the fact that the new constitution provided for the creation of a Senate, a Tribunate, and a Legislative Body, which could have represented in principle—but did not offer in reality—an effective countervailing power to the executive.

Necker began by pointing out the most important and conspicuous shortcoming of the Constitution of 1799: this government that called itself republican did not grant any significant part of political power to its citizens and refused to allow the nation to play a direct role in the administration of the country.[155] The right of the nation to exercise political power was replaced in the new constitution by a highly complex and inefficient system of lists of "eligible" citizens that constituted "*un grand echaffaudage,*"[156] incomprehensible to the population at large. "All this organization," Necker argued, referring to articles VII-XIII of the constitution inspired by Sieyès, "is simultaneously a subject of irritation for the general mass of citizens, an attack on their rights, and an embarrassment for the government, detrimental to the good of the state."[157] The very nature and existence of the republic were called into question by the fact that the people would not effectively participate in the nomination of magistrates and the election of legislators.

In Necker's view, the 1799 constitution also suffered from a serious want of proportions, as illustrated by the highly complex and ultimately inefficient relationship between the Senate and the two parts of the legislature: the Tribunate and the Legislative Body. Necker was especially concerned by the excessive authority granted to the head of state and the reduced attributions of the legislature (especially the Senate), which created a situation in which the legislative arm could not exercise any effective control over the executive. The constitution was equally unsuccessful in its attempt to combine the political responsibility of the ministers with the inviolability of the head of state. Such a combination, Necker argued, was possible only in a constitutional monarchy and was not suitable to a republican regime.[158] The provision according to which the Senate had the right to invalidate unconstitutional acts was meaningless so long as its members feared that, in so doing, they risked arousing the wrath of the First Consul.[159] Necker further opposed granting the right of legislative initiative only to the executive power and expressed concern that the Legislative Body was to play too limited a role in this process, being entitled only to accept or refuse the proposals submitted to its consideration. This, he opined, represented a move from one extreme—denying the executive any role in the legislative function—to the other extreme, which denied the deputies the right of legislative initiative and restricted their role to simply saying "yes" or "no" to the proposed laws. Necker insisted that the right to initiate legislation must never be solely in the hands of any single power, but ought to be shared in different degrees between the legislative and the executive bodies.[160]

Overcoming Rousseau's Spell: "Complex Sovereignty" and Necker's Critique of Equality

It should be obvious by now that Necker's writings affirmed a set of values and principles belonging to the pantheon of classical liberalism—individualism, liberty, pluralism, and limited power (constitutionalism)—which he shared with the other members of the Coppet group. He introduced a number of important themes that drew upon—and sometimes went beyond—Montesquieu's conceptual framework and departed from the ideas of Rousseau, the nemesis of all nineteenth-century French liberals.[161] These concepts were: complex sovereignty; neutral power; and the intertwining of powers based on a seminal distinction between the separation of powers, the balance of powers, and the union of powers.[162]

The concept of "complex sovereignty" deserves special consideration since political life during the revolution and the Directory was dominated by an unprecedented battle between competing theories of sovereignty and political obligation. Many French political thinkers endorsed the idea of indivisible sovereignty, which rendered the concept of a mixed or divided sovereignty problematic. Necker participated in this debate, criticizing the theory that the legislative assembly was the unique (and reliable) interpreter of the general will of the nation. In so doing, he grappled with the specter of Rousseau, whose monist theory of sovereignty set the terms of subsequent debates by asserting that the will of the people could only be represented by a single and simple organ (a legislative body). Rousseau, who regarded plurality of interests as a synonym for disunion and factionalism, took issue with the theory of the balance of powers in part because he believed that "limited sovereignty" was a contradiction in terms and that sovereignty could never be divided in practice. A few decades before Sieyès criticized *le système des contrepoids*, Rousseau had rejected the system of checks and balances, claiming that such a system was incompatible with the indivisible sovereignty of the people. Consequently, Rousseau's theory of sovereignty amounted to a direct attack on the ideas of mixed and balanced constitutions, two concepts that loomed large in the writings of the Coppet group half a century later.

In *Réflexions philosophiques sur l'égalité*,[163] published as an appendix to *De la Révolution française* (1796), Necker rejected Rousseau's conceptual framework and provided a trenchant critique of the notions of the sovereignty of the people and undivided sovereignty. He described popular sovereignty as a monist concept incompatible with a "salutary balance between the different political powers"[164] in the state. The sovereignty of the people, Necker remarked, is an abstract ideal, "for there can never exist a perfect accordance of wills among the numerous individuals of whom a great nation is composed; the diversity of characters and of their interests opposes it."[165] If this diversity is ignored, any attempt to put popular sovereignty into practice is likely to lead to despotism or anarchy. In Necker's view, constitutions must acknowledge the existence of natural superiorities in society arising from different levels of wealth, knowledge, and education.[166] Comparing popular sovereignty to other concepts in circulation during the revolution, Necker criticized the French propensity for abstractions. Abstract ideas, he wrote, "impose upon us like phantoms, by their vague, confused, indeterminate forms; and it is thus the abstraction of liberty, the abstraction of equality, the abstraction of the sovereignty of the people, and the abstraction of the rights of man, that have captivated the homage and the faith of a credulous people."[167] Under the spell of these abstract theories, previous legislators subjected tribunals and assemblies to continual renewal procedures, rendered all authorities unstable and all powers temporary, and prepared "the arrival of despotism by the weakness of men and the confusion of things."[168]

Necker drew a seminal distinction between *le vœu de la nation*, the long-term and unchanging will of the nation, and *la volonté de la nation,* the transitory and ever changing will of the people. "A will without rule and without hold," he claimed, "is not less irreconcilable with the sovereignty than a will without instruction; but such is still the necessary character of the will of the people; they take its force and impetuosity for a constant movement, and yet this movement is never determined but by the passions. The multitude resemble the waves of the sea that always roll together, but change their direction with the first wind."[169] Because the nation's representatives express the changing will of the nation, they ought not to be taken as the infallible representatives of *le vœu de la nation*: "It is in their wishes and not in their wills that nations are constant, but their wills alone govern; their wills alone relate to the exercise of sovereignty; yet these two expressions, these two ideas, the wish and the will, become by their confusion a great source of error."[170] The wills of individuals, subject to the influence of fluctuating passions and momentary interests, are always in tension with one another, making it difficult to infer from them what the general interests of the nation might be. "The unanimity of wills and of enlightened wills, the constant unanimity, if it were possible, would represent, at least in appearance, the general interest," Necker wrote. "But in a political society, where all fortunes, where all situations are different, a mere superiority of suffrages cannot serve as a title for the indefinite exercise of the sovereignty, without the absolute overthrow of all principles of justice, principles anterior to the sovereignty itself, because it was for their preservation that that sovereignty was invented."[171]

By distinguishing between *vœu* and *volonté*, Necker sought to redefine the terms of the debate on equality, liberty, sovereignty, and limited power. To this effect, he denounced the mistake made by previous legislators who "inconsiderately placed liberty between two encroaching principles, the sovereignty of the people and absolute equality," and who " instead of giving support to that liberty which they appeared to cherish . . . have deprived it of its strength, and drained its sources of life."[172] Necker, who defined true equality as "equality of happiness" rather than political equality, also took to task the *philosophes* whose understanding of civil and political equality, he believed, was in opposition to morality, liberty, and public order and contradicted the nature of things and the order of nature.[173] Among the effects of (extreme) equality, Necker mentioned centralization, rivalry, restlessness, general uncertainty, vanity, incivility, fanaticism, rudeness, and the emergence of a "bellicose" spirit in society inimical to the development of arts, religion, and industry. The attempt to establish absolute (political) equality, he warned the levelers of his day, would inevitably lead to the reign of force and the tyranny of numbers. Under the reign of "absolute" equality, which fosters the centralization of power, public opinion can no longer fulfill its seminal role as a reformer of abuses, and a new form of despotism comes into being in the name of the people. Necker deplored the insufficient attention that the *philosophes* and the legislators had paid to examining the roots of political obedience and authority, a neglect that he believed had blinded them to the importance of the complex structure of ranks, orders, duties, and respect without which social order and public liberty cannot be properly preserved. Authority, he insisted, can neither be created merely through new laws, nor by placing power in the right hands. Rather, authority is the product of existing customs and mores and builds upon the lessons of experience rather than against them.

Starting from the premise that there can be no true liberty in a state if there is in its middle an unbalanced and unchecked authority, Necker endorsed the concept of *complex sovereignty*, thereby criticizing both the Jacobin and the ultraroyalist conceptions of sovereignty. "The sovereignty in a free country, in a wisely organized political society," he argued, "can never exist in a simple manner,"[174] and a mere majority may never serve as a justification for the unlimited exercise of sovereignty. In order for sovereignty to be limited, it must never be simple: "The sovereignty, not in its abstraction but in its reality, must be considered as a mixed idea, as a compound institution, and its primary elements are eternal reason and eternal justice."[175] It is worth noting here that Necker regarded reason and justice primarily as *moderating* principles, that is, as principles anterior to sovereignty. In his view, the vote of the deputies could not be regarded *a priori* as a definitive criterion of legitimacy:

> It is necessary to consult the perpetual representative of its interests, its rights and duties, and this perpetual representative, whose throne is built upon everlasting foundations, is no other than the unalterable justice. The sovereignty of the people in a kingdom consisting of twenty-six millions of souls is a perfect abstraction; for the innumerable wishes and sentiments of a master like this can never be known by the small number of persons appointed to be the interpreters of them. Under such a reign, therefore, every plan, every measure, every system, in whatever legal form it may be clothed, will be usurpation, if it does not bear the stamp of reason, justice, and sound policy.[176]

Accordingly, Necker praised the wisdom of those forms of government in which the institutionalization of complex sovereignty leads to a system of *intertwined* rather than separated powers. What he had in mind were those regimes (like the English constitutional monarchy) where "sometimes an hereditary chief, sometimes an elective chief, participate in that legislation, either by their concurrence, or by their sanction, or by their initiative."[177]

Necker's endorsement of complex sovereignty was an expression of his belief that we should be skeptical toward simple (moral and political) principles, since they cannot account for the complexity of our social and political world. The first principles guiding our reflections on morality and politics, he argued, "must be considered, not such as they are in their abstraction, but such as they come to us, such as they are modified amidst social institutions, and by the conflict of our interests and of our passions."[178] No simple theory could reduce the complexity and infinite diversity of our universe to basic units entirely accessible to reason. The view of the entire world, Necker claimed in a beautiful passage reminiscent of Pascal, can be clear only to the sight of the sovereign author of universal harmony, not to our intellect. We are destined to remain "spectators at the extremity of the most mysterious, the most complicated work, whose smallest parts exhaust, in some manner, our attention by their infinite diversity."[179]

Beyond the Separation of Powers: *L'entrelacement des pouvoirs*

Another major concept that Necker reformulated in his writings was the separation of powers as a key principle of representative government. The previous sections showed that Necker conceived of the role of the executive power in modern society and the necessary links between the legislative and the executive in a way that challenged the conventional interpretation of the separation of powers. If Necker did not advocate the *strict* version of this principle, did he believe that the latter ought to play no role whatsoever in the government of society? Did he, perhaps, endorse instead the related concept of the balance of powers, and if so, how did he account for the differences between a separation and a balance of powers?

As already mentioned, these two principles must be seen as distinct, the latter being only one of the forms in which separation can appear.[180] As a reader of Montesquieu, Necker was aware that his predecessor had emphasized the blending rather than the strict separation of powers, insisting that in moderate monarchies, both parliament and the king have a share in the exercise of the legislative and executive functions. In *Du pouvoir exécutif*, Necker granted the executive pride of place in the architecture of representative government, arguing for a simultaneously *strong* and *limited* executive power. Both Montesquieu and Necker shared a common admiration for the unwritten English constitution, though they understood differently some of its principles, most notably the participation of the monarch and his ministers in the exercise of the legislative function.[181]

Necker's argument can be divided into two basic parts. First, he challenged the view according to which the supreme power in a state is the legislative power, seen as the unique representative of the nation. The formation of the legislative power, Necker argued, is not a difficult practical issue and does not require "a precise rule, an exact conformity, from which it would be dangerous to depart."[182] The situation is entirely different in the case of the executive power, for this is the supreme power in a state, whose proper institutionalization constitutes "the essential and perhaps sole difficulty of every system of government."[183] A properly circumscribed executive power is essential to the constitution of a free state: "When it passes certain limits, this power is alarming to liberty, and may endanger the constitution itself; and when stripped of the prerogatives that compose its strength, it is incapable of fulfilling its important destination, and its place remains as it were vacant amidst the social edifice."[184] Therefore, Necker argued, special attention must be paid to ensuring the efficacy of this power by using "the most exact combinations, where all is proportion and every thing in equipoise."[185]

The second and, as Henri Grange has demonstrated,[186] the more important part of Necker's argument comprises his redefinition of two key concepts of our conventional political vocabulary: the executive and the legislative powers. In a well-constituted government, he argued, both are supposed to share in the exercise of the legislative and the executive *functions*. On this view, the executive power means *organe de gouvernement* (leadership), while legislative power is an *organe de contrôle* (supervision). The most significant implication of Necker's bold conceptual innovation was to replace the theory of the (strict) separation of powers with *l'entrelacement des pouvoirs*, loosely translated as the "intertwining of powers." In practice, this called for the existence of effective links between the executive and the legislative. In the absence of such links, Necker maintained, "all would be contest and confusion"[187] and mistrust and suspicion would dominate the political scene.

It was within the larger framework of *l'entrelacement des pouvoirs* that Necker interpreted the classical doctrine of the separation of powers. His fundamental premise was that it would be impossible to establish effective cooperation between different powers solely through the exercise of constant watchfulness and mutual distrust:

> The powers of which a government is composed, powers *intermixed* in various ways, and the exercise of which devolves on men subject to frailties and passions, are not to be retained in their place but by means of reciprocal relations nicely graduated. Were we to discard these principles of *union*, and substitute laws of equilibrium in their stead, it would be necessary, if I may so express myself, to place a sentinel on the confines of every vanity, every sort of self-love, every individual ambition.[188]

In Necker's view, harmonious links between powers were essential to creating a sound and balanced constitution, because these ties make possible dialogue and cooperation. When such links are absent or weak, contest and confusion prevail and the members of the legislative power lack the knowledge of details necessary to drafting good laws. "They are *ties* then, not counterpoises, *proportions* not distances, fitnesses (*convenances*) not vigilance, which most contribute to the *harmony* of government," Necker argued; "and the reason that we are continually calling the attention of legislators to the necessity of balancing one power by another, and not to the advantage of *blending* them by judicious and natural means is, that in moral ideas, as in physical objects, the transitions and shadings escape us, while contrasts attract instant observation and never fail to impress us."[189] In conclusion, Necker recommended that the executive be granted both the right of legislative initiative and sanction.

The need for intertwined powers was demonstrated by the success of two concrete examples to which Necker drew attention: the effective sharing of the legislative function between the executive and legislative bodies in England and the United States. Across the Channel, Necker noted, the king's ministers were almost always *de facto* members of the parliament (mainly the House of Commons) and played an important role in parliamentary deliberations by contributing their knowledge of affairs and their judgment of circumstances. The presence of ministers in the two chambers, he insisted, did not infringe upon the "separation" that ought to be maintained between the legislative and executive *functions*. According to Necker,

> Nothing less is necessary [to liberty] than the perpetual presence of ministers in parliament, their capacity of representatives, and their personal merits, to the creation of that perfect and harmonious sympathy between the executive and the legislative powers, which is indispensable to the health of the state. . . . The veritable participation of the executive power in legislation does not properly consist in the constitutional necessity that the monarch should execute the acts of his parliament, but in the intervention of ministers in the deliberations which precede these laws.[190]

The ministers' participation in the exercise of the legislative function made the exercise of the royal veto unnecessary in practice, for the bills presented to the king had previously benefitted from the advice and knowledge of his ministers.

A similar situation, Necker remarked, could be found in the United States, where the executive power had close ties with the legislative. Necker called upon French legislators to study the principles of the U.S. Constitution.[191] The Americans, he argued, grasped that "legislation and execution must be kept separate, but in spirit they must be blended with each other."[192] On the one hand, they refused to make of the executive power the blind agent of the (will of the) legislature; on the other hand, they realized that it would be a great mistake to imagine that, in order to secure the cooperation between the executive and the legislative powers, it would be sufficient to hold the ministers politically accountable. Moreover, the founding fathers of the U.S. Constitution understood that they could not simply rely on the good intentions of the government, and that the members of the executive power must comprehend and identify with the laws whose execution is entrusted to them.

At first sight, Necker's argument in favor of the "union of powers" might appear as a departure from—or even an attack upon—the classical principles of constitutionalism. Appearances notwithstanding, it would be inaccurate to conclude that, because he defended the intertwining of powers, Necker was a critic of constitutionalism and an opponent of limited power and divided sovereignty. In fact, nothing would be farther from the truth. If Necker defended the intertwining of powers, it was because he thought that *l'entrelacement des pouvoirs* properly conceived was the essential condition of liberty in a modern representative state. The key idea at the heart of his political philosophy—to which he always remained faithful—was that there is no real freedom if there exists in the state an authority without counterpoise. Moreover, in order for powers to be effectively limited, they must have proper means both of acting in concert and of being able to hold each other in check. A few years later, Necker reiterated this point when making a renewed case for a constitutional framework in which powers would exercise mutual circumspection and effective vigilance over one another. "We ought, therefore, to endeavour to establish a constitutional alliance between the executive and legislative powers," he wrote; "we ought to consider that their *prudent association*, their *artful intertwining*, will always be the best security for mutual circumspection and efficacious vigilance."[193] In his view, the executive power must have effective (if limited) means of proposing and participating in the drafting of laws, which ought to remain the supreme prerogative of the legislative.

Necker's constitutionalism based on the artful intertwining of powers prevailed neither in 1795 nor in 1799, when the French took a different course of action. Furthermore, in spite of the moderate nature of the Charter of 1814, his ideas had little influence upon its authors, who looked across the Channel for a model. Yet, Necker's constitutional vision did not disappear altogether. Four decades later, it inspired another member of the Coppet group, Sismondi, who, in a chapter of *Études sur les constitutions des peuples libres* (1836; 2nd ed. 1839) presented his own version of the "union" of powers. Without insisting as much as Necker did on the preeminence of the executive power, Sismondi affirmed a viewpoint that had strong affinities with his predecessor's:

> It is not true, as it has often been said, that liberty consists in an equilibrium of powers assuring every power a degree of resistance equal to the action of others. The consequence of such a tempering (*pondération*) of powers would be absolute immobility. The machine must properly function. . . . It does not need the separation of powers, but their cooperation toward the same goal; it does not need the balance of forces but their union. Finally, it is necessary that a single will results from the friction and fusion of diverse wills, but in such a way that all these wills have been taken into account, all interests consulted, and all causes presented.[194]

The idea that the constitution must create the conditions for cooperation among powers and should avoid their strict separation was Necker's legacy and its articulation by Sismondi a testimony to the enduring appeal of Necker's political philosophy.

The Failure of Virtuous Moderation?

Composed at different stages of the revolution, Necker's works articulated a courageous and complex political agenda revolving around the idea of moderation in opposition to arbitrary power and violence.[195] More so than any other thinker studied in these pages, Necker illustrates all four of the meta-narratives that constitute the core of the present book: the twofold nature of moderation as character trait and as embodied in a comprehensive institutional-constitutional framework; the affinity between political moderation and institutional/constitutional complexity; moderation as "trimming" between extremes; and the eclecticism of moderation. In addition to all this, Necker's writings also shed light on an additional dimension of moderation that has not yet been emphasized: namely, the connection between political moderation and religion.

If Necker's moderation owed much to his long experience as a banker and to his personal temperament, it also had deep roots in his religious and moral views, which are fundamental for understanding his political thought. As he himself acknowledged in 1791, "I cannot separate my cause from that of reason and virtue."[196] Commenting on Necker's life and works, both Mme de Staël and Auguste de Staël emphasized the unity of his thought along with the centrality of morality and religion to his political views.[197] Religion, Auguste de Staël wrote, was the true center of his grandfather's life and politics. "What characterized his spirit," his daughter wrote, "was the art of finding resources in almost all difficult situations, and his character had this rare reunion of prudence and activity which provides for everything without jeopardizing anything."[198] Necker's religious views played a key role in this regard.

Necker's agenda is so interesting for us today because he effortlessly combined liberal principles (accompanied by a dose of skepticism toward the effects of political equality) with a coherent religious vision of the world that respected the liberty and equality of individuals. In the preface to *De l'importance des opinions religieuses* (1788),[199] a work that had obvious affinities with the Scottish Enlightenment, Necker posited a close relationship between administration, politics, and religion, affirming that the prosperity of modern states depends on the harmonious alliance between the administration of worldly affairs and a judicious commitment to moderation. Rejecting at the same time both the dogmatic rigidity of religious inquisitors and the superficiality of those "inconsiderate philosophers" who refused to grant religion any role in society, Necker argued that "one must seek to carve out a path among these extreme feelings and in the middle of these equally dangerous differences."[200] The social utility of religion derives from the fact that it "completes in a certain way the imperfect work of legislation"[201] by complementing the insufficient means at the disposal of government. Necker distinguished between religion in the service of justice and liberty and religion as a rampart for despotism.[202] Statesmen, he argued, must meditate on and take their cue from "morality fortified by religion,"[203] because the latter is a constant reminder of our imperfection and human limits and promotes moderation and self-restraint, two virtues indispensable in politics.

I mentioned at the outset that Necker's writings and politics were never an object of indifference among his contemporaries. Some like Mounier praised his moderation, probity, and dedication to liberty and applauded his qualities as an administrator, while others criticized Necker's combination of realism with idealism. Sieyès is reported to have described him as the only man capable of combining the rigor of a banker with the imagination of a poet (hardly a compliment in Sieyès' view).[204] Finally, Roederer, who admired Necker's moderation, thought that his political and historical writings were not easy to read because Necker mixed historical and theoretical considerations with attempts to justify his personal conduct during the revolution, thus making it difficult to distinguish polemical from impartial observations. "In administration," Roederer claimed, "Necker relates everything to reality; in politics, everything to illusions."[205]

To paraphrase a claim once made by Hume,[206] Necker was always more fond of promoting moderation than zeal, and he understood that the best way of producing moderation in every party was to increase zeal for the public welfare. Interested first and foremost in governability, he conscientiously assumed "the role of a political practitioner preoccupied with the problems of the means of government as opposed to actors obsessed with the problems of principles."[207] Necker respected the demands of public opinion and treated political issues not in an abstract manner, but always in keeping with the demands of morality and pragmatism. As his daughter remarked, in this, as almost on every other point during his career, Necker observed a medium and acted like a moderate.[208] He assumed his role as mediator between parties fully aware of the countless challenges he faced, and he viewed himself as a *trimmer* seeking to keep the ship of the state on an even keel:

> It was in openly resisting the usurpations of the National Assembly, or in disputing against its errors, that I singularly and unceasingly exposed that popularity so eagerly sought after by others. Thus also, in all my memorials to the National Assembly, and at the certain risk of incurring its displeasure, I continued to recall its attention to the importance of the executive power, and to the danger to which it was exposing public order, in neglecting to invest the mon-

arch with the prerogatives necessary to his authority. . . . Thus also, speaking in the name of the Prince, and defending a forsaken cause, I reclaimed the justice of the National Assembly in favour of the ecclesiastics robbed of their estates, and the proprietors of every kind, who had become victims to the depredations and violence which the public authority was unable to repress.[209]

As a trimmer, Necker found himself isolated (in 1789) between two prominent political forces—the National Assembly and the Court—which proved to be anything but moderate. He described them as two superior orders which, burdened by their prejudices, had remained too much behind the times. The impetuous assembly, Necker claimed, "addressed its compositions and thoughts to an imaginary posterity," while the Court, dominated by nostalgia and fear, became "wavering and unsteady." In this context, Necker went on, he fulfilled "a difficult duty, if not skillfully, if not with success, yet at least as an honest man committed to liberty as a moral (and religious) imperative. But being always in the center of events, and appearing to influence them, it has been easier to impute to me those very errors and faults against which I have exerted myself the most."[210]

As Marcel Gauchet once noted, Necker the trimmer has never recovered from a twofold charge of inconsistency: "He is accused by some of unwittingly wrecking the monarchical tradition, by others of irresolutely defending a lost cause."[211] To be sure, in spite of his principled trimming in favor of liberty and his strong commitment to morality and religion, Necker was criticized for his (sometimes) excessive scrupulousness in fulfilling his duties as a politician and for carefully cultivating his image as an upright public man. Pointing to Necker's alleged pedantry of virtue, as demonstrated by the lengthy defense of his actions made in *Sur l'administration de M. Necker*, some of Necker's critics compared his strict (and sometimes defiant) adherence to the principles of morality to the stern and inflexible attitude of Cato in ancient Rome. Necker, they claimed, expected too much from the ascendancy of morality and did not understand the "logic of passions"[212] that characterized his times and to which he should have adapted his actions.

Although he understood the influence of destructive passions in politics, Necker seems to have lacked the means to effectively confront the dark side of politics; nor was he able to effectively combat the influence of factions, an inability perhaps related to his propensity toward moderation. Because he lacked Mirabeau's talent for manipulating the people, that "tribune by calculation, patrician by taste, and always immoral,"[213] Necker did not form or lead a great party, being excessively cautious and inclined to hesitation and too susceptible to self-reproach, traits both Mme de Staël and Malouet remarked.[214] Others alleged that he may have been "radically insensitive to what was profound in the aspiration to equality,"[215] being overly critical of political equality and too blind to the demands put forward by its defenders. Still others like Constant thought that Necker, who never fully shed his technocratic Colbertist proclivities, may had been overly confident in the authority of the executive power, maintaining to the very end the tone of the former minister of Louis XVI, preoccupied above all with governability and governing techniques rather than with the preservation of individual rights and liberties. Finally, some of his harshest critics like Ginguené accused Necker of lacking political realism and failing to understand the legitimacy of republican ideals.

If Necker's trimming agenda might be described as lukewarm and hesitant, it is also true that he had the courage to swim against the current when his proposals or actions were out of sync with his times. "Even during the reign of the first National Assembly," Necker recalled, "I dared to develop its faults, and the imperfections of its work. During the threatening empire of a blind fanaticism, I dared attack the favorite system of equality, and point out afresh the sacrifices that reason and morality demanded of liberty; at a time when all the existing authorities, together with all the passions, appeared to have conspired the destruction of the most unfortunate of princes, I appeared the foremost in the band of his defenders."[216] Being a moderate by nature, he understood the difficulty of holding a middle course in a climate of intransigence and radicalism in which extremist views thrive, using ignorance, fear, and force as means to power.

It is therefore fitting that we give Necker the last word in explaining the kind of moderation to which he was committed, "this virtue of the heart and mind [which] will never be united with ignorance."[217] Fully aware that it takes courage to remain loyal to moderate opinions when passions are running high and people are prone to various forms of enthusiasm, Necker viewed his entire political career as illustrating

> . . . the persecutions to which a spirit of moderation exposes public characters in times of trouble and agitation. They find themselves surrounded by party rage without being in favour with any side, and have for them only the uncertain chance of the justice of posterity, or the low, and trembling voice of the honest men of their age. They are struck by all the crossing hands, and as they are passed by the accelerated march of the passions, as they are left behind by new ideas and modern systems, they fall into disrespect, and their character is accused of feebleness.[218]

Moderation, Necker believed, always demands a special kind of courage and nobility, which are the marks of those who are firm enough to remain faithful to moderate ideas and principles when everyone around them is willing to abandon them.[219] The next chapters will continue presenting their story by focusing on two of Necker's main disciples, Mme de Staël and Benjamin Constant.

FIVE
MODERATION AFTER THE TERROR
Madame de Staël's Elusive Center

Le temps, la sagesse, la modération, voilà les seuls moyens avec
lesquels on peut fonder la justice et l'humanité.
        —Mme de Staël

In a text written during the Directory, as France was trying to come to terms
with the legacy of the Terror, Mme de Staël claimed: "Time, wisdom, moderation: these are the only means with which one can found justice and humanity."[1] While France badly needed moderation to return to a minimal
sense of normalcy, this virtue proved out of reach for Mme de Staël's generation, engaged in a prolonged struggle to constitutionalize the liberties of
1789 and end the long revolutionary cycle that had begun with the fall of
the Bastille. Resigned, she came to acknowledge that, during revolutionary
periods, "one needs fanaticism to win, and a moderate party will never inspire fanaticism."[2]

Mme de Staël's works and personal trajectory constitute a particularly interesting case study for the student of moderation.[3] A Protestant in a predominantly Catholic country, a woman with major literary and political ambitions, this *dame célèbre* elicited both strong admiration and powerful
contestation from her critics and rivals. Whether described as the spoiled
daughter of a rich man, as an ambitious and vindictive woman, as a high-
class *conspiratrice* attempting to bring to power her friends, or as a disguised
friend of the aristocrats conspiring against the revolution, Mme de Staël was
never an object of indifference. Her reputation was such that in 1814 she
was regarded in many powerful circles as one of the three great independent
powers in Europe, along with England and Russia.[4] Rivarol, no stranger to
irony, once wryly remarked that she had more *esprit* than talent,[5] while
Byron is reported to have said of Necker's daughter: "I never go near her—
her books are very delightful, but in society I see nothing but a very plain
woman forcing one to listen and look at her with her pen behind her and her
mouth full of ink."[6] Others, like Rosalie Constant, were not reluctant to acknowledge Mme de Staël's irresistible charm: "One is swept along, subju-
gated by the force of her genius. It follows a new path; it is a fire which lights
the way, which sometimes blinds you but which cannot leave you cold or
indifferent."[7] Her cousin, Benjamin Constant, agreed: "No volcano in the
world blazes as much as she does,"[8] he wrote in his diary. And what a volcano she was indeed!

Mme de Staël's intense personal life that blended love and politics in an
original way accounts for the high prestige she enjoyed throughout her en-

tire life. A Romantic of soul, she felt compelled to write in order to fight against her inner restlessness and to understand man's spiritual existence on Earth. In her unfinished book on the role of the passions, she confessed: "I have written to find myself, through so many sorrows, to free my faculties from the slavery of feelings, to elevate myself to a kind of abstraction that will let me observe the pain of my soul, to examine in my own impressions the movements of social nature, and to generalize the experience provided by thought."[9] One of the last masters of the art of conversation, Mme de Staël was also "*une grande salonnière*,"[10] the heir to a long French tradition of *civilité* whose apprenticeship she made in the Parisian salon of her mother. "Nature," she once said, "has made me for conversation. . . . For me, to talk about politics is to be alive."[11] Although she never occupied any political position in her entire life (women were not allowed then to play a political role in those days), Mme de Staël's intense social and political activism, along with her books and her unique talent for conversation, made her a political force *sui generis* with which everyone had to reckon. If she felt herself condemned to celebrity without being really understood, she managed to turn that social handicap of her gender into an invaluable asset, becoming one of the first (non-aristocratic) women whose voice was listened to and respected at the principal courts of Europe.[12]

The vagaries of French politics condemned Mme de Staël to a life of constant movement and uncertainty, marked by periods of exile and persecution. She was a suspect in the eyes of three regimes, having left France in early 1793, just in time to avoid the Terror. The republican regime during the Thermidor and the first years of the Directory also viewed her with skepticism and monitored her movements. (She had to fight to have her French citizenship officially recognized in 1795–96.) In 1797, she cofounded with Benjamin Constant the Constitutional Circle (also known as the "Club de Salm") as an alternative to the influential ultraroyalist Club de Clichy. She eventually became one of the most vocal critics of Napoleon, with her salon at Coppet serving as a major center of opposition to the First Consul. The price she paid for her bold opposition was far from insignificant: ten years of exile in Switzerland, Russia, and England that took a high toll on her health. As the latter began to decline in late 1816, Mme de Staël had the opportunity to reflect one more time on her prodigious life and achievements. In a letter to Chateaubriand from this period, she confessed: "I have always been the same: lively but sad. I love God, my father, and liberty."[13]

Her untimely death in Paris on July 14, 1817, at the age of fifty-one, cut short a remarkable life and a unique mind. "It is a great loss for the world," her friend Sismondi remarked upon learning of Mme de Staël's passing away. "Her talent would have taken a new form. . . . She could have lived another thirty years, and during this time she might have enriched the world with something that no one else would ever be able to offer."[14] In addition to her unflinching commitment to liberty, there were a few related themes that defined her political outlook: her opposition to despotism and arbitrary power and her defense of representative government.[15] Above all, Madame de Staël's biography and works reveal a strong and sustained commitment to political moderation. In her view, moderation was essential to the pursuit of happiness, defined as "the union of all contrary things."[16] It was, to be sure, a particular form of moderation, inseparable from her passion for ideas, her romantic thirst for adventures and glory, and her defense of enthusiasm in the service of liberty.[17]

Was the Revolution of 1789 Inevitable?

It is possible to grasp the magnitude and complexity of the political challenges faced by a liberal-minded thinker such as Mme de Staël by examining the debates on the origins, nature, and legacy of the French Revolution to which she contributed. The intensity of these debates can be explained by the highly fragmented political and intellectual scene after 1795. While reopening the controversy over the legitimacy of the principles of 1789, the French had to come to terms with the violent episodes of the revolution and had to decide whether the fall of the Old Regime had been inevitable, or whether *l'ancien régime* could have been reformed by peaceful means.

Not surprisingly, many historical writings of the period display a high degree of political partisanship. Historians and politicians of all persuasions turned to Clio in order to find proofs and arguments in favor of or against the legitimacy of the principles of 1789 and to explain the causes of the Terror of 1793–94. Liberals insisted that the opening episodes of the revolution should be seen neither as a prelude to the Terror, nor as a complete break with the feudal past, but as the inevitable outcome of past factors and trends. As Susan Tenenbaum remarked, "by identifying the 'true' revolution as a period of moderation, the liberals might have left unclear what accounted for its classification as a revolution."[18] The liberal catechism, based on a selective reading of the past, which insisted on discontinuities or long-term social, cultural, and political patterns, was memorably captured by Mme de Staël in her claim that in France liberty was ancient and despotism modern.[19] French liberals shared two other things: they defended the principles of representative government (either as constitutional monarchy or republic) and admired the English model for its harmonious synthesis between order and liberty.

Mme de Staël's political writings—in particular, *Des circonstances actuelles qui peuvent terminer la Révolution et des principes qui doivent fonder la République en France* and *Considérations sur les principaux événements de la Révolution française*—contributed to this rich and intense historical debate. "Who can be alive at this time," she once wrote, "who can write, without feeling and thinking about the French Revolution?"[20] She endorsed the attempts of the French nation to improve its system of national representation and approved of the right of the Third Estate to be properly represented on the political scene in 1789. At the same time, she emphasized the French Revolution's debt to the past and its continuity with the entire course of the nation's history.

The *longue durée* of Mme de Staël's perspective is evident from the very first page of *Considérations* in striking contrast to the approach of another political moderate, Edmund Burke, for whom the French Revolution was the result of accidental forces that brought forth the sudden collapse of the Old Regime in 1789. Burke denied that the events of 1789 were inevitable and believed that the institutions of the Old Regime could have been reformed if another path had been chosen. Mme de Staël disagreed. The French Revolution, she argued, was *not* the outcome of accidental forces, as some of its critics argued. On the contrary, "the Revolution of France is one of the grand eras of social order. Those who consider it as the result of accidental causes have reflected neither on the past nor on the future; they have mistaken the actors for the drama; and, in seeking a solution agreeable to their prejudices, have attributed to the men of the day that which had been in a course of preparation for ages."[21] By espousing this long-term perspective, Staël's analysis anticipated Tocqueville's meticulously researched diagnosis of the internal crisis of the Old Regime. After highlighting the lack of public spirit and the absence of a genuine constitution prior to 1789, she claimed that the revolution was an irreversible phenomenon that arose in response to the deep structural problems, which impaired the functioning of the institutions of the Old Regime. Although she stopped short of claiming, like Tocqueville, that the real revolution had actually occurred *prior* to 1789, Mme de Staël's account gives the reader a strong sense of the inevitability of the events of that year, though without endorsing a deterministic view of history.

As Benjamin Constant pointed out,[22] this long-term view enabled Mme de Staël to argue that the true authors of the French Revolution were not the actors who suddenly appeared on the political scene in the spring and summer of 1789. They were only the revolution's instruments. The real actors and causes were those that had furthered the decline of the Old Regime to the point that it ultimately became impossible to reform its institutions by peaceful means. On this view, the true "authors" of the revolution were Cardinal de Richelieu and his tyrannical government; Mazarin and his ruses, which discredited authority; and Louis XIV, whose prodigality, along with his politics of intolerance, had ruined the country. Accordingly, the true causes of the revolution were the growth of royal absolutism and arbitrary power, as well as the arrogance of the nobles whose main concern was the defense of their privileges at all costs.[23]

Hence, far from being fortuitous, the fall of the Old Regime in 1789 had, in fact, been inevitable, the outcome of a long historical evolution that could not have been blocked or delayed by the efforts of a few individuals. Moreover, Mme de Staël argued, the events of 1789 were also consonant with the overall development of European civilization,[24] representing the culmination of an evolution that spanned three eras: the feudal age, the age of despotism, and the age of representative government. The same social and political forces that had brought about the two revolutions of 1648 and 1688 in England were also prime causes of the revolutionary wave that swept France a century later: "Both belong to the third era in the progress of social order—the establishment of representative government."[25]

These ideas loomed large in the first part of Mme de Staël's *Considérations,* where she reflected on the state of public opinion in France at the accession of Louis XVI and discussed Necker's plans for finance and administration. In an important chapter (XI) of book 1, she claimed that, because France lacked a real constitution, it was deprived of the possibility of having a moderate government.[26] Of all modern monarchies, Mme de Staël opined, "France was certainly the one whose political institutions were most arbitrary and fluctuating."[27] Like her father, she was interested in the ambiguous relationship between royal power, the Estates-General, and the *parlements,* and partly shared Necker's skepticism that the latter, as intermediary bodies, would be capable of curbing the power of the monarch. Noting that the privileges of these bodies were undefined, she remarked that "the king was at one time kept in tutelage by them, and they, at another, were trampled underfoot by the king."[28] Although the *parlements* invoked from time to time the "fundamental laws of the state" and asserted their right to "register" the laws after they had been "verified," they were never able to impose effective limits on royal authority. The absolute power of the king (*Si veut le roi, si veut la loi*) was incompatible with the principles of moderate government.

Therefore, on the eve of the revolution, according to Mme de Staël, France was a country with no fixed political principles existed, where the elites were absorbed in the pursuit of power under the domineering effect of vanity and arrogance, and laws counted for very little. "France," she wrote, "has been governed by custom, often by caprice, and never by law. . . . The course of circumstances alone was decisive of what everyone called his right."[29] It is revealing that Mme de Staël listed a long series of royal abuses to buttress her claim, including arbitrary imprisonments, ordinances, banishments, special commissions, and *lits de justice.* In her view, the history of France was replete with attempts on the part of the nation and the nobles to obtain rights and privileges, while the kings aimed at enlarging their prerogatives and consolidating their absolute power. "Who can deny," she concluded, "that a change was necessary, either to give a free course to a constitution hitherto perpetually infringed; or to introduce those securities, which might give the laws of the state the means of being maintained and obeyed?"[30]

Consequently, in her view, the events of the summer of 1789 were justified insofar as the deputies sought to put an end to arbitrary power and eliminate a social structure based on obsolete and illegitimate privileges. Nonetheless, while the revolution as an adjustment of political institutions to the new social order might have been inevitable, the actual course taken by events was not. According to Mme de Staël, the explanation for all these missed opportunities in the spring and early summer of 1789 must be sought in the peculiar social condition of France, a country in which there was at the time a marked discrepancy between its political institutions and its social condition. Shortsightedness, stubbornness, self-interest poorly understood, and the lack of political experience prevented the political elites from making the necessary concessions, such as giving up their fiscal privileges or recognizing the importance of bicameralism as a pillar of liberty.[31]

In this regard, there was a great difference between France and England, the country of moderation *par excellence*. Across the Channel, Mme de Staël argued, on all political principles public opinion was in harmony with the constitution and the political institutions of the country. In France, no such concord existed, which made the success of moderate ideas virtually impossible in a nation where the political elites and citizens lacked genuine political experience. The republic arrived too early, for there was in France no set of republican principles and mores to guide the functioning of republican institutions. Public opinion alone, drawing on an abstract knowledge of politics taught by books, was not a sufficient substitute for missing political institutions.[32] What followed was a tragic reminder of the consequences of immoderation in politics.

The Constituent Assembly and the Constitution of 1791

As already noted, nowhere were these missed opportunities and immoderate decisions more obvious than in the Constituent Assembly. Although the first two years of the revolution were marked by intense political conflict, social and political life had a particular charm which Mme de Staël evoked in a short chapter in book 2 of her *Considérations*. She fondly recalled the brilliance of French society during that period when the promise of liberty came to be united with the communication of superior minds and the elegance of aristocratic mores:

> Never was that society at once so brilliant and serious as during the first three or four years of the Revolution, reckoning from 1788 to the end of 1791. As political affairs were still in the hands of the higher classes, all the vigor of liberty and all the grace of former politeness were united in the same persons. . . . And the highest questions to which social order ever gave rise were treated by minds the most capable of understanding and discussing them.[33]

Liberty of speech allowed gifted orators to freely express their views at the tribune and answer the challenges of equally brilliant colleagues. The time of the scaffolds had not yet arrived.

Not surprisingly, Mme de Staël's account of the Constituent Assembly was more positive than Burke's, which dwelt upon the immoderation, excesses, and limitations of the French deputies. Unlike Burke, Mme de Staël thought that the achievements of the assembly ultimately outweighed its shortcomings in light of the abuses it abolished and the institutions it created. "We are indebted to the Constituent Assembly for the suppression of the privileged castes in France, and for civil liberty to all,"[34] she wrote. It was the Constituent Assembly that effaced ancient and pernicious barriers between classes, rendered taxes uniform, and proclaimed complete freedom of worship. It modernized the administration of the country by dividing it into eighty-three departments that removed ancient separations and established provincial assemblies, thus lessening the influence of the capital over local matters. Moreover, the Constitution of 1791 provided for an unprecedented extension of the practice of popular election of local officials.[35] The deputies also reformed criminal jurisprudence by abolishing torture and other judicial barbarities, creating the institution of juries, and depriving the *prevôtal* courts of some of their powers. By removing artificial and burdensome restraints on industry and suppressing the unfair advantages of older corporations and wardenships, they fostered the spirit of enterprise, spreading new life, energy, and knowledge into the provinces.[36]

At the same time, in spite of the many wrongs that the Constituent Assembly righted, the deputies committed serious errors when it came to building new institutions on the ruins of the Old Regime. In the footsteps of her father, Mme de Staël criticized the assembly for having displayed an immoderate "philosophic enthusiasm," proceeding, in part, from its excessive reliance on the example of the American constitution. She also took the deputies to task for ignoring the lessons of the English constitution, which emerged in the last part of her book as the model that could have saved France from ruin. The Constituent Assembly, Mme de Staël remarked, proceeded with too much precipitation and immoderation in its plans of reform: "A mania of vanity, something like that of a man of letters, prompted the French to innovate in this respect; they had all the fastidious apprehension of an author who refuses to borrow either character or situations from existing works."[37]

Drawing upon Necker's critique, Mme de Staël faulted the assembly for paying insufficient attention to the organization of the executive power, for failing to see in it an indispensable safeguard of liberty. By drafting the constitution as a treaty between two rival parties rather than as a work based on a necessary compromise between various social and political interests, the Constituent Assembly "formed a constitution as a general would form a plan of attack"[38] and thus failed to establish a sound balance of powers. All the subsequent mischief proceeded from the decision of the deputies to preserve monarchy while stripping the king of his royal prerogatives necessary for properly fulfilling his duties. They were wrong to make of the king a public functionary absolutely dependent on an all-powerful assembly. They should have fully acknowledged that in a constitutional monarchy, the monarch is one of the independent powers in the state and must have a share in the sanction of the laws. Moreover, a single chamber with almost unlimited authority was wholly incompatible with the principles of moderate government; the deputies' preference for monocameralism had delayed the creation of an effective system of checks and balances such as might have limited the power of the legislature.

Of particular interest is Mme de Staël's description of the balance of power within the assembly and of the differences of opinion between and within different groups, two topics which she first addressed in a 1791 essay, *A quels signes peut-on connaître quelle est l'opinion de la majorité de la nation?* In this early defense of constitutional monarchy, she attempted to bring moderate republicans and moderate royalists closer by pointing to the overlap between their fundamental political principles. Her essay ended on a hopeful note, drawing attention to the prospects for moderation in revolutionary times, which, she remarked, depended on "the coalition between reason and conscience."[39] In order to succeed, moderation needed two strong parties that would defend their agendas with courage and determination. Most of the divisions within the Constituent Assembly, she added, were founded not on questions of principle, but on personal interests and rivalries, which fueled a rhetoric of intransigence and prevented various groups in the assembly from making reasonable compromises and concessions in due time.

The general inflexibility of the deputies and the mutual distrust between them account for the precarious position of moderates within the assembly. It was the aristocrats' strong misgivings about constitutional moderates that led them to join hands with radicals in rejecting moderate proposals (such as bicameralism) in the hope of "obtaining good by the excess of the evil."[40] If a single chamber were adopted it would, they hoped, discredit the work of the assembly and prepare the way for an eventual return to the old order of things. As for the popular party, Mme de Staël noted that it was divided into four groups, with the Mountain forming the fourth party. Those leaders of the left side of the assembly who were not altogether hostile to the preservation of monarchy, were nonetheless unwilling to ally themselves with moderates such as Mounier and Necker, because they did not want to play a subordinate role in the course of events. Thus, Mme de Staël claimed, "they carried all the foppery of a court into the cause of democracy"[41] and sought to gain ascendancy in the assembly by attacking or ridiculing the moderates, "as if moderation were weakness, and they the only men of energy."[42]

Their partisan and uncompromising spirit came to the fore during the debates on the royal veto. Those for whom the very word "absolute" veto amounted to a blank check handed to royal despotism referred to the veto in the streets of Paris "as of a monster that would devour little children."[43] Overconfident in their influence within the assembly, Sieyès and his supporters thought themselves capable of restoring the authority of the throne, only to discover later that they had undermined it through their previous actions. "How many distresses would have been saved to France," Mme de Staël exclaimed, "if this party of young men had united its forces with the moderates!"[44] Constitutional monarchy could have survived in France and the country might have been spared the Terror if all the friends of freedom had rallied round the party that was the "least bad" among their adversaries, even though the principles of that party were still remote from their own views.[45]

These tensions and contradictions, Mme de Staël insisted, became visible in the text of the Constitution of 1791 that united a great deal of knowledge with many errors, all of which were attributable (in her view) to the lack of moderation displayed by the leaders of all parties. Swayed by a passion for abstract ideas, the assembly came to be entirely dominated by rumors and fears of conspiracy. The deputies constantly tried to second guess the king's thoughts and plans in order to ascertain if he was truly resigned to the restraints imposed upon him by the new political context. This climate of distrust made the passing of salutary articles (such as bicameralism) virtually impossible. Many deputies described bicameralism as a conspiracy against the sovereign will and interests of the nation, while deputies who otherwise were inclined toward two chambers became alarmed at being called "aristocrats" and being branded enemies of the people. The deputies also refused to grant the king the right to dissolve the legislative body; they made the revision of the constitution extremely cumbersome, and adopted a decree forbidding the deputies from being elected to the subsequent legislative assembly.[46] Last but not least, the voluntary decision of many nobles to leave the country rendered constitutional monarchy impracticable in the absence of a strong and viable aristocratic intermediary body.[47] The road to Jacobin dictatorship was thus open at the very moment when people were celebrating in the streets the ratification of a constitution that had made the king and a long chapter of French history virtually irrelevant.

The Anatomy of Political Fanaticism

An abyss separates this early period of the revolution from its later stages, especially from the Reign of Terror.[48] How is one to account for the fourteen months that followed the proscription of the Girondists on May 31, 1793, how explain the rise of Robespierre and Danton to absolute power?

Of all political passions, Mme de Staël argued, it was fanaticism and the passion for equality, "the subterraneous volcano of France,"[49] that came to dominate and transform the French political scene beginning in the second half of 1792. The link between the two was not accidental and Mme de Staël dwelt upon it in *Des circonstances actuelles*, describing fanaticism as the antonym of moderation. A few years later, she also drew a famous distinction between fanaticism and enthusiasm in *De l'Allemagne*, whose final chapter described enthusiasm as an elevated and powerful passion, qualitatively different from *Schwärmerei* and blind fanaticism.[50] Enthusiasm, she argued, allows us to elevate ourselves above the level of utilitarian activities by giving us the opportunity to pursue the truth disinterestedly, to contemplate the beautiful, the good, and the noble things in life as ends in themselves, without being distracted by their practical aspects.

In *Considérations*, Mme de Staël devoted only a surprisingly short five-page chapter to the Terror, preferring instead "to take a philosophical view of events"[51] (she discussed political fanaticism in another separate chapter). She identified fanaticism as the main cause of the Terror and claimed that *l'esprit de parti* taken to extremes and a faith in abstract ideas were at the root of political fanaticism and intolerance.[52] The analysis of fanaticism and the other factors responsible for the Terror occupied a rather small space in *Considérations*, but they loomed large in Mme de Staël's earlier political works. If in her book on passions written in 1796, she had referred to the Terror as a historical "anomaly" produced by fortuitous and unique circumstances,[53] two years later she espoused a different approach. She still rejected the notion that the Terror was the inevitable outcome of the principles of 1789, but she was now prepared to argue that the Terror followed a more systematic and calculated plan of destruction than previously admitted, a view which she restated in *Considérations*. Mme de Staël noted that the Committee of Public Safety did not rule alone but in conjunction with other powerful state institutions, such as the Committee of General Security (which controlled the police) and the *Commune insurectionnelle* of Paris (which held military power after the fall of the monarchy on August 10, 1792). Although the direction of affairs, with the exception of the conduct of the war, was at this time nothing else than "a mixture of grossness and ferocity," it was a "mixture" that did not follow any coherent recipe "except that of making one half of the nation butcher the other."[54] While the government of the Terror distinguished itself by the unprecedented atrocity of its crimes, the authority of the Jacobin leaders consisted in an unusual form of power. "Springing out of popular fanaticism, it struck alarm into the very persons who commanded in its name."[55] The measures taken by the government spread fear and mutual distrust throughout the entire population, not least among the leaders of the revolution.

Mme de Staël found it difficult to explain the unprecedented frenzy that seized the Jacobins and made them trample underfoot the last remnants of legality and morality. Such a phenomenon, she remarked, defied human understanding. "We seem," she confessed, "to be descending, like Dante, from circle to circle, always lower in hell."[56] The members of the Committee of Public Safety scrupulously followed two principles: unlimited exercise of arbitrary will and the pursuit of power founded upon the degradation of individuals. They sacrificed morality to circumstances and created a formidable system that upset social order, treating political issues as principles of faith requiring absolute obedience and spontaneous consent. In *Réflexions sur la paix* addressed to William Pitt in December 1794, she remarked that the entire power of the French Revolution consisted in *"l'art de fanatiser l'opinion pour des intérêts politiques,"*[57] through which political principles were transformed into dogmas. In particular, it was the principle of equality, developed into a virtual religion, that fueled the rise of fanaticism, by joining political enthusiasm, inspired by faith in metaphysical abstractions, to the political ambitions of the Jacobin leaders.

In *Réflexions sur la paix intérieure*, Mme de Staël referred to fanaticism as a singular passion combining the "power of crime and the exaltation of virtue."[58] As the opposite of moderation, fanaticism is the outcome of an extreme partisan spirit and, though pretending to speak on behalf of virtue, equality, and morality, is instead one of the most dangerous of political passions.[59] At the same time, she admitted that a certain dose of fanaticism (*sui generis*) might sometimes be needed during revolutionary times when immoderate means are the only way to triumph over one's enemies. The fanatic mind, Mme de Staël argued, is dangerous because it knows no limits, is incapable of self-restraint, and admits of no guilt. Fanatics demand unconditional obedience and uniformity of thought, and they have no scruples about sacrificing the fate of current generations to the hypothetical happiness of future ones. They tend to reduce every political and moral issue to one single problem (or dimension) on which they focus blindly.[60] Fanaticism is a malady of the spirit, more dangerous than the passion for vengeance or domination, because it so easily masks its true face under a veil of generosity and humanity. In reality, fanaticism effaces all traces of pity and compassion and elevates concern with the preservation of its dogmas above anything else. By refusing compromise and espousing dogmatic rigidity, those who are led by such an extreme form of partisan spirit resemble dangerous forces of nature that rush headlong, unhindered by any obstacles in their path.[61]

Mme de Staël also discussed the concept of fanaticism as an antonym of moderation in *Des circonstances actuelles*, a book in which she sought to demonstrate "the absurdity of political intolerance"[62] in a republic that had come into being prematurely and needed a spirit of moderation and compromise in order to achieve social peace. Referring again to fanaticism as "the most formidable of all human passions,[63] she alleged that fanaticism corrupts any valid principle or idea (such as equality or virtue) by drawing extreme implications that distort its true meaning. It has its origin in a vague principle from which positive duties and obligations are then derived until everything is finally deduced from one single idea—equality, reason, justice, liberty, or *salus populi*[64]—which, in turn, is used to legitimize all kinds of oppression. Mme de Staël made a distinction between fanaticism, bad faith, and wickedness, noting that fanaticism, the most irrational of the three, comes in two forms, either political or religious, both of which distinguish themselves through their intransigence to reason. Fanatics may be perfectly virtuous in everything that does not directly relate to their consuming idea or principle, but with regard to the latter they are dogmatic, ruthless, and inflexible.[65] As such, fanaticism stems from an intransigent monist perspective that rejects pluralism and toleration and stands in stark opposition to a fundamental principle endorsed by moderates. The latter hold that nothing in the moral world is ever true absolutely, but only relatively, and that the meanings of ideas and principles depend on—and vary with—different contexts in such a way that what may be suitable in one situation may be inapplicable in others.[66]

The Elusive Center

Had a schism not developed in the summer of 1794 that divided the Convention deputies, the government of the Terror might well have lasted longer, for the guillotine at the time exercised virtually unlimited power. Although the aftermath of Robespierre's fall ushered in a period of instability and crises, it gave Mme de Staël a much-awaited opportunity to become involved in politics while also pursuing her literary and intellectual interests. Her *Réflexions sur la paix* (1794) rejected political fanaticism and denounced the "chimerical system of equality," which had become a sort of political religion in France. Her text called also for the formation of a moderate party to further the principles of 1789 and pave the way for peace with England. Along with Benjamin Constant, whom she had met for the first time in September 1794, she returned to Paris in the spring of 1795, accepting the republican regime as a *fait accompli*.

Mme de Staël's correspondence during that period shows an optimism that is rare in her later writings. In a letter to her lover Ribbing sent from Mézery on January 23, 1795, she reported: "The news from France is better every day: success abroad, humanity and liberty at home, and attachment to the republican government."[67] In *Considérations*, however, her tone was different. Thermidor was described as an epoch of true anarchy. The practices of the Old Regime had corrupted the people and public morality but, she argued, they had also paved the way for the horrors of the revolution by instilling in the lower classes a desire for vengeance and a profound hatred of inequality and all distinctions of rank.[68] Although the general wish of the French nation was to establish free institutions, there was a high level of political instability, which was matched only by the general ideological confusion. This uncertain climate was ripe for opportunism.[69]

If the legacy of the Terror was evident everywhere, it was arguably nowhere more apparent than in the legislative realm. Many of the laws passed during Robespierre's reign continued in effect; although never properly implemented, the Constitution of 1793 had not been abrogated yet. The former power of the Jacobins still inspired fear and the political agenda of the ultraroyalists was dominated by their desire for revenge, as illustrated by the famous Verona Declaration issued in 1794 by Louis XVI's brother.

Under the influence of vocal ultraconservatives such as the Comte d'Antraigues, the future king Louis XVIII rejected all the changes that had been made in France since 1789, thus giving the impression that the only possible way out of the crisis was a return to the institutions of the Old Regime. Moreover, the new regime not only refused to give the nobles and clergy the same legal securities as other citizens enjoyed, but showed a willingness to resort to extreme revolutionary measures that belied any appearance of legality and shut many individuals out from the protection of the law.

It was against this background that the decree of October 24, 1795 was passed, excluding from any public employment the relatives of émigrés and all those who had voted for liberticidal projects. The decree signaled the fact that the new regime was intent on banishing or imprisoning those suspect of being attached to the Old Regime, as well as other categories of individuals whose commitment to the republic was regarded as dubious. The republic was now in the hands of the members of the Convention. This, Mme de Staël noted, was a great misfortune, because many of the deputies had contracted indelible "habits of servility and tyranny"[70] and had been tainted by their association with the government of the Terror.

Coming to terms with the institutional and moral consequences of the latter proved to be a daunting task, one carried out amidst a general cacophony of self-incrimination and moralizing that blurred the lines between good and evil. "The apologies of those who shared in the Reign of Terror," Mme de Staël remarked,

> . . . formed truly the most inconceivable school of sophistry which it was possible to witness. Some said that they had been constrained to whatever they had done, though a thousand actions of spontaneous servility or cruelty might have been cited against them. Others pretended that they had sacrificed themselves to the public good, though it was known that they had thought only of self-preservation; all threw the evil upon some individuals . . . several political leaders gave fear, and nothing else, as a sufficient excuse for their conduct.[71]

All this made it difficult to find a simple and convincing explanation for the errors of the past, difficult even to distinguish between the agents of evil and their victims. Against those who insisted that republican principles and ideas were responsible for the Terror, Mme de Staël argued that the best proof of the excellence of republican principles was that the revolution could be brought to an end only with their aid. Republican principles, she insisted, were the only means of closing the revolutionary chapter and founding the new institutions that the country so badly needed.[72] The errors of the past, she opined, could be accounted for by the existence of a strong opposition to the revolution and by the fact that the republic had arrived in France prematurely, before the advent of republican ideas and mores, which alone could have ensured a firm foundation for the new republican institutions.[73] The proliferation of revolutionary laws made things worse, since they tended to make crises permanent, thus opening the door to arbitrariness.

Did moderation have a real chance in this unstable environment fraught with uncertainty and riven by moral and ideological confusion? What could a moderate voice have done to promote a coherent and successful reformist agenda? Upon her return to Paris in April 1795, Mme de Staël lost little time in attempting to secure a new place for herself in the midst of once-brilliant Parisian society. She acted the part of a political force, commanding respect and attention and taking a strong interest in the deliberations of the constitutional committee entrusted with the drafting of the Constitution of 1795. She reopened her salon on the rue du Bac, which attracted this time an eclectic audience mirroring the fragmented political landscape of the time. The house of Mme de Staël, La Revellière and Thibaudeau noted (not without irony), was the influential center of a "*coterie*" desirous of playing a great role in public affairs.[74] Among her guests were influential politicians and writers such as Boissy d'Anglas, Lanjuinais, Lezay-Marnésia, and Roederer.

Mme de Staël summarized her new republican (moderate) political agenda in *Réflexions sur la paix intérieure* which, unlike the previous reflections addressed to Pitt, were printed but never distributed, mostly out of prudential considerations, at the recommendation of her close friend, François de Pange (only a few copies of the original print survived).[75] In a letter sent to the editors of *Des nouvelles politiques, nationales et étrangères* on June 3, 1795, Mme de Staël reaffirmed her attachment to the values and principles of the French Republic in unambiguous terms. Responding to accusations that had appeared in the press casting doubt on her republican credentials, she stated that she sincerely desired "the consolidation of the French Republic upon the sacred foundations of justice and humanity," adding that under the then existing circumstances only a republican government could give France the peace and liberty that the country needed.[76] She attempted to rally all the friends of liberty against the twin dangers of anarchy and royalist extremism. "Since the revolution of the 9th Thermidor," she wrote in early June 1795, "there are, in France, only two influential parties: the friends of a just and free Republic, whom all the enlightened and patriotic French citizens want to join; and the agitators promoting a bloodthirsty anarchy which everyone must reject."[77] Although at first she seemed more concerned about the extreme left than about the ultraroyalists, she eventually came to believe that the existence of both extremes threatened to destabilize the new regime. In her view, the survival of the latter depended on the creation of a *parti mitoyen*, a political center large enough to include moderates from all camps, including surviving Girondists and committed Thermidorians, who, by putting aside for a moment their differences, could agree on a set of common values capable of restoring social peace and promoting institutional stability.

Establishing such a center, however, proved impossible. The moderates, who were expected to occupy or lead it, were far from being united.[78] And Mme de Staël, given her own political situation, was not prepared to play the role of the presumptive leader of such a party. Necker's name was still on the list of émigrés, and his assets had not yet been returned to his family. In spite of her declaration of allegiance to the French Republic, her status remained uncertain; she was still considered a foreigner (and she would have to lobby hard to have her French citizenship recognized).[79] As wife of the Swedish ambassador to Paris, she had hoped that Sweden's *ouverture* toward republican France would benefit her image and status. But on August 18, 1795, shortly before the adoption of the new constitutional text, Legendre denounced Mme de Staël in the Convention as the greatest protector of the émigrés. She was criticized for playing the role of a *"sirène enchanteresse,"* seeking to corrupt the leaders of the republic and plotting with the royalists to topple the government.[80] A few months later, in October 1795, the authorities ordered her to leave France within ten days, and then placed her under constant surveillance in Switzerland, soliciting and receiving from its informants detailed reports about her whereabouts.[81] Monachon, one of the spies paid by his superiors in Paris to follow her activities, commented on the alleged versatility of Mme de Staël, accusing her of insincerity and criticizing her desire to ingratiate herself with all parties. According to him, she made every effort to appear as a royalist among the émigrés and as friend of democracy among the patriots.[82]

It did not take Mme de Staël long to discover that in such a climate of intransigence, extreme opinions were more likely to attract followers than moderate ideas. She eventually came to doubt that reason could triumph over fanaticism,[83] but continued to believe that pluralism and moderation could act as a rallying point for all friends of liberty and a stabilizing force for the French Republic. In particular, she opposed any form of political Puritanism, arguing that a one-size-fits-all approach was unsuitable to a context in which everyone had previously made compromises and bowed under the yoke of circumstances.[84] To deal with such a complex situation, Mme de Staël argued, moderation was needed, along with a (legal) "dictatorship of institutions," which she contrasted with a dictatorship based on persecutions and arbitrary power. Only such a *dictature des institutions* could promote the rule of law and foster liberty and morality in the long-run.[85]

She embraced the ideal of a liberty *above* or *beyond* all parties, believing that one must support whatever government had the best chance of promoting civil and political liberty: "It is around the sacred love of freedom, around this feeling that requires all the virtues, which electrifies all souls . . . it is around its real meaning that one must rally."[86] While most people want to be free, she argued, many abuse liberty; only enlightened minds know how to become and remain free.[87] In fact, during the revolution no word had been abused more than "liberty." It had been invoked by its overzealous friends to justify the elimination of their opponents, denounced as enemies of the republic. "Liberty" had been on the lips of those who took part in the fall of the Bastille and of those who drafted and ratified the Constitutions of 1791 and 1793. Yet, genuine political liberty had long eluded France. Indeed the country seemed destined to rove the political seas forever in search of its final haven, that elusive political center reflecting the country's emerging pluralism.

"Everything which partakes of reason, justice, and humanity," Mme de Staël wrote, "demands attention, concessions, and a reason always adjusted to the present moment without losing sight of the future; and it is honorable for the public person in charge of the interests of the nation to seek compromises in each case."[88] In particular, she criticized the inflexibility and stubbornness of radicals on both sides, whose rigid adherence to principles was not, she contended, a virtue in this conflict-ridden post-revolutionary context, which demanded instead prudent concessions and accommodation. Praising flexibility, she renewed her call for a center between all parties, insisting that the pursuit of absolute principles (perfect justice or equality) was a costly illusion. Many flawed constitutions and forms of injustice had arisen from the legislators' lack of pragmatism, illustrated by their failure to consider all the facets of political affairs and their inability to understand the inherent complexity of the political sphere:

> Everything is exchange, everything is compensation, everything is a calculation of surplus. Where, on this planet, does one see a good without any inconveniences? . . . A legislator can always endorse only the law or the institution which contains a greater dose of good than evil. Any absolute [principle] is a true impossibility. In the political realm, utopians dream of a kind of moral fairytale whose miracles would be worth the enchanted cup, the horn of Astolphe. Their readers do not always see the supernatural in the abstraction and believe in these metaphysical miracles, as our children do in the wonders of the golden lamp.[89]

Nothing illustrates better Mme de Staël's moderate political agenda than her ideas in *Réflexions sur la paix intérieure,* a sophisticated manifesto at the heart of which lies the concept of political moderation. Her text advocated three principles which had also been endorsed by Necker: bicameralism, a strong and independent executive, and respect for private property. She avoided highly controversial topics, such as the renewal of the Convention, a subject likely to deepen further the rifts between competing parties.[90] Seeking to reach out to moderates on both sides, her text was an invitation to reconciliation addressed to partisans of limited monarchy and defenders of an elitist form of republicanism based on limited suffrage, whom she invited to rally around a common value, "the sacred love of liberty."[91] On the one hand, Mme de Staël appealed to constitutional royalists who were committed to political and civil liberty but still reluctant to accept the legitimacy of the new republican principles. On the other hand, she reached out to moderate republicans concerned with order and legality but as yet unwilling to cooperate with partisans of monarchy, including constitutional royalists. She sought to mobilize all these moderates to form a strong center which, she believed, was seminal for the stability and future of the republic. In her opinion, apart from their attachment to monarchy, the principles of royalist constitutionalists coincided with the interests of moderate republicans. She referred to the two groups as belonging to the same "party," pursuing similar goals by different means, and invited them to seek a middle ground where they could reconcile their differences through mutual concessions, leaving aside, as much as possible, personal rivalries and dreams of vengeance. She warned both groups not to misjudge their allies and own forces and asked them to focus on their common interest in strengthening the executive power. "In the end," Staël argued,

> Republicans and royalists, the friends of freedom, regardless of their opinion on the future, must follow the same road. If you are a republican, you must strengthen the executive power so that anarchy does not bring back the monarchy. If you are a royalist, you must strengthen the executive power so that the nation becomes accustomed again to being governed, and the spirit of uprising is contained. If you are a republican, you must wish that positions be occupied by honest individuals who will make the new institutions dear to the people. If you are a royalist, do not give up on elections, and try to make that people choose the most virtuous ones as their representatives.[92]

She added that one group "must sacrifice monarchy to the certainty of liberty," while the other should be prepared to sacrifice "democracy to the guarantee of public order."[93] An alliance between constitutional republicans and moderate royalists, she maintained, was both necessary and timely, and it was the only coalition that could have save the republic from ruin.

A couple of years later, Mme de Staël renewed her call to compromise in a letter to Roederer (April 1797), the editor of the *Journal de Paris*, a republican who had remained skeptical toward the Directory. Once again, she resorted to a powerful rhetorical arsenal in order to convince him to rally to the support of the endangered republic. The republicans, she admitted, had committed injustices, but they represented the lesser evil and deserved to be supported by all friends of liberty. The new political circumstances did not allow for hesitation or impartiality: faced with the possibility of a right-wing reaction, one had to be either for or against the Directory.[94] Mme de Staël's claim that the greatest danger came from the ranks of the ultraroyalists might have been a rhetorical exaggeration on her part, signaling a shift from her earlier belief that the greatest danger to the republic was posed by the Jacobins. Whether this argument was a mere sophism used by proponents of the center to discredit their extremist opponents is a different question. Suffice it to say that such an interpretation would not render justice to the complexity and richness of Mme de Staël's republican agenda. The only lasting cure for fanaticism, she averred, was the sovereignty of law and a wise blending of institutions capable of promoting the interests of disparate social and political groups.

It was in this context that Mme de Staël renewed her appeal for moderation and reasonableness, inviting moderates from both camps to join the "real" majority which, she opined, could alone express the permanent interests of the French nation.[95] She took to task radical republicans for having been immoderate in their attachment to democratic principles, and reminded them that only an ordered form of liberty could effectively defuse political fanaticism. The antidote to anarchy lay, she insisted, in moderation and the rule of law. The "torches of the furies" could be extinguished only through the principles of representative government. Only they could adequately promote limited power, create a proper balance of powers in the state, and provide for the orderly participation of the people (through their representatives) in the exercise of legislative power. The republicans' agenda, she went on, must aim at strengthening their electoral and political base by recruiting new members from the ranks of moderate royalists. Mme de Staël called upon republicans to avoid appearing weak and hesitant and argued that they ought to be generous and open toward their opponents as well as firm in their commitment to governing the country. Their moderation of method and tone, she added, had to be combined with a bold political agenda and firmness in exercising political power: "Today, a new system must guide the ruling party. The latter had previously been violent and detached, and must now be ambitious and moderate. It must relinquish power under no pretext, and, step by step, it should rally around it the support of the majority of the nation."[96] Worth noting here is the association between moderation, assertiveness, and power, and the implication that one can (and should) act like a moderate not only in opposition, but also while in power. This boldness is the mark of "good" moderation, and distinguishes it from the kind of moderation that has its origin in fear, timidity, powerlessness, or indifference.[97] As such, "true" moderation is *not* incompatible with passionate commitment to a cause—in this case, republicanism and representative government—and ought *not* to be interpreted as an expression of weakness or indecisiveness.

Mme de Staël's appeal to moderation, which she sought in a hypothetical *juste milieu* between extremes, did not bear fruit and ultimately made her suspect in the eyes of many, both monarchists and republicans. Even Thibaudeau, who shared Staël's republicanism, expressed skepticism toward her moderate agenda because it came from a person "who was receiving the Jacobins in the morning, the émigrés in the evening, and everyone else at dinner."[98] While it is true that Mme de Staël counted among her guests members of the republican government, former émigrés, and writers seeking the favors of the new regime, it is also possible to interpret her ecumenical attitude as an expression of her commitment to moderation and an attempt to find a political anchor in a new environment. She defended moderation while also appearing as an immoderate partisan of the new republican regime. Was this an example of her alleged versatility, or a necessary concession to circumstances? Did her attitude repose upon a set of principles that she never abandoned? In a *"république des girouettes,"*[99] almost anything was possible, including being a republican of the "extreme center."

Rebuilding Representative Government: The Constitution of 1795

Mme de Staël's *Réflexions sur la paix intérieure* and *Des circonstances actuelles* were important contributions to the debate on "ending" the French Revolution. Though the main principles defended in these writings overlapped with those of Necker, she parted company with her father when it came to the preferred form of government. In a 1795 letter to Henri Meister, Necker distanced himself from his daughter's new republican faith, indicating that, like Constant, she seemed "a little too much inclined" to forgive the means employed by the new republican government in the pursuit of its goals. "I am far from seeing things in the same way," Necker acknowledged.[100]

Mme de Staël's declaration of republican faith is particularly interesting because it demonstrates that moderation can go hand in hand with assertiveness and strong political (even partisan) commitments. Her allegiance to republican principles did not rely on a putative belief in the superiority of the republican form of government, and should not be regarded primarily as a simple emotional attachment or an opportunistic change of mind courting the favor of the new government. Mme de Staël thought that a free and just republic was called forth and justified by the new political circumstances rather than by abstract principles. "I sincerely wish the establishment of the French Republic upon the sacred bases of justice and humanity," she confessed. "I desire it because it has been made clear to me that, under the current circumstances, only the republican government can give France peace and liberty."[101] In a letter to Alexandre Lameth dated November 24, 1794, she justified her allegiance to the First Republic by arguing that remaining uncommitted between the republican regime and the "monarchy of Condé" was an irresponsible position. In her view, it was reasonable to endorse the republican regime and try to prudently guide it by grounding it on the principles of justice and humanity.[102] The republic was a *fait accompli* and any attempt to subvert it was likely to create even more instability and anarchy in a country already exhausted by six years of revolutionary turmoil. Mme de Staël appeared now as a genuine supporter of the republic, even though she continued to believe that republican institutions had been introduced in France abruptly, before the corresponding mores that should have served as their foundation were in place. These republican principles and institutions had, at least, the advantage of being perfectible and could eventually bring forth liberty, stability, and peace.

Two words stand out in Mme de Staël's passionate plea for an ordered republic in 1795: "to calm" and "to console." France, she argued, needed internal peace and reconciliation in order to exit the revolutionary orbit, which had so depleted its human and material resources. The republican constitution enjoyed a great advantage; it would be readily endorsed by all parties if only because the people were weary of the revolutionary turmoil:

> It can be implemented effortlessly and will come into being, if nobody opposes it; the force of inertia works in its favor; the government only needs to promote peace. . . . But if people want to fight, the fate of freedom will be uncertain. If nobody wants to reopen any wounds . . . if people move forward without destroying, the republic will be consolidated, almost unnoticed by those who do not want it. . . . In France, with the exception of the Vendée, there is currently no fanatic allegiance to the monarchy; all reasonable individuals are in favor of the republic. . . . It is thus necessary to calm and console; this simple idea is the key secret of this moment. Even within the most radical parties, people are tired. The constitution must accommodate all those who are tired of revolutions; we must welcome them, and put an end to all the misfortunes which it is still in our power to redress.[103]

France, Mme de Staël continued, had missed the opportunity to create a constitutional monarchy à l'anglaise in 1789–1791 and a second chance at such a form of government, she averred, would be possible only after the country had passed through a period of military government: "France can stop at the republic; but in order to arrive at a mixed monarchy, it will have to pass through a military government."[104] France had few sound political institutions and too many revolutionary laws impeding their proper functioning; hence, it needed new institutions capable of creating a genuine balance of power and promoting constitutional peace in keeping with the principles of republican government and equality under the law.[105] The latter, Mme de Staël added, demanded recognizing the right of each man who fulfils the conditions required for citizenship to participate, through his representatives, in the drafting of the laws. Representative institutions and principles alone could achieve this task because they express "the immutable principle of equality of political rights."[106]

The fact that Mme de Staël referred to representative government rather than democracy should not go unnoticed. Her views on representative government reflected, in fact, the conventional wisdom of her time, privileging an elitist form of republicanism (purified of its extreme democratic tendencies) and the liberty of the moderns, grounded in respect for individual rights and security of property.[107] Since democracy was equated with mobocracy and a corrupted form of popular sovereignty that had been used to legitimize the Jacobin dictatorship, moderating and purifying democracy became a priority for French post-revolutionary liberals, including Necker and Mme de Staël. To this effect, they advanced a nuanced critique of equality, emphasizing the importance of property qualifications for granting political rights. Mme de Staël cast doubt on the necessity for two-degree elections and rejected hereditary privileges, calling for rethinking the principle of representation and the frequency of elections. The final goal was, in her own words, the creation of *"une aristocratie des meilleurs"*[108] capable of correcting the shortcomings of extreme equality. Such a system, defined as "the government by the few, with power placed in the hands of the most enlightened, most virtuous, and most courageous,"[109] was, in her view, better suited than political democracy to meet the needs of French post-revolutionary society.

Mme de Staël insisted that a well-ordered representative government based on free elections was not incompatible with the presence of a "natural" aristocracy such as would recognize the presence of natural superiorities in society and prevent leveling in the name of a fictitious equality. "Those who govern must own property," she confidently wrote, adding that representing the interests of the propertied classes must be complemented by acknowledging the role of *"les vertus et les lumières"* in the representation of the entire society.[110] Hence, the task of the government was to reward the "natural superiorities" existing in society by giving them the opportunity to participate in central and local government.

The following fragment clearly illustrates Mme de Staël's skepticism toward political democracy, which can also be found in many other writings of the period. The future of property and the association of thirty million individuals were important questions that required prudent and thoughtful deliberations:

> These two great modifications of natural freedom demand first representative government instead of personal democracy, the division into two assemblies, and a strong executive power. Thus, strictly speaking, there is no democracy in the French constitution. It is a natural aristocracy, in opposition to a factitious aristocracy; it must be the government of the best. . . . This kind of government which promotes natural inequality in order to destroy more effectively an artificial inequality . . . is an entirely new political system and we misunderstand it when we confuse it with the laws of democracy.[111]

Worth noting here is the link between representative government, property, liberty, and the balance of powers, as well as the idea that political democracy, if not properly purified of its (allegedly) radical tendencies, fails to give due consideration to all these principles and values.

The concept of a "modern liberty," which would be elaborated by Constant two decades later, played a central role in Mme de Staël's political writings during the Directory (the concept had previously been used by Sieyès in a different context). She argued that in modern society, laws must protect private property and the private sphere from any form of illegitimate interference. "The liberty of present times," Staël wrote, "consists of everything that guarantees the independence of citizens against the power of the government."[112] She contrasted modern societies, in which citizens were allowed to freely pursue their self-interest, with ancient republics that gave priority to civic virtue and asked their citizens to sacrifice their individual interests for the sake of the common good. Such a demand, Mme de Staël argued, ceases to be legitimate in the context of modern society in which it is no longer possible to expect citizens to spontaneously identify with the "common good." What motivates modern individuals is, instead, the pursuit of private interests, and these must be duly respected by the laws.

Hence, protecting modern liberty and personal interests was the only way to end the revolutionary cycle and make representative institutions work: "In order to finish the revolution, one must find a center and a common link. . . . This center which we need is property; this link is personal interest."[113] Mme de Staël insisted, moreover, that representative government must rely upon a sound distribution of powers and a proper representation of interests, defined as "the political combination through which the nation is governed by people who are chosen and combined in such a way that they have the will and interests of all."[114] By simply increasing the number of representatives, she warned, the legislators might paradoxically strengthen the spirit of faction. When the spirit of faction dominates a legislative body, the principle of representation becomes corrupted and the will of the people no longer has a trustworthy interpreter and defender. A well-designed representative system, she believed, must therefore be an adequate reflection in miniature of public opinion at large, and ought to take into account the interests of both the progressive and conservative elements in society, by trying to reconcile civil equality with political and economic inequality.[115]

Most of these principles, including bicameralism, were enshrined in the final text of the Constitution of 1795 voted by the Convention on August 22. Of all the members of the Commission of Eleven, Mme de Staël was particularly close to Boissy d'Anglas and Lanjuinais, whom she praised as "names that always meet us whenever a ray of freedom gleams over France."[116] She welcomed the pragmatic spirit evinced by the members of the commission who drew upon the American and English constitutions in order to give a more solid anchor to the new republican institutions in France. She also agreed with the proposed eligibility criteria for the legislative body that reintroduced property qualifications and limited suffrage. Most importantly, she was pleased that the Constitution of Year III endorsed the principle of bicameralism, which she regarded as a moderating element indispensable to securing *la pondération des pouvoirs*. At the same time, like Necker, Mme de Staël was concerned that the new constitutional text did not create an adequate balance of powers, opting instead for a system in which the executive and legislative powers did not share in the exercise of the legislative function.[117]

Mme de Staël had already commented on the right of veto in *Réflexions sur la paix intérieure*, and she returned to it a few years later in *Des circonstances actuelles*, where she examined the veto in connection with the role of the executive power. From the very beginning, she expressed her hope that the country would have the wisdom to learn from the mistakes of the past. "The suspensive veto," she remarked, "produced within the Convention the same effect that M. Lally's proposal on bicameralism had caused in the Constituent Assembly. Will the executive power have to pay the same price in order to obtain the strength necessary to the maintenance of the government and consequently, of the republic?"[118] The political context in 1795 was, however, radically different from that of 1789 in one important respect. France now had a republican regime, and the absolute veto was regarded by some as incompatible with republican principles and popular sovereignty. In a republic, Mme de Staël remarked, the idea that a single person should be capable of opposing and obstructing the will of the majority was illegitimate, and in fact impossible. An absolute veto was the attribute of a monarch and so could not be granted to a republican government.

She drew a seminal distinction between "countering" and "enlightening" a will, between *arrêter* and *éclairer la volonté*, insisting that only the second was an essential condition for the proper functioning of representative institutions. There is a great difference between the two. The knowledge and information that only the executive power possesses are necessary to the elaboration of the laws. If the executive were not able to make suggestions for the revision of a decree deemed to be dangerous, the laws could not be properly applied.[119] She reminded her readers that, in England, the veto power was never exercised because the monarch had at his disposal other means of exercising influence over the executive power, the most important being the presence of his ministers in the House of Commons. Using a striking metaphor that anticipates Constant's notion of "neutral power," Mme de Staël argued that the constitutional monarch remains aloof, in a "cloud" above political battles and untouched by them: "In England, the king could remain for the entire life in a cloud without affecting the work of the government. It is only necessary to know up to which point the mystery of this cloud is necessary in order to countervail all individual ambitions."[120] On this view, the executive power should have the right of veto and the right to choose its members among the deputies in the lower chamber. While the directors must be granted absolute inviolability, except in cases of rebellion, their ministers must be held politically responsible, being obliged to resign if they should lose the confidence of the legislative body.[121]

The implications of this view are worth spelling out. First, in the footsteps of Necker, Mme de Staël considered the executive power the representative of the nation and made an important distinction between the executive and administrative power, insisting that the directors did not have the right to dismiss the administrators chosen by the people. Second, she claimed that the co-participation of the executive power in the exercise of the legislative function was essential to the smooth functioning of representative institutions and the application of the laws. The members of the executive power, Mme de Staël argued, possess valuable information and can contribute significantly to legislative debates. To properly discharge this role, they must never be forced to execute a law of which they disapprove and should have statutory means of asking the legislative power to take a second look at the laws that had been adopted.[122] This stipulation, Mme de Staël believed, would make the notion of ministerial responsibility effective and avoid the awkward circumstance of a power condemning or rejecting what it is supposed to execute.

Third, Mme de Staël argued against the strict separation of powers, endorsing instead a *union of powers* reminiscent of Necker's *entrelacement des pouvoirs*. "An eloquent thinker has argued that it is the union of powers that we must seek," she wrote; "and yet people generally confound the necessary separation of functions with the separation of powers which inevitably makes them mutual enemies."[123] A real balance of powers represents much more than an equilibrium of forces; it is a certain form of the "intertwining" of powers by dint of which both the executive and the legislative are able to curb each other's tendency to overstep their legitimate boundaries:

> The balance of powers does not mean one power pitched against the other one, which, in other words, would refer to a balance of forces that would constantly incite them to wage war against each other in order to obtain a decisive advantage. The [true] balance of powers is the outcome of the combinations which make them agree with each other, and, in a free state, only public opinion in all its strength can force one of these two powers to concede to the other, if disagreements between them arise.[124]

The best expression of Mme de Staël's views on the relationship between the executive and legislative power can be found in an important letter of June 9, 1795 sent to Roederer, in which she referred again to *l'union des pouvoirs* as the most difficult political question. Arguing against creating an executive power strictly separated from the legislative, she declared that ministers must be allowed to participate in the deliberations of the lower chamber because their administrative experience and knowledge are essential to raising the level of legislative debates. This "union" of powers, she emphasized, must be properly distinguished from a confusion of powers (which is the opposite of constitutionalism), as well as from their pure opposition (which would lead to political stalemate):

> People speak a lot about the separation of powers, and it is perhaps their union which is the most challenging question. An executive power which is not involved in the making of the laws is naturally the enemy of those that subject it to decrees which go against its views and interfere with its means of execution. For this reason, people have felt the need to give the right of sanction to the king. It is impossible to grant so great an influence to a republican executive power. Consequently, would it not be necessary to choose the ministers among the representatives of the Senate? By joining together two titles they would gain more respect; they would intervene in the debates and, as in England, they would have the advantage of preventing the problems arising from implementing the proposed laws. . . . The first reaction to this idea is to mention the confusion of powers . . . Nonetheless, is there any confusion of powers in America and England because the ministers are at the same time the representatives of the people? It is the opposition and the collision of powers that pave the way for the invasion of one of these two powers, and it is through their reunion that they can maintain themselves. But if there are no permanent public relations between deputies and ministers, a rivalry will emerge between the power sought by deputies and the one held by ministers.[125]

Worth noting in this passage is the emphasis on several key themes such as "opposition and collision of powers," and, more importantly, "union of powers," which Mme de Staël distinguished from "confusion" of powers. She concluded that an executive power that did not participate in the elaboration of the laws was a merely instrumental and passive power, with little interest in the proper application of the laws.

She drew attention also to the composition and role of the Council of the Ancients, pointing out that its members must have life tenure and ought to be considered candidates for the position of directors. She also believed that the Council could fulfill the role of a "neutral" power (*sui generis*) "superior to all others,"[126] and argued that there was no need for a new institution such as the constitutional jury proposed by Sieyès.[127] The key role that Mme de Staël granted to the Council of the Ancients illustrates her belief that democracy could be adequately moderated with the aid of "aristocratic" elements. Her claim that strengthening popular institutions required the selective use of aristocratic ideas and elements anticipated one of Tocqueville's most important insights, for he also believed that democracy tends to go astray if its principles are taken to extremes.[128] The democrats, she noted, know how to take possession of new rights and liberties, while aristocrats are often skilled at preserving their privileges. After their triumph, the first must carefully study the means used by the latter and should adopt such "aristocratic" principles as could contribute to the consolidation of fledgling democratic institutions.

The Failure of Moderation and the Rise of Napoleon

As we have seen, the constitutional text adopted in August 1795, which sought to charter a new course in French post-revolutionary history, was destined to have a short life. The conventional interpretation of its failure points to the peculiar conditions of political life under the Directory, which made the implementation of a moderate (republican) constitution virtually impossible. According to this view, the constitution failed not so much because of its shortcomings as because the environment was unfavorable to moderation and the *juste milieu* endorsed by Mme de Staël and other like-minded liberals. There is some truth to this analysis, as the ever-present specter of reaction and Jacobinism rendered the task of moderates extremely difficult. Moreover, the political personnel of the Directory were corrupt and unable to properly fulfill their tasks. Another line of interpretation emphasizes the inherent limitations of the Constitution of 1795, most notably the lack of adequate legal means for resolving conflicts between the two main powers in the state, as demonstrated by the events of 18th Fructidor and 18th Brumaire. Other problems were the rigid separation of powers envisioned by the French legislators, the annual elections, and the rather odd provisions for the renewal of the personnel of many institutions, including the Directory (every year a new director was supposed to be elected, along with a third of each of the two councils). It was this intense pace of political life that made Barras declare that the country resembled a besieged citadel which, from time to time, had to resort to risky counteroffensive measures in order to win some breathing space.[129]

Mme de Staël attributed the defeat of moderates not only to the volatile environment in which they operated, but also to "that extreme self-love which does not allow men to tolerate any other ideas than their own,"[130] a form of vanity that characterized the nobles and radicals. They would pay a high price for their stubbornness and poor judgment. The internal dysfunction of the Directory became evident on the eve of 18th Fructidor, when the fear of a counterrevolution created public confusion and blurred the dividing line between the friends of liberty and the partisans of arbitrary power. As Thibaudeau remarked in his memoirs, the Directory was confronted with a choice between overcoming the royalists by force of arms or by strengthening the constitutionalist party around which supporters of the rule of law rallied. "In the first case," he remarked, "it would have ruined the constitution and the republic; in the second, it is likely that it would have saved them."[131]

Unfortunately, the directors chose the first solution. Their *coup* was made easier by the fact that the executive power did not have the right to dissolve the legislative power in case of political gridlock. Two of the directors, Barthélemy and Carnot, were rumored to share the radical views of some members of the Council of the Five Hundred, which further compounded the situation. The remaining three directors, Reubell, Barras, and La Réveil-lière, made a bold decision that, although initially endorsed by some liberals (including Constant and Mme de Staël), proved to have disastrous long-term political consequences. They sent soldiers to arrest the recalcitrant members of the Council of the Five Hundred, expelled almost two hundred deputies, and proceeded to remove from the political scene the two dissenting directors. No less than 163 opponents of the regime were condemned to deportation overseas, military commissions were set up, and freedom of the press was abolished once again, this time in light of Art. 355 of the Constitution of 1795, which allowed for a one-year suspension of liberty of the press in exceptional circumstances. The subsequent reception given by the Directory to General Bonaparte, whom Talleyrand himself called "the liberator of Italy and the pacificator of the Continent,"[132] epitomized the irreversible subduing of the national representation by military power and demonstrated the fragility of the Directory and its representative institutions.

It may seem surprising then that a liberal like Mme de Staël did not originally oppose the events of 18th Fructidor and that, despite her liberal constitutionalism, she endorsed the use of nonconstitutional means to save the First Republic. In *Considérations*, she has surprisingly little to say about the role she and Constant played during the crisis leading to the *coup d'état* that opened a deep rift within the camp of moderates. Eventually, Mme de Staël came to regret her initial position and denounced the events of 18th Fructidor while seeking to justify her initial decision:

> The journals whose office it was in 1797 to insult all the friends of liberty have pretended that, from a predilection for a republic, I approved of the affair of 18th Fructidor. I certainly would not have counseled, had I been called upon to give advice, the establishment of a republic in France; but when it once existed, I was not of the opinion that it ought to be overturned. Republican government, considered abstractedly and without reference to a great state, merits the respect which it has inspired; the Revolution of 18th Fructidor, on the contrary, must always excite horror, both for the tyrannical principles from which it proceeded and for the frightful results which were its necessary consequence.[133]

As Talleyrand remarked, "Mme de Staël had approved of 18th Fructidor but not of the events of the 19th."[134] He was right. The *coup d'état* signaled that the directors had too much arbitrary power and too little legal power and demonstrated the rising power of the army, the most ominous development during the second half of the Directory. "No epoch of the Revolution was more disastrous than that which substituted military rule for the well-founded hope of a representative government," Mme de Staël wrote. "For it was so contrary to the spirit of a republic to employ the soldiers against the representatives of the people that the state could not fail to be destroyed in the very attempt to save it by such means."[135]

Des circonstances actuelles was Mme de Staël's attempt to sketch a constitutional agenda that could save the republic from ruin. What makes this seminal text so interesting is that its author adopted a partisan tone while pretending at the same time to be the voice of moderation in search for a necessary consensus among all the friends of liberty in France. Described by some commentators as "one of the most representative texts of republican constitutionalism"[136] ever written, a true "discourse of method of the new republicanism,"[137] Mme de Staël's book manuscript sought to express "the theoretical opinions of the conquerors and the sentiments of the vanquished."[138] A republican treatise and a textbook of political cohabitation, it articulated an ambitious agenda aimed at rallying all moderates around a set of republican ideas and principles that could bring much-needed social peace and act as a countervailing force to fanaticism and intolerance. To this end, she had to walk a narrow path, seeking to persuade, convince, and pressure the undecided sympathizers of the republic. She expressed concern over the low public spiritedness of the French, which she regarded as a corollary of civic apathy and post-revolutionary fatigue.[139] In order to "end" the revolution, as already mentioned, she favored an elitist form of republicanism based on political rights, popular sovereignty, representative government, and respect for private property. She also expressed optimism about the possibility of a new science of politics modeled upon the natural sciences. Such a science, she hoped (in a surprisingly Hobbesian vein), would be capable of submitting political passions to rigorous analysis and would view politics as a rational and quantifiable object of investigation.[140]

The policy of cohabitation that Mme de Staël recommended in 1798 had important similarities with the strategy of accommodation outlined in her earlier writings. Her credo remained unchanged: the republic could be saved only if all *honnêtes hommes* rallied to support republican institutions and moderate principles.[141] And yet, there was something surprisingly radical in Mme de Staël's approach which, at first sight, seems to contradict her image as a proponent of moderation. Consider, for example, the confident tone and bold advice she gave to the government: it must preserve its monopoly on power at all costs. Power should not escape from the hands of a party supporting the republic, she argued, adding that the republicans should never agree to share power with another party. Instead, they must consolidate their position in spite of the fact that public opinion was against them.

At the same time, her call to firmness and assertiveness was tempered by her appeal to moderation in the exercise of power.[142]

Given the partisan tone espoused by Mme de Staël, her plea for bipartisan collaboration might well have seemed purely rhetorical to those who were skeptical about the intentions of the Directory. Her endorsement of strict measures meant to restrict freedom of the press certainly worried republicans; she agreed that books should be published freely, but accepted the censorship of journals.[143] Similarly, her argument in favor of national reconciliation might not have persuaded the Anglophiles who believed that only an open and unrestricted competition for power among robust parties could further the consolidation of republican institutions. One might then argue that Mme de Staël's position remained faithful to an old way of interpreting politics that did not have much room for open confrontation between political parties. Finally, rallying all reasonable monarchists—Mme de Staël's most important target audience—to support the cause of the republic was plausible only because the project of moderate (tempered) monarchy, Necker's preferred regime, had become impossible in the context of the Directory. If a *monarchie modérée* might have been possible and desirable in 1789–1791, it was no longer an appealing project in 1798. Under then-current circumstances, she would have to work hard to convince defenders of constitutional monarchy that the only reasonable course was to create a "moderate republic" by enlisting the support of all of the friends of liberty in France.

The moderate republican political agenda of *Des circonstances actuelles* had little chance of influencing the French political scene, and it is revealing that the text was never published.[144] A year later, Napoleon's coup of 18th Brumaire officially ended the Directory, marking the second time since the revolution when civil power was humiliated by the military.[145] Deputies favorably disposed toward Napoleon met and created a Consular Commission that included Napoleon and two directors (Sieyès and Ducos). As already noted,[146] the new constitution of Year VIII (drafted by Sieyès) reduced the role of popular elections and made the government no longer representative in the proper sense of the term. The events of 18th and 19th Brumaire marked the moment when the moral force of national representation was annihilated by the power of the sword, and the legislative body became, in the eyes of the military, an irrelevant assemblage of men whom they could easily dispose of whenever it became convenient to do so. Eventually, some of Mme de Staël's friends—Talleyrand among them—abandoned her, and the "republic" established by the Constitution of Year VIII was exposed as an empty shell, with all power placed in Bonaparte's hands. The way was cleared for the proclamation of the First Empire in 1804.

Mme de Staël's independent personality was bound to clash with Bonaparte's plans. Her courageous stance toward the latter proves that political moderation is not the mark of lukewarm and hesitant characters, as is sometimes alleged. She had met the General for the first time in 1797 in Talleyrand's house and, in his presence, she had immediately felt unable to breathe, realizing that no emotion of the heart could influence this man.[147] Napoleon, for his part, had few reasons to like Mme de Staël. He detested women who meddled in politics and, in particular, outspoken and intelligent challengers of his authority. During the early days of the Consulate, Mme de Staël unsuccessfully reached out to Napoleon who did not reciprocate. He was interested, however, in winning the backing of former nobles and the clergy, and eventually managed to remove from the Tribunate the most vocal members of the opposition (among them, Benjamin Constant). To Mme de Staël's critical remarks, the First Consul furiously replied, in a private conversation with his brother Joseph: "So she wants war, does she? . . . Advise her not to block my path, no matter what it is, no matter where I choose to go, otherwise I will break her . . . I will crush her."[148] A few years later, the Emperor, at the height of his power, acknowledged: "There is no truce nor peace possible between us; she asked for it, let her suffer the consequences."[149] The publication of Necker's *Dernières vues* gave Napoleon an additional pretext to persecute Mme de Staël who, he thought, had connived with her father to block his rise to power.

After being placed under tight surveillance, Mme de Staël was ordered to leave Paris and was forced into exile in late 1803.[150] At Coppet, she formed around her a powerful opposition to Napoleon that brought together many friends of liberty who had become the Emperor's staunchest critics. Her unfinished memoir *Dix années d'exil* recounts the story of her peregrinations in Europe and, along with Parts III and IV of *Considérations*, illustrates how one of the most brilliant minds of Europe became an object of constant persecution by Bonaparte. Mme de Staël offered a precise anatomy of the system of absolute power that Napoleon incarnated and brought to perfection. "I flatter myself," she wrote, "with having estimated him as all public men ought to be estimated: with reference to the effects of their conduct on the prosperity, information, and morality of nations."[151] She claimed that Bonaparte, who was unlike any other human being, represented a whole system of power that ought to be examined like a great political puzzle relevant to many generations: "No emotion of the heart seemed to be able to really move him, and he always regarded his fellow citizens as mere things and means rather than equal creatures worthy of respect and consideration. What made him unique was that he was "neither good, nor violent, nor gentle, nor cruel. . . . Such a being had no fellow, and therefore could neither feel nor excite sympathy."[152]

Intoxicated with the "vile draught of Machiavellianism"[153] and resembling in many respects the Italian tyrants of the fourteen and fifteenth centuries, Napoleon managed to enslave the French nation through the shrewd application of three strategies. He sought to satisfy men's interests at the expense of their virtues, disregarded public opinion, and gave the French nation war for an object instead of liberty. Mme de Staël emphasized not only Napoleon's unbounded egotism and pernicious intoxication with power, but also his unsettling air of vulgarity and the political cunning that allowed him to lay hold of the imagination of his people. He was able both to dazzle the masses and corrupt individuals by acting upon their imaginations and captivating them with a false sense of his greatness. Under his reign, nothing was carried out properly with the exception of extravagant military campaigns, all other matters were willfully neglected.

Mme de Staël also pointed out how Napoleon's rise to absolute power had been made possible by the progressive leveling and atomization of French society. Napoleon, she argued, appeared in the eyes of many as the legitimate child of the revolution, ready to bring the revolutionary chapter to an end, and willing to serve the interests of the nation. Thus, his triumph, in both France and Europe, was based on a "great equivocation"[154] that caused him to appear as the defender of the rights and interests of the people at the very moment when, in reality, he was becoming their greatest enemy. Napoleon destroyed republics and unseated legitimate monarchs, and yet many people were convinced that all this was going to usher in a period of liberty and peace. He managed to reestablish order, having been endowed by nature with a unique gift for leadership that allowed him to grasp that he could rule not against, but only with the aid of the selfish passions triggered by the revolution. He was astute enough to make himself obeyed and respected by those whom he degraded and turned into mere subjects,[155] but the corruption of character he fostered did a great harm to the cause of liberty.

Napoleon's fall from power, Mme de Staël argued, could be ascribed to many factors, among which she counted the influence of public opinion and the limitations inherent in any form of despotism that ends up losing contact with reality. In the end, it became evident that Napoleon's power rested upon fragile foundations. "Of the whole inheritance of his dreadful power," she wrote, "there remains nothing to mankind but the baneful knowledge of a few secrets the more in the art of tyranny."[156] The emperor left a nefarious legacy: "All France had been cruelly disorganized by the reign of Bonaparte. What forms the strongest charge against that reign is the evident degradation of knowledge and virtue during the fifteen years that it lasted."[157] Napoleon founded a pernicious system built of egoism, oppression, and corruption that derailed the natural political evolution of the country, wasting countless resources. In particular, Mme de Staël deplored the absence of the rule of law in France and the fact that public opinion was powerless without the authority of the law and the independent organs to express it.

The political changes that Napoleon promised to implement during the Hundred Days did not convince Mme de Staël that he would ever be able to transform himself into a constitutional sovereign. Some of her closest friends, like Constant and Sismondi, thought otherwise, encouraged by Napoleon's assertion that he was prepared to make a series of liberal concessions to the advocates of the principles of representative government and constitutional monarchy. In April 1815, he signed an "Additional Act to the

Constitutions of the Empire" drafted by no less a figure than his former opponent, Benjamin Constant. The preamble of the Act clearly indicated the new spirit that ruled over the country, mentioning that the Emperor acknowledged the importance of representative government. Nonetheless, Mme de Staël remained skeptical of Napoleon's true intentions, and suspected that "it was degrading the principle of liberty to clothe them in a former despot."[158] Subsequent developments proved her right.

The Charter of 1814 and England's "Happy Constitution"

Upon her return to Paris from her long European exile on May 12, 1814, Mme de Staël found a capital dominated by foreign troops. "To see Paris occupied by them," she confessed, "the Tuilleries, the Louvre guarded by troops who had come from the frontiers of Asia, to whom our language, our history, our great men were all less known than the meanest Khan of Tartary—this was insupportable grief."[159] Only a tyrant such as Napoleon could have left a great country like France in such a deplorable state. The next day, after his fall from power, there was no activity in France except in Paris, and even there it was reduced to people running after money and governmental positions. Dignity of character, consistency of opinion, and inflexibility of principle no longer existed among the people previously formed and employed by Napoleon; they combined all the blind passions of the revolution with all the vanities of the old regime. Although intelligent, ambitious, and dexterous, they possessed a servile mentality that rendered them capable only of showing obedience toward power and of deceiving others.

On the positive side, the epoch of confiscation, exile, and illegal arrests was now a thing of the past, and free thought was beginning to replace the reign of bayonets and censorship.[160] Would the new epoch witness the triumph of political moderation? The new constitution granted by Louis XVIII seemed to be a step in the right direction. The Charter of 1814 sought to bring social peace in a country divided among rival factions and groups fiercely opposed to one another. Though it was not in the proper sense of the term a "contract" between the monarch and the people, the Charter recognized the new civil rights and created a two-chamber parliament, the Chamber of Deputies being elected by electoral colleges according to a narrow franchise. As a moderate, Mme de Staël was favorably disposed toward the document, because, among other reasons, it contained many of the articles previously endorsed by Necker. At the same time, she expressed concern regarding the long-term viability of the text, an odd mixture of royal *octroi* (concession) and political contract, which, she argued, was inferior in many respects to the unwritten English constitution.[161]

All these ideas appeared in the last two books of *Considérations,* which shed light on the complex relationship between freedom, constitutionalism, and moderation. In book V, she examines the system that the Bourbons and the friends of liberty ought to have followed in 1814 to create a French constitutional monarchy. Book VI contains Mme de Staël's analysis of liberty in England. Her interpretation belongs to a distinctively French tradition of political rhetoric and engagement and should not be read as a work of pure historiography.[162] It was to become Mme de Staël's most significant *political* work, more important than *Des circonstances actuelles,* which remained to a great extent caught up in the orbit of the controversy over republicanism under the Directory and beyond. *Considérations* gave voice to her belief that republican principles had not lived up to their potential and were responsible, to some extent, for the failure to carve out a much-needed center between extremes after 9th Thermidor. Yet, this should not obscure the fact that her reflections developed further the Thermidorian case for bringing the revolution to an end and dealt with the contested legacy of the revolutionary years.

Mme de Staël did not intend to offer a purely historical work retracing step by step the main events and phases of the French Revolution and its aftermath. Her initial goal was to write a book examining the actions and ideas of her father; in the end, she went beyond that goal to articulate a liberal agenda at the heart of which lies the idea of political moderation. The title, indicative of her main goal and method, was probably a rejoinder to two other influential interpretations: Joseph de Maistre's *Considérations sur la France* (originally published in 1796 and reedited in 1814) and Montlosier's *De la monarchie française depuis son établissement jusqu'à nos jours* (1814). At once personal testimony, historical narrative, and a justification of her father's actions and of the Charter of 1814, *Considérations* was a book in which the author reflected on past events with a view to providing enlightened guidance to those interested in France's future. To this end, Mme de Staël sought to adopt the point of view of the future and to paint on a broad canvas the march of history, without dwelling too much on personal anecdotes and particular historical details. "My ambition," she wrote on the first page, "shall be to speak of the age in which we have lived, as if it were already remote."[163] She combined the perspective of a witness with that of a detached actor, relying upon historical analogies and a comparative approach (between England and France). She distinguished between principles and circumstances, the general and the particular, and pointed to unexploited possibilities, missed opportunities, and lost chances that might have saved liberty and spared the country military dictatorship. Without displaying any political nostalgia, she invites the reader to imagine what might have been the future of liberty in France if Necker's plans for reform had been adopted in 1789, if the moderates' agenda had been supported by the aristocrats, and if 18th Fructidor had failed, thus delaying or perhaps blocking Napoleon's rise to power.

Mme de Staël's *Considérations*, a true manifesto of moderation, elicited vigorous responses in the press, being regarded as a first-rate contribution to an important ongoing political and historical debate on representative government and its institutions in nineteenth-century France and Europe. Nonetheless, the reactions were far from uniformly positive.[164] Mme de Staël's critics argued that she had failed to understand and explain the true significance of the events and the principles of the revolution. She was taken to task for ignoring economic factors and focusing mostly on what happened in the capital, thus glossing over equally important social and political developments in the provinces. Others took issue with the eclecticism of the book, criticizing her for attempting to be simultaneously "an ultraroyalist and ministerialist, a liberal and a *philosophe*, impious and devout, English, French, and German."[165] In *Examen critique de l'ouvrage posthume de Mme. la Baronne de Staël, ayant pour titre: Considérations sur les principaux événements de la Révolution française* (1818), J.-C. Bailleul disagreed with Mme de Staël's views on the roles of the monarchy and aristocracy in the Old Regime and claimed that her idolatry of her father rendered her account of the revolution subjective and unreliable. Still others objected to her enthusiastic apology for England and her unqualified defense of the Directory, or (like Stendhal) were put off by her exceedingly harsh treatment of Napoleon. Other liberals were attracted to the book because it cast their hero, Lafayette, in a positive light. Finally, *Considérations* was also warmly received by the French Doctrinaires. In 1818, Charles de Rémusat dedicated a long article to Mme de Staël in which he discussed the importance of the book's main theses for his young generation.[166]

Mme de Staël paid particular attention to the ultraroyalists who dreamt of restoring the Old Regime and undoing the legacy of the revolution. Not surprisingly, the most vocal critics of her book came from the right. One of them was Louis de Bonald, author of *Observations on the Work of Mme de Staël Entitled 'Considerations on the Principal Events of the French Revolution'* (1818).[167] In Bonald's view, Necker's daughter failed to give an impartial account of the revolution, preferring instead to reinterpret the significance of its main events in such a way as to vindicate her father's actions and legacy. Bonald then went further to attack the political ambitions of Mme de Staël's book, along with its liberal principles and Protestant outlook. He also disagreed with her emphasis on the inevitability of the revolution and rejected her claim that France did not have a proper constitution prior to 1789.[168]

Although Mme de Staël was aware that the Charter was a moderate constitution, she feared that its limitations did not bode well for its future.[169] The new constitution, she argued, ought to have been based on a contract with the nation confirming both the rights of the throne and those of the nation and would, consequently, have inspired greater confidence in the durability of the document. As written it failed also to deal adequately with the legacy of Napoleon and the Terror. Those who committed crimes during the revolution, who enriched themselves by their servile acquiescence to tyranny, and who, setting aside all political scruples, brought their science of despotism to the throne of Bonaparte, should have not been allowed to play a prominent political role during the Restoration. The rebuilding of the country should have been entrusted to "men whose principles are invariable"[170] rather than to those who believed that flexibility represents the apex of political art and considered politics "a maneuver to be regulated by the prevailing winds."[171]

She accused the king's ministers of having no concerted vision and of being moved mostly by personal ambitions and motives, rather than by a desire to follow the constitutional system with the energy and sincerity that circumstances demanded of them. They did not take the articles of the Charter seriously and in private professed little respect for the rights of the nation enshrined in the new constitutional text. To a moderate like Mme de Staël, hypocrisy in the pursuit of liberty was more repellant than its complete denial. The Law on freedom of the press (October 1814) was an example of the unwillingness of the new government to fully accept the principles of representative government.[172] The ministers did not understand that "in a country intoxicated with military ardor, the freedom of debate is a protection rather than a danger, since it adds to the strength of the civil power."[173] In flagrant violation of the principles of representative government, "the direction of that opinion by which they are to be tried and enlightened"[174] was put into their own hands, allowing them to remove disobedient individuals from office and replace them with cronies.

The last book of *Considérations* reflects Mme de Staël's political moderation and her famous Anglophilia, so reminiscent of Necker's.[175] She believed that, in the attempt to overcome its deeply rooted legacy of despotism and centralization, France should have drawn inspiration from England, without however carrying imitation of the English to extremes.[176] The French, she argued, were not destined to be governed despotically forever. Although some considered them frivolous and unfit for liberty, no decree of Heaven condemned them to despotism. If the French had not achieved lasting liberty yet, this was not due to flaws inherent in their national character, for "every country, every people, every man are fit for liberty by their different qualities; all attain or will attain it in their own way."[177] She warned that any attempt to recreate the edifice of old prejudices and privileges would amount to building a castle of cards on shifting sands. There were, she continued, only two forces in the country that had to be reckoned with: "public opinion, which calls for liberty, and the foreign troops who obey their sovereigns: all the rest is mere trifling."[178] All attempts to sail against the new democratic torrent, she added, were destined to fail in the long-term: "Let this torrent enter into channels, and all the country which it laid waste will be fertilized."[179]

She recommended four effective means for combating Napoleon's legacy of centralized despotism: decentralization, self-government, the rule of law, and respect for public opinion. "Public opinion bears the sway in England," she wrote, "and it is public opinion that constitutes the liberty of a country."[180] Comparing the pattern of centralization in France to local liberties in England, she noted with admiration that one of the wonders of the latter was the great number of individuals who were free and willing to occupy themselves with the interests of each locality, and who were respectful of other people's rights and mindful of all citizens' duties. In France, the situation was different: intrigues, love of money and titles were the chief arenas in which many individuals exercised their talents.[181] It was of great importance then "to establish local authorities in the towns and villages, to create political interest in the provinces in order to diminish the ascendancy of Paris."[182] Mme de Staël also believed that decentralization ought to have been accompanied by the creation of a new system of public education that should have mandated the establishment of schools in all the departments for what was then known as "mutual education," a form of learning in which the instructor was helped by the best students in class.[183] She also favored a lower age qualification and a different mode of election for the Chamber of Deputies and believed that the Chamber of Peers should not have admitted all the former senators, but only those distinguished by personal merit. The two chambers taken together should have fostered a "constitutional blending"[184] of classes and ranks without which there could be nothing but arrogance and servility at the extremes of the social spectrum. Nor should the debates in the Chamber of Peers have been made secret. The lower Chamber should have had a more numerous body—at least six hundred deputies—for that would have given it greater respectability and fostered better debates, from which the ministers themselves would have benefitted.

In Mme de Staël's view, the most distinctive trait of the moderation built into the English constitution was its "possibility of improving itself without convulsion."[185] This allowed its leaders to successfully engraft new forms onto the old by dint of gradual reforms, giving liberty both the advantage of an ancient origin and the benefits of prudent innovation. Moderation, she noted, acted as a guarantee of individual security and promoted the common good and free political competition, while also ensuring that fidelity to a party was founded on respect for public opinion. Moreover, moderation in England acted as an effective countervailing force to radicalism by fostering a politics and culture of compromise. The differences between the political views of the two major parties—the Whigs and Tories—were only a matter of shades: "Tories approve of liberty and love monarchy, while Whigs approve of monarchy and love liberty; but between these two parties, no question could arise about . . . the old or the new dynasty, liberty or servitude; in short, about any of those extremes and contrasts which we have seen professed by the same men in France."[186] On this view, political moderation does not exclude partisanship, and fidelity to a party is not incompatible with liberty as long as freedom of debate is universally respected and the fact of being a member of a party does not compromise one's commitment to the public good and the spirit of honor. It is not surprising that

Mme de Staël wanted to create a viable parliamentary system in France by invoking English ideas, but in doing so she sometimes ignored the reality of British parliamentary politics, structured as it was around two strong parties competing for power, and representing many rotten boroughs in need of urgent reform. At any rate, the idea of political parties as promoters of freedom should have appeared as a novelty to the French who were still unsure as to how to regulate political contestation.[187]

Finally, there are a few distinctively Burkean tones in Mme de Staël's *Considérations*—the claim, for example, that what makes England distinctive is "a mixture of chivalrous spirit with an enthusiasm for liberty."[188] This combination fostered a sound balance between all social classes in such a way that "the English nation seems . . . one entire body of gentlemen."[189] Unlike the French nobles, English aristocrats were united to—and identified themselves with—the nation at large and did not form a privileged caste detached from the management of local affairs. Mme de Staël also explored the seminal influence of religion and morals on political liberty, anticipating Tocqueville's analysis of religion as a bulwark of political freedom in America. "In England," she wrote, "all is constituted in such a way that the interest of each class, of each sex, of each individual lies in conforming themselves to morality. Political liberty is the supreme instrument of this admirable combination."[190] It is to this dignified and enlightened form of liberty that the prosperity of England can be ascribed. Liberty also promotes moderation and common sense. It is no coincidence that "that admirable good sense which is founded on justice and security" exists nowhere but in England and its offspring, America. Finally, borrowing a theme from Montesquieu, Mme de Staël commented briefly on the moderating effects of commerce which, "placing men in relation to the interests of the world, extends ideas, exercises judgment, and, from the multiplicity and diversity of transactions, makes the necessity of justice continually felt."[191] It is commerce that teaches toleration, a certain disposition to compromise, and a proper sense of justice, all of which are essential to promoting political moderation.

An Enthusiastic Moderate

"If she knew how to govern herself, she would have ruled over the entire world,"[192] Benjamin Constant once said of his longtime friend who left such a deep trace on her age and whose influence crossed national borders, cultures, and disciplines. The intellectual and political trajectory of Mme de Staël is particularly relevant to our history of political moderation for several reasons. First, in her works one can find a passionate commitment to promoting political moderation and a constant preoccupation with securing and protecting individual and civil liberties—freedom of association, freedom of thought, and religious freedom. Second, Mme de Staël's writings shed fresh light on the affinities between political moderation and institutional complexity, one of the major meta-narratives of this book. Third, the readers might pause for a moment to reflect on her search for a "complex" center as the locus of the type of political moderation to which she was committed during her entire life. Fourth, political moderation is a particularly interesting topic in Mme de Staël's writings, since she was not a moderate temperament and rarely followed a moderate path in her private life. The marriage between an immoderate soul and a politically moderate thinker demonstrates that moderation should never be reduced to a character trait and must instead be studied in all of its institutional and political embodiments.

Although Madame de Staël never explicitly defined moderation, the latter is omnipresent, in one form or another, in all of her political works. Understanding the centrality of moderation to her outlook requires then a sophisticated reconstruction and archeology which must take into account related concepts such as fanaticism, enthusiasm, and extremism, her discussion of passions and happiness, and her (sometimes immoderate) praise of the English constitution and society. Mme de Staël stopped short of inferring that moderation is best defined as a collective attribute of a nation's civic culture (namely, England's), but she noted the existence of several distinctively English traits emblematic of moderation (a commonplace in the literature). Above all, England emerged as an exemplary synthesis of liberty and order, of imperialism and constitutionalism. But moderation, like liberty, should not be viewed as the asset of a single country. Even the French, Mme de Staël argued, could become free and moderate if they would only take the necessary steps.

In her case, then, we have an immoderate soul with a politically moderate sensibility, an original if uneasy combination that we also find in Benjamin Constant's writings. In her works dating from 1796 to 1798, Mme de Staël devoted illuminating pages to a discussion of moderation as an individual disposition and passion, to which she opposed fanaticism, *l'esprit de parti*, and extremism. What makes her position original is that she did not see any *a priori* incompatibility between moderation and enthusiasm. On the contrary, as an enthusiastic moderate, she believed that moderation *is* compatible with strong commitments, passionate beliefs, a powerful imagination, and exalted feelings, and depends, in fact, on achieving a subtle alchemy between all of these. In a period when the ideas of the *philosophes* were deemed responsible for the greatest errors of the revolution, Mme de Staël did not hesitate to express her enthusiasm for philosophical ideas, which, she believed, could become agents of moral and political change.[193] At the same time, she unambiguously denounced those fanatics who distorted noble principles (liberty, equality, virtue) by drawing extreme consequences from them.

In the concluding chapter of *De l'Allemagne* she went so far as to try to rescue enthusiasm from its negative association with fanaticism: "Let me repeat: enthusiasm has nothing to do with fanaticism and cannot lead people astray. Enthusiasm is tolerant—not out of indifference, but because it makes us feel the interest and beauty of everything."[194] In her opinion, a properly exercised form of enthusiasm does not lead to error; on the contrary, only enthusiasm can elevate our souls to the comprehension of superior truths that have no direct or immediate bearing on our worldly interests. One possible implication is that only enthusiastic spirits can practice "true" moderation, combining attachment to reason with proper appreciation for *les raisons du cœur*. Mme de Staël believed that finding this synthesis between enthusiasm and moderation, between reason and sentiment is the key to happiness that allows us to overcome two of our greatest enemies, spiritual apathy and laziness of soul.

Finally, Mme de Staël's commitment to moderation was demonstrated not only by her firm condemnation of fanaticism and factionalism, but also by her constant search for a *parti mitoyen* (which she dreamt of forming from 1791 until her death), or a *juste milieu* between extremes. As she once wrote, "the extremes are in the minds of the people, but not in the nature of things."[195] At the same time, she understood that it is important to have a grain of boldness in everything, and that sometimes, even a virtue like moderation should be temporarily replaced by immoderation. One such example is the use of extreme measures in order to effectively countervail the pernicious effects of *l'esprit de parti*.[196] She emphasized that even truth must be pursued with prudence, for those who claim to be committed to a politics of truth are apt to reduce the complexity of the world to a single dimension, principle, or idea. "Nature," Mme de Staël affirmed, "is not subject to the empire of a single law. Madness is the domination of a unique idea."[197] This drive to simplification, she insisted, is the root of fanaticism and "bad" philosophy, while "good" philosophy recognizes and respects the inherent and ineradicable complexity of social and political practices and institutions. As such, the search for the truth in politics implies and requires pursuing many paths and endorsing many values and principles.[198] It follows a complex and contorted route. The way is never linear, never simple, as radicals and extremists tend to believe.

Mme de Staël's political thought evolved over many years in a social and political context marked by high polarization and protracted political conflict. Yet, in spite of the uncertainty and turmoil of her times, her reflections retained a remarkable thematic and conceptual unity and coherence. Her political moderation wore various masks, defying a simple definition, although they all shared several features that point to a common denominator. She always took liberty to mean the opposite of despotism and endorsed constitutionalism, rejecting the ideological arsenal of the Jacobins and Napoleon. She detested the political opportunism of some of her former friends and associates (such as Talleyrand) whose clever policy of always sailing with the wind bordered on servility and immorality. In this regard, her political ideas were close to Necker's, yet there were also important differences between them in temperament and in their views on republicanism, the scope of the executive power, and bicameralism.

The development and transformation of Mme de Staël's ideas, which have puzzled some of her interpreters, offer us a unique vantage point from which to follow the challenges faced by French moderates during and after the revolution. In 1789–1791, she was among those who defended constitutional monarchy; a few years later, in 1795, she became a partisan of an elitist (conservative) form of republicanism, which sought to bring back limited suffrage and, unlike classical republicanism, allowed the executive power to play a significant role. A decade and a half later, her allegiances shifted back to constitutional monarchy, and her last book ended with an eloquent commentary on English politics and society that marks the highest moment of Anglophilia in nineteenth-century French political thought.

The peculiar nature of Mme de Staël's republicanism has recently led some commentators to argue that the republican constitution she endorsed would frighten today's liberals.[199] In my view, this is an overstatement that does not take adequate account of the fundamentally *moderate* and *liberal* core of Mme de Staël's political philosophy. In this regard, I agree with G. E. Gwynne that we can find in her writings an "unshaken fidelity to a small number of fundamental principles which constitute the remarkable identity of [her] thought."[200] If we adopt this view, then it is possible to argue that Mme de Staël's republicanism rested on a combination of principled realism and calculation and that, from her advocacy of republicanism in the 1790s to her endorsement of constitutional monarchy in 1814, the conceptual core of her political outlook remained more or less unchanged, as is demonstrated by her constant search for *via media*, a prominent theme in all of her political writings.[201]

Her moderate agenda had, however, an *eclectic* core, seeking to achieve in France what England was famous for: "a reconciliation of republican liberty with monarchical calm, the emulation of talents with the silence of factions, a military spirit abroad and respect for laws at home."[202] Not surprisingly, Mme de Staël identified this form of eclecticism with political happiness, a topic that unfortunately remained undeveloped in her writings. While it is true that she eventually placed individual liberties and rights at the center of her later political writings, and became more skeptical toward equality, a quintessentially republican principle tainted by its association with Jacobin democracy, Mme de Staël remained committed to a set of liberal values and principles clustered around the concept of political moderation, *le fil directeur* of her political thought. If she had completed the second part of *De l'influence des passions*, the promised testament of her thought, it would in all likelihood have been a hymn to political moderation.

SIX

MODERATION AND "NEUTRAL POWER"
Benjamin Constant's pouvoir modérateur

Pour faire marcher la liberté, il faut être partial pour la liberté.
—Benjamin Constant

An Enigmatic Character

Benjamin Constant's last book, *Mélanges de littérature et de politique* (1829), begins with the following declaration: "For forty years, I have defended the same principle, liberty in everything, in religion, in philosophy, in literature, in politics: and by liberty I mean the triumph of individuality over the authority which would like to govern despotically as well as over the masses that claim the right to subject the minority to the majority."[1] In spite of such an unambiguous commitment to liberty, Constant remains an enigma for many of his readers.[2] The complexity of his political thought and the strategies Constant used to promote liberty defy any single interpretation, but there is another unifying theme in his writings which might be even more important than liberty in defining his political outlook: moderation.

To be sure, Constant's works[3] illustrate, arguably better than those of any other author examined in this book, the paradoxes and challenges of political moderation as well as its complex institutional elements and arrangements calculated to uphold and protect individual liberty. Although Constant's political views were moderate, he was at the same time a restless spirit, perpetually dissatisfied with his intellectual and political achievements, and always in search of an elusive spiritual ideal. Constant thought highly of his talents but was prone to *ennui* and melancholy. He feared dejection as one of the great scourges to which human beings are subject and was painfully aware that "reaching the end is always sadder than being on the journey, when one is constantly being distracted by the objects one passes."[4] It is impossible, indeed, not to be impressed by the contrast between the thinker, who emphasized the importance of responsibility and morality in society, and the individual who, in his personal life, was always ready to take extreme risks[5] and to engage in relationships which were, to say the least, spectacularly passionate and complicated.[6]

Moreover, as one of Constant's first critics (Sainte-Beuve) argued, there was something unusual about a man who wrote a book about love (*Adolphe*) without being capable of truly loving anyone, and another one on religion (*De la religion*) without really believing in God.[7] Nor is it easy to explain why, during the Hundred Days, after having written an entire book in which he denounced Napoleon's absolute power, Constant joined forces with the latter, agreeing to write a new (liberal) constitution for the Emperor.[8] During the Directory, Constant found himself in yet another paradoxical situation; that of defending the monopoly on power exercised by a republican government that worked for a legitimate cause—the consolidation of the republic—but did not have a majority in the legislature. As already noted, it was this regime that, in order to prevent the return to power of ultraroyalists and the Jacobins, resorted to extra-constitutional means which ultimately eroded the legitimacy of the First Republic, paving the way for Napoleon's rise to power. Finally, although Constant's name has often been identified with the "liberty of the moderns" and individual rights, in all of his political writings, with the exception of his late two-volume commentary on Gaetano Filangieri,[9] he did not endorse a pure version of "negative" liberty (freedom from state interference), nor was he a simple defender of small government and individual rights. During the Directory, when he leaned to the left, Constant advocated in fact an energetic form of government, while in his later writings, he expressed support for a judicious combination of the two forms of liberty (ancient and modern), considering political participation an essential element of political liberty and a means of self-improvement as well. Finally, it is also worth remembering that Constant lived as a Swiss citizen and a Protestant in a country (France) that was predominantly Catholic and was reluctant to extend the benefits of French citizenship to foreign nationals.

Emphasizing the contrast between his personal and public life may not, however, be the best way of studying Constant's moderation or trying to understand his complex *persona*. A better point of departure might be his early writings during the Directory and the Consulate,[10] which are full of interesting ambiguities. Some of Constant's interpreters condemned him for his endorsement of the *coup d'état* of 18th Fructidor (1797). The events of 18th Fructidor posed a particular challenge to republican constitutionalists such as Mme de Staël and Benjamin Constant because it raised the issue of whether it was ever legitimate to use non-constitutional means to save the republic.

I shall begin by examining Constant's lesser-known political writings from 1795 to 1799 and then turn to his better-known works written during the First Empire and the Bourbon Restoration. Interpreting Constant's writings poses interesting hermeneutical challenges. For one thing, he was a prolific writer who took extensive notes and used them in his numerous writings, making occasional but significant changes and additions to his texts. For example, his most important political book, *Principes de politique*, exists in two versions (1806–1810 and 1815), which are, in fact, two more or less different books.[11] The 1806 manuscript offered a powerful antidote to Napoleon's power, while the second edition appeared in late April 1815, by which time Constant had rallied to Napoleon's cause. Moreover, Constant left unpublished[12] a major political work, *Fragments d'un ouvrage abandonné sur la possibilité d'une constitution républicaine dans un grand pays* (drafted around 1802), in which he took up the important issue of the compatibility between a large state and a republican regime. Perhaps even more surprising, Constant regarded as his masterpiece neither *Principes* nor *Fragments*, but the five-volume *De la religion*, which he called "the only consolation" of his life. Helena Rosenblatt has recently argued that Constant's religious ideas and his Protestantism were inseparable from his political views and require special consideration. Without taking account of the religious and moral convictions that informed his individualist form of political liberalism, therefore, we risk getting only a distorted and truncated view of Constant's theory of liberty as a means of self-development.[13]

Constant's Middle Way during the Directory

It is possible to interpret Constant's political thought as a development of many of the themes that also preoccupied Necker, Mme de Staël, and Sismondi, such as liberty, moderation, and limited power. Yet, while Constant belonged to Necker's school[14] and was the closest intellectual companion of Mme de Staël, they did not always agree in their political and personal views, even when claiming to represent a middle way between revolution and reaction during the Directory. If the dialogue between Necker and Constant remains to be fully analyzed, the story of the complex relationship between Constant and Mme de Staël has been explored in detail by their biographers, old and new.[15] There is little doubt that in their close intellectual collaboration they enriched each other's political vision in numerous ways, although their personal relationship was often tumultuous.[16] Some of Constant's recent interpreters have claimed that, while his experience paralleled that of Mme de Staël, he was, arguably, a "more explicitly reflective and systematic political thinker."[17] Nonetheless, it is in the political writings of Mme de Staël from the 1790s rather than in those of Constant (during the same period) that we find the first coherent and sustained treatment of constitutional issues. Both thinkers saw their intellectual and political engagement as an attempt to find a center between revolution and reaction, and both mobilized an unprecedented arsenal of forces and energies to establish such a *juste milieu* between extremes.

Constant published three influential pamphlets in 1796 and 1797 that are essential to understanding his political agenda. Completed in December 1795, *De la force du gouvernement actuel de la France et de la nécessité de s'y rallier* appeared first at Lausanne in March 1796. *Des réactions politiques* and *Des effets de la Terreur* came out a year later in 1797. During this period, Constant also published a number of short essays[18] that shed light on the evolution of his ideas and the ways in which he responded to changing circumstances. If Constant was a moderate searching for a center, what type of moderate was he, and what kind of center did he envisage? How can we account for his notorious political versatility, which made him change some of his positions while also appealing to universal principles that commanded unconditional allegiance? And finally, was there a rift between his early writings and the two editions of his *Principes de politique* (1806–1810 and 1815), in which his constitutional thought found its most coherent expression?

The texts Constant published between 1795 and 1799 have often been viewed as mere *écrits de jeunesse* that preceded the crystallization of his political thought, which arguably took place around 1806, when he drafted the first version of *Principes*. Many scholars, including Stephen Holmes and Biancamaria Fontana, have paid particular attention to his famous speech on the liberty of the moderns and the liberty of the ancients given at the Athénée Royal in Paris in 1819. A few others, however, such as Mauro Barberis, Stefano de Luca, K. Steven Vincent, and Étienne Hoffman,[19] have pointed to the importance of Constant's early pamphlets which, in their opinion, represent an original and valuable attempt to link principles and circumstances, or, in other words, theory and political practice. According to these authors, the early writings of Constant contained all of the essential elements of his mature liberal doctrine and must be seen as much more than circumstantial works defending momentary causes. In these writings, Constant articulated a powerful defense of the liberal-republican agenda of the Directory, used historical insights to argue for the necessity of specific institutions and principles, and participated in a larger debate on the meanings, causes, and legacy of the French Revolution, having as interlocutors major thinkers such as Necker, Mme de Staël, Burke, Kant, Maistre, and Lezay-Marnésia. Like Mme de Staël, Constant took a *longue durée* view of the French Revolution which, he argued, was not an accidental event, but had been in the making for a long time. The veritable authors of the revolution, Constant maintained, were political actors such as Richelieu, Mazarin, and Louis XIV, their despotic ministers, and the arrogant nobles who exercised or endorsed absolute power, wasted the resources of the country, and persecuted dissenters.[20] Furthermore, along with Necker's and Mme de Staël's works, the texts written by Constant during the Directory represented one of the first attempts to rethink in a systematic way the possibility of a moderate constitutionalist agenda in France after the Terror.

The evolution of Constant's political ideas over the two decades separating the Thermidor from the Bourbon Restoration constitutes a fascinating case study that would exceed the scope of this chapter. Suffice it to say that, in spite of their partisan and occasionally propagandistic tone, Constant's texts from 1795 to 1799 offer a special point of entry into his political thought. Although these early writings were conceived under the pressure of circumstances, in the middle of intense political battles whose end was not always in sight, they shed fresh light on the development of Constant's political views and clarify for us the ways in which he tried to navigate the stormy waters of the Directory, amidst a rapidly changing and unstable political climate. Moreover, Constant's later endorsement of constitutional monarchy during the Restoration was, to use Stefano de Luca's own words, *"la traduzione monarchica di un assetto costituzionale per la repubblica"*[21] elaborated between 1795 and 1803. For in Constant's early writings, we find a lucid analysis of the risks inherent in the democratic principle as well as a strong critique of political arbitrariness and the corruption of popular sovereignty. We see Constant commenting on the possibility of a republic in a great state and highlighting the challenges posed to a fledgling representative regime by opponents who wished a return to the previous order. Last but not least, in these texts we discover Constant developing ingenuous political and rhetorical strategies meant to support the government, while also trying to give his position a more solid theoretical foundation.

As we have seen, in the summer of 1795, a year after 9th Thermidor, the political landscape was still dominated by the ghosts of the Terror and the stability of the new republican institutions was threatened by the ideological intolerance of the Jacobins and the émigrés. In Constant's view, what the enemies of the new republican government had in common was a preference for arbitrary power, a propensity to intransigence, and a blatant disregard for publicity and the rule of law.[22] The line between suspects and innocents was thin, while fear and a desire for revenge contributed to the creation of a climate of uncertainty and intolerance.[23] The prevailing anxiety was exacerbated by the imminent end of the Convention and the forthcoming elections, which seemed to favor the extreme right. Anticipating a comeback of the ultraroyalists at polls that threatened to bring about the end of the republic, the members of the Convention wanted to avoid committing the same error as their predecessors four years before. They decided to pass two decrees on August 22 and 30, 1795 stipulating that two thirds of the members of the new assembly would be chosen from the ranks of the Convention and only a third would be elected in genuinely free elections.[24] Thus, they attempted to secure for themselves the majority in the future assembly by infringing upon one of the fundamental principles of the fledgling republic: liberty of suffrage.

Soon after he arrived in Paris with Mme de Staël in May 1795, Constant was drawn into the debates on the new constitution and on the causes and meanings of the Terror. The events of 1st Prairial Year III (May 20, 1795), when a Jacobin rebellion was defeated, and the insurrection of 13 Vendémiaire (October 5, 1795), when the army put down a royalist insurgence, loomed large on Constant's mind. He was also eager to refute those who viewed the Terror as a necessary or inevitable period in the unfolding of the revolution. To this effect, he worked arguably harder than anyone else to separate the revolution from the Terror and to save the moment of 1789 from that of 1793.[25] In his writings of this period, Constant called upon all the constitutionalists—republican and monarchical—to rally to the republican cause in order to create a common front against the dangers posed by counter-revolutionary and Jacobin factions. Referring to all the constitutionalists as friends of liberty, he asked them to support the republic and its institutions, much as Mme de Staël did in her *Réflexions sur la paix intéri-*

eure, the text she completed at about the same time as Constant's three *Letters to a Member of the Convention* published in *Nouvelles politiques, nationales et étrangères*. Constant's letters, which marked his political debut, appeared on June 24, 25, and 26, 1795.[26] His critique of the two-thirds elicited several critical responses, most notably from the pen of Jean-Baptiste Louvet (1760–1797). Barely a month later, Constant joined his former critic in drafting a few speeches in which Louvet defended the controversial decrees. Constant's change of mind is a fascinating illustration of the ambiguities and paradoxes of moderation. It might be explained, to some extent, by the ideological confusion that prevailed in France during the summer of 1795, but we should also grant that he might have learned from experience and from the criticisms of his colleagues.

In the first letter, Constant dismissed the analogy with the Constituent Assembly as being unfounded and argued that the political circumstances of 1795, when the country was searching for a new synthesis between order and liberty, were entirely different from those of 1791, when liberty trumped all other principles. The new deputies, Constant argued, could represent their constituencies with dignity and confidence only if chosen in free elections open to primary assemblies.[27] In the second letter, he insisted that the decrees of the two-thirds were counterproductive and predicted that they would have perverse consequences, irritating the people.[28] Finally, in his third letter, Constant claimed that it was in the real interest of the Convention to give up the idea of preserving a two-thirds majority in the new assembly by resorting to a blatantly unconstitutional measure. Constant's letters triggered widely different reactions among republicans, who were dismayed by them, and among royalists, who welcomed Constant's critique of the two-thirds decrees. While the republicans criticized Constant for failing to understand that free elections would usher in a powerful ultraroyalist majority which could jeopardize the survival of the republic, the royalists mistook Constant for a supporter of monarchy and invited him to join their ranks.

A month later, Constant changed gears and claimed that those who criticized the decrees were wrong to apply abstract principles without paying due consideration to shifting circumstances.[29] He collaborated with Louvet in drafting three important discourses which the latter gave in the Convention on August 21 and 22, 1795.[30] Louvet believed that the priority for the members of the Convention was the preservation of the republic and argued that the Convention rather than primary assemblies ought to have been given the choice of the controversial two thirds. Primary assemblies, Louvet argued, were nests of intrigue and extremism in which the true friends of the republic were a minority. Unfortunately, Louvet's fears were borne out by subsequent developments. The newly elected assembly came to be dominated by royalists whose political agenda threatened the stability of the new government.

Along with the speeches given at the Constitutional Circle in 1797–98, the three books published by Constant in 1796 and 1797 put forward a compelling case for the Directory and confirmed his attachment to the (liberal) principles of 1789, a stance that remained, in the words of Steven Vincent, "remarkably consistent."[31] Although the issue of individual rights did not loom large in these early texts, the reader will find in their pages many of the themes that eventually became central to Constant's later political outlook, such as his opposition to political arbitrariness and extremism and his commitment to moderation and pluralism. Key questions emerged as well: What are the limits of legal repression of political abuses? How can political responsibility be properly secured? At the same time, it must be pointed out that Constant's tone in these early writings seems anything but moderate (if we take moderation to be incompatible with strong partisanship). Although he was attracted to the moderates in the Convention, his texts contain many strongly polemical and partisan claims that stand in an uneasy relation with his image as a defender of the center, which was supposed to bring together all the friends of liberty and moderation in France.

To be sure, Constant was extremely vocal in his support for the republican government and resorted to a complex rhetorical strategy, which went so far as to include veiled threats. He defended the necessity of republican institutions in France, rejected Montesquieu's claim that republics could survive only in small countries, and sketched a philosophy of history grounded in the idea of progress.[32] Finally, he outlined a bold agenda addressed to all friends of freedom with a view to overcoming their inner divisions. He described the political scene in terms of the stark contrast between moderates and radicals, insisting that a gulf separated the two camps. "On one side are ranged the moderate men, on the other the violent," Constant wrote. "Only these latter, however, remain united a long time.... Moderate men, not being under the sway of a dominant preoccupation, lend their ears readily to individual considerations. Pride awakens in them, courage is shaken, their steadfastness wearies, personal calculation, repulsed for a moment, takes up the charge again."[33] Post-revolutionary periods, he argued, pose daunting challenges to the defenders of liberty, because during these times the voice of passions tends to be stronger than reason, and virtue, fear, vanity, and pride coexist with the desire for revenge, cupidity and ruthless self-interest. The political scene is filled not only with "mediocre talents, joined with subaltern natures"[34] who set themselves up as guardians of thought, but also with shrewd opportunists, moved by ignoble desires. "The apostates of all opinions gather swiftly.... Crafty turncoats, famous in the annals of vice, slip into place; at all times they blight everything good, belittle everything elevated, and insult everything noble."[35] Furthermore, as intelligence is separated from conscience, "the weirdest doctrines are arrogantly advanced and the prejudices of all the ages and the injustices of all countries are brought back together as materials of the new social order.[36]

Given this complex situation, Constant called upon the all friends of freedom to carefully "distinguish those who really hate the cause of liberty from those who have the misfortune to distrust its effects; to examine every division of the enemy's army, with a view either to recognize their old allies, or to encourage new deserters."[37] In order to be successful, the real friends of freedom should "exclude and repulse none but the degraded partisans of pure despotism, or the ferocious advocates of crimes and barbarity."[38] They must not compromise with the agents of reaction over their fundamental principles—republicanism, the rule of law, opposition to despotism—and ought to vigorously affirm their principles and beliefs. Situated in a besieged middle exposed to the crossfire of extremes, they should remain firmly attached to their fundamental values "in order to establish and consolidate the reign of principles."[39] They must not follow the whims of public opinion, but should try to prudently moderate and, when appropriate, educate it. Furthermore, Constant added, they should oppose arbitrariness and endorse the rule of law, while also exposing the prejudices of their enemies and highlighting the contradictions in their arguments.

We must avoid drawing hasty conclusions when interpreting Constant's endorsement of republican institutions, particularly in *De la force du gouvernement actuel* (1796), a controversial and partisan book, warmly received by some and harshly criticized by others.[40] There is no need to question the sincerity of his allegiance to the French republic, but we should not forget that, in his view, all forms of government were less important than the goals they served, their ultimate aim being the protection of freedom and individual rights. Constant urged his audience to support the republican regime by describing the latter as a *fait accompli* that already commanded the allegiance of a majority of French citizens:

> The Republic has one primary advantage, which does not seem to be sufficiently attended to, that of being actually established. . . . One half of France, at the least, is at present attached to the Republic by its interests. . . . Thus the Republic has in its favor, besides the circumstance of being established, the interests of a numerous body of men; and those of the most ardent and enthusiastic part of the nation.[41]

In making this point, Constant challenged those who questioned the legitimacy of the new republican institutions and wished to overturn the regime. He accused them of being "dupes of words" and took them to task for forgetting that "a counter-revolution would be, in fact, nothing but a new revolution."[42] To all these opponents of the Directory, he issued a strong warning: the government was prepared to do everything in its power to protect itself against their attacks. It would mount a powerful response to any challenge. It was ready, in fact to use nonconstitutional means if exceptional circumstances required them. Among such possible means, Constant mentioned recourse to "terrorists" who, he added, "may be considered as the artillery of the government: always concealed, but always formidable; and which, whenever they are forced to employ them, will grind all their adversaries to dust."[43]

A great deal of Constant's ire was directed at the journalists who had attacked the Convention after 9th Thermidor and whose republican allegiance seemed doubtful. The treatment he reserved to them in the first chapter of the book illustrates the latter's highly polemical and partisan tone. Constant described them as "a class of men, scrupulous, discontented, and fond of disputing about trifles, well meaning and possessed of considerable talents, but unforgiving and intolerably vain," who "set an equal value upon all their own opinions [and] insist, with the same warmth and obstinacy, upon the slightest grievances, and the most important questions."[44] These perennially dissatisfied critics, Constant opined, "are not only useless, but essentially dangerous, during revolutions and in new governments."[45] Accusing them of misreading the political scene and letting themselves be guided by their vanity and petty ambitions, he challenged them to have "confidence of success and the enthusiasm which promises victory."[46] Constant called upon all undecided friends of liberty to support the new republican government: "Away therefore with your doubts, fatigue us no longer with your skepticism, but assist us in consolidating liberty."[47] He insisted that no one could afford the luxury of remaining impartial in times of crisis. All must stand by the Directory when its legitimacy and stability were threatened:

> Justice is the sacred duty of all those who govern, but impartiality would be both weak and criminal. Before a man can hope to make any institution succeed, it is requisite that he should himself feel a partiality for it. It would be absurd to become a political doubting philosopher, and to employ oneself in collecting doubts, comparing probabilities, and eternally asking the majority if it persevered in preferring the present form of government. The mind of man is so changeable, that the systems by which he is governed ought to be made as stable as possible. The majority ought to be supported and encouraged, by putting it in mind of its former wishes and of its present duty.[48]

As Lezay-Marnésia argued, there was something odd about Constant's immoderate call for supporting the republic at all costs, for it would have been equally legitimate to ask the government to bend to public opinion, which was opposed to many of the Directory's policies. Constant was undisturbed by this paradox, for he believed that public opinion was ultimately unreliable. It was excessively influenced by *l'esprit de parti*, and so could not be seen as truly representative of the wide gamut of opinions and interests in society: "At a moment when the agents of the government are first invested with great powers, which, though their limits are exactly traced out by the constitution, are not yet rendered sacred by custom; it is advantageous, I will even say necessary to the establishment of liberty, that these agents should be in opposition to public opinion."[49] Moreover, Constant added, the tensions between government and public opinion could be beneficial if properly monitored and moderated, and if the actions of the agents of government were kept under close public scrutiny. On the contrary, Constant went on, when the government is fully supported by public opinion, there remain few checks on its power, and laws may become powerless in restraining its sphere of action.[50]

Constant's argument in favor of political flexibility did not amount, however, to a blank check given to political arbitrariness, as one might infer from the previous quotes. In *Des réactions politiques* (1797), he denounced in unambiguous terms the lack of respect for rules and forms along with the ruthless pursuit of personal interest at the expense of the common good.[51] The partisans of arbitrariness, Constant claimed, reject principles, preferring instead to invoke whatever circumstantial pretexts suit their momentary interests. If everyone paid attention only to circumstances and behaved opportunistically, the outcome would be chaos, instability, injustice, and arbitrariness, defined as the absence of any fixed rules and limits:

> If there are no principles, nothing is fixed; what are left are only circumstances and everyone is free to judge them as he thinks fit. People will go from one circumstance to another one, without their claims having any firm foundation. For there can be no stable ground where everything fluctuates. What is just and unjust, what is legitimate and illegitimate will cease to exist because all these elements are founded upon principles and disappear with them. What is left are the passions which will draw upon arbitrariness, the bad faith which will abuse arbitrariness, and the spirit of resistance which will seek to control it; in one word, arbitrariness will rule alone. . . . Arbitrariness is the absence of rules, limits, definitions, in one word, the absence of everything precise.[52]

Circumstantial considerations and transitory interests, Constant insisted, should never trump principles, and those who exercise power must always follow the rule of law rather than seeking the fleeting approval of unstable majorities. "What is passionate, personal, and transitory must be related and subservient to what is abstract, fixed, and immutable," he argued. "The government should reject this revolutionary habit which makes it look for justifications which do not come from the laws. It must be praised for following the document where its duties are written—the constitution which is always the same—and not in the transitory applause of versatile opinions."[53] In particular, Constant criticized those who, in the footsteps of Burke, opposed abstract principles in the name of the allegedly higher call of prudence and practical wisdom in response to the pressure of circumstances. In his view, rejecting *a priori* theoretical principles and relying upon "prejudices" and recollections was an unacceptable position because it did not rule out arbitrariness.[54] Nonetheless, though Constant disagreed with Burke's critique of the original principles of the French Revolution, he fully shared his opposition to arbitrariness and radicalism. Constant identified two forms of arbitrariness, which he unambiguously rejected: one arising from the absence of any principles whatsoever, the other stemming from a rigid interpretation of principles that ignored historical and political contexts. The second form of arbitrariness, Constant argued, had emerged during the later phases of the revolution, when general principles such as equality and fraternity were embraced so dogmatically as to make political compromises virtually impossible. Because these principles were not mediated by what Constant called necessary "intermediary" principles, they remained confined to an abstract sphere, being generally perceived as destructive of—or foreign to—the real interests and needs of the country.

Moderation and the Republic of the "Extreme Center"

Denounced by some as a mere rhetorical position devoid of any coherent or positive doctrine, the political center had an undeniable complexity and surprising fluidity during the Directory. According to Pierre Serna, it was a powerful rhetorical trope used by various political actors to defend a wide range of agendas.[55] Though its essence and contours ultimately depended upon the fluctuating vitality and strategies of the extremes, the ideas used to justify the *juste milieu* that lay between them triggered lively political debates.

One such debate focused on the possibility and desirability of a "third" power, on which the stability of the republic arguably depended. Far from being a novelty, the concept of a *troisième pouvoir* was an offshoot of the doctrine of the balance of powers and could be found, for example, in Roederer's public lectures of 1793, in which he analyzed the causes that had led to the defeat of a third (moderating) party in 1792.[56] The dream of establishing such a party in France remained unfulfilled, as political events turned unfavorable to the friends of moderation. Their status became at once both tragic and ironic. Tragic, because the eventual silencing of moderates after 18th Brumaire meant that their short spring of liberty came to an abrupt end before the institutions of the republic were consolidated. Ironic, because through the strategies and temporary alliances they formed in their quest of the ever-elusive center, the moderates in the end created the conditions for Napoleon's rise to absolute power.[57] If the center, the *locus* of moderation, remained a utopian goal during the Directory, this was not because it lacked a coherent set of principles or a solid doctrine. In reality, the search for the center became a pretext for endorsing a variety of ideological positions pretending—sometimes rhetorically, other times in good faith—to see farther and better than the extremes. Interested in consolidating the republic around an "extreme center,"[58] the moderates like Constant or Mme de Staël proceeded to stigmatize and neutralize centrifugal and radical forces. They claimed that that their center represented the only possible means of pacifying the country, healing the wounds inflicted by the revolution, and creating effective representative institutions in France.

It has been argued that Constant's position may be regarded as truly moderate only *after* the coup of 18th Fructidor. Before that date, he had positioned himself to the left of center in his attempt to rally support for the besieged republican government.[59] At first sight, this claim seems to be true. In spite of the avowedly centrist agenda pursued by Constant, the concept of moderation occupied only a small place in the three pamphlets he published in 1796 and 1797. What is remarkable is that, in 1796, Constant spoke in support of the virtues of the French Republic while encouraging the government *not* to practice them, or to do so only sparingly and when it suited its agenda. This endorsement of *Realpolitik* was surprising on the part of a thinker who a year later claimed that a strict adherence to principles was the only way of effectively neutralizing the nefarious influence of "circumstances."[60] And yet, a closer look at the agenda pursued by Constant shows that the theme of moderation was not at all absent from his early writings.[61] In fact, he distinguished between "true" and "false" moderation, while arguing for a flexible type of moderation based on "principles."[62]

This distinction deserves special attention. Constant took to task "those eternal and unabashed panegyrists of change who, always looking for the middle ground, remain midway, and do not believe that social order can be established on a firm foundation."[63] These false moderates, he claimed, pretended to be neutral between error and truth (in the sense of not caring whether something is true or not) when, in reality, they were pursuing only their own interests and were not committed to fixed principles. For Constant, a genuinely centrist agenda could not dispense with the latter: "There is a middle ground between changes which hinder and exaggerations which mislead. This middle consists of principles ... in all their force and as a whole, according to their natural order and their necessary logical sequence, principles adopted in totality, properly gathered and arranged, and supporting each other."[64]

Not all liberals, however, were convinced by Constant's arguments. A part of what was informally known as *le parti constitutionnel* remained skeptical toward his call to form a new center. Although the importance of this group has often been downplayed by historians, its members, as Henri Grange has argued,[65] mounted a significant challenge to the Directory, even if they remained committed to liberal and republican principles. As the victim of the coup d'état of 18th Fructidor, *le parti constitutionnel* had sufficient reasons for being skeptical toward Constant's centrist rhetoric. For one thing, the latter had significant political implications and connotations with which the members of the "constitutionalist party" disagreed. Among other things, they must have remembered that Constant had worked hard to cast doubt on the possibility and desirability of a two-party system in France, similar to the one existing in England. His quest now for a third party—the party of the center—illustrated his distrust toward the possibility of a two-party system (in France), in which the governing party was expected to have the majority of the legislative power. This position was certainly surprising in the case of a declared Anglophile like Constant, who should have noticed that a *parti mitoyen*, which he deemed to be fundamental to the political stability of France, did not exist in England and did not seem to be essential to the preservation of liberty across the Channel.

The topic of a putative "third party" became the subject of an interesting dialogue between Constant and Adrien de Lezay-Marnésia (1769–1814). A close friend of Mme de Staël, Lezay disagreed with Constant in an important pamphlet whose suggestive title was intended to remind his readers that the Directory did not have the majority on its side: *De la faiblesse d'un gouvernement qui commence, et de la nécessité où il est de se rallier à la majorité nationale* (1796).[66] Lezay-Marnésia did not think that a third centrist party could play a significant role in strengthening representative institutions in France. The ideology of the center, he argued, had in fact been opportunistically used by a wide array of politicians with strikingly different political allegiances. Many of them had previously been Jacobins under Robespierre and anti-Jacobins after 9th Thermidor; some of them condemned the "terrorists" after 1st Prairial as strongly as the ultras, while yet others appeared to be even more radical than the members of the Mountain after 13th Vendémiaire.[67] Because of the diversity of their ideas, they would not possibly be able to form a stable and strong party, let alone articulate a coherent doctrine capable of gaining wide political support.

Furthermore, according to Lezay-Marnésia, this *parti sans bannière*[68] did not have a solid anchor in the views held by the majority of the people and could not legitimately claim to represent "the middling opinion"[69] of the country. As such, it was confined to pursuing an uncertain and incoherent *politique de bascule*, allowing various groups to come to power through temporary but ultimately questionable alliances. Acting as a rallying point for all the opportunists excluded from other parties, this middling party was (in Lezay-Marnésia's words) nothing more than a *parti de sable*, a "party made out of sand, which the smallest wave can divide or throw, as the wind blows, against one of the rocks on the left or the right."[70] It was a "party without force" because it was not connected to the country and did not reflect its long-term interests. In particular, Lezay-Marnésia criticized the claim of the partisans of the center that they alone represented public opinion. Such a claim blurred the distinction between the "legal" majority (defined as the numerical majority of the electors of a nation who manifest their positive will at polls) and the "real" or "natural" majority, which forms itself spontaneously whenever the nation experiences a major change and also includes the voices of those—women, children, servants—who do not belong to the "legal" majority. This "real" majority of the nation, Lezay-

Marnésia insisted, was the natural one, while the legal majority was an artificial construct.[71]

He added that the presence of a third party claiming to represent the center in the assembly would constitute a threat to the stability of the latter, by condemning it to remain at the mercy of unstable and fleeting coalitions and majorities. "As long as this third party exists," Lezay-Marnésia wrote, "an assembly would be in perpetual motion. It can recover its equipoise only when it is reduced to two well-established parties, one supporting the prerogative of the government against the invasions of the lower classes, and the other supporting the freedom of the people against the encroachment of the government."[72] Hence, Lezay-Marnésia concluded, the efforts made by the partisans of the center to discredit the left and the right had a paradoxical implication which was an unintended outcome of their (arguably good) intentions: it *prevented* the consolidation of a stable bipolar political system, which alone could have brought about the desired order and stability. An important upshot of his critique is that political moderation depends on— and is enhanced by—the existence of a two-party parliamentary system in which both parties freely compete for the votes of the electorate. On this view, a party of the center is unlikely to contribute significantly to the consolidation of a parliamentary system regulated by the alternation in the majority/ minority status of two parties. The only way a third party might thrive would be to adopt the shrewd rhetorical and political strategy of exaggerating the dangers posed by extremes and pursuing an opportunistic policy of recruitment of those dissatisfied with the agenda espoused by the two parties.

That Lezay-Marnésia's critique of the centrist rhetoric of the period was aimed at a real phenomenon is amply demonstrated by a cursory look at some of the most important newspapers published during this period. The ideology of the center and the theme of a "republic of the center" were omnipresent in influential newspapers, such as *La Décade, Le Conservateur, Le Journal de Paris,* or *L'Ami des Lois,* in which one can find a remarkable display of rhetorical skills meant to convince a skeptical audience of the power and legitimacy of the center and of the nefarious influence of centrifugal (allegedly radical) forces threatening to destabilize the republic. Four major themes loomed large in the articles published on this topic in the aforementioned journals: the idea of political moderation; the portrait of the centrist citizen as a loyal subject of the republic; the justification of the support for the Directory and its republican institutions; and finally, the legitimization of a strong executive power allowed to use, in exceptional circumstances, extra-constitutional means to save the republic. These articles sought to demonstrate the need for—and the reasonableness of— compromise for the sake of preserving republican institutions allegedly endangered by the radicalism of "extremists." Their authors endorsed flexibility and prudence and redefined common sense as a form of moderation and a pillar of the besieged center, with a view to bringing reluctant moderates to support the Directory. The authors of these articles imagined a new class, *la classe mitoyenne*, which they presented as the locus of reason-ableness and the only "intermediary" body upon which the liberty and order of the republic could safely rest.

Worth noting in all these texts is the simultaneously open and exclusive nature of the center which included, in fact, several groups separated by significant differences of opinion. In an article published in *La Décade* (1798), Jean-Baptiste Say identified three categories of radicals whom he wanted to exclude from a hypothetical party of the center because of their lack of allegiance to the Directory:[73] royalists dreaming of restoring the Old Regime; fomenters of anarchy; and ruthless opportunists seeking to profit from the republic in order to gain wealth and personal influence. "When the Republic will be fully consolidated and when the still powerful parties of royalism and the Terror will no longer exist," Say predicted, "these people will be the first ones on the list of those to be excluded."[74] The "true" center, he opined, did have a positive and clear agenda resting on a few fundamen-tal principles and values such as common sense, moderation, and honesty: "The middling ground between ostentatious wealth and poverty has always been and still is the one which has most virtue and knowledge."[75] These virtues alone, Say concluded, could heal the wounds of the revolution by reinvigorating economic life and promoting social trust.

Equally bold and confident was the tone espoused by Say in another ar-ticle published in *La Décade* on May 19, 1798, in which he endorsed the use of extra-constitutional means to defend the besieged republic against its alleged enemies. Say's position (also shared by Constant[76] and Staël) nicely shows the ambiguities of moderation and the center during the second half of the Directory. He began by admitting that the question of justifying the temporary violation of constitutional principles is perhaps one of the most difficult problems in theory. The difficulty lay in the fact that all parties tended to be hypocritical when addressing this issue: "All parties want to seem to respect principles at the very moment when they are forced to vio-late them." Say went on to explain why the partisans of the republic and the friends of liberty had to "defend themselves with equal weapons" by resort-ing to the same discourse and tactics as their opponents. In the past, the "honest, enlightened, and humane partisans" of the French Revolution had been the constant victims of royalism and Jacobinism "as long as they scru-pulously respected principles."[77] The time had finally come for a radical change of strategy, Say concluded. It was necessary to strengthen the be-sieged center and the executive power so that they would both become ca-pable of acting swiftly and effectively in emergency situations such as 18th Fructidor.

It is important to stress that the rhetoric of an "extreme center"[78] was *not* uncommon among those who claimed to represent moderate views during the Directory and whose political agenda was anything but lukewarm and indecisive. They put forward a thorough analysis of the causes of the revo-lution and the Terror identified the enemies of the republic, denouncing their strategies and highlighting the alleged anachronism of their political views. At the same time, they sought a much-needed consensus around a set of principles and institutions capable of "ending" the revolution by opposing political arbitrariness, the corrupting vice and "germ of death" of all institutions.[79]

All these ideas can be found in the speeches Constant gave at the short-lived Constitutional Circle in 1797–98. Founded shortly before 9th Messidor (June 27) 1797, le *Cercle constitutionnel* was originally conceived as a counterpart to the ultraconservative Club de Clichy. Its founding occurred after the turn of the Legislative Body to the right, a development that fueled speculation about a possible counter-revolution prepared by ultraroyalist circles that seemed to be in a "permanent conspiracy against the Republic."[80] The very title—*Circle* instead of *Club*—is revealing because it shows that, from the very beginning, it sought to avoid the image of a political club liable to being outlawed by the Constitution of 1795. Dissolved on July 24, following the Directory's temporary ban on all political associations, it was reopened a few weeks later, after the Directory lifted the ban during the night of 18th-19th Fructidor. The Constitutional Circle received support from the government, with one of its directors, Barras, acting as the patron of the new group.[81] The most important task that the members of the circle set for themselves was to offer accurate and pertinent analyses of the ongoing political situation in order to better countervail the initiatives of the government's opponents.

Constant played an important role in the founding of this group, which had strict criteria for membership (potential members were carefully vetted and approved after rigorous scrutiny).[82] He benefitted from participating in its activities, which raised his political visibility and allowed him eventually to make many useful political connections. Less than two weeks after the coup of 18th Fructidor, on September 16, 1797, Constant gave an important speech in which he addressed the connection between moderation and the center.[83] Paradoxically, his position contained a good measure of intransigent partisanship that, again, was hardly moderate. Constant deliberately cast all radical positions in a pejorative light and glossed over the nuances and differences between them. He then justified the events of 18th Fructidor as a prelude to reestablishing the rule of law. He did it, however, in a sober manner, by warning the government not to make a habit of invoking the pressure of circumstances to justify resorting to extra-constitutional means. Instead, France needed strong institutions capable of putting an end to political arbitrariness. Constant asked the partisans of the republic not to bind themselves by self-imposed (legal) constraints that might limit their freedom of action and favor other factions. Impartiality, apathy, and skepticism, he maintained, were the enemies of republican institutions and principles. Instead of being impartial and tolerant toward their opponents, republicans should tighten their grip on power. They should exercise it confidently and firmly:

Citizens, let us condemn this system of indifference which one adorns by the name of impartiality. We were deluded for far too long. Let us not confuse any more impartiality with justice. Justice is a government's duty; impartiality is only madness and crime. In order to promote liberty, one must be partial in favor of liberty; and when one sees it attacked by its enemies, one must not make a stupid merit from remaining neutral between them, in the middle.[84]

Like Say, Constant recommended that the government purge from all levels of administration anyone who did now show the required solidarity with and fidelity to republican institutions.[85]

Constant's speech of 9th Ventose, Year VI (27 February 1798) was written in the same mold and raised similar questions. Denouncing the neo-Jacobins as ignorant zealots, he accused them again of acting against the fundamental principles and values of the republic.[86] What is remarkable about this discourse is that, while Constant labeled the neo-Jacobins "criminals" worthy of being exterminated, he also sketched a theory of constitutionalism and political guarantees that would become an essential component of his later liberal doctrine. At the same time, he worried that the constant invocation of real or imaginary enemies and plots against the republic and the habit of resorting to non-constitutional means were likely to subvert the legitimacy of the very regime that promised to consolidate the legacy of the revolution. Constant called again upon his audience to regard the future with confidence and remain committed to a few principles, as the best protection against the malignant influence of factions. These principles were: liberty, equality, the respect for property, and opposition to arbitrariness and hereditary privileges.

Constant declared that arbitrariness had a corrupting effect on all institutions and maintained that any form of liberty, security, and progress was incompatible with it. It was dangerous not only to the governed, but also for those in power who resorted to it. Constant reiterated the importance of morality and constitutional limits on power as well as the responsibility of the agents of government. To live decently, he affirmed, people need fixed rules and guidelines. These rules are given to individuals by morality and to those in power by the laws and the principle of political responsibility:

People need fixed rules and firm guides. For individuals, it is morality; for governments, it is the law; compared to the law, arbitrariness is what superstition is to morality: it distorts and misleads. What protects us from arbitrariness is the observance of forms; forms are the tutelary gods of all human associations. . . . Without them, everything would be obscure and dependent on individual consciousness and changing opinions; only forms are visible and it is to them alone that those who are oppressed can appeal. Ultimately, the remedy to arbitrariness is the responsibility of the agents of power. . . . Every time I shall see in a nation an arbitrarily imprisoned citizen without seeing immediately the officer who arrested him also thrown in the same prison, along with the warden who accepted him, and the bold individual, whoever he might be, who violated the forms of justice, I shall say: this people may wish to be free, may deserve freedom, but they are not familiar yet with the first elements of liberty.[87]

Constant's two speeches and Say's essays from *La Décade* are particularly interesting for students of moderation, because they show how two moderates sailed the muddy waters of the Directory and endorsed strong prerogatives for the executive power that seemed to contradict the spirit of the principle of the balance of powers, a fundamental tenet of all moderates. They maintained that the government should be prepared, if circumstances demand it, to *forgo* moderation and ignore constitutional norms in order to prevent the enemies of the republic from gaining power. With the benefit of hindsight, one can argue that there was a great deal of confusion, illusion, and partisanship in Constant's and Say's positions. It is revealing that in the same speech of 30th Fructidor Year V in which Constant justified the earlier *coup* as a prelude to the reestablishment of the rule of law, he also made an apology of the progress of knowledge and ideas. When those who strive for military glory will also be among the most enlightened, he opined, there will be nothing more to fear from a military government. Two years later, Constant's confident words—"*Alors, nous n'aurons plus à craindre le gouvernement militaire*"[88]—would seem hopelessly naive.

Limited Sovereignty and Individual Liberty

The concept of limited sovereignty occupied a crucial place in all of Constant's political writings. As early as 1797, he stressed the urgency and importance of limiting sovereignty as opposed to merely transferring it from the hands of the few into the hands of the many, without limiting the total sum of power invested in society. In Constant's view, undoubtedly influenced by Necker, no unlimited power should ever exist in society. Only the proper limitation of sovereignty through a complex set of laws, institutions, and practices could create the necessary conditions for liberty.[89] Twenty years later, Constant returned to this point, denouncing the Terror as a conscious and systematic attempt to implement a flawed and pernicious theory of sovereignty and liberty. His interpretation of the Terror stressed that the latter was not the outcome of fortuitous circumstances, but the fruit of a perverted "revolutionary mentality steeped in archaic political myths and lacking historical understanding, totally incapable of understanding the nature and requirements of modern society."[90]

Constant participated in a lively debate on the meanings of the Terror, in which many other important French political thinkers of his time—among them Robert Lindet, Joseph de Maistre, Adrien de Lezay-Marnésia, and Louis de Bonald—also took part. That so many publicists on both sides felt compelled to take issue with the meanings and legacy of the Terror is hardly surprising. No one had been left untouched by the events of 1793–94, which continued to loom large on the post-revolutionary mind. The greatest challenge in interpreting the episode was to properly distinguish between what had to be attributed to human will or the (alleged) coalition of internal and external "enemies" of the revolution, and what was the outcome of political circumstances beyond human control. In assessing human agency, the question that arose was whether there were only a handful of guilty individuals, or whether the responsibility was shared by many more actors, both active and passive instruments of the Terror. Moreover, some saw the revolution and the Terror as inseparable, while others drew a clear distinction between 1789 and 1793. Still others claimed that the Terror had been an accident and refused to admit that the significance and legacy of the revolution could be reduced to its darkest episode. On the extreme right, some regarded the Terror as divine punishment for the hubris of revolutionary leaders. This view amounted to denying human beings the ability to direct political events, implying that it was events that led individuals against their will.[91]

Constant's *Des effets de la Terreur*[92] was written as a point-by-point refutation of Lezay-Marnésia's *Des causes de la Révolution et de ses résultats* (1797), an ambitious and anonymously published work in which the author reflected on the causes of the French Revolution by placing them within a larger historical context.[93] In spite of their fundamental disagreement, the two authors were in accord on a few major points. They both held that France had no true constitution during the Old Regime when the power of the monarch was absolute.[94] Constant was also in agreement with Lezay's justification of the overall achievements of the revolution, in particular with his claim that its most durable outcome was "a spirit of liberty" opposed to any form of tyranny.[95] On this view, it was wrong to reject the revolution as a whole in spite of the violence that it engendered.

Where the two authors differed most was in their account of the inevitability of the Terror. Constant was particularly troubled by Lezay-Marnésia's focus on "circumstances" and his implicit legitimization of violence as a necessary phase in modern revolutions. Lezay-Marnésia made no distinction between the liberal moment in 1789 and the illiberal phase of 1793, and argued that the great changes brought forth by the French Revolution could not have occurred without its violent episodes. There always is in the middle of popular revolutions, he wrote, a phase marked by extreme violence, which gives renewed vigor to extremist forces and emboldens radicals to action. Lezay also maintained that the Terror was not a sudden event but one anticipated by the previous phases of the Revolution. The events of

1793–1794 followed their own logic which owed little to individual actions and almost everything to factors beyond human control.[96]

Regarding the true causes of the revolution, Lezay-Marnésia and Constant were not as far apart as they might have initially thought. The revolution, the first claimed, had little to do with the actions of individuals, and owed a lot to the advance of knowledge, the progress of *lumières*, and the changes fostered by Protestantism. As such, the revolution brought forth much more than a mere change in the form of government. It led to a profound transformation of mores, habits, conditions, and interests, and altered the structure of property and the entire constitutional landscape of the country. Finally, Lezay-Marnésia refused to admit that the causes of the revolution could be reduced to a single factor, and made a plea for a nuanced analysis of its origins.

Constant should have been in agreement with Lezay's argument that the deeper causes of the revolution were to be attributed to the advance of *les lumières*. In a lesser-known (but important) text, *Histoire abrégée de l'égalité*,[97] Constant expressed the belief that the progress of history was coeval with the growth of equality, which he equated with justice. Keen on preserving the distinction between 1789 (made possible, in his opinion, by the advance of liberty) and 1793 (caused by an excess of equality), and professing to be indulgent toward individuals (who had made the Terror possible) while remaining irremediably opposed to its principles,[98] Constant vigorously opposed all attempts at justifying the necessity and inevitability of violence. The Terror, he maintained, was not necessary to the safety of the republic. On the contrary, it undermined its foundations and corrupted its principles (virtue, popular sovereignty), delaying the consolidation of republican institutions in France. The Terror also made possible the appearance of new forms of fanaticism and extremism, which corrupted the public spirit, fostering fear and civic apathy.[99] All of these ideas would reappear in Constant's later writings, especially in the two versions of *Principes* (1806–1810, and 1815), in which his thoughts on moderation and sovereignty overlapped with reflections on the ancient polis, legitimacy, authority, the distribution of powers, political responsibility, and the limits of political obligation.

No account of Constant's ideas on sovereignty can be complete without commenting on his engagement with Rousseau, which led to a rich intellectual dialogue that makes clear both Constant's deep fascination for the latter and his opposition to the political implications of Rousseau's *Du contrat social*.[100] It is fair to say that Constant's Rousseau was not the same figure as the real author bearing this name, for Constant paid virtually no attention to Rousseau's constitutional writings on the government of Poland and Corsica, focusing instead on his theory of the social contract.[101] On the one hand, he referred to Rousseau as "that sublime genius" and praised him for his pure love of liberty and courage in denouncing some of the most unjust institutions of modern society. He also shared Rousseau's critique of the inequalities of the Old Regime, and must have been impressed by his diagnosis of the artificiality of modern society, although he did not endorse Rousseau's opposition to private property. Equally important, as Constant's essay "*Histoire abrégée de l'égalité*" shows, he partly shared Rousseau's views on equality, believing that human beings are born equal and that an artificial inequality comes into being only later by dint of flawed institutions. Equality, Constant argued, is the original law of society, and the desire for equality must be recognized as the most natural of our sentiments; whoever refers to justice also implies equality and vice-versa.[102]

On the other hand, without seeking to lay the blame on Rousseau for all the evils of the French Revolution, Constant believed that he had been a "blind architect" of freedom, who became the father of tyranny, in spite of the brilliance of many of his ideas. Rousseau's theories, Constant claimed, legitimated many fatal errors and furnished the most terrible auxiliary to all forms of despotism. Constant opposed the doctrine of the general will on the grounds that it endorsed a degree of power that was simply too great to be manageable and threatened to become an evil in itself regardless of the hands in which it was placed: "Entrust it to one person, to several, to all, you will still find it an evil . . . . There are things too heavy for human hands."[103] He also criticized Rousseau's concept of general interest for ignoring individual (private) interests and proposing a flawed image of a fictitious unitary body politic inspired by Sparta.[104]

In lieu of Rousseau's holistic view of the social, Constant proposed a more nuanced model that recognized the sanctity of the private sphere and the importance of securing individual rights, two central themes for all the members of the Coppet group. "The management of public affairs belongs to everyone," he maintained. The key principle is that "what interests only a fraction of citizens must be decided by that group. Whatever affects only the individual must be subject to the jurisdiction of that individual." Hence, he concluded that, "when it goes beyond its legitimate sphere, the general will is no more respectable than the individual will.[105] Against Rousseau, Constant asserted that individuals have imprescriptible rights upon which no earthly authority may ever infringe. There is a part of human existence, he argued, that must remain always individual and independent from state interference, and which is by right *beyond* all social and political jurisdiction.[106] Any claims made by the state on this sphere are illegitimate, even when advanced in the name of the will of the entire nation: "On those [issues] on which the law must not pronounce, the wish of the majority is no more legitimate than that of the smallest minorities."[107]

Moreover, unwilling to forget the darkest moments of the French Revolution, Constant questioned the validity of Rousseau's theory granting sovereignty to the individual will. He was concerned about the political implications of the principle according to which individuals have the right to make and unmake political institutions as they please. While rejecting the idea that society as a whole is ever entitled to exercise unlimited sovereignty over its members, Constant warned that, under certain circumstances, the rule of the people might turn into a new form of despotism. Popular sovereignty is not a reliable safeguard of individual freedom, for unlimited power is equally dangerous in the hands of the people and in the hands of absolute monarchs. The power of the people ought not to be confounded with the liberty of the people. Constant explained the errors of the revolution by arguing that, instead of destroying absolute power once and for all, the French legislators thought only of displacing it, without addressing the root of the problem: "Their wrath has been directed against the wielders of power and not the power itself. Instead of destroying it, they have dreamed only of relocating it."[108]

The lesson that Constant drew from their experience was that all precautions against absolute power are futile so long as sovereignty is not properly divided: "If political authority is not limited, the division of powers, ordinarily the guarantee of freedom, becomes a danger and a scourge."[109] When no limit to the authority of the legislative body is acknowledged and sovereignty is unlimited, the people's leaders and representatives are no longer defenders of freedom, but "aspiring tyrants,"[110] and there is no means of protecting individuals from potential encroachment upon their liberties. Rousseau's general will, Constant maintained, contained dangerous seeds of despotism. "You can try a division of powers," he went on, "but if the sum total of powers is unlimited, the divided powers have only to form a coalition for despotism to be installed without remedy."[111] Constant added that "the important truth, the eternal principle to be established is that sovereignty is limited, and that there are desires that neither the people nor their delegates have the right to entertain."[112] In other words, there are acts which not even the consent of the majority may ever justify, and "the assent of the majority is not enough in all circumstances to render its actions lawful."[113] Hence, Constant insisted, the abstract limitation of sovereignty is never sufficient to prevent the usurpation of sovereignty and protect the sanctity of the individual sphere. Individuals, Constant insisted, have rights independent of any social and political authority, and the majority is never entitled to do anything they please. If the majority of the people seek to judge acts that are not within their legitimate sphere of authority, they cease to be a legitimate majority and may become a faction. One of the implications of Constant's critique of Rousseau is that if sovereignty and power are unlimited, it does not really matter in whose hands they are placed. The real question is not *who* exercises power, but *how* power is exercised, and how it should be limited in order to prevent despotism.

Since the fall of the Old Regime and the Terror of 1793–94 had demonstrated the illegitimacy of the "divine right" of kings and cast doubt as well on the practical application of the sovereignty of the people, there was a pressing need to find new ways of conceptualizing sovereignty, political power, and authority. All this became evident once again in 1814–15 when the Bourbons returned to the throne of France. In the footsteps of Necker, Constant argued that new representative institutions would have to be built according to the principle of a "complex" sovereignty that would combine "the interests of the different holders of power so that their most apparent, most durable and most certain advantage would be to remain within the limits of their respective attributions."[114] This is why legislators must begin by delimiting proper spheres of authority as well as the limits of sovereignty before turning to constitutional details. In *Principes de politique* (1815), Constant insisted that the first question that must be solved when writing a new constitution is about the nature and limitation of sovereignty.[115] In an essay written in 1818 as a companion to *Principes*, Constant admitted that, "if it is recognized that sovereignty is not without limits, that is to say, that there is no unlimited power on earth, then nobody will ever dare to claim such a power."[116]

The affinity between Constant's and Necker's ideas on sovereignty should be obvious by now. To be sure, echoes of Necker's theory of "complex sovereignty" can be found in Constant's argument in favor of a mixed form of sovereignty, and in his belief that no authority on earth may be unlimited, neither that of the people nor that of their representatives, nor finally that of the law. Both authors believed that recognition of an abstract "sovereignty of the people" does not automatically increase individual liberty. Whether or not Constant also came close to advocating mixed government is a different question. He did not specifically refer to mixed government in his constitutional writings, but it might seem at first sight that his views on sovereignty were, to some extent, close to Sismondi's, who did advocate mixed government as the only regime suitable to modern society, in which all parties must have a constitutional place and a proper share in decision-making. Sismondi believed that aristocracy and democracy are the two elements necessary to all forms of good government and that they are pernicious when they become exclusive, both being "essential to the happiness of nations when they are skillfully combined, so as to work together."[117] As Paulet-Grandguillot showed, in Constant's works, much more than in Sismondi's, the limitation of power by a *balance* of powers is less important than the limitation of social authority by individual *rights*. Protecting individual independence was of paramount significance for Constant, and the first step was not to organize and balance powers but to limit the total sum of what he called *"autorité sociale"*—an authority that belongs to the collectivity, yet does not enjoy absolute sovereignty, being limited by individual rights so that no unlimited power may exist in the state.[118]

The Architecture of Representative Government

What are the implications of Constant's defense of limited sovereignty and individual independence for our analysis of political moderation? To answer this question, let us examine his conception of constitutions as "guarantees" of rights and liberties. *Pace* Rousseau and his disciples, Constant insisted that the real parameter in judging them must be the "right" rather than the law, even when the latter is the expression of the general will (or precisely for that reason). Constant underscored the importance of constitutional guaranties by arguing that, if one single individual or element of the social order is not fully protected from arbitrariness, the guarantees enjoyed by the rest are uncertain and may be easily undermined.[119] Constant regarded constitutions as expressions of mistrust and defiance essential to the preservation of liberty and was concerned by the proliferation of laws and the illegitimate extension of social authority.

What makes Constant's reflections on the architecture of representative government particularly interesting is that, during the Directory, he had to grapple with the weakness of the executive power, whereas during the Consulate and the First Empire, it was the growing power of the First Consul and the Emperor and the weakness of the legislative body that represented the main threats to liberty. This situation gave Constant the chance to reflect on the fundamental guarantees that a constitution should provide against the abuses of both the executive and legislative powers, and led him highlight the importance of bicameralism, the right of veto, political responsibility, and the independence of the judiciary. Constant's views on all these topics were developed in several writings, beginning with *Fragments* and continuing with the two editions of *Principes* (1806–1810; 1815), *Réflexions sur les constitutions* (1814), and *De la responsabilité des ministres* (1815). Constant's constitutional views reflected his belief that liberty can be secured only by limiting political and social authority through a proper distribution and balance of powers, in such a way that the total sum of powers is never unlimited. Central to his vision were two ideas: (1) power must always be circumscribed within precise and proper limits; and (2) far from weakening the executive and the legislative power, the limits placed on them could, in fact, make them stronger and more effective: "Freedom gains everything from government's being severely confined within the bounds of its legitimacy; but it gains nothing from government's being feeble within those bounds. . . . Wisely established limits are the good fortune of nations because they circumscribe power, in such a way that no one can abuse it."[120] In the absence of such limits, the effectiveness of government and parliament is affected and their members might be encouraged to usurp or abuse power.

Another illustration of Constant's moderation can be found in his account of the shortcomings of the Constitution of Year VIII. Taking up the relationship between the legislative and the executive power, he justified the right of veto on the ground that investing the executive with this right was essential to improving not only cooperation between the two powers, but also the overall quality of legislation. To achieve this goal, Constant claimed, veto power must be absolute, for an attenuated form of veto (the suspensive one) would be ineffective in the long-run and would diminish the consideration due to the executive power. In his view, granting the right of veto to the executive power also required giving the latter the right to dissolve legislative assemblies in times of crisis.[121] By drawing on the example of England, Constant sought to teach French legislators an important lesson. The success of the English constitution, he remarked (in Necker's footsteps), owed a great deal to its sound balance of powers, as illustrated, among other things, by the fact that the king's ministers were allowed to participate in the debates of the House of Commons:

> If the ministers sat in the Assembly among the deputies, they would discuss among themselves the measures necessary to the administration of the country; they would bring into the Assembly their knowledge of facts which only the exercise of power can give. . . . By bringing individuals together while distinguishing powers among themselves, one would have a harmonious government, instead of creating two camps ready to go to war against each other.[122]

Constant also believed that it would be a great advantage if deputies shared in the exercise of the executive function as members of the elected Chamber; and he maintained that they should be allowed to stand for reelection (in his view, the impossibility of reelection was a grave political error that had to be avoided at all costs). If the two powers were strictly separated, the members of parliament might perceive the government as their greatest enemy rather than their necessary partner. On the contrary, if deputies had a share in the exercise of the executive function, they would, when criticizing the executive, focus on its agents rather than on the institution of government as a whole. Similarly, if ministers were allowed to attend parliamentary debates and had the right to examine and discuss draft laws in the lower chamber, their input could enhance the quality of legislation and prevent flawed legislative initiatives from being adopted by the assembly.[123]

It might be useful at this point to compare Constant's ideas with Necker's views on the relationship between the executive and legislative powers. While they agreed in their accounts of the constitutional failures of 1789, 1793, and 1795, they differed with regard to what they considered to be the supreme power in society. Unlike Necker, Constant believed that this power was the legislative, though at the same time he was fully aware of the challenges that legislative assemblies had posed to the consolidation of liberty in France since 1789. A great deal of the country's previous problems, he argued, did not have their source in the initiatives of the executive power, but in the erratic behavior of legislative assemblies to which previous constitutions had failed to assign fixed limits and rights. What the French failed to grasp was that, while legislative assemblies are essential to the preservation political liberty, the power of the nation's representatives must be properly limited. Constitutions ought to provide guarantees against the excesses and errors not only of kings, but also of legislative assemblies.[124] The Constituent Assembly, Constant remarked, included enlightened individuals, but those individuals voted laws inimical to liberty. Four years later, the authors of the Constitution of 1795 also failed to incorporate an effective countervailing power to the authority of the legislative, refusing to give the executive the right of veto and the right to dissolve the legislative assembly.[125] At the same time, Constant warned against taking skepticism toward the legislative or the executive to extremes. In his view, the weakness of a single power—either the legislative or the executive—could cause a fundamental imbalance within the political system that would threaten its stability.[126]

Constant believed that the supreme power was the legislative, but the role he reserved to the executive power was by no means an insignificant one. A useful way to explore his views on this issue would be to start from his claim (in *Fragments*) that there is an incompatibility between political liberty and a unitary form of executive power, for the latter is irreconcilable with a genuine balance of powers. Constant preferred a complex form of executive power, observing that when a people gave up a unitary executive power to adopt the latter type, they were able to maintain their liberties, while those who preserved the former often lost their liberties (as in the case of Rome). A complex executive power requiring extensive deliberations among its members would be hesitant to take extreme measures (such as going to war) and would be more likely to listen to its critics and to minority opinions.[127] And yet, Constant insisted, even the existence of such a complex executive power would not be in itself a sufficient condition for the preservation of liberty. The French Directory, for example, represented such a complex authority, but in reality enjoyed none of its presumed advantages, being deeply fragmented and lacking the minimal degree of unity required for properly performing its tasks. This was not so much the fault of the directors themselves as of the structure imposed by the Constitution of 1795, whose stipulations created internal dissension among the five directors. Under the pretext of furthering the common good and public tranquility, each director could use his power to strengthen his own position at the expense of the other four colleagues.[128]

Although, like Necker, Constant believed that liberty could not survive if the executive power was weakened, his skepticism toward power marked a clear departure from Necker's position. Constant thought that Necker's theory of intertwining of powers did not offer sufficient guarantees against real or potential abuses of power, even if one assumed that the agents of government were animated by good intentions. The preservation of liberty, Constant argued, requires a simultaneous retrenchment of the means of government and administration and of the attributions of the government, along with a sound equilibrium between powers. The contrast with Necker's emphasis on the superiority of the executive power in modern society is worth noting because it points to two different approaches to power, one that emphasizes the rights of individuals in a slightly libertarian tone (Constant), the other focusing on governability and announcing, *toutes propor-*

tions gardées, the modern welfare state. In the 1806–1810 edition of *Principes,* Constant was not shy in voicing his skepticism toward Necker's elevation of the executive power to the rank of tutor of public happiness. "M. Necker," he wrote, "is not free from the errors with which I reproach those who favor an increase in political authority. He calls the sovereign power the tutor of public happiness and, when he deals with commercial prohibitions, he constantly assumes that individuals let themselves be dominated by short-term considerations, and that the sovereign power understands their long-term interests better than they themselves."[129]

Heir to a long French statist tradition that included Colbert and Turgot, Necker saw in government "a more extensive means of benevolence and good works" and defined government as "the interpreter and trustee of social harmony,"[130] something to which Constant strongly objected. In response to Necker, he argued that rulers are not necessarily less liable to error than the governed; on the contrary, "it is always likely that the governors will have views which are less just, less sound, and less impartial than those of the governed."[131] Constant cast doubt on the allegedly superior knowledge possessed by the members of the executive power, and feared that any increase in the authority vested in rulers would be at the expense of civil freedoms. Moreover, he added, the mistakes of the government are often far more dangerous than the errors made by ordinary citizens:

> Doubtless individuals can make mistakes too; but several basic differences make theirs far less fatal than those of government. If individuals go astray, the laws are there to check them. When government goes wrong, however, its mistakes are fortified with all the weight of the law. Thus the errors of government are generalized, and condemn individuals to obedience. The mistakes of individual interest are singular. One person's mistake has absolutely no influence on the conduct of another.[132]

It is in this context that Constant's reflections on political responsibility must be analyzed. Along with his theory of *pouvoir neutre,* they represent the cornerstone of his doctrine of representative government. Constant's thoughts on this topic followed again in the footsteps of Necker.[133] In *Dernières vues,* Necker had recognized the seminal importance of political responsibility and the difficulty of implementing it in practice, without affecting the dignity of the executive.[134] He drew a fundamental distinction between the inviolability of the monarch and the political responsibility of his ministers, and was skeptical that this distinction could be effectively applied to republican regimes. Necker's argument must have influenced Constant who took up the question of the viability of a republic in a large state. What are the proper means for ensuring political responsibility while also giving the executive and legislative powers effective means for holding each other in check? Constant believed that the participation of ministers in parliamentary debates would facilitate the enforcement of political responsibility. Referring to the accusations that might be brought against ministers, Constant wrote:

> If they were guilty, they would be attacked much more easily, because it would be enough to answer to them without having to denounce them. If they were innocent, they would exonerate themselves more easily, because every day they could explain and motivate their behavior. . . . Another result would be that an incompetent minister or one of whom the majority of the national assembly is suspicious could not remain in power. In England, a cabinet minister loses his function if he finds himself in minority.[135]

A decade later, as Constant was pondering the principle of political responsibility in a constitutional monarchy, he would write an entire book on this topic,[136] and he returned to the issue of the responsibility of ministers and their subordinates in *Principes* (1815), devoting no less than three chapters to the topic. It is in these pages that we see Constant reflecting upon the inviolability of the head of state (which he distinguished from the political responsibility of ministers), analyzing the right of the executive power to dissolve legislative assemblies, and criticizing the Constitution of Year III for not granting such a right to the Directory.

De la responsabilité des ministres was published on February 1, 1815, almost a month and a half before Napoleon's return. Organized in fourteen chapters and amounting to over one hundred pages, Constant's book was a vigorous call to the rule of law after more than a decade of absolute power.[137] It began with a straightforward statement about the importance of the principle of ministerial responsibility and posited a fundamental distinction between royal power and executive and ministerial power. "The responsibility of the cabinet ministers is the necessary condition of any constitutional monarchy," Constant wrote. "It is this responsibility that places the king in a separate sphere, above all the commotions of the government properly speaking. By distinguishing between royal power and the executive (or ministerial) power, it makes the first a neutral authority which preserves the system and separates the active powers when they disagree."[138] Royal power must remain unaffected by the controversies between other powers in order to be able to restore the peace and facilitate their cooperation. Constant then described the king as performing the role of a "neutral" power essential to the preservation of the balance of powers in the state. The last chapter, "*Dernières réflexions sur la liberté individuelle*," the longest—twenty-two pages—of the entire book, offered a summary of Constant's views on the guarantees of individual liberty and on political arbitrariness. It is here that we find one of the best expressions of his critique of the Directory's shortcomings,[139] and one wonders if Constant's assessment also implied *eo ipso* a critical reevaluation of his previous pro-Directory views. He now insisted that repeated violations of liberty are never conducive to the preservation of the latter and must be strongly opposed, *regardless* of circumstances.

Some of the ideas in this book reappeared three months later in *Principes* (1815), the volume published during the brief return of Napoleon, after Constant was appointed *conseiller d'État* by the Emperor. During the Hundred Days, Constant also drafted a new constitution known as *L'Acte additionnel*, whose Part IV was entitled *"Des ministres et de la responsabilité."*[140] The analysis of political responsibility in *Principes* (1815) comes after the discussion of limited sovereignty, neutral power, elections, and representation, and should read in relation to another important topic: trial by jury.[141] Chapter 9, entitled "On the responsibility of ministers" is, in fact, the longest of the entire book, amounting to no less than fifteen pages; and to these one should add the extra eight pages on related issues discussed in chapters 10 and 11. In total, the space devoted to political responsibility amounts to twenty-three pages, exceeding the number of pages devoted to elections (twelve pages), neutral power (eleven pages), sovereignty and property (eight pages), and individual liberty (six pages).

How can we account for Constant's strong interest in a topic that may seem to us purely technical? Constant's answer was straightforward. In his view, the importance of the principle of responsibility derived from its twofold goal. On the one hand, in its narrow sense, it was intended to deprive guilty ministers of their power by removing them from office if it could be proven that they had made illegal use of their authority. On the other, according to its larger sense, the principle of political responsibility was expected to keep alive in the nation, "through the watchfulness of her representatives, the openness of their debates, and the exercise of freedom of the press applied to the analysis of all ministerial actions, a spirit of inquiry, a habitual interest in the maintenance of the constitution of the state, a constant participation in public affairs, in a word a vivid sense of political life."[142] The successful enforcement of political responsibility was, moreover, essential to both public and individual security. "For my part," Constant acknowledged,

> I do not know of any public security without individual guarantee. I believe that public security is especially compromised when the citizens see in the authority a danger rather than a safeguard. I believe that arbitrary power is the real enemy of public security; that the obscurity with which arbitrary power shrouds itself can only increase this danger; that there can be public security only in justice, justice only in the law, and laws only in definite procedures.[143]

In this larger sense, ministerial responsibility became for Constant one of the key elements of representative government and of his theory of political moderation. Instead of focusing on the classical distinction between political and penal responsibility, he distinguished between the legal uses of power, inevitably subject to political contestation and sometimes impossible to define with apodictic certainty, and the illegal uses of power (in other words, he distinguished between error and arbitrariness, to use Édouard Laboulaye's terms).[144] According to this principle, "ministers will only be accused for their abuse or misuse of their legal power, through illegal acts prejudicial to the public interest, and yet bearing no direct relation on particular individuals."[145] Such illegal uses of power arise when ministers "introduce into the government what is most contrary to the security and the honor of any government, that is, arbitrariness."[146] As such, the enforcement of political responsibility is supposed to act as a buffer against arbitrary power, albeit an imperfect one.

One final point is in order here. For Constant, the principle of political responsibility was not enough to secure political liberty. He candidly admitted that "responsibility can never be free from a certain degree of arbitrariness."[147] He was not willing, however, to grant the legislative body the right to dismiss the executive, refusing to follow in this regard the example of the England, where a government is automatically dismissed when it loses its majority in parliament. Surprisingly for a declared admirer of the English constitution, Constant remained unconvinced by this principle. He reserved the right of dismissal for the monarch as the head of state, whom he invested with the authority of a neutral power, conceived of as "the judiciary power of other powers."[148] It is not a mere coincidence that Constant described the monarch as "neutral power" in chapter 10 of *Principes* (1815), entitled "On the declaration that ministers are unworthy of public trust," which immediately followed the long discussion of the concept of ministerial responsibility in chapter 9.

Neutral Power as *pouvoir modérateur*

The concept of *pouvoir neutre*[149] is the *clef de voûte* of Constant's theory of representative government and illustrates his attempt to offer a concrete and viable solution to the question of how the institutionalization of complex (limited) sovereignty was to be accomplished. *Pouvoir neutre* or *pouvoir préservateur* (as Constant sometimes called it) has an interesting genealogy. It might seem surprising that the concept did *not* appear in Montesquieu's *Spirit of the Laws,* which offered the classical account of English constitutionalism, nor was it present in the vocabulary of the English political thinkers of that period. This detail is surprising and could be taken to mean that the concept of neutral power might not be essential to constitutionalism, as Constant suggested. Moreover, there had been many interesting proposals in both the Constituent Assembly and the Convention to create such a "neutral" (or "third") power endowed with important functions, among them deciding the constitutionality of laws and defining the limits of legislative power. As Carl Schmitt noted in *Verfassungslehre*, the idea of a "neutral" power has never fully disappeared from constitutional debates in Europe and had sometimes been invoked in relation to the prerogatives of the heads of state in republican countries.[150] The concept has also appeared in non-European contexts. For example, Title V (Art. 98ff) of the Brazilian Constitution of 1824 referred to the Emperor of Brazil as a *pouvoir modérateur*, representing the constitution's key organizing principle. Such a power, it was stated, "is exclusively delegated to the Emperor as the supreme head of the nation in order to watch over the maintenance of the independence, equilibrium, and harmony of the other political powers."[151]

The idea that a third power could have a salutary moderating effect was not a new topic when Constant proceeded to make it the pillar of his constitutional outlook.[152] A few years before, a disciple of Sieyès, Polverel, had argued in favor of creating a fifteen-member *conseil de révision* endowed with the right of veto over the laws passed by the elected assembly. Similar proposals for setting up a moderating power came from the pen of Abbé Brun de la Combe (who endorsed the formation of a "supreme tribunal" as a *conseil examinateur*) and Lavicomterie, who justified the creation of a countervailing power—which he dubbed a "tempering power"[153]—strong enough to contain the executive within legal bounds. Others, such as Hérault de Sechelles, called for the formation of a neutral power in the form of a "national jury"[154] empowered to protect citizens against the potential domination of the legislative and executive powers. Finally, addressing the Jacobins whom he sought to convince that there must exist a third power above the executive and the legislative, Pétion warned that, in the absence of a third regulating power which, through its influence, could alone restore the equilibrium of power in society, the republic would become vulnerable and its institutions susceptible to collapse.[155]

In the end, the French, who had previously rejected the absolute royal veto and bicameralism, also opposed the idea of creating such a third moderating power to oversee all other political forces and capable of balancing and tempering them. Wary of erecting an authority superior to that of the legislative, which represented the unity of the nation, they discarded all of the proposals on offer. Nonetheless, the specter of a *pouvoir modérateur* reappeared during the debates on the Constitution of Year III, only to go down to defeat once again, as did proposals for an absolute royal veto and an "aristocratic" second chamber. Attempts to erect a third power did however have the effect of triggering interesting debates, which led to the publication of several important tracts. The author of *Le Balancier politique* (1795), for example, argued that, while it was relatively easy to determine the limits of the two rival powers, the more difficult and important task was to create a third countervailing power that could prevent the others from overstepping their legal boundaries.[156]

The most coherent proposal for creating such a higher power was made by Sieyès in two seminal discourses of 2nd and 18th Thermidor 1795, in which he proposed the creation of a constitutional jury (*jury constitutionnaire*) as a form of neutral power *sui generis*. Sieyès admired Rousseau's ideas and, like him, was skeptical toward any notion of complex sovereignty. Yet, at the same time, he had reservations about Rousseau's endorsement of virtually unlimited legislative power. To the system of countervailing powers—"*le système de contrepoids*"—endorsed by Necker, Constant, and the monarchiens, Sieyès opposed his system of "*organized unity*" emphasizing the separation of powers. He believed that "unity alone is despotism, division alone is anarchic; division with unity gives the social guarantee without which all liberties are precarious."[157] Although the ultimate purpose of Sieyès' *jury constitutionnaire* was to safeguard the constitutionality of the laws, in reality, as Michel Troper has demonstrated, it was not meant to serve as a proper constitutional court in the modern sense of the word.[158] Given the general definition of the law in the Constitution of Year III, the jury envisaged by Sieyès was expected to judge only the acts (broadly defined) of the Council of the Ancients and the Council of the Five-Hundred. In the end, the notion of a *jury constitutionnaire* was dismissed as unconventional and Sieyès' proposal rejected. It received support from only a few lone voices such as Lamare and Eschassériaux.[159]

The idea of a *pouvoir neutre*, unrelated to oversight of the constitutionality of the laws, had also appeared previously in Necker's works. He emphasized the inviolability of the monarch and made a fundamental distinction between royal and ministerial (or executive) power, a distinction taken up by Constant in his writings on ministerial responsibility.[160] Necker never fully developed the concept of neutral power, however, which might explain why it made only a brief appearance in Mme de Staël's texts during the Directory.[161] Its most explicit formulation—again, unconnected with judgments regarding the constitutionality of the laws—can be found in Constant's theory of representative government at the heart of which lies his theory of a moderating power situated above all other powers in the state, and entrusted with an important and difficult task: maintaining the balance between powers and arbitrating any conflicts that might arise among them.

Constant offered a first sketch of his theory of neutral power in *Fragments*,[162] in which he devoted an entire book (VIII), almost one hundred pages, to discussing this concept. His main purpose was to show how the concept of *pouvoir neutre* would apply to a republican constitution in a large modern state. Among the conditions for eligibility to neutral power in a republic, Constant listed the following three: no one could be a member of the neutral power if he was younger than forty; if he did not have a certain amount of wealth (landed property) as a guarantee that he would have an interest in the maintenance of the constitution and the social order; and if he had not previously been a member of the executive or legislative power.[163] Only those fulfilling these criteria, Constant believed, could possess interests independent of the executive and the legislative as well as of the people,[164] and would be able to properly discharge their role, "to separate the executive and the popular power when they fight against each other, protect the first from the attacks of the second, and strengthen the latter if it was forced to bend under the yoke of the former."[165] A decade later, after rallying to the cause of the Bourbons, Constant returned to the concept of neutral power, this time seeking to apply it to constitutional monarchy. To this effect, he began his *Réflexions* by highlighting the seminal role which neutral power could play in settling disagreements between the legislative, executive, and the judiciary powers. He argued that constitutional monarchy presents the great advantage of creating such a power in the person of a monarch who rules but does not govern. The monarch as neutral power does not privilege one power over others, but is interested in ensuring that the legislative and the executive act in concert when addressing important political issues.[166] A year later, after Napoleon returned to Paris during the Hundred Days, Constant wrote an entire chapter on neutral power (chapter 2) in *Principes* (1815), in which he reiterated his previous arguments.

As Constant lost confidence in the future of republicanism in France, he realized that a republican power renewable periodically could not effectively act as an effective neutral power, standing above all powers and unanswerable to no one. Moreover, in a republic such a power "in no way strikes the imagination."[167] The situation is different in a constitutional monarchy in which the monarch lives, as it were, in a citadel above all political parties, "in a fixed, unassailable point which passions cannot reach. . . . Nothing of the kind happens in a republic, where all citizens may rise to supreme power."[168] And there was, Constant noted, yet another reason why it would be difficult to establish an effective neutral power in a republic, and this had to do with the issue of political responsibility. "Republics," he argued, "are forced to make the supreme power responsible. But then this responsibility becomes illusory"[169] because, if exercised, it would remove from office men whose fall might abruptly interrupt foreign relations or jeopardize the internal machinery of the state. As such, Constant warned, "the remedy would always prove more repellent than a moderate evil and responsibility would be void, because it has been set too high."[170] Constitutional monarchy, Constant argued, has none of these problems, because it creates this neutral power in the person of the head of state whose true interest "is not that any of these powers should overthrow the others, but that all of them should support and understand one another and act in concert."[171] Constant conceived of royal power as "neutral" power with the main goal of facilitating harmonious cooperation between the executive, the legislative, and the judiciary. He believed that, in order for liberty to exist, there should always be a discretionary authority in the state, but that authority should never be absolute or condone arbitrary power, and should have clearly circumscribed attributions that could never be transgressed unpunished. Because the nature of such a neutral power was sometimes misunderstood, its discretionary power came to be identified with arbitrary power.[172]

In making these arguments, Constant resorted to the lessons of experience and practice rather than abstract speculation. History taught the necessity of creating an authority independent of the people (represented by the elected chamber) and the executive power. The failure to create such a neutral power had been quite possibly the greatest shortcoming of all previous French constitutions. It represented the main flaw in the Constitution of 1791, which placed a great part of political authority into the hands of the legislative power, without proper regard for creating the mechanisms that would ensure its necessary collaboration with the executive.[173] The Constitution of 1791 thus lacked an institution for solving in a timely and effective manner conflicts between the legislative and executive powers and restoring the necessary concord between them. This could only have been remedied, Constant insisted, by creating a third "neutral" power between the legislative and executive, capable of maintaining equipoise between the two rival powers and thereby preserving the stability of the government.[174]

In *Réflexions* and *Principes* (1815), Constant justified neutral power as a prudential tool for solving constitutional crises and, to some extent, as a mechanism for oversight of the constitutionality of the laws. Only such a *pouvoir neutre* could moderate rivalry between powers, preventing disagreements from degenerating into open war; only a neutral power could effectively prevent the formation of temporary alliances between the two main powers in the state that might usurp civil liberties. Neutral power acts as "the judiciary power of the other powers" when the latter are divided and unable to compromise.[175] But this goal can be achieved only if those who exercise neutral power are different from those who govern, and if their interests partly overlap with those of the people, while being independent of the latter. In a republic, for example, those who exercise neutral power should not be subject to dismissal or term limits but must be allowed to serve for life. They should not be eligible for any other position under a republican regime, and that ineligibility must be compensated by their having other eminent functions that allows them to exercise their ambitions within legal bounds.

Constant thought that the usurpation of neutral power was to be feared mostly in republics since in constitutional monarchies no one would try to rival the authority of the monarch. He pointed out that it is the distinction between ministerial and royal power that makes political responsibility easily enforceable in a moderate monarchy, warning at the same time that "we can lose this immense advantage either by lowering the power of the monarch to the level of the executive power, or by elevating the executive power to the level of the monarch."[176] If the two powers—royal and executive— were confused, the dismissal of members of the executive power would become problematic and political responsibility would be rendered effectively meaningless. It is only when the constitutional monarch is considered inviolable that he can successfully hold the members of the executive power politically accountable, and only then would it be possible to separate ministerial responsibility from neutral power. A hereditary monarch can and must be answerable to no one, while his ministers are and must be held politically responsible.[177]

If, on Constant's view, neutral power was supposed to act like a "trimmer," seeking to keep the ship on an even keel, it was certainly invested with significant attributions and rights. Among them, Constant mentioned the right to dissolve legislative assemblies and dismiss those who exercise executive power if they commit crimes—though "without staging a trial or passing judgment against them."[178] Constant's constitutional monarch combined, in fact, two powers: the royal and the executive. The first relied upon memory, tradition, and religious symbolism;[179] only in the second capacity could the monarch serve as a "neutral" power between the people, their representatives, and the king's ministers. And it is only to this neutral power, Constant opined, that the constitution must grant the right to dismiss members of the executive and legislative power for crimes or violations of the constitution.

Is then the existence of such a discretionary power compatible with liberty? Constant had no hesitation in responding in the affirmative to this question. He was quick to point out several guarantees against potential abuses of neutral power, that is, against the very things that neutral power may never do.[180] It has been remarked that his model of constitutional monarchy rests not on three, but on *five* powers: royal power, executive power, representative power of long duration (the hereditary assembly), representative power of public opinion (the elective assembly), and judicial power.[181] As *pouvoir préservateur* or *pouvoir modérateur*, "the royal power is in the middle, yet above the four others, as superior and at the same time intermediate authority, with no interest in disturbing the balance, but on the contrary, with a strong interest in maintaining it."[182] The monarch must remain confined to a separate, sacred precinct in which he is protected against the passions of the moment. "Your concerns, your suspicions, must never touch him. He has no intentions, no weaknesses, no connivance with his ministers, because he is not really a man but an abstract and neutral power above the storms."[183] As such a neutral power, the monarch serves an indispensable tempering and moderating function in the state: "The king never acts in his own name. Placed at the summit of all powers, he creates some, *moderates* others, directs political life in this way, *tempering* without taking part in it. It is from this that his inviolability derives."[184] He cannot condemn, imprison, despoil, or proscribe anyone, his authority being limited to that of depriving of their authority those members of the assembly and the executive power who have proved incapable of properly discharging their role and who represent a danger to public order and liberty.[185] As a moderating force immune to all political passions, the constitutional monarch "floats, so to speak, above human anxieties" and represents "amidst those dissensions . . . an inviolable sphere of security, majesty, impartiality, which leaves those dissensions to develop without danger, provided they do not exceed certain limits, and which, as soon as some danger becomes evident, terminates it by legal constitutional means, without any trace of arbitrariness."[186]

As such, Constant insisted, neutral power properly circumscribed and exercised may never be arbitrary. To ensure that this is always the case, its discretionary authority should be limited in such a way that those who exercise neutral power may never pass judgment on individual actions and may never be in charge of elections. If this power were ever to acquire the status of a judiciary power, Constant warned, "it would be the most abominable of all tyrannies. The neutral power which would have pronounced any punishment against citizens, regardless the pretext invoked, would have corrupted its function and given up its nature."[187] Furthermore, neutral power may never simultaneously dissolve the legislative and the executive power in order to become the sole power in the state. If the government is dismissed, then "the neutral power must not be authorized to nominate, even for a single moment, the temporary holders of the executive power; I would grant the nomination to the second chamber, without the participation of the first."[188]

It is essential then that neutral power always remain a purely "constitutional" power whose main duty is to prevent from exercising political power "those whom the assemblies thought to be too dangerous to hold power."[189] The decisions made by the neutral power may not aim at favoring or harming particular individuals, but must always maintain a certain level of generality and neutrality. As such, neutral power may endorse no individual opinion and may favor no individual project, its main task being the protection of individual rights from encroachment by the legislative or the executive.[190] Finally, neutral power does not have the right to change the constitution; proposals for the revision of the constitution should come from both the executive and legislative power, and any revision must always be the outcome of their concerted efforts. Neutral power has only the right to sanction these proposals for the revision of the constitution.[191]

Yet, in spite of Constant's repeated insistence on the many things which neutral power may not do, there is something unmistakably paradoxical and unsettling about this concept in his writings. In its most developed form (in a constitutional monarchy), Constant's theory amounts to affirming that, in order to preserve liberty, we must acknowledge the existence of a supreme power that is *neither* elected *nor* born out of the consent of the governed. As Constant himself acknowledged, this is a real political puzzle, since there can be no additional constitutional guarantees against potential abuses of the neutral power. Did Constant contradict himself when arguing that, as *pouvoir neutre*, the constitutional monarch has both limited prerogatives and great authority, all placed in the hands of one person, and that his prerogatives are compatible with—and, indeed, essential to—political liberty? Did he ask too much from a constitutional monarch living, as it were, in a "cloud" above all political parties? And how can we square all this with the classical principle of the separation of powers and limited government?

Constant, for one, did not see any contradictions here. On the one hand, he insisted that the power exercised by the constitutional monarch as *pouvoir neutre* would always be limited, since he may make legislative proposals only through the intermediary of his ministers and "never orders anything which they have not signed as a guarantee to the nation of their responsibility."[192] On the other hand, he insisted that, as the judiciary power (*sui generis*) of other powers, the constitutional monarch has the right to make nominations, dismiss ministers, create new peers, and dissolve the elective chamber in order to ensure that public order is preserved.

Benjamin "Inconstant" and the Paradoxes of Moderation

Constant may have been one of the leading liberal voices on the eve of the Revolution of 1830, the endpoint of our journey in this book, but his star fell in the years following his death. He was not, however, the only liberal to suffer this fate. (Mme de Staël's *Considérations* were reprinted only in 1983 and most of Necker's political writings are still out of print in France!) Lucien Jaume, who described Constant as the founding father of an individualist type of liberalism, attributed his eclipse to the fact that Constant's brand of liberalism fell out of fashion as the French scene came to be dominated by a "liberalism by the state," as illustrated by Guizot and his fellow doctrinaires. Not surprisingly, individualist liberalism has remained a minority variant in France to this day, and the rediscovery of Constant as a major political thinker came very late, in 1980, when Marcel Gauchet published a remarkable collection of his most important political writings.[193]

Over the years, Benjamin Constant had many unsympathetic readers and critics. One of them was Karl Marx who, in *The Eighteenth Brumaire of Louis Bonaparte*,[194] took him to task as a mediocre spokesman for bourgeois economic interests, who had little or nothing to say about class struggle and the poverty of the working class. Others, like Sainte-Beuve and Émile Faguet criticized Constant for his alleged hypocrisy and opportunism. They also suggested that it was Constant's egoism, the "foundation of his entire political system,"[195] and his "secret disdain for people"[196] that explain why he insisted so vehemently on a right to personal autonomy. Guizot regarded Constant as "a skeptical and mocking sophist, with no convictions, no consideration."[197] Others were slightly more generous, although not entirely convinced by his genius. Tocqueville, for example, did not feel inclined to really engage with Constant's ideas and made only a few references to his writings during the Directory in the unfinished second volume of *L'Ancien Régime et le Révolution*.

In a letter of September 1820 to his cousin Rosalie, Constant confessed: "Despite all the interest which politics must and do inspire in me in my present situation, I sometimes get terribly tired of my job as a schoolteacher, having to repeat again and again the same ideas."[198] Toward the end of his life, Constant himself foresaw that his sustained commitment to the cause of liberty would not bear fruit during his lifetime. What is remarkable is that Constant tirelessly sought to create a system of liberty at the core of which lies the individual, the alpha and omega of social life.[199] As a result, the issue of individual liberty and the guarantees necessary for its protection occupied a fundamental place in all of his political writings. At the same time, one is at pains to explain Constant's political *girouettes,* which have made him the paradigmatic figure of political opportunism in France, as Henri Guillemin's controversial book described him. Hence, one cannot avoid asking whether Constant's confession, quoted at the outset of this chapter was not, after all, mere lip service or a rhetorical attempt to consolidate his (contested) image as a defender of liberty, an image challenged by those who criticized Constant's approval of extreme measures (the "extreme center") during the Directory and his endorsement of Napoleon during the Hundred Days.

Be that as it may, it seems impossible to describe the restless author of *Adolphe* as a one-track thinker, obsessed with one single idea or principle. One may wonder if it might not be possible to add to the invocation of liberty (in this chapter's opening quote) another value that was central to Constant and the Coppet group: political moderation. Borrowing and paraphrasing Bernard Manin's distinction between two types of liberalism—*la règle et la balance*[200]—I would like to argue that Mme de Staël and Sismondi might be viewed as advocates of a "moderation of balance" that gives priority to fostering a vibrant social, economic, and political pluralism in society, while Constant could be seen, all things considered, as a proponent of a "moderation of rule" that gives pride of place to the protection of the individual from any undue interference. This distinction must be taken with a grain of salt, because Constant's theory of neutral power indicates a concern with the preservation of balance between powers and might be construed as a proof that he also defended a moderation of balance, as Steven Vincent has recently argued.[201] What is beyond doubt is that, although these thinkers were condemned to live in a state of tension and uncertainty, their political agenda, flexible as it may have been at times, did not degenerate into a mere arithmetic of opportunistic deal-making. On the contrary, it had a firm and inspiring polestar: the "animated moderation"[202] that was related to their belief in pluralism and reasonable compromise, and relied upon a complex view of human nature that took into account the key role of passions (fear, interest, and enthusiasm) and sentiments in shaping human behavior.[203]

Nonetheless, describing Constant as a moderate is not an easy task. The intensity of his personal life (in which he was anything but moderate) and his fluctuating political commitments (for and against Napoleon) belie that description. But moderation *was* present in all of his works and defined his political vision, which shows a deep affinity between political moderation and institutional/constitutional complexity. The constitutional aspects of moderation come to the fore in his writings more so than in those of any other author studied in this book, including Montesquieu. Haunted probably by the specter of Rousseau's omnipotent legislator who could entirely (re)shape society at will, Constant felt the need to qualify Montesquieu's famous statements that moderation must be the spirit of the legislator and that legislation ought to be adapted to the condition of each people. In one of his late (and lesser-known) works, *Commentaire sur l'ouvrage de Filangieri* (1822, 1824), he insisted that legislators must also have their hands tied by constitutional rules and should not forget that there is a sphere of human life that ought always to remain free from the interference of any laws, good or bad. As several passages from *Commentaire* show, even legislation that is good (on paper), if separated from constitutional limits and rules, does not offer sufficient guarantees of the protection of individual freedom and rights. To bring everything under the competence of the laws and try to regulate with them all the spheres of life would amount to tyranny. "Let us distrust today more than ever any attempt to turn our eyes away from politics in order to fix them upon legislation," he told his contemporaries, who could still remember Napoleon's Code and the other legislative initiatives that ultimately robbed them of their freedom. "When governments offer legislative improvements to their people, the latter must respond by demanding constitutional institutions from them. Without a constitution, the people cannot have any certainty that the laws will be obeyed."[204] Espousing a decidedly libertarian tone, Constant rejected the idea that legislation must adjust to the social and moral condition of each country, and denied that legislators should be entrusted with the task of enlightening public opinion, governing minds, encouraging talent, preventing errors, regulating luxury, and creating or redistributing wealth. Legislation, Constant claimed, should serve only two central purposes: to prevent internal disorders and repel foreign invasions.[205] On this view, the functions of governments are purely *negative*: they "must repress disorders, remove obstacles, in one word prevent evil from happening. Beyond that, one can trust individuals for finding the good."[206]

Constant, whose liberalism rejected both revolutionary utopianism and ultraconservative traditionalism, was conscious of the centrality of moderation to his political thought. He was also aware that moderates always face tough challenges in their courageous attempts to defend liberty, reason, honor, and virtue in dark times. He liked, in fact, to compare himself to the unsung heroes whom he described in the final pages of *Principes* (1806–1810), as "unrecognized, suspected, surrounded by men incapable of believing in impartiality, courage, disinterested conviction. . . . They have always wandered the earth, the butt of all parties, isolated in the midst of generations sometimes raging, sometimes depraved. It is on them, however, that the hope of the human race rests."[207] In my view, this was more than mere rhetoric on Constant's part, for he was sincere in belief that moderates were called to play a seminal role in defending truth and decency in modern society. That he considered himself a member of this select group is also evident from his writings. What made his moderation unusual was his conviction that, in order to remain true to their long-term goals (such as the preservation of liberty and republican institutions), moderates sometimes had to resort to radical or extra-constitutional means to save the republic. In so doing, they relied on "intermediary principles"[208] that provided the necessary links between universal principles (such as liberty and rights) and fluctuating circumstances. On this view, it is "intermediary" (mediating) principles rather than abstract theories or principles that allow us to continually adjust our short-term strategies to changing contexts. Moderates, Constant concluded, might not triumph during their lifetime, but "when they are no more, the truths they have repeated in vain will be listened to. . . . It is a matter only of knowing how to struggle long-term, perhaps all one's life."[209] This might be, after all, the best portrait of Constant we have, and it is no accident that it explicitly places moderation at the heart of his liberal political thought.

EPILOGUE
MODERATION, "THE SILKEN STRING RUNNING THROUGH THE PEARL-CHAIN OF ALL VIRTUES"

Tout vouloir est d'un fou. L'excès est son partage/ La modération est le trésor du sage.
— Voltaire

"Our life is like a house built on sand and full of weariness," Mme de Staël wrote to Benjamin Constant shortly before her untimely death in 1817.[1] The touch of sadness in her words reflects the sober mood of the thinkers whose ideas form the core of this book. Engaged in an epic struggle against despotism and tyranny, most of them did not live to see a free regime consolidated in France. Were their efforts useless after all? And what does their tumultuous history tell us about the chances of moderation and about the tradition of political moderation in general?

With the exception of Montesquieu, the writers studied here were caught in the orbit of the French Revolution, which I have used as a kind of "prism" to examine the various faces of moderation in modern French political thought. They acknowledged the complex nature of politics and the fragility of political liberty and the social order, and they attempted "to disintoxicate minds and calm fanaticism."[2] Our authors believed that in politics one can make sensible decisions even in the darkest of times and that most political questions admit of a middle, which can be found through trial and error.[3] Their works show that political moderation forms a distinct and diverse tradition of thought, resembling an *archipelago* consisting of various "islands" that represent a wide array of ideas and modes of argument and action, an archipelago whose precise contours are yet to be discovered and fully appreciated by political theorists. This tradition, which lacks well-defined boundaries, includes values, ideas, principles, institutions, and political strategies that are not shared by all moderates, or are shared only in varying degrees. I have identified family resemblances between these islands, a network of overlapping affinities between the various arguments, ideas, themes, and concepts developed by the modern French thinkers who are the central players in this book. Theirs is, however, only a part of the large archipelago of moderation. After 1830, French thinkers as different as Guizot, Tocqueville, Cousin, Montalembert, Chateaubriand, and Laboulaye were confronted with a new challenge: how to reconcile the egalitarian social condition with the rise of political democracy and the new social question. Their responses to this dilemma will be examined in a sequel to the present book.

"Animated Moderation"

I have argued that the ideas of the moderates examined in the previous chapters can and ought to be studied as a whole rather than in isolation one from the other, despite the important differences between them. If I had to propose one term to describe what they all shared, I would use a phrase coined by Walter Bagehot in *Physics and Politics* (1872): "animated moderation." Defined as that virtue which allows us to see things in the right proportions and makes us willing to refrain from using hyperbole and violence, "this union of life with measure, of spirit with reasonableness"[4] makes a moderate (and middling) mind at once firm and flexible, full of common sense, vivacity, and buoyancy. The "animated moderation" of our authors did not make them all intellect, did "not "sickly them o'er with the pale cast of thought."[5] It weeded out rigidity and dogmatism. It enlivened their social relations and gave to their debates a good-tempered cast that encouraged their search for the golden mean. At the same time, their "animated moderation" was inseparable from a certain ideal of civility and decency guided by its own laws of measure and self-restraint.[6]

The moderation of the authors studied in this book was, moreover, neither a "halting between extremes"[7] nor a form of wavering lacking firmness of purpose. It is best described as a mixture between, on the one hand, responsibility, prudence, and civility, and, on the other hand, enthusiasm and passionate commitment to a distinctive set of principles and institutional arrangements. Far from being a shy, lukewarm, or meek virtue, this animated moderation was strong, combative, and energetic—"*la modération avec transport*" of Montlosier,[8] the enthusiastic moderation of Mme de Staël, or the extreme center endorsed by Constant. As such, it must be clearly distinguished from the "counterfeits of pusillanimity and indecision"[9] invoked by Burke or the meekness praised by Norberto Bobbio.[10] The "animated moderation" that is the subject of this book was above all a *political* virtue that thrived on partisanship and did not search for a cozy (and ultimately illusory) political consensus on divisive and complex issues. Our authors did not propose a "Parnassian retreat" from the turmoil of power struggle into a sphere of art or literature, free from the "impurity" of politics.[11] On the contrary, they searched for a "complex center"[12] that would help them navigate better in a world of conflicting and competing ends and ideals. Last but not least, they agreed with Burke's claim that "political reason is a computing principle: adding, subtracting, multiplying, and dividing, morally and not metaphysically or mathematically, true moral denominations."[13] As such, they maintained a healthy dose of skepticism toward any form of zealotry and rejected all attempts to impose the absolute rule of a single idea or political principle.[14]

The "Decalogue" of Moderation

In the prologue, I referred to four major meta-narratives which constitute the overarching themes of the present book. It is time to return to them now and, in light of the arguments of the previous chapters, to draw ten conclusions in the form of a "Decalogue" *sui generis* about the nature of political moderation. Needless to say, the term "Decalogue" must be taken here with a grain of salt, especially when applied to such a complex concept as moderation, which admits no apodictic laws or categorical imperatives. It is meant to serve as a convenient heuristic device, helping the reader grasp what I have tried to achieve in this book and how I would answer the skepticism toward moderation discussed in the opening chapter.

The staunchest critics of moderation (Nietzsche, for example) claimed that the latter is a vague and weak virtue for hesitant souls, incapable of strong feelings and bold actions. They have dismissed moderation because of its assumed relationship to opportunism and conformism, its supposed preference for the *status quo*, and its alleged inability to promote democratic reforms. As Nancy Rosenblum has remarked, "moderation and accommodation can indicate complacency in the face of remediable injustice," and flexibility, along with the disposition to compromise, may be interpreted as a disquieting sign of immoralism.[15]

In the present book I have tried to counter these critiques by examining a defining period in the history of modern French political thought (1748–1830). While the first meta-narrative shed light on the transformation of moderation from an individual virtue (or character trait) into a set of concrete institutional and legal arrangements (conclusions 1–3 below), the second meta-narrative focused on the strong affinity between political moderation and institutional/constitutional complexity (conclusions 4–5). The third narrative (conclusion 6) illustrated an important face of moderation—trimming between extremes—while the fourth one revealed the eclecticism of moderation, which cannot be analyzed solely with the aid of our traditional political vocabulary (conclusions 7–9). All four narratives suggest that moderation is a complex, difficult, and sometimes risky virtue, one whose effectiveness depends on many factors, some of which may be beyond our control (conclusion 10).

Here, then, are the ten conclusions that should answer the questions: What is moderation? What do moderates stand for, and what do they oppose?

One. Do not assume that moderation has only one face.

The authors analyzed in these pages demonstrate that moderation has *many* faces. They regarded it as a cardinal virtue that enables us to regulate and control our desires, emotions, and passions, and viewed the "golden mean" between extremes as instrumental in preserving freedom, order, and rule. Defined as a virtue opposed to fanaticism and extremism, moderation represented for them, as Bishop Joseph Hall so nicely put it four centuries ago, "the silken string running through the pearl-chain of all virtues."[16] Thus, it is possible to define moderation as middlingness, as the antidote to zealotry and fanaticism, as a form of civility, as temperance, or as a disposition to compromise.

At the same time, in addition to its *ethical* meaning, moderation can also have a distinctively *political* and *institutional* dimension, being linked to the balance of powers, social and political pluralism, and mixed government. As our discussion in chapter 6 suggested, we can identify two variants of constitutional moderation: a moderation of balance and a moderation of rule. As chapter 2 showed, it is also possible to speak of penal and fiscal moderation, two topics on which Montesquieu had important things to say. In order to understand why he and his followers regarded moderation (rather than justice) as the supreme virtue of the legislator, it became necessary to examine not only the uses of the term "moderation" in their works, but also related concepts such as "complex sovereignty," "intertwining of powers," "*parti mitoyen*," "third power," and "neutral power," moderation as trimming or balance, "moderate government," and moderation as a center or *juste milieu* between extremes. All these concepts show that, in spite of the existence of many faces of moderation, the latter is *not* a vague or fuzzy virtue, and that a proper study of moderation requires that we take into account all of its ethical, institutional, and constitutional dimensions.

Two. Try to understand why some people are temperamentally inclined to moderation while others are not.

With regard to moderation as a character trait, our analysis suggests that one can be moderate not only by temperament (Necker), but also out of fear (Montesquieu), necessity (Mme de Staël, Constant), or as a matter of principle (Mounier, Malouet). In some cases, moderation is a way of trimming and blending opposites, which explains why it is so difficult (but still possible) to be a principled moderate combining "a tough mind with a tender heart"[17] and a strong fist. Thus defined, moderation can be a fighting and combative virtue and should not be equated with indecision, shyness, and submissiveness.

Moreover, nothing prevents one from being a moderate both out of fear and as a matter of principle, or from being moderate in some respects and radical (immoderate) in others. Moderation as a matter of principle is arguably the most intriguing variety. We have seen Mounier proudly responding to Napoleon (who remarked that Mounier had remained the man of 1789) that times change but principles do not. This form of "principled" moderation may be commendable and worthy of our admiration. But it is less so when it implies, in a curiously dogmatic way, that *only* political moderation can serve as the basis of liberty and as a rampart against anarchy and despotism. Because this claim might sometimes turn into something close to an ideology, it should be taken with a grain of salt, a conclusion buttressed by our analysis of the rhetoric of the ("extreme") center in the writings of Benjamin Constant and Mme de Staël. The first type of moderation—out of temperament—also has its own charming ambiguities. Sometimes, as the intellectual and political trajectories of Mme de Staël and Constant illustrate, political moderation can be married to an immoderate soul, giving birth to an original mixture that makes moderates unpredictable, idiosyncratic, restless, and highly individualistic. In other cases (Necker), moderation may, in fact, be subordinated to morality and religion, playing a subordinate role and making one's behavior (more) predictable and constant.

Three. Pay special attention to the constitutional elements of moderation.

Moderation is neither a fixed ideology (a party platform), nor a merely positional virtue. It must *not* be interpreted *solely* as a peculiar trait of (personal or national) character, a state of mind, a habit/disposition, or an ethos, as it is too often the case.[18] For, as we have already seen, moderation is also an important *constitutional* principle with significant implications for *institutional* design. This was illustrated by the debates on the royal veto, bicameralism, and neutral power. The importance of the constitutional aspects of moderation—which constitutes one of the main themes of this book—is borne out by the detailed analysis of the *Declaration of the Rights of Man* and the Constitutions of 1791, 1795, and 1799 examined in chapters 3 through 5, as well as the detailed discussion of a "third" or "neutral" power in chapter 6. Finally, habits of moderation owe a lot to—and can be fostered through—institutional design (the same can be said about habits of immoderation!). Thus, it is no mere coincidence that the moderates discussed in this book defended bicameralism and the royal veto and insisted on the need for a (third) moderating power, situated above the other powers, and capable of tempering their rivalry.

Four. Examine the concrete ways in which moderate agendas promote pluralism and the balance of powers, values, and interests while also fighting for the preservation of individual rights.

The discussion of Mme de Staël's and Constant's views on representative government along with the brief references to Sismondi's ideas pointed out that political moderation is compatible with *both* a liberalism of *rule* and a liberalism of *balance*.[19] We have also examined the connection between moderation and mixed government (mixed constitution), and the interdependence of mutually limiting powers and authorities, as illustrated, for example, by Cicero's metaphor of *symphonia discors*. At the heart of this form of government one finds the doctrine of the balance of powers (Montesquieu's famous *pouvoirs distribués*) rather than the strict separation of powers. As Mogens Hansen has recently pointed out, the doctrine of the *separation* of powers, which insists on the *division* between three different functions (the legislative, the executive, and the judiciary), does not entirely reflect the complexity of contemporary constitutional arrangements based on the *balance* of powers, which seeks to provide various mechanisms for *cooperation* between those who share in the exercise of the three powers. That is why we may want to return to Montesquieu's analysis of the mixed constitution, which could be used as "a corrective to the prevailing view that Western states are pure democracies, that is, rule by the people."[20] In reality, modern democracies must be regarded as *mixed* forms of representative government in which several institutions and powers share in the exercise of one function (legislative, executive, or judicial), and those who perform one function are also entitled to exercise a part of the power inherent in one or both of the other functions.

Five. Remember that moderates do not lack political vision.

The authors studied in this book, beginning with Montesquieu, belonged to the *pluralist* camp and rejected any monist definition of the political good, insisting on the fundamental indeterminacy of the latter (without at the same time being relativists!).[21] In their view, the greatest challenge came from those who, temperamentally inclined toward monism and a politics of faith, intransigently divided the world between the pure and the impure, being incapable or unwilling to accept the essential ambiguity of our social and political universe. These intransigent apostles of the truth tend to view politics as being similar to the exact sciences, where the validity of axioms and laws does not vary with time and place. Such a position was rejected by the moderates examined in these pages. In Montesquieu's eyes, for example, a political science *more geometrico*, such as the one proposed by Hobbes and Spinoza (and later by Condorcet), was to be avoided at all costs. He warned that legislators who take their cues from geometry misunderstand the complex and unique nature of politics and legislation. In Montesquieu's view, it was wrong to claim that a good law was good for all people and valid for all times.

Our authors also drew attention to the seminal connection between moderation and institutional complexity, one of the meta-narratives of this book. Moderate governments, they argued, are complex forms of government in which institutional checks and balances regulate the competition for power and are instrumental in securing social order. Hence, their interest in "moderating" various types of government or forms of political engagement, and their belief that prudent "temperings," agreements, and corrections—the terms belong to Montesquieu—are essential to successful statesmanship. All things considered, their vision was one that put a great emphasis on balance and equipoise, and this explains why their efforts to carve out a center between extremes earned them the reputation of "trimmers."

Six. Honor those who try to keep the ship of the state on an even keel!

The texts examined in this book confirm the existence of a close relationship between moderation and the center, a key theme of Aristotle's political philosophy, in which the center, embodying the principle of moderation, was seen as a balance between too little and too much. Yet, it is possible to go beyond this classical definition of the center as balance or scale—an always reasonable center that never exaggerates and does not lose its equipoise—to imagine a bolder and somewhat riskier center, which seeks to protect and foster moral, ideological, and institutional complexity in volatile environments that make compromises, errors, and even exaggerations inevitable. While this center rarely allows us to control the intensity of political conflicts, it gives us the opportunity to preserve and nurture the pluralism of ideas, principles, and interests essential to freedom in modern society.[22] The question remains: Is such a center possible and realistic after all, or is the center by nature the *locus* of pragmatic deal-making myopically focused on short-term gains?

In a comparative study published over four decades ago that examined the doctrine of the *juste milieu* in nineteenth-century France and England, Vincent Starzinger noted the following paradox. "There may be something about the center position per se," he wrote, "which inclines it also to theorize in unreal terms, despite the perennial claim of the middling mind to understand practical necessity."[23] Does our story confirm this claim? Might it be the case that the center invoked by our authors was nothing more than a vague concept supported by a questionable centrist rhetoric that sometimes abused its claim to represent the only reasonable option against the extremes?

To be sure, the center envisioned by the authors studied in this book was not entirely free of these problems, especially given their sometimes overstated claims about the reasonableness of their centrist agenda and the alleged irrationality (or extremism) of their opponents. The objections raised by the latter against the attempts of the moderates to carve out a center between extremes must, therefore, not be dismissed too quickly.[24] It would seem however, that their center did, in reality, rest on a concrete and bold institutional vision that required determination, courage, and firmness, along with a great deal of non-conformism. If partisans of the center like

Constant and Mme de Staël sometimes positioned themselves between political parties, their moderation was nonetheless not incompatible with responsible political commitment, nor was it a synonym of political isolation, indecision, or powerlessness. The fact that their trimming agenda meant choosing one side or another, though not always the same side, gave their choices an air of unpredictability (Necker was the exception in this regard).[25]

While it may be possible to criticize some of our thinkers for their alleged opportunism, I prefer to view them as *trimmers* whose primary loyalty was to principles rather than individuals, and who avoided one of the greatest sins in politics—single-mindedness—being sometimes of several minds and uncertain which way to go. As Nancy Rosenblum has argued, "the moderate middle is not single-minded, nor are ordinary partisans. They are of several minds, and their partisan hearts and minds are not always in sync."[26] At the same time, I am fully aware that commitments to principles (whether to a single principle or to several), if not properly moderated by other value(s), can sometimes be as problematic as blind loyalty to individuals. The case of Constant is particularly intriguing in this respect, since in the preface to his last book published in 1829, he described himself as having devoted his entire career to upholding one fundamental abstract principle: individual liberty. His example suggests that there might not be a contradiction between grounding oneself on a single principle—in this case, political liberty as non-interference—and endorsing at the same time political moderation, which recognizes the fundamental indeterminacy of the political good. It is also equally possible to infer that, in pursuing his centrist agenda, Constant had not one, but two guiding principles—liberty *and* moderation— and that the latter exercised a salutary tempering influence on the pursuit of the former, even if it did not prevent Constant from switching sides or abjuring some of his previous commitments.

Be that as it may, under the crossfire of their opponents, Constant and our other authors pursued a vigorous politics of the center, which sought to promote a balance of ideas and principles (complex sovereignty, intertwining of powers, neutral power). If their approaches were sometimes eclectic and partisan, they were nonetheless based on a strong commitment to creating and maintaining institutional and political balance in a world in constant flux. They understood that no political question could be decided by taking into consideration one single principle or viewpoint (hence their rejection of single-mindedness as the root of fanaticism), and were aware that human actions have unintended consequences which can jeopardize the implementation of even the best plans. Their centrist policy fostered social, political, and moral complexity and promoted a mixture of institutions, ideas, and principles such as pluralism, the balanced constitution, and mixed government. The principle to which they were committed—trimming—can be summarized as follows. If we know how society is unbalanced at any point in time, then we must add weight to the lighter side of the scale in order to maintain or restore its fragile equilibrium.[27] As David Brooks has recently remarked, "if moderation has any meaning, I suppose it is acknowledging that with many issues there are two opposing and partially true points of view, and that it's best to try to balance both truths. . . . Moderation doesn't mean picking whatever policies are in the center at any one time. It means practicing prudence, striking balances, and picking an agenda that is right for the moment rather than one that fits some universal ideological system."[28]

This point adequately reflects the outlook of the moderates studied in this book. They were, again, *trimmers* who, by adopting the soundest attitudes and principles of all parties, sought to facilitate agreements between them that could prevent the country from slipping into anarchy or civil war. As Joseph Hamburger noted in his study of Macaulay, "there is a tradition here, one that can accommodate men with radically different outlooks in normal times. But this tradition attracts those who are sensitive to crisis and who give priority to the problem of maintaining the legacy of rules and procedures and civilized habits that provide the framework within which party and even ideological politics is permissible."[29] This is often a "party without banners," to use Lezay-Marnésia's phrase (from chapter 6).

Trimmers attempt to keep the ship on an even keel and are convinced that the absolute domination of any single party or group would spell the end of freedom and the rule of law. It is by paying attention to this final goal—the preservation of political balance—rather than to abstract theories of liberty, equality, or justice that we can know when compromise and accommodation are necessary, desirable, and possible, and when they are not. The adjustments made by our trimmers were not, however, aimed exclusively at expediency. They attempted to preserve the balance between various social and political forces and interests on which political pluralism, order, and freedom ultimately depend. Although this required them to change their political allegiances in response to shifting circumstances, or to endorse certain means or courses of action that seemed to go against their initial agenda, their trimming was not an expression of political opportunism. This last point was demonstrated by the case of the monarchiens, whose political doctrine, as one of their critics claimed, far from being opportunistic, may have been, in fact, too rigid and hence unable to adjust to shifting circumstances.

Seven. Pay due attention to the eclecticism of moderation.

The diversity of viewpoints expressed by our authors proves that, for all their warm praise of "moderate government" broadly defined (as a constitutional monarchy, a republic based on limited or universal suffrage, or as a democracy), there is, after all, neither a single model of political moderation, nor an infallible recipe that guarantees good legislation (one of Montesquieu's most important lessons discussed in chapter 2). In reality, in light of its inherent *eclecticism*, moderation can accommodate a wide range of political ideas, views, laws, and forms of government (the accompanying danger, of course, is that moderation might suffer from what I referred to in the prologue as semantic bleaching). Hence, moderation cannot—should not—be interpreted as an ideology with fixed contours, one which affirms that moderation must always trump all other principles (e.g., justice). Since the mean is always multi-dimensional, what is or may seem moderate today might very well be immoderate tomorrow, and no party of moderates is likely to flourish or survive for a long time. This is why moderation is a difficult virtue, a philosophically and politically perplexing one, which has many dimensions and can take various forms.

At the same time, the chapters of this book show that it would be an error to regard moderation only as a positional virtue, entirely dependent upon the vitality of the extremes. While it is impossible to deny that the latter posses "a great advantage in often laying down the ideological categories of the dispute,"[30] it is equally important to acknowledge that the moderates studied here adopted highly combative attitudes, seeking to define the rules of the political game in which they were involved. In other words, they did not limit themselves to reacting to the extremes, but delineated a broad range of constitutional options and policies which they courageously defended, albeit with mixed results. These points were illustrated by the writings of Constant and Mme de Staël, two thinkers who, as we have seen, switched their political allegiances from constitutional monarchy to republicanism and back while remaining steadfastly committed to a moderate political agenda opposing fanaticism and dogmatism. At the same time, their example also suggests that moderates may sometimes benefit from partisanship and polarization insofar as the exposure to the crossfire of radicals can stimulate their imagination by encouraging them to develop original political and institutional responses to their problems.

Eight. Do not assume that moderation is in its essence only a conservative virtue.

Challenging the common view of moderation as an exclusively or essentially conservative virtue (a mask for conservatism, some critics would say), the chapters of this book confirm that political moderation cuts across contemporary ideological distinctions and cannot be properly analyzed or understood solely with the aid of our conventional political vocabulary. Moderation has affinities with *different* political traditions. Moderates can exist on the left or at the center, as well as on the right side of the political spectrum. The *eclectic* tradition of moderation presented in this book overlaps to a certain degree with liberalism in the European sense of the word, understood as a doctrine of the center, which in America might be seen as conservative. Nonetheless, not all liberals or conservatives have endorsed moderation and not all moderates have been "liberals" in this strict sense of this word. Political moderation, as Benjamin Constant's forceful critique of Filangieri's theory of legislation shows, can even have a libertarian ring, insisting that the government and the laws must have only purely negative (and strictly limited) functions.

Nine. Do not forget that moderates can sometimes promote radical ideas and that moderation is not a synonym of apathy, complacency, or indecisiveness.

In other words, the phrase "an ambitious moderate" or "a bold moderate" is not an oxymoron. The moderates studied in this book were sometimes obliged to incline toward extremes in order to find and hold onto the putative middle ground between them. In other cases, they were confronted with paradoxical and difficult situations, which either admitted of no middle or proved that compromises between the extremes are not always legitimate. Several sections of the book (such as the chapter on the monarchiens and the discussion of the "extreme center" during the Directory) shed light on the radicalism (*sui generis*) of moderation, while others highlighted its conservative side as demonstrated by those thinkers, like Necker, who endorsed moderation as a means of "purifying" democracy of its anarchic and revolutionary elements. Yet, for all its close relationship with prudence and its acknowledgment of the existence of a higher moral order to which we owe unconditional allegiance, the conservative type of moderation was neither a simple allegiance to custom, convention, and continuity, nor a recognition of the body social as a kind of "spiritual" corporation, two of the main tenets of conservatism.

Hence, it is important to remind those who see in moderation only a conservative virtue upholding the *status quo* that, during the Old Regime, moderation became a powerful tool for criticizing absolute power and promoting political reform, albeit in a gradual manner. A few decades later, Mounier and his fellow monarchiens endorsed bold and far-reaching constitutional and political reforms challenging the existing social and political hierarchies and proving (*pace* Jonathan Israel's claim) that political moderation can promote democratic ideals. During the Directory, Constant, who was also a political moderate, positioned himself to the left of Mme de Staël and Necker, whose commitment to ending the revolution he shared. Last but not least, Constant's critique of Burke's elevation of prudence over philosophical "principles," or the tense (and ultimately failed) dialogue between Burke and the monarchiens prove the existence of significant differences between all of these thinkers who, nonetheless, shared a strong commitment to political moderation.

Ten. Remember that moderation is not a virtue for everyone or for all seasons.

The previous chapters suggest that, for all its positive aspects, moderation is *not* an absolutely and universally positive virtue. They also leave open the possibility, indicated by Condorcet in his critique of Montesquieu, that the first duty of any legislator is justice rather than moderation. The case of the monarchiens discussed in chapter 3 is revealing in this regard, because it shows the inherent limitations of moderation in dark times when, in spite of its reasonableness, moderation is hardly a winning card. Furthermore, there are cases in which the middle cannot be found or simply does not exist, and there are situations when no one is willing to risk their life for moderation. In such circumstances, moderation does not work because it demands too much from those who need instead clearly defined distinctions to help them decide which politicians and policies to endorse. Finally, as Uwe Backes has recently argued, "political extremisms that act in the framework of legality can, like poisons that in small dosages develop healing effects, give an impetus to course corrections."[31]

That is why, although this book reflects my appreciation for many of the ideas and initiatives of the moderate thinkers studied here, I do not believe that moderates are (always) on the "good" side of history and opponents of moderation (always) on its dark side. Similar to the distinction between virtuous and pernicious enthusiasm (or fanaticism),[32] one can argue that there are good and bad forms of moderation (and of radicalism), a fact that French moralists like La Rochefoucauld knew very well. Aristotle was the first to remind us that moderation ought to be pursued with caution and prudence, according to circumstances, at the right moment, toward the right objects and people. Sometimes, the world is "in dire need of creative extremists,"[33] so long as they work for the right causes (such as justice or liberty). At other times, the exact opposite is true. Hence, as character trait, moderation is not a virtue for all seasons and all persons. But all the same, as an institutional principle, it does carry concrete implications and connotations derived from a certain view of what we take to be a decent and free society.[34]

As for political philosophers, I tend to agree with Hume that their main task is to serve as mediators between contending parties. They must seek in earnest to encourage moderate opinions and to find "the proper medium" in all disputes, while trying to persuade each party that its opponents may sometimes be in the right.[35] This is a necessary but difficult task, as the examples of Necker and Mounier showed, but it is also a lonely and, at times, heroic endeavor, as Constant reminded us. A century and a half ago, Frédéric Bastiat affirmed that only those who endorse extreme views are likely to succeed in politics, while moderates will always be abandoned and vanquished in the middle.[36] Does the story told in these pages confirm his claim?

If moderates have often been routed, criticized, or vilified for their beliefs, their ideas have nonetheless *not* been delegitimized. Overall, I am prepared to endorse again Hume's realistic assessment of moderation, one to which the authors analyzed in this book also subscribed. "Extremes of all kinds," Hume wrote, "are to be avoided, and though no one will ever please either faction by moderate opinions, it is there we are most likely to meet with truth and certainty."[37] I have written this book to prove that moderation is a noble virtue for courageous minds, one that, for all its ambiguities and limitations, can make our world better, safer, and more humane.

Notes

Prologue: Why Moderation?

1. *The Political Writings of John Adams*, George A. Peek, ed. (Indianapolis, IN: Bobbs-Merrill, 1954), 92.

2. Aurelian Craiutu, *Liberalism under Siege: The Political Thought of the French Doctrinaires* (Lanham, MD: Lexington Books, 2003); "The Virtues of Political Moderation," *Political Theory*, 29-3 (2001): 449–68; "Tocqueville's Paradoxical Moderation," *Review of Politics*, 67-4 (2005): 599–629; *Elogiul moderaţiei* [*In Praise of Moderation*] (Iaşi: Polirom Publishing House, 2006).

3. I borrow this concept from Reinhart Koselleck; see *Futures Past* (Cambridge, MA: MIT Press, 1985); *Critique and Crises: Enlightenment and the Pathogenesis of Modern Society* (Cambridge, MA: MIT Press, 1998); and *The Practice of Conceptual History: Timing History, Spacing Concepts* (Stanford, CA: Stanford University Press, 2002). Koselleck initially referred to it as *Sattelzeit* and, later, as *Schwellenzeit*. See Reinhart Koselleck, "A Response to Comments on the *Geschichtliche Grundbegriffe*," in *The Meanings of Historical Terms and Concepts*, eds. Hartmut Lehmann and Melvin Richter (Washington, DC: German Historical Institute, 1986), 68–70. On the contemporary relevance of the French Revolution, see François Furet's *Débats autour de la Révolution*, reprinted in Furet, *La Révolution française* (Paris: Gallimard, 2007), 821–915.

4. The influence of Rousseau's ideas in France was analyzed by Jean Roussel, *Jean-Jacques Rousseau en France après la Révolution, 1795–1830, lectures et légende* (Paris: Armand Colin, 1972).

5. I borrow this metaphor from Halifax (see chapter 1 below).

6. In an excellent recent study, *Libéralisme et démocratie: De Sismondi à Constant à partir du Contrat social (1801–1806)* (Geneva: Slatkine, 2010), Emmanuelle Paulet-Grandguillot has shed fresh light on the intellectual dialogue between Sismondi, Rousseau, and Constant, touching on several issues discussed in the present book, such as mixed government, limited sovereignty, and the balance of powers.

7. Jean-Denis Bredin, *Sieyès: La clè de la Révolution française* (Paris: Editions de Fallois, 1988). On Sieyès as the precursor of Constant, see chapter 6 below.

8. For a recent overview, see Philipp Blom, *Enlightening the World: Encyclopedia, the Book that Changed the Course of History* (London: Palgrave MacMillan, 2005). Liberty Fund will soon publish a new anthology from the *Encyclopédie*, edited and translated by Henry Clark.

9. See Edward Shils' essay "Ideology and Civility," reprinted in *The Virtue of Civility* (Indianapolis, IN: Liberty Fund, 1997), 25–62; also Michael Oakeshott's critique of ideological politics in *Rationalism in Politics and Other Essays*, 2nd ed. (Indianapolis, IN: Liberty Fund, 1991), 5–42.

10. Seneca, "On Tranquility of Mind," in *Dialogues and Letters*, C.D.N. Costa, ed. and trans. (Harmondsworth: Penguin, 1997), 58.

11. "A grain of boldness is everything. This is an important piece of prudence" (Baltasar Gracián, *The Art of Worldly Wisdom*, trans. J. Jacobs [New York: Shambala, 2000], 74).

12. Seneca, "On Tranquility of Mind," 58.

13. Ran Halévi, "La modération à l'épreuve de l'absolutisme. De l'Ancien Régime à la Révolution française," *Le Débat*, 109 (2000): 73–98.

14. Quentin Skinner, "Meaning and Understanding in the History of Ideas," in *Visions of Politics*, vol. 1: *Regarding Method* (Cambridge, MA: Cambridge University Press, 2002), 57–89.

15. My eclectic method combines the approaches of the Cambridge school, the *Begriffsgeschichte*, and the tradition of inquiry developed by François Furet and continued by his former collaborators in France. The *Begriffsgeschichte* school allows us to study conceptual change and political innovation over time, especially during and after revolutionary periods, when key concepts are contested and undergo profound transformations. By treating language and political actions as interdependent, it enables us to notice contradictions that were originally overlooked and allows us to imagine alternative possible trajectories; in so doing, it connects the history of concepts to social history and the history of mentalities, something that the Cambridge school does not do systematically. See, in particular, the *Handbuch politisch-sozialer Grundbegriffe in Frankreich, 1680–1820*, edited by Rolf Reichardt and Eberhard Schmitt in collaboration with Gerd van den Heuvel and Anette Höfer (18 vols.) and the *Geschichtliche Grundbegriffe* edited by Otto Brunner, Werner Conze and Reinhart Koselleck (since 1975). The following chapters of the *Handbuch* are of special interest to the topic of moderation: "Terreur, Terroriste, Terrorisme" (3: 89–132), "Civilité" (4: 1–49), "Fanatique, fanatisme" (4: 51–115), "Honnête homme, Honnêteté, Honnêtes gens" (7: 7–73), "Constitution, constitutionnel" (12: 31–64), "Modération, modéré, modérantisme" (16: 123–58). A good commentary on the *Begriffsgeschichte* school can be found in Melvin Richter, *The History of Political and Social Concepts* (Oxford: Oxford University Press, 1995). For two different French versions of this approach, see *Interpréter les textes politiques,* eds. Lucien Jaume and Alain Laquièze, *Les Cahiers du CEVIPOF* 39 (2005), http.cevipof.msh-paris.fr; and Pierre Rosanvallon, *Democracy Past and Future* (New York: Columbia University Press, 2006), chapters 1–2.

16. Originally, the word "*modérantisme*" was used by the enemies of moderation to denounce their moderate opponents. In *Trésor de la langue française* 11 (Paris: Gallimard, 1985), the concept is broadly defined as the political doctrine of the moderates during the revolution. The dictionary also lists a claim attributed to Sénac de Meilhan (1797), identifying the defenders of *modérantisme* with former "terrorists."

17. See Thomas Schleich, "Fanatique, fanatisme," in *Handbuch*, 4: 51–115; Werner Conze and Helga Reinhart, "Fanatismus," in *Geschichtliche Grundbegriffe,* 2: 303–27. For a recent treatment, see Alberto Toscano, *Fanaticism: On the Uses of an Idea* (London: Verso, 2010), especially chapters 1–3, and the conclusion. Toscano identifies several key interlinked dimensions of fanaticism, such as the refusal of mediation or representation, the negation of the world, and the celebration of antagonism and violence (ibid., 27).

18. See chapter 1 below; also Anette Höfer and Rolf Reichardt, "Honnête homme, Honnêteté, Honnêtes gens," in *Handbuch,* 7: 7–73; Roger Chartier, "Civilité," *Handbuch,* 4: 7–50; and the article on civility by Jaucourt in the *Encyclopédie*.

19. See Werner Conze, "Mittelstand," in *Geschichtliche Grundbegriffe* (Stuttgart: Klett-Cotta, 1978), 4: 49–92.

20. From a text published in 1792, quoted in Thomas Schleich, "Fanatique, fanatisme," in *Handbuch,* 4: 98.

21. Fanaticism in the service of liberty can also be sometimes interpreted as a

virtue. See, for example, the following claim from a letter of Abbé Rive to Desmoulins: "Si le fanatisme est un crime en religion, il est un devoir en liberté, et il ne faut avoir du fanatisme que pour elle" (quoted in *Handbuch*, 4: 99).

22. The phrase is Antoine Meillet's, as quoted in Melvin and Michaela Richter, "Introduction: Translation of Reinhart Koselleck's 'Krise' in *Geschichtliche Grundbegriffe*," *Journal of the History of Ideas*, 67-2 (2006): 353.

23. See, for example, the contributions of Walter Kuhfuß, "Modération: Die Ideologisierung eines politischen Begriffs im Französischen," *Romanische Froschungen*, 87–3 (1975): 442–81; Georges Benrekassa, "Modération, Modéré, Modérantisme" in Rolf Reichardt & Hans-Jürgen Lüsebrink, *Handbuch politisch-sozialer Grundbegriffe in Frankreich, 1660–1820*, Heft 16–18 (Munich: R. Oldenbourg Verlag, 1996), 125–58; and Halévi, "La modération à l'épreuve de l'absolutisme," which discusses the transformation of moderation into an important political weapon during the Old Regime. Harry Clor's *On Moderation: Defending an Ancient Virtue in a Modern World* (Waco, TX: Baylor University Press, 2008) makes a cogent case for moderation as a political, individual and philosophic virtue. For a recent analysis of political extremism, see Uwe Backes, *Political Extremes: A History of Terminology from Ancient Times to the Present* (London: Routledge, 2009). Robert McCluer Calhoon's *Political Moderation in America's First Two Centuries* (New York: Cambridge University Press, 2008) explored political moderation in America from 1713 to 1884 as an integral element in political culture and the product of religious belief and practice. Vincent Starzinger's *Middlingness*, 2nd ed. (New Brunswick, NJ: Transactions Publishers, 1991) examined the concept of *juste milieu* in nineteenth-century France and England. In *The Politics of Faith and the Politics of Skepticism* (New Haven, CT: Yale University Press, 1996), Michael Oakeshott commented on the relationship between skepticism, moderation, and trimming. Other important studies are: Lucien Jaume, *L'individu effacé ou le paradoxe du libéralisme français* (Paris: Fayard, 1997); Annelien de Dijn, *French Political Thought from Montesquieu to Tocqueville: Liberty in a Levelled Society* (Cambridge: Cambridge University Press, 2008); J.A.W. Gunn, *When the French Tried to be British: Party, Opposition, and the Quest for Civil Disagreement, 1814–1848* (Montreal and Kingston: McGill and Queen's University Press, 2009); Paulet-Grandguillot, *Libéralisme et démocratie;* and K. Steven Vincent, *Benjamin Constant and the Birth of French Liberalism* (Basingstoke: Palgrave Macmillan, 2011) Julien Boudon's *La passion de la modération* (Paris: Dalloz, 2011) and Jean-Pierre Rioux's *Les Centristes: De Mirabeau à Bayrou* (Paris: Fayard, 2011) touch on several topics discussed in this book, including the political dimension of moderation. Also of interest is William Egginton, *In Defense of Religious Moderation* (New York: Columbia University Press, 2011).

24. Michel de Montaigne, *The Complete Essays*, trans. M. A. Screech (London: Penguin, 1987), 458.

25. Edmund Burke, *A Philosophical Enquiry into the Origin of our Ideas of the Sublime and Beautiful* (Oxford: Oxford University Press, 1990), 50.

Chapter One: In Search of a Lost Archipelago

1. Montesquieu, *The Spirit of the Laws*, trans. Anne M. Cohler, Basia Carolyn Miller, and Harold Samuel Stone (Cambridge: Cambridge University Press, 1989), 426 (henceforth abbreviated as *SL*).

254 • Notes to Chapter One

2. *The Political Writings of John Adams*, 89.

3. Edmund Burke, *Reflections on the Revolution in France*, Connor Cruise O'Brien, ed. (Harmondsworth: Penguin, 1969), 374.

4. Clor, *On Moderation*, 5.

5. This is the so-called "Okrent's law" in political science.

6. One notable exception is Jonathan Israel, whose history of the Enlightenment is based on the seminal distinction between moderate and radical Enlightenment. See Israel, *Radical Enlightenment* (Oxford: Oxford University Press, 2001), *Enlightenment Contested* (Oxford: Oxford University Press, 2006) and *Democratie Enlightenment* (Oxford: Oxford University Press, 2011). For a summary of Israel's view, see *A Revolution of the Mind: Radical Enlightenment and the Intellectual Origins of Modern Democracy* (Princeton, NJ: Princeton University Press, 2009).

7. In *Trésor de la langue française*, vol. 11, moderation is defined as temperament, as the antonym of extremism, and as the synonym of the center and *juste milieu* between extremes. The opposition between moderation and stupidity or madness appears, for example, in the following German proverb: "*Zu wenig und zu viel / Ist aller Narren Ziel.*"

8. Germaine de Staël, *Considerations on the Principal Events of the French Revolution*, Aurelian Craiutu, ed. (Indianapolis, IN: Liberty Fund, 2008), 306 (henceforth abbreviated as *CPE*).

9. Friedrich Nietzsche, *Daybreak: Thoughts on the Prejudices of Morality*, Maudemarie Clark and Brian Leiter, eds., trans. R. J. Hollingdale (Cambridge: Cambridge University Press, 1997), 167.

10. For a similar point, see Clor, *On Moderation*, 5.

11. See, for example, the following remark: "Presque toujours les hommes que l'on décore du nom de modérés sont des caractères indécis" (quoted in the entry on "*modéré*" in *Grand dictionnaire universel*, Pierre Larousse, ed. [Paris: Administration du Grand dictionnaire universel, vol. 11, 1877], 361). Also see Nietzsche's critique of moderation and "petty politics" in *Beyond Good and Evil*, trans. Walter Kaufmann (New York: Random House, 1966), 131–32.

12. Charles Fourrier, *Théorie des quatre mouvements et des destinées générales* (Paris: Société pour la propagation et la réalisation de la théorie du Fourrier, 1846), 185.

13. A paraphrase of Marx's epigraph to the *Introduction to the Critique of Hegel's Philosophy of Right*.

14. La Rochefoucauld, *Maxims*, trans. Stuart Warner and Stéphane Douard (South Bend, IN: St. Augustine's Press, 2001), 61. For a contemporary view on the role of passions in political thought, see Michael Walzer, "Passion and Politics," *Philosophy and Social Criticism* 28-6 (2002): 617–33.

15. Isaiah Berlin, *Personal Impressions* (Oxford: Oxford University Press, 1982), 27.

16. On "meekness" as another face of moderation, see Norberto Bobbio, *In Praise of Meekness: Essays on Ethics and Politics*, trans. Theresa Chataway (London: Polity, 2000), 19–38.

17. Ibid., 26–27.

18. Alexis de Tocqueville, *The Old Regime and the Revolution*, vol. 2, trans. Alan S. Kahan (Chicago: University of Chicago Press, 2001), 30.

19. See Israel, *Enlightenment Contested*, 866.

20. Israel, *A Revolution of the Mind*, 236. On the distinction between "moderate" and "radical" Enlightenment, see Israel's works cited above, and especially chapter 7 of *A Revolution of the Mind* which emphasizes the "irreconcilability" of the two forms of Enlightenment. For two critical assessments of Israel's "radical-moderate Enlightenment" dichotomy, see Anthony J. La Vopa, "A New Intellectual History: Jonathan Israel's Enlightenment," *Historical Journal* 52-3 (2009): 731–38; and Harvey Chisick, "Interpreting the Enlightenment," *The European Legacy* 13-1 (2008): 35–57.

21. This aspect is well highlighted in Jacques Proust's classic study, *Diderot et l'Encyclopédie*, 2nd ed. (Paris: Armand Colin, 1967), chapters X–XI (341–448).

22. See chapter 3 below.

23. "The instinct of the herd," Nietzsche wrote, "considers the middle and the mean as the highest and most valuable: the place where the majority finds itself; the mode and manner in which it finds itself. It is therefore an opponent of all orders of rank. . . . The herd feels the exception as something opposed and harmful to it. . . . Fear ceases in the middle: here one is never alone, here there is little room for misunderstanding; here there is equality (Friedrich Nietzsche, *The Will to Power*, trans. Walter Kaufmann [New York: Vintage, 1967], 159).

24. Edmund Burke, *Further Reflections on the Revolution in France*, Daniel E. Ritchie, ed. (Indianapolis, IN: Liberty Fund, 1992), 16.

25. The comparison of the serpent to the dove can be found in aphorism no. 256 of Baltasar Gracián's *Oráculo manual* (translated as *The Art of Worldly Wisdom*).

26. Horace, *Odes* 2.10.5.

27. http://nothingistic.org/library/confucius/mean/mean01.html (accessed April 10, 2010). Also see *The Bhagavad Gita*, trans. F. Edgerton (New York: Harper Torchbooks, 1964), 33.

28. On the relation between moderation and extremes in classical thought, see Backes, *Political Extremes*, 16–50. An overview of the different meanings of moderation in the history of philosophy can be found in *Historisches Wörterbuch der Philosophie* (Basel/Stuttgart: Schwabe & Coag, 1980), 838–41. The key primary texts include: Aristotle's *Politics*, especially 2:1–6, 3:11, 3:13, 4:11; chapter 3 of Polybius' *History of Rome*; and Cicero, *On the Commonwealth*, especially book 1.

29. See books 4 and 6 (485a4–487a8) of Plato's *Republic*. For two different readings, see John F. Wilson, *The Politics of Moderation: An Interpretation of Plato's Republic* (Lanham, MD: University Press of America, 1984), especially 35–54, 185–200; Melissa Lane, "Virtue as the Love of Knowledge in Plato's *Symposium* and *Republic*," in *Maieusis: Essays in Ancient Philosophy in Honour of Myles Burnyeat*, Dominic Scott, ed..(Oxford: Oxford University Press, 2007), 44–67. For a treatment of moderation as an individual virtue in the *Charmides*, see W. Thomas Schmid, *Plato's Charmides and the Socratic Ideal of Rationality* (Albany, NY: SUNY Press, 1998). Schmid identified four conceptions associated with *sophrosyne* in Greek ethical thought, which Socrates addressed in *Charmides*: quietness or peaceful orderliness (*Charmides*, 158e6–160d4); shame as a form of moral consciousness (160d5–161b4); doing one's own and not invading the affairs of others (161d4–164d3); self-knowledge (164d3–165b4).

30. Schmid, *Plato's Charmides and the Socratic Ideal of Rationality*, 161.

31. E. P. Panagopoulos, *Essays on the History and Meaning of Checks and Balances* (Lanham, MD: University Press of America, 1986), 6–9.

32. Aristotle, *Nichomachean Ethics*, 1106b35 (trans. W. D. Ross) in *The Basic Works of Aristotle*, Richard McKeon, ed. (New York: Random House, 1941), 959.

33. Ibid., 1107a6. On this issue, see Ioannis D. Evrigenis, "The Doctrine of the Mean in Aristotle's Ethical and Political Theory," *History of Political Thought* 20-3 (1999): 393–416 and Boudon, *La passion de la modération*, 19–32. For an interesting account of the enduring relevance of Aristotle's categories, see Richard Godkin's *The Tragic Middle: Racine, Aristotle, Euripides* (Madison: University of Wisconsin Press, 1991); Ezequiel Adamovsky, "Aristotle, Diderot, Liberalism, and the Idea of Middle Class," *History of Political Thought* 26-2 (2005): 303–33. On Aristotle's views on prudence, see Pierre Aubenque, *La prudence chez Aristote* (Paris: PUF, 1963).

34. Aristotle, *Nichomachean Ethics*, 1106b5–10, in *The Basic Works of Aristotle*, 958.

35. Distinguishing between philosophical and practical wisdom, Aristotle argued that the latter is concerned primarily with human things, about which it is possible and necessary to deliberate, while the former only with universal things, which allow for no deliberation. On this view, practical wisdom is concerned with both universals and particulars.

36. Aristotle also adds a further requirement: having a certain "state of character" (*Nichomachean Ethics*, 1139a35). The "particulars" Aristotle referred to include changing circumstances, shifting goals, the presence of other actors, and alternative courses of action.

37. Ibid., 1109b1–7, in *The Basic Works of Aristotle*, 963. A similar point can be found in Sophocles: "A wise man . . . knows he does not have to be rigid and close-hauled. / You've seen trees tossed by a torrent in a flash flood: / If they bend, they're saved, and every twig survives, / But if they stiffen up, they're washed out from the roots. / It's the same in a boat: if a sailor keeps the footline taut, / If he doesn't give an inch, he'll capsize, and then— / He'll be sailing home with his benches down and his hull to the sky" (*Antigone*, trans. Paul Woodruff [Indianapolis, IN: Hackett, 2001], 31).

38. On prudence and political judgment, see Richard Ruderman, "Aristotle and the Recovery of Political Judgment," *American Political Science Review* 91-2 (2007): 409–20; and Wynne Walker Moskop, "Prudence, Imprudence, and the Puzzle of Bill Clinton," in *Tempered Strength,* Ethan Fishman, ed. (Lanham, MD: Lexington Books, 2004), 151–80.

39. Aristotle, *Nichomachean Ethics*, 1109b22–1109b27, in *The Basic Works of Aristotle*, 964.

40. James M. Blythe, *Ideal Government and the Mixed Constitution in the Middle Ages* (Princeton, NJ: Princeton University Press, 1992), 11. Other important analyses of mixed government can be found in: George Aalders, *Die Theorie der gemischten Verfassung im Altertum* (Amsterdam: A. M. Hackert, 1968); Paula Zillig, *Die Theorie der gemischten Verfassung in ihrer literarischen Entwicklung in Altertum and ihr Verhältnis zur Lehre Lockes und Montesquieus über Verfassung* (Würzburg: Stürz, 1916). On the connection between mixed government, checks and balances, and balanced constitutions, see John Morrow, *History of Western Political Thought: A Thematic Introduction,* 2nd edition (Basingstoke: Palgrave Macmillan, 2005), 227–47; M.J.C. Vile, *Constitutionalism and the Separation of Powers,* 2nd ed. (Indianapolis, IN: Liberty Fund, 1998), chapters 2–3; Backes, *Political Extremes,* 25–50; and Panagopoulos, *Essays on the History and Meaning of Checks and Bal-*

ances, 1–44. For a recent interpretation, see Mogens Herman Hansen, "The Mixed Constitution Versus the Separation of Powers: Monarchical and Aristocratic Aspects of Modern Democracy," *History of Political Thought* 31-3 (2010): 509–31. He insists that "by contrast with the theory of the separation of powers, the theory of the mixed constitution did not assign one function to one institution" (522).

41. The contrast between mixed government and simple forms of government, subject to corruption and decay, was a common trope in the writings of many ancient authors, from Solon, Thucydides, and Plato to Polybius and Cicero. In their view, the best way to check political power was to distribute it among several classes, groups, interests, and institutions in order to achieve a moderate blending, in the interests of both the few and the many. On the concepts of mixed and balanced government in the writings of the Founding Fathers, see Gordon Wood, *The Creation of the American Republic, 1776–1787* (New York: Norton, 1972), 197–255.

42. Aristotle, *Politics*, 1304b1 (trans. Benjamin Jowett), in *The Basic Works of Aristotle*, 1239.

43. Ibid., 1295b5–6, in *The Basic Works of Aristotle*, 1220. Also see Fred D. Miller, Jr., "Aristotle and American Classical Republicanism," in *Justice v. Law in Greek Political Thought*, Leslie G. Rubin, ed. (Lanham, MD: Rowman & Littlefield, 1997), 183–94; Creed, "Aristotle's Middle Constitution," *PSA Study Group in Greek Political Thought* 8 (1989): 2–27; Thomas Lindsay, "Aristotle's Qualified Defense of Democracy through 'Political Mixing,'" *Journal of Politics* 54-1 (1992): 101–19.

44. An earlier endorsement of mixed government as a "moderate blending" between the interests of the few and the many can be found in book 8 of Thucydides' *History of the Peloponesian War* (8: 97).

45. See Plutarch's essay on Lycurgus in *Plutarch's Lives*, vol. 1, Arthur Hugh Clough, ed., trans. Dryden (New York: Modern Library, 2001), 52–80.

46. See Polybius, *The Rise of the Roman Empire*, trans. Ian Scott-Kilvert, F. W. Walbank, ed. (Harmondsworth: Penguin, 1979), 302–18, 338–52.

47. See Kurt von Fritz, *The Theory of the Mixed Constitution in Antiquity: A Critical Analysis of Polybius' Political Ideas* (New York: Columbia University Press, 1954).

48. Cicero, *On the Commonwealth and On the Laws*, James E. G. Zetzel, ed. (Cambridge: Cambridge University Press, 1999), 52. Cicero, who considered moderation (*modestia*) to be a cardinal virtue along with justice, wisdom, and magnanimity, discussed its relevance in book 1 of *On Duties*, where he defined it as "the knowledge of putting in their place things that one says or does" (*On Duties*, M. T. Griffin and E. M. Atkins, eds. [Cambridge: Cambridge University Press, 1991], 55).

49. Cicero, *On the Commonwealth and On the Laws*, 167–68.

50. Ibid., 31. Underlying this view there was also an implicit endorsement of moderation as the opposite of excess. See for example, the following claim of Cicero: "Anything that is too successful . . . generally turns into its opposite, and that is particularly true of commonwealths: extreme liberty, both of the people at large and of particular individuals, results in extreme slavery" (ibid., 30).

51. Ibid., 56–57. This metaphor also appeared in Horace's *Ars poetica*. It is possible that Cicero was inspired by Plato's description of a well-ordered soul in book 4 of the *Republic*. Cicero's contribution to the general theory of republican constitutionalism is discussed in Neal Wood, *Cicero's Social and Political Thought* (Berkeley:

University of California Press, 1991), 159–75; Nicholas Buttle, "Republican Constitutionalism: A Roman Ideal," *Journal of Political Philosophy* 9-3 (2001): 331–49.

52. *The Desert Fathers: Sayings of the Early Christian Monks*, Benedicta Ward, trans. and ed. (Harmondsworth: Penguin, 2003), 106.

53. Josef Pieper, *The Four Cardinal Virtues: Prudence, Justice, Fortitude, Temperance* (Notre Dame, IN: University of Notre Dame Press, 1966), 3–4.

54. Ibid., 6–7.

55. Daniel M. Nelson, *The Priority of Prudence: Virtue and Natural Law in Thomas Aquinas and the Implications for Modern Ethics* (University Park, PA: Pennsylvania State University Press, 1992), ix.

56. St. Thomas Aquinas, *Summa Theologiae* 36: "Prudence" (2a2ae, 47–56), Thomas Gilby, ed. (Cambridge: Blackfriars, 1974), 11.

57. Ibid., 41.

58. Romans 8:6.

59. Aquinas, *Summa Theologiae* 36, 43.

60. Ibid., 63.

61. The topic of the mixed constitution was also addressed by Francesco Guicciardini in his work on the government of Florence. Guicciardini's reformulation of the theory of mixed government is analyzed in Blythe, *Ideal Government and the Mixed Constitution*, 292–97. On moderation in early modern French thought, see Kuhfuß, "Modération: Die Ideologisierung eines politischen Begriffs im Französischen," 442–81; Halévi, "La modération à l'épreuve de l'absolutisme," 79–86 and Boudon, *La passion de la modération*, 32–39. On the concept of *juste milieu* during the Renaissance, see Emmanuel Naya and Anne-Pascale Pouey-Mounou, eds., *Éloge de la médiocrité: le juste milieu à la Renaissance* (Paris: Rue d'Ulm, 2005), 137–234.

62. See Machiavelli, *Discourses*, book 1, chapters 2, 4.

63. Seyssel as quoted in Nannerl Keohane, *Philosophy and the State in France* (Princeton, NJ: Princeton University Press, 1980), 35; all emphases added. On Seyssel and Le Roy as precursors of Montesquieu (with regard to moderate monarchy), see Kuhfuß, *Mäßigung und Politik: Studien zur politischen Sprache und Theorie Montesquieus* (Munich: Wilhelm Fink, 1975) 175–87; Blythe, *Ideal Government and the Mixed Constitution*, 265–69; Keohane, *Philosophy and the State in France*, 84–87; and Halévi, "La modération à l'épreuve de l'absolutisme," 79–80.

64. Keohane, *Philosophy and the State in France*, 35.

65. On Pasquier, see Keohane, *Philosophy and the State in France*, 42–49 and Donald R. Kelley, *Foundations of Modern Historical Scholarship: Language, Law, and History in the French Renaissance* (New York: Columbia University Press, 1970), chapter 10.

66. Montaigne, *The Complete Essays*, 225. On Montaigne's injunction to live temperately, see Sarah Bakewell, *How To Live? Or a Life of Montaigne in One Question and Twenty Attempts at an Answer* (New York: Other Press, 2010), 195–202.

67. Montaigne, *The Complete Essays*, 1258–59. The French term is "*à propos*".

68. Ibid., 1261.

69. Ibid.

70. "Les extrémités sont vicieuses et partent de l'homme: toute compensation est juste, et vient de Dieu" (La Bruyère, *Les Caractères* [Paris: Garnier-Flammarion, 1965], 411).

71. See Pascal, *Œuvres Complètes,* Louis Lafuma, ed. (Paris: Seuil, 1963), 526–27. Richard Godkin's *The Tragic Middle* explores the issue of moderation in the works of Racine.

72. "The security of prudence," he wrote, "consists in inner temperance" (Gracián, *The Art of Worldly Wisdom,* 73).

73. Ibid., 34.

74. Ibid., 22.

75. Ibid., 15. The reference to "judicious" or "wise" moderation appears in aphorism no. 33.

76. This concept is discussed in Helmut Jansen, *Die Grundbegriffe des Baltasar Gracián* (Geneva and Paris: Droz and Minard, 1958), 33–35.

77. Quote in Benrekassa, "Modération, Modéré, Modérantisme," 130.

78. *Dictionnaire universel,* vol. II, Antoine Furetière, ed. (Hague and Rotterdam: Arnout & Reinier Leers, 1690; reprint Geneva: Slatkine, 1970), F-O. "Modérateur" was defined as a "dogmatic" term, referring to the person who governs or rules; the entry gave God as an example of "le modérateur du monde."

79. "*Vertu qui porte à garder une sage mesure en toutes choses, surtout à ne se point laisser aller à la colère, au luxe, à l'orgueil*" (quoted in Benrekassa, "Modération, Modéré, Modérantisme," 128).

80. Writes Jaucourt: "La prudence dirige notre ame à rechercher la meilleure fin, & à mettre en usage les moyens nécessaires pour y parvenir; c'est pourquoi la véritable *modération* est inséparable de l'intégrité, aussi-bien que de la diligence, ou de l'application. Elle se fait voir principalement dans les actes de la volonté & dans les actions; c'est la marque d'un esprit sage, & c'est la source du plus grand bonheur dont on puisse jouir ici bas" (*Encyclopédie, ou dictionnaire raisonné des sciences, des arts et des métiers,* Denis Diderot and Jean le Rond D'Alembert, eds. [University of Chicago: ARTFL Encyclopédie Project (Spring 2010 Edition), Robert Morrissey, ed.: http://encyclopedie.uchicago.edu/, accessed December 28, 2010]).

81. See Höfer and Reichardt, "Honnête homme, Honnêteté, Honnêtes gens," in *Handbuch,* 7: 7–73; Jolanta Pekacz, *Conservative Tradition in Pre-revolutionary France: Parisian Salon Women* (New York: Peter Lang, 1999), 20–72.

82. This is the definition given by Chévalier de Méré around 1680 (as quoted in Höfer and Reichardt, "Honnête homme," 22). The social ideal of *l'honnête homme* was outlined in Nicolas Faret's *L'honnête homme ou l'art de plaire à la cour* (1630).

83. See the remark of Le Maître de Claville as quoted in Pekacz, *Conservative Tradition in Pre-revolutionary France,* 28.

84. See Pekacz, *Conservative Tradition,* 28.

85. See, for example, aphorism no. 308 in La Rochefoucauld, *Maxims,* 61.

86. Ibid., 104 (withdrawn maxim no. 106).

87. Ibid., 58 (maxim no. 293).

88. Henry Home, Lord Kames, *Elements of Criticism,* vol. 1, Peter Jones, ed. (Indianapolis, IN: Liberty Fund, 2005), 149.

89. See Halifax, *Complete Works,* J. P. Kenyon, ed. (London: Penguin, 1969) and Mark Brown's general introduction to *The Works of George Saville Marquis of Halifax,* vol. 1, Mark N. Brown, ed. (Oxford: Clarendon Press, 1989), xix–xliii.

90. Plutarch, *Selected Lives and Essays* (Roslyn, NY: Walter J. Black, 1951), 160.

91. Halifax, *Complete Works,* 50. For additional information about the various meanings of "trimmer" in the epoch, see Brown's introduction to *The Works of George Saville,* vol. 1, 42–43. In 1664, "Trimmers" designated the evangelical or

left-wing Anglicans who were the target of Sir Roger L'Estrange's critique later that year. For more information, see Donald R. Benson, "Halifax and the Trimmers," *Huntington Library Quarterly* 27 (1963): 115.

92. David Hume, *Essays. Moral, Political, and Literary*, Eugene Miller, ed. (Indianapolis, IN: Liberty Fund, 1985), 507.

93. Ibid., 494.

94. David Hume, *The History of England*, vol. 6 (Indianapolis, IN: Liberty Fund, 1983), 418.

95. Macaulay's account of Halifax is revealing in this regard. "In temper," he wrote, "Halifax was what, in our time, is called a Conservative; in theory he was a Republican (Thomas Babington Macaulay, *The History of England from the Accession of James the Second*, vol. 1, Charles H. Firth, ed. [London: Macmillan, 1913], 234).

96. Hume, *Essays*, 78.

97. See Deleyre's article on fanaticism in *Denis Diderot's The Encyclopedia: Selections*, ed. and trans. Stephen Gendzier (New York: Harper Torchbooks, 1967), 104. Also see Schleich, "Fanatique, fanatisme," in *Handbuch*, 4: 51–115; Dominique Colas, *Civil Society and Fanaticism: Conjoined Histories*, trans. Amy Caobs (Stanford, CA: Stanford University Press, 1997), 8–20.

98. Deleyre, "Fanaticism," *The Encyclopedia*, 104.

99. Quoted in Schleich, "Fanatique, fanatisme," 69. For a survey of the meanings of "enthusiasm" in the history of modern Europe, see Lawrence E. Klein and Anthony J. La Vopa, eds., *Enthusiasm and Enlightenment in Europe, 1650–1850* (San Marino, CA: Huntington Library, 1998), especially the essays of J.G.A. Pocock, "Enthusiasm: The Anti-self of Enlightenment" (7–28), Antony La Vopa, "The Philosopher and the *Schwärmer*: On the Career of a German Epithet from Luther to Kant" (85–116), and Lawrence E. Klein, "Sociability, Solitude, and Enthusiasm" (153–77); also John Christian Laursen, "Bayle, Hume y Kant. Sobre la superstición y el fanatismo en politica," in Gerardo López Sastre, *David Hume. Nuevas perspectivas sobre su obra* (Cuenca: Ediciones de la Universidad de Castilla-La Mancha, 2005), 65–85; James Farr, "Political Science and the Enlightenment of Enthusiasm," *American Political Science Review*, 82-1 (1988): 51–69.

100. Voltaire, *Dictionnaire philosophique*, René Pomeau, ed. (Paris: Garnier-Flammarion, 1964), 189–91. On Voltaire's critique of fanaticism, see Peter Gay, *Voltaire's Politics: The Poet as Realist* (New York: Vintage, 1965), 249–58.

101. Jean-Jacques Rousseau, *Émile or On Education*, trans. Allan Bloom (New York: Basic Books, 1979), 236; also see ibid., 313, 354.

102. Ibid., 312.

103. Also see the epilogue of this book.

104. The contemporary relevance of this theme is highlighted in Hansen, "The Mixed Constitution versus the Separation of Powers."

105. For an account of the concept of balance in modern thought, see Kurt Kluxen, "Zur Balanceidee im 18. Jahrhundert," in *Vom Staat des Ancien Regime zum modernen Parteienstaat. Festschrift für Theodor Schieder*, Helmut Berdin, Kurt Düwell, Lothar Gall, Wolfgang Mommsen, and Hans-Ulrich Wehler, eds. (Munich: R. Oldenbourg Verlag, 1978), 41–58; also Hans Fenske, "Gleichgewicht," in *Geschichtliche Grundbegriffe*, vol. 2, 959–96. On the place occupied by moderation in the *Encyclopédie* as an essential virtue instrumental in achieving social and political

balance, see the entries on "government" (by Jaucourt) and "representatives" (by d'Holbach), partially translated by Gendzier in *The Encyclopedia*, 124–25, 214–22. Also see Israel, *Democratic Enlightenment*, 56–92.

106. d'Holbach, "Representatives," ibid., 221.

Chapter Two: The Architecture of Moderate Government

1. Montesquieu, *SL*, 602. The original text of *De l'Esprit des lois* can be found in Montesquieu, *OCM*, II: 227–995. The references to the English text are inserted in the main text; Roman numerals correspond to the book numbers, and Arabic numerals correspond to the chapter numbers, followed by the page numbers to which references are made. The Pléiade edition also contains important additional documents on the writing and significance of *SL* (see especially Montesquieu, *OCM*, II: 1121–1200). On Montesquieu's intellectual ambition, see *OCM*, II: 1039–41, especially aphorisms no. 198, 200–206.

2. See Goyard-Fabre, *Montesquieu, la Nature, les Lois, la Liberté* (Paris: PUF, 1993), 153–54.

3. See Paul Rahe, *Montesquieu and the Logic of Liberty: War, Religion, Commerce, Climate, Terrain, Technology, Uneasiness of Mind, the Spirit of Political Vigilance, and the Foundations of the Modern Republic* (New Haven, CT: Yale University Press, 2009), 75.

4. Some of the main themes of *SL*, especially the relationship between political liberty, despotism, and moderation, had already appeared a decade and a half earlier in *CR* (1734), and had also been present to some extent in Montesquieu's *PL* (1721). For a treatment of moderation in *PL*, see Donald A. Desserud, "Virtue, Commerce, and Moderation in the 'Tale of the Troglodytes:' Montesquieu's Persian Letters," *History of Political Thought* 12-4 (1991): 605–26. The claim that moderation is the supreme virtue of legislators, along with his theory of moderate government in *SL*, is the solution proposed by Montesquieu to the dilemmas raised in *PL*.

5. The classical biography remains Robert Shackleton, *Montesquieu: A Critical Biography* (Oxford: Oxford University Press, 1961). The genesis and plan of *SL* are discussed in Catherine Volpilhac-Auger, "Une nouvelle 'chaîne secrète' de *L'Esprit des lois*," in *Montesquieu en 2005*, Catherine Volpilhac-Auger, ed. (Oxford: Voltaire Foundation, 2005), 85–180; and Jean Ehrard, *L'Esprit des mots: Montesquieu en lui-même et parmi les siens* (Geneva: Droz, 1998), 179–91. For more information on the reception of *SL*, see Israel, *Enlightenment Contested*, 824–39; David Carrithers, "Introduction" to *Montesquieu's Science of Politics: Essays on The Spirit of the Laws*, David Carrithers, Michael Mosher, and Paul Rahe, eds. (Lanham, MD: Rowman & Littlefield, 2001), 1–6. On the reception and influence of Montesquieu in America, see Anne Cohler, *Montesquieu's Comparative Politics and the Spirit of American Constitutionalism* (Lawrence, KS: University Press of Kansas, 1988); Paul Merrill Spurlin, *Montesquieu in America, 1760–1801* (Baton Rouge: Louisiana State University Press, 1940). The larger philosophical implications of Montesquieu's ideas are explored in Pierre Manent, *The City of Man*, trans. Marc A. LePain (Princeton, NJ: Princeton University Press, 1998), chapter 1; Thomas Pangle, *The Theological Basis of Liberal Modernity in Montesquieu's Spirit of the Laws* (Chicago: University of Chicago Press, 2010); and Guillaume Barrera, *Les lois du monde*.

262 • Notes to Chapter Two

Enquête sur le dessein politique de Montesquieu (Paris: Gallimard, 2010), especially 117–50; 352–79. There are numerous other excellent studies that analyze Montesquieu's thought in relation to that of his predecessors, contemporaries, and followers. From this long list, I would like to single out the following: Cecil P. Courtney, *Montesquieu and Burke* (Oxford: Blackwell, 1963); Melvin Richter, "Introduction" to *The Political Theory of Montesquieu* (Cambridge: Cambridge University Press, 1977), 1–110; Bertrand Binoche's *Introduction à l'Espirit des Lois* (Paris: PUF, 1998); *Montesquieu and the Spirit of Modernity*, David Carrithers and Patrick Coleman, eds. (Oxford: Voltaire Foundation, 2002); *Lectures de l'Esprit des lois,* T. Hoquet and Céline Spector eds. (Bordeaux: Presses Universitaires de Bordeaux, 2004); *Montesquieu and His Legacy*, Rebecca Kingston, ed. (Albany: State University of New York Press, 2008). A more recent account of Montesquieu's political theory of moderation in relation to Hobbes and Locke can be found in Duncan Kelly, *The Propriety of Liberty: Persons, Passions, and Judgment in Modern Political Thought* (Princeton, NJ: Princeton University Press, 2011), 59–116. Montesquieu's account of monarchy is examined in Michael Sonenscher, *Before the Deluge: Public Debt, Inequality, and the Intellectual Origins of the French Revolution* (Princeton, NJ: Princeton University Press, 2007), 95–153. For an analysis of moderation in the context of the Old Regime, with reference to Montesquieu, see Halévi, "La modération à l'épreuve de l'absolutisme," and Mark Hulliung, *Montesquieu and the Old Regime* (Berkeley: University of California Press, 1976). On the role of moderation in Montesquieu's thought, see Walter Kuhfuß, *Mäßigung und Politik: Studien zur politischen Sprache und Theorie Montesquieus*; Henry J. Merry, *Montesquieu's System of Natural Government* (West Lafayette, IN: Purdue University Press, 1970), chapter 8; Anne M. Cohler, *Montesquieu's Comparative Politics*, chapter 4; Andrea Radasanu, "Montesquieu on Moderation, Monarchy, and Reform," in *History of Political Thought* 31-2 (2010): 283–307, and Boudon, *La passion de la modération*, 38–48.

6. Carrithers, "Introduction," 3.

7. The phrase belongs to La Beaumelle as quoted in Israel, *Enlightenment Contested*, 820. If Montesquieu's moderation earned him the respect of his admirers, it also elicited the ire of those who disagreed with his conclusions. Some accused Montesquieu of endorsing a pernicious form of natural religion, others took him to task for being a defender of the *status quo*. Although initially the Jesuits acknowledged the erudition of Montesquieu's book, they eventually expressed their dissatisfaction with the underlying religious and political message of *SL* which advocated toleration. A year after the publication of Montesquieu's book, it became the target of a sustained Jansenist attack which denounced Montesquieu's materialism and his alleged failure to give religion its due. Finally, in November 1751, *SL* was put on index by the Vatican. Montesquieu answered his critics in *Défense de l'Esprit des Lois*, published anonymously in Geneva in February 1750. He defended himself against the charge of "Spinozism" by pointing to the numerous references to a divine creator and natural law in his book.

8. See Catherine Volpilhac-Auger, "*L'Esprit des lois*, une lecture *ad usum Delphini?*" in *Le Travail des Lumières. Pour Georges Benrekassa*, Caroline Jacot-Grapa et al., eds. (Paris: Honoré Champion, 2002), 157–72; Ehrard, *L'Esprit des mots*, 11–24.

9. *SL*, xliv.

10. See, for example, the surprising invocation to the muses at the beginning of

Part IV of *SL* (Book XX) or the epigraph from Ovid at the beginning of Book XXVIII.

11. See *OCM*, II: 1249–50.

12. *SL*, XI: 20, 186.

13. This is how Albert Sorel described Montesquieu's style: "The artist in Montesquieu was as exacting as the thinker. . . . He was less anxious 'to be read than to stimulate thought.' He always desired to leave something to be guessed, that the reader might be complimented and his discernment be flattered, by thus becoming a partner in the work. . . . He is a master . . . in the art of planning by-paths, of opening up vistas, of making the most of resting-places" (Albert Sorel, *Montesquieu* [Port Washington, N.Y.: Kennikat Press, 1969], 94–95). As Paul Carrese put it, Montesquieu "blends a poet's perception of the passions, a modern scientist's mathematical views of motion, and a realist's eye for the dynamics of politics" (Paul O. Carrese, *The Cloaking of Power* [Chicago: University of Chicago Press, 2003], 239). On this issue, also see Ehrard, *L'Esprit des mots*, 11–24; Thomas L. Pangle, *Montesquieu's Philosophy of Liberalism* (Chicago: University of Chicago Press, 1975), 11–19. On Montesquieu's use of (what Simone Goyard-Fabre's called) *tableaux de pensée*, see Goyard-Fabre, *Montesquieu*, 271. Also worth consulting are two essays by David Young, "Montesquieu's Methodology: Holism, Individualism, and Morality" and Emile Durkheim, "Montesquieu's method," reprinted in *Charles-Louis de Secondat, Baron de Montesquieu*, David Carrithers, ed. (Farnham and London: Ashgate, 2009), 131–46, 147–58.

14. See Pangle, *Montesquieu's Philosophy of Liberalism*, 12.

15. See *SL*, XI: 5, 156; also see *OCM*, II: 1138. I also want to draw attention to Montesquieu's wonderful *Essai sur le goût dans les choses de la nature et de l'art*, originally published in vol. VII of the *Encyclopédie* and reprinted in *OCM*, II: 1240–1263.

16. *SL*, preface, xliii–xliv. On the importance of understanding the "chain" connecting all of Montesquieu's ideas see *OCM*, II: 1038, 1161, 1243.

17. See in particular Ehrard, *L'Esprit des mots*, 179–91.

18. "It is not a matter of indifference," Montesquieu acknowledged, "that the people be enlightened. I would consider myself the happiest of mortals if I could make it so that men were able to cure themselves of their prejudice" (*SL*, preface, xliii).

19. *OCM*, II: 229–31; 1037.

20. In *Pensées* (no. 21), Montesquieu suggested that moderation and frugality were the means by which he managed to build a considerable fortune; also see Kuhfuß, *Mäßigung und Politik*, 22.

21. For a similar view, see Bernand Manin who emphasizes the duality of moderation as the virtue of the good legislator and as a feature of a particular social state ("Montesquieu et la politique moderne," *Cahiers de philosophie politique* 2-3 [1985], 185).

22. Scholars continue to disagree as to Montesquieu's actual views on mixed government. See Vile, *Constitutionalism*, 89–94.

23. See Sonenscher, *Before the Deluge*, 135–39. The complex nature of modern monarchies in Europe and the distinction between absolute and arbitrary power are explored in Hans Blom, John C. Laursen, and Luisa Simonutti, eds., *Monarchisms in the Age of Enlightenment: Liberty, Patriotism, and the Common Good* (Toronto: University of Toronto Press, 2007). Chapter 7 (written by Gianni Paganini) examines

the affinities between Montesquieu's and Condilliac's critiques of despotism and their views on moderate monarchy. An indispensable book on this topic remains Élie Carcassonne, *Montesquieu et le problème de la constitution française au XVIIIe siècle* (Geneva: Slatkine, 1970; originally published in Paris in 1927), whose first part examines the conceptions of monarchy in France before Montesquieu.

24. Lee Ward, "Montesquieu on Federalism and Anglo-Gothic Constitutionalism," *Publius* 37-4 (2007): 569.

25. *CR,* 103.

26. *SL,* XXII: 12, 415. In Part IV, by emphasizing the centrality of commerce to modern life, he seems to imply that Rome could no longer serve as a viable political model for modern commercial European nations, because "commerce was not a part of the Roman spirit" (*SL,* XXI: 15, 383). See Larrère, "Montesquieu on Economics and Commerce," in *Montesquieu's Science of Politics,* 354.

27. See *CR,* 87.

28. Ibid., 93.

29. Ibid., 94.

30. *OCM,* I: 1450. In *SL,* he also accounted for the decay of Roman institutions as a consequence of the waning of the balance of powers: "The patricians alone had obtained all the sacred, political, civil, and military employments; an exorbitant power had been attached to the consulate; the people were subjected to outrages; finally, they had almost no influence left in the voting" (*SL,* XI: 14, 173).

31. I use the translation from Keohane, *Philosophy and the State in France,* 396. For the original text, see *Considérations sur les causes de la grandeur des Romains et de leur decadence,* Jean Ehrard, ed. (Paris: Garnier Flammarion, 1968), 82. The importance of this passage is also highlighted in Ehrard, *L'Esprit des mots,* 23–24.

32. On this issue, see Leo Spitzer's erudite and rich *Classical and Christian Ideas of World Harmony: Prolegomena to an Interpretation of the Word 'Stimmung'* (Baltimore: Johns Hopkins Press, 1963), 72–75 and passim. Leo Spitzer examined the semantic field *concentus-temperare* which he linked to the old metaphor of musical discordant accord and *harmonia mundi.*

33. Also: "La raison pourquoi la plupart des gouvernements de la Terre sont despotiques, c'est que cela se fait tout seul. Mais, pour des gouvernements modérés, il faut combiner, tempérer, les puissances; savoir ce qu'on donne à l'un, ce qui reste à l'autre; enfin, il faut un système, c'est-à-dire une convention de plusieurs et une discussion d'intérêts. Le gouvernement despotique est uniforme partout: il saute aux yeux" (*OCM,* I: 1429).

34. Keohane, *Philosophy and the State in France,* 399.

35. In this respect, see Vile, *Constitutionalism,* 89; Lee Ward, "Montesquieu on Federalism," 551–577.

36. See Vile, *Constitutionalism,* 93.

37. See Goyard-Fabre, *Montesquieu,* 262–69.

38. See *SL,* V: 2–3, 42–43; III: 3, 22. The opposition between a humane and cruel way of exercising power is a major theme distinguishing Montesquieu's minimalist "liberalism of fear," which sought above all to avoid cruelty and intolerance, from other forms of perfectionist liberalism. The phrase "liberalism of fear" was coined by Judith Shklar in an essay with the same title, originally published in 1989 and reprinted in Shklar, *Political Thought and Political Thinkers,* Stanley Hoffmann, ed. (Chicago: University of Chicago Press, 1998), 3–20.

39. See *SL,* VI: 9, 83.

40. See Goyard-Fabre, *Montesquieu*, 259; Keohane, *Philosophy and the State in France*, 412. As Kuhfuß remarked, "für Montesquieu, ist die Mäßigung der politischen Freiheit übergeordnet" (*Mäßigung und Politik*, 150).

41. *SL*, XI: 2, 154. For an analysis of liberty in connection with moderation in Montesquieu's writings, see Kuhfuß, *Mäßigung und Politik*, 70–91; Goyard-Fabre, *Montesquieu*, 147–57; Cohler, *Montesquieu's Comparative Politics*, 66–97.

42. It is prudent to steer clear from extreme interpretations such as that Montesquieu was nothing more than a closet Hobbesian or that he had no natural standard of justice at all. Nonetheless, Montesquieu's position on natural right remains a complex and vexing question for his interpreters. Although he harbored skepticism toward foundational principles (such as natural right), he did refer in various places to the "cosmic analogy" of order, put natural right in the context of a variety of kinds of law, and was at times quite close to the anti-perfectionism of Hobbes (with regard to avoiding the *summum malum*, in spite of his criticism in *SL*, I: 2). Montesquieu probably believed that all of these statements can be correct without contradiction, but his interpreters agree that this is not the case in any obvious or self-evident way. On Montesquieu's engagement with the natural law tradition, see C. P. Courtney, "Montesquieu and Natural Law," in *Montesquieu's Science of Politics*, 41–67. Thanks to Lee Ward for drawing my attention to these issues.

43. On this issue, also see Goyard-Fabre, *Montesquieu*, 244–87.

44. Here is what Montesquieu actually wrote: "De là, il faut conclure que la liberté concerne les monarchies moderées comme les républiques, et n'est pas plus eloignée du trône que d'un sénat" (*OCM*, I: 1152).

45. See Céline Spector, *Le vocabulaire de Montesquieu* (Paris: Ellipses, 2001), 45.

46. See *SL*, V: 16, 66.

47. I borrow this phrase from Judith N. Shklar, *Ordinary Vices* (Cambridge, MA: Harvard University Press, 1984), 7-44; 237–39.

48. "In aristocratic government, the nobles form a body which, by its prerogative and for its particular interest, represses the people; having laws is enough to insure that they will be executed" (*SL*, III: 4, 24).

49. See David W. Carrithers, "Montesquieu and the Liberal Philosophy of Jurisprudence," in *Montesquieu's Science of Politics*, 291–334. For an excellent discussion of penal moderation, also see Binoche, *Introduction à l'Esprit des Lois*, 271–78.

50. Montesquieu also paid special attention to the constitution of the judiciary power. After discussing the English model in book XI, he wrote: "Among a free people who have legislative power, the masterwork of legislation is to know where properly to place the power of judging. But it could not be placed worse than in the hands of the one who already had executive power" (*SL*, XI: 11, 169).

51. "Liberty can be founded only on the practice of this knowledge," Montesquieu insisted (*SL*, XII: 2, 188).

52. The same connection is restated in books XIX and XXIX of *SL*.

53. I follow here Carrithers, "Montesquieu and the Liberal Philosophy of Jurisprudence," 301–12.

54. See *SL*, VI: 9, 82–83.

55. "Everything is turned upside down if speech is made a capital crime instead of being regarded as the sign of a capital crime" (*SL*, XII: 12, 199).

56. See *SL*, XII: 12, 197.

57. See *SL*, VI: 9–21, 82–95; also XII: 5, 192.

58. *SL*, V: 16, 66. Montesquieu added: "Judgments should be fixed to such a de-

gree that they are never anything but a precise text of the law. If judgments were the individual opinion of a judge, one would live in this society without knowing precisely what engagements one has contracted" (*SL*, XI: 6, 158); also see VI: 2–3, 75–76. Montesquieu was skeptical of the institution of the jury and expressed doubt about the accuracy of many of the verdicts reached by jurors, preferring instead those handed down by judges. He thought, moreover, that it was appropriate for judging to be done differently in France and England.

59. *SL*, VI: 1, 72. The situation differs significantly from the one to be found in despotic states where law is only the will of the prince (*SL*, V: 16, 66).

60. See *SL*, VIII: 6, 117; VI: 5, 79. Note also the difference between the monarch's council and tribunals (*SL*, VI: 6, 80).

61. A better translation would be "the life of the lowest citizen is esteemed."

62. In despotic governments, notes Montesquieu, power is not mediated and "passes entirely into the hands of the one to whom it is entrusted" (*SL*, V: 16, 65).

63. See *SL*, III: 8, 27. Compare this to the situation in a despotic regime where "one has received the order and that is enough" (*SL*, III: 10, 29). On the general spirit of compromise in moderate governments, see *SL*, III: 9, 28.

64. On fiscal moderation, see Binoche, *Introduction*, 279–89.

65. "All is lost," Montesquieu wryly notes, "when the lucrative profession of tax-collectors, by its wealth, comes to be an honored profession" (*SL*, XIII: 20, 227). While this may be necessary in despotic regimes, it is not appropriate to republics, because it can stifle honor and the desire to distinguish oneself through work and achievement.

66. Larrère, "Montesquieu on Economics and Commerce," 344.

67. *SL*, XX: 4, 340–41.

68. I follow here the argument of Céline Spector, *Montesquieu et l'émergence de l'économie politique* (Paris: Honoré Champion, 2006), 382–85.

69. Montesquieu, *Pensées*, no. 831, also quoted in Keohane, *Philosophy and the State in France*, 398, fn. 17. Also see chapter IX of *CR*.

70. Kuhfuß, *Mäßigung und Politik*, 182.

71. The literature on this topic is extensive. Among the classical interpretations are: Charles Eisenman, "L'*Esprit des lois* et la séparation des pouvoirs," and "La pensée constitutionnelle de Montesquieu," *Cahiers de philosophie politique* 2–3 (1984–1985): 3–66; Vile, *Constitutionalism*, 83–106; Robert Shackleton, "Montesquieu, Bolingbroke, and the Separation of Powers," *French Studies* 3-1 (1949): 25–38. For recent interpretations, see Sharon Krause, "The Spirit of Separate Powers in Montesquieu," *Review of Politics*, 62-2 (2000): 231–66, and *Montesquieu's Constitutional Legacies*, Rebecca Kingston, ed. (Albany: State University of New York Press, 2008).

72. See Vile, *Constitutionalism*, 94–97.

73. Michel Troper, *La Séparation des pouvoirs et l'histoire constitutionnelle française* (Paris: Librairie générale de droit et de jurisprudence, 1980).

74. Ibid., 121.

75. Ibid., 125. The view according to which the theory of balance of powers (or theory of the balanced constitution) was introduced in order to correct the effects of the "pure" theory of separation of powers must therefore be amended. This latter interpretation was defended by Vile, who traced the development of the doctrine of the separation of powers back to the particular circumstances of the Civil War in mid-seventeenth-century England. Initially, the doctrine was expressed by using the

vocabulary of the prevailing legislative-executive division of functions. With the Glorious Revolution, Vile argued, the "pure doctrine" of the separation of powers was amended to allow for the development of a theory of balanced (or mixed) government. Although the main points of the previous doctrine were not forgotten, they were woven into a complex amalgam of mixed government, legislative supremacy, and the separation of powers, all of which were blended into a widely accepted theory of English government: the theory of the balanced constitution. See Vile, *Constitutionalism*, 59.

76. Eisenman, "L'*Esprit des lois* et la séparation des pouvoirs," 4.

77. On the principle of distribution of powers in Montesquieu's writings, see Charles Eisenman's two seminal essays, "L'*Esprit des Lois* et la séparation des pouvoirs" and "La pensée constitutionnelle de Montesquieu." As Vile argued, Montesquieu "did not maintain the pure doctrine of the separation of powers, for he combined with it the ideas of mixed government and checks and balances" (Vile, *Constitutionalism*, 99). Shackleton defended a different view, insisting on the differences between the separation of powers and the doctrine of mixed government (see Shackleton, "Montesquieu, Bolingbroke, and the Separation of Powers," 27).

78. *SL*, XI: 6, 162. Almost half a century later, Benjamin Constant would go a step further and refer to the constitutional monarch as a "neutral power."

79. *SL*, XI: 6, 164. Moreover, the army must be dependent on the executive power, not on the legislative body. Otherwise, notes Montesquieu, "the government will become military" (ibid., 165).

80. On this point, see Eisenman, "L'*Esprit des Lois* et la séparation des pouvoirs," 26–28. He distinguished between the parliamentary regime and the cabinet government, adding that the former adds to the latter the principle of the political responsibility of the cabinet before parliament.

81. See Vile, *Constitutionalism*, 101. On the relationship between balanced government and the English constitution, see Sonenscher, *Before the Deluge*, 41–67.

82. *SL*, XI: 6, 164; emphases added.

83. Also see Eisenman, "L'*Esprit des Lois* et la séparation des pouvoirs," 29.

84. The original text in *SL*, XI: 7 is: "Les trois pouvoirs n'y sont point (dans les monarchies que nous connaissons) distribués et fondus sur le modèle de la Constitution dont nous venons de parler." The Cambridge translation reads: "The three powers are not distributed and cast . . . ." It fails to render accurately the important point made by Montesquieu when he speaks about the *fusion* of powers. Eisenman summarizes Montesquieu's recommendation as follows: "obliger les deux organes à s'accorder chacun avec un organe qui échappe à sa prise, qu'ils ne puissent donc briser. . . . Ils ne pourraient rien l'un contre l'autre ni l'un sans l'autre" (Eisenman, "L'*Esprit des Lois* et la séparation des pouvoirs," 28).

85. Ward, "Montesquieu on Federalism," 552.

86. In *SL*, XXX: 21, Montesquieu also comments on the territorial justice of the churches.

87. Ward, "Montesquieu on Federalism" 557.

88. For more details, see Ray Forrest Harvey, *Jean-Jacques Burlamaqui: A Liberal Tradition in American Constitutionalism* (Chapel Hill: University of North Carolina Press, 1937).

89. Jean-Jacques Burlamaqui, *Principles of Natural and Politic Law*, trans. Thomas Nugent, Peter Korkman, ed. (Indianapolis, IN: Liberty Fund, 2006), Part 1,

Chapter 7 ("*Of the essential characters of sovereignty, its modifications, extent, and limits*"), § 4 ("Of Fundamental Laws"), 320–21. The importance of Burlamaqui's theory of balanced sovereignty and its influence on the Coppet group is highlighted in Paulet-Grandguillot, *Libéralisme et démocratie*, 306–32.

90. Burlamaqui, *Principes*, Part 2, chapter 1 ("Of the various forms of government"), 333. For a detailed analyis of Burlamaqui's political thought and his legacy in America and Europe, see Forrest Harvey, *Jean-Jacques Burlamaqui,* and Bernard Gagnebin, *Burlamaqui et le droit naturel* (Geneva: Éditions de la Frégate, 1944).

91. Charles Eisenman endorsed a similar view of Montesquieu; see Eisenman, "*L'Esprit des Lois* et la séparation des pouvoirs," 30.

92. Spector, *Le vocabulaire de Montesquieu*, 45. Also see Spector, "La mesure du droit dans *l'Esprit des lois*," in *Montesquieu en 2005*, 219–42.

93. Take, for example, justice. On the one hand, it can be obstructed and delayed by the existence of too many formalities and rules: "The formalities of justice are necessary to liberty. But their number could be so great that it would run counter to the end of the very laws establishing them: suits would be interminable; the ownership of goods would remain uncertain" (*SL*, XXIX: 1, 602). On the other hand, the absence of these formalities of justice leads to chaos and political instability, paving the way for arbitrary power. The desirable solution, Montesquieu suggests, always lies in a *juste milieu* between two extremes. Spector points to the comparison between politics and medicine in *Pensées*, no. 172. For more detail, see Spector, "La mesure du droit dans *l'Esprit des lois*," in *Montesquieu en 2005*, 229, fn. 50.

94. See Pangle, *Montesquieu's Philosophy of Liberalism*, 44. Also Manin, "Montesquieu et la politique moderne," 167.

95. See Condorcet's *Observations on the Twenty-ninth Book of the Spirit of the Laws*, published as an appendix to Antoine Louis Claude Destutt de Tracy, *A Commentary and Review of Montesquieu's Spirit of the Laws*, trans. Thomas Jefferson (New York: Burt Franklin, 1969), 278–79. On Condorcet and Montesquieu, also see Keith M. Baker, *Condorcet: From Natural Philosophy to Social Mathematics* (Chicago: University of Chiocago Press, 1975), 260–63, 353–54.

96. See Radasanu, "Montesquieu on Moderation, Monarchy, and Reform," 286–90.

97. See *SL*, XIV: 10, 239-40.

98. See Binoche, *Introduction*, 140–42; also, *SL*, XIX: 4, XIV: 5, XVI: 8.

99. See *SL*, XVI: 12, 273.

100. See *SL*, XIV: 5, 236. Also see the editor's introduction to *The Spirit of the Laws by Montesquieu: A Compendium of the First English Edition*, David W. Carrithers, ed. (Berkeley: University of California Press, 1977), 48–51.

101. Condorcet, *Observations*, 273. On Condorcet's critique of Montesquieu, see also Ehrard, *L'Esprit des mots*, 295–306; and Bradley Thompson, "The American Founding and the French Revolution," in *The Legacy of the French Revolution*, Ralph Hancock and Gary Lambert, eds. (Lanham, MD: Rowman & Littlefield, 1996), 130–34.

102. Destutt de Tracy, *A Commentary*, 257.

103. Condorcet, *Observations*, in ibid., 261, 262.

104. Ibid., 261.

105. Ibid., 262.

106. Ibid., 274. On Condorcet's political thought, see David Williams, *Condorcet and Modernity* (Cambridge: Cambridge University Press, 2007); Keith M. Baker,

Condorcet: From Natural Philosophy to Social Mathematics (Chicago: University of Chicago Press, 1974).

107. Condorcet, *Observations*, 261; emphases added.

108. *SL*, XXIX: 18, 617.

109. For a view emphasizing Montesquieu's debt to the tradition of natural law, see C. P. Courtney, "Montesquieu and Natural Law." Also see note 42 above.

110. "Perfection," Montesquieu maintained, "does not concern men or things universally" (*SL*, XXIV: 7, 464).

111. See *SL*, XXVI: 16, 512.

112. See, for example, *SL*, VII: 4, 100.

113. Note the similarity with Machiavelli's argument from *Discorsi*, book 1, chapter 34, where the Florentine pointed out that, of all the institutions of Rome, it was dictatorship created according to public law and not usurped by individual authority that contributed most to her greatness and dominion. On the intellectual dialogue between the two authors, see Etorre Levi-Malvano, *Montesquieu and Machiavelli*, trans. A. J. Pansini (Kopperl, TX: Greenvale Press, 1992); also Robert Shackleton, "Montesquieu and Machiavelli: A Reappraisal," in Shackleton, *Essays on Montesquieu and on the Enlightenment*, eds. David Gilson and Martin Smith (Oxford: Voltaire Foundation, 1988), 117–31. As Paul Rahe has argued (*Montesquieu and the Logic of Liberty*, 259, fn. 24), it is likely that Montesquieu reread Machiavelli's *Discorsi* in the original after his return to France from England.

114. On the subject of emergency powers in general, see John Ferejohn and Pasquale Pasquino, "The Law of Deception: A Typology of Emergency Powers," *International Journal of Constitutional Law* 2-2 (2004): 210–39; Nomi Claire Lazar, *States of Emergency in Liberal Democracies* (Cambridge: Cambridge University Press, 2009).

115. The people must constantly be shown tangible proofs that they are well administered and the laws ought to encourage the nobles to pay attention to the interests of the people, while holding magistrates accountable (*SL*, V: 8, 52–53).

116. On this view, the more an aristocratic regime approaches democracy, the better it will be; correspondingly, "to the degree it approaches monarchy, the less perfect it will become" (*SL*, II: 3, 17).

117. *SL*, II: 4, 18. The words "subordonate and dependent" were not printed in the original manuscript and were added subsequently. Montesquieu's decision to add them at a later point shows perhaps his prudence and fear of censorship. See Jean-Ehrard, " 'Subordonnés et dépendans': un *mystère* vraiment *dévoilé?*" in *Le Travail des Lumières*,129–38.

118. See *SL*, VIII: 6, II: 4, V: 16.

119. "Monarchical government is that in which one alone governs, but by fixed and established laws" (*SL*, II: 1, 10).

120. See *SL*, V: 14, 61.

121. *SL*, V: 11, 57.

122. The *parlements* were sovereign courts of law and also served as final courts of appeal for the judicial districts of the country. In 1789, there existed thirteen such *parlements* in the country and four other "sovereign councils" (similar to the *parlements*). The *parlements* were, in fact, more than mere courts of law, and attempted to play an active role in both the local administration through their power to issue *arrêts de règlements* on various local issues, and in the legislative process, through their right to "register" new laws and royal edicts and their related right of "remon-

strance," which entitled them to signal shortcomings and incompatibilities in these texts. For more information, see John J. Hurt, *Louis XIV and the Parlements: The Assertion of Royal Authority* (Manchester: Manchester University Press, 2002); and William Doyle, "The Parlements," in *The Political Culture of the Old Regime*, 157–67.

123. Echoing Machiavelli, Montesquieu argued that the people, "are admirable for choosing those to whom they should entrust some part of their authority. They have only to base their decisions on things of which they cannot be unaware and on facts that are evident to the senses" (*SL*, II: 2, 11). But although the people may be most of the time capable of selecting virtuous and worthy individuals as their representatives, they often do not know how to govern themselves.

124. "An equal division of lands," Montesquieu pointed out, "cannot be established in all democracies" (*SL*, V: 7, 49).

125. See Binoche, *Introduction*, 24; also *SL*, XI: 8.

126. Rousseau's letter to Mirabeau (July 26, 1767), quoted in Keohane, *Philosophy and the State in France*, 443.

127. See Goyard-Fabre, *Montesquieu*, 268.

128. For a similar view, see Manin, "Montesquieu," 197, 213–14.

129. *SL*, XIX: 9, 313; see also XIX: 11, 314.

130. This point was emphasized by Isaiah Berlin, "Montesquieu" in *Against the Current* (Harmondsworth: Penguin, 1982), 130–61; Manin, "Montesquieu et la politique moderne," 192–93, 213–14.

131. According to Pierre Manent, Montesquieu's position amounts to arguing that "good results are more assuredly attained in politics by fleeing evil than by pursuing good" (Pierre Manent, *The City of Man*, trans. Marc LePain [Princeton, NJ: Princeton University Press, 1998], 41–42). This perspective is also endorsed by Judith Shklar and Betrand Binoche.

132. See Albert Hirschman, *Passions and Interests* (Princeton, NJ: Princeton University Press, 1977). The overlap and difference between Montesquieu's views on commerce and liberty and those of Voltaire from *Lettres philosophiques* (1734) are discussed in Sonenscher, *Before the Deluge*, 101–102. Of special interest are chapters 8 ("Sur le Parlement"), 9 ("Sur le gouvernement"), and 10 ("Sur le commerce") from Voltaire's book.

133. England also makes a quick appearance toward the end of chapter VIII of *CR*. Montesquieu's *Notes sur l'Anglettere* can be found in *OCM*, I: 875–84; the letter to Domville in *OCM*, I: 1447–50. On Montesquieu's nuanced attitude toward England, see Sharon Krause, "The Spirit of Separate Powers in Montesquieu;" Rahe, *Montesquieu and the Logic of Liberty*, 86–102. More generally, see Édouard Tillet's comprehensive account in *La Constitution anglaise, un modèle politique et institutionnel dans la France des Lumières* (Aix-en-Provence: Presses Universitaires d'Aix-Marseille, 2001), especially 249–76 (Montesquieu's "errors" are examined on pp. 354–57). Abbé de Bonnaire accused Montesquieu of having made of the English people "*un produit de son imagination*" (354).

134. Sonenscher, *Before the Deluge*, 41.

135. *SL*, II: 4, 1819. On Montesquieu's reservations about liberty in England, see Ward, "Montesquieu on Federalism and Anglo-Gothic Constitutionalism;" and Sonenscher, *Before the Deluge*, 41–43, 107–108. The complexity of Montesquieu's account of England in *SL*, XI: 6 and XIX: 27 is discussed in detail in Tillet, *La Constitution anglaise*, 249–69; Barrera, *Les lois du monde*, 134–50, 268–71, 356–79. For

a different view, see Pangle, *Montesquieu's Philosophy of Liberalism*, 46, 114. According to Pangle, England represented for Montesquieu "the rational solution of the problem of human nature" (ibid., 114).

136. See for example, Rahe, *Montesquieu and the Logic of Liberty*, 99–102; Manin, "Montesquieu et la politique moderne," 183.

137. It was Montesquieu's praise of commerce that made him, in the eyes of many commentators, a defender of market capitalism before Adam Smith. Voltaire, too, was favorably disposed toward the spirit of capitalism. For more details, see Spector, *Montesquieu et l'émergence de l'économie politique*, 163–228. A good overview can be found in Larrère, "Montesquieu on Economics and Commerce," in *Montesquieu's Science of Politics*, 335–74. For the general background, see *Commerce, Culture, and Liberty: Readings on Capitalism before Adam Smith*, Henry C. Clark, ed. (Indianapolis, IN: Liberty Fund, 2003).

138. See *OCM*, I: 880.

139. Krause, "The Spirit of Separate Powers in Montesquieu," 242, 253. It would be interesting to compare in this regard Montesquieu's reflections on liberty and individualism with Tocqueville's ideas on liberty in America.

140. *PL,* 53 (letter 11).

141. Many of the entries in the *Encyclopédie*, such as those signed by Diderot and Jaucourt, acknowledged their debt to Montesquieu whose conception of political liberty they endorsed. In turn, Blackstone and Burke paid due tribute to Montesquieu's ideas, as did Voltaire in spite of his usual jibes. Furthermore, it is not a mere coincidence that Édouard Laboulaye, the "spiritual" father of the Statue of Liberty, was a fervent disciple of Montesquieu whose writings he edited in the 1870s (Montesquieu, *Œuvres Complètes*, 7 vols., Édouard Laboulaye, ed. [Paris: Garnier, 1875–1879?])

142. Unlike them, Pierre Manent once argued, Montesquieu "is liberal not only in his principles but also in his mood or tone" (Manent, *An Intellectual History of Liberalism*, trans. Rebecca Balinski [Princeton, NJ: Princeton University Press, 1994], 53). Also see Barrera, *Les lois du monde*, 60–76, 171–205, 471–80.

143. Also see Manin, "Montesquieu et la politique moderne," 224–26.

144. The preface to *SL* ends with a rather unusual confession. After outlining the plan of his book, Montesquieu compares himself to an enigmatic painter—Correggio—whose stylistic innovations paved the way for significant developments in Baroque art. In the final sentence of the preface, Montesquieu quotes a remark—*Ed io anche son pittore!*—attributed to the Italian painter upon seeing Raphael's portrait of St. Cecilia. Montesquieu concludes: "'And I too am a painter' have I said with Correggio!" (*SL*, preface, xlv). The method, means, and objectives of Montesquieu's new science of politics are analyzed in Binoche, *Introduction*, 29–196.

145. "To carry back to distant centuries the ideas of the century in which one lives," Montesquieu warned, "is of all sources of error the most fertile" (*SL*, XXX: 14, 636).

146. Kelly, *The Propriety of Liberty*, 96.

Chapter Three: The Radical Moderates of 1789

1. This detail is reported in Robert Griffiths, *Le Centre perdu: Malouet et les 'monarchiens' dans la Révolution française* (Grenoble: Presses universitaires de

Grenoble, 1988), 104; first mentioned in *Courrier français*, 258 (September 15, 1791): 230.

2. See Halévi's entry on the Feuillants in *CDFR*, 343–50.

3. See Griffiths, "Le 'monarchienisme' et la 'monarchie limitée. Malouet et les monarchiens," in *Terminer la Révolution*, François Furet and Mona Ozouf, eds. (Grenoble: Presses Universitaires de Grenoble, 1990), 44. One must use the term *monarchiens* with due caution as there were important differences among them on the role of the Constituent Assembly and the optimal relationship between the legislative and executive power. See Griffiths, *Le Centre perdu*, 110, 135–38, 140, 163, 175.

4. For more information about the life and writings of the monarchiens, in addition to Griffiths' path-breaking book, the reader can consult the excellent biographical notes (by Furet and Halévi) in *ORF*, an indispensable source for the study of the monarchiens. Also important are the memoires of Malouet (*Mémoires*, 2 vols. [Paris: Didier, 1868]), as well as Mounier's *Exposé de ma conduite* (reprinted in *ORF*, 908–97). Jean Egret's *La Révolution des notables: Mounier et les monarchiens* (Paris, 1950) and L. Lanzac de Laborie's *Un royalist libéral en 1789: Jean-Joseph Mounier, sa vie politique et ses écrits* (Paris: Plon, 1887) focus on the politics and ideas of Mounier. His political doctrine is also discussed in Roberto Moro, "La dottrina politica di J. J. Mounier e l'ideologia monarchica alla vigilia della Rivoluzione," *Rivista internazionale di filosofia del diritto* 4-46 (1969): 440–73. Moro's article, which focuses on Mounier's works prior to the summer of 1789, does an excellent job of highlighting the virtues and shortcomings of Mounier's *modérantisme*, especially as illustrated in his *Nouvelles Observations*. Mounier's works are also discussed in Israel, *Democratic Enlightenment*, 773–78, 927–28. For a biography of Clermont-Tonnerre, see Charles du Bus, *Stanislas de Clermont-Tonnerre et l'échec de la révolution monarchique* (1757–1792) (Paris: Félix Alcan, 1931); the book also contains a chapter on *Le club des Impartiaux* founded in 1790. *Terminer la Révolution* contains important essays by F. Furet, W. Doyle, R. Griffiths, and P. Pasquino examining the monarchiens' political doctrine. Also see: Ran Halévi, "Monarchiens," in *CDFR*, 370–79; Griffiths, "The Legacy of the Monarchiens in Contemporary France," *The European Legacy* 1-1 (1996): 84–89; François Furet and Ran Halévi, *La monarchie républicaine* (Paris: Fayard, 1995). The monarchiens and their dialogue with Mallet du Pan are also discussed in Bradley Thompson's essay "The American Founding and the French Revolution," in *The Legacy of the French Revolution*, 109–50. On Mallet du Pan, see Frances Acomb, *Mallet du Pan (1794–1800): A Career in Political Journalism* (Durham, NC: Duke University Press, 1973). His political thought is discussed in particular by N. Matteucci, *Jacques Mallet Du-Pan. Ginevra, l'Illuminismo, et la Rivoluzione francese* (Lungro di Cosenza: Marco Editore, 2004), and Julien Boudon, "La voie royale selon Mallet du Pan," *Revue française des idées politiques* 1 (2008): 3–41. They spell out in detail the complexity of Mallet du Pan's political agenda, from his initial critique of the abuses of the Old Regime and his commitment to a "moderate liberalism" to his later loss of faith in the power of moderate ideas.

5. "C'était un homme passionnement raisonnable," Mme de Staël said of Mounier (quoted in Laborie, *Un royaliste liberal*, 1). For a self-portrait of Mounier, see *CSG*, 4.

6. R. R. Palmer, *The Age of Democratic Revolution*, (Princeton, NJ: Princeton University Press, 1969), I: 489ff.

7. Most of these speeches were published in *Collection des opinions de M. Malouet, député à l'Assemblée Nationale*, 2 vols. (1791).

8. The program of *the Club des Impartiaux* was published in early January 1790 and reprinted in Malouet, *Mémoires*, I (Paris: Didier, 1868): 375–79. In volume 1 of his memoirs, Malouet devoted an entire chapter to discussing the activities of this club (374–412), and reprinted an important *Lettre aux amis de la paix* (January 2, 1790), in which the Impartiaux outlined their political philosophy (397–405). This text is also fundamental for understanding the political moderation of the monarchiens.

9. Malouet, *Mémoires, I*: 402–403.

10. I use the term "revolutionary" in a general sense here, but I am well aware of its complex nature. The latter was highlighted by Timothy Tackett in *Becoming a Revolutionary: The Deputies of the French National Assembly and the Emergence of a Revolutionary Culture (1789–1790)* (University Park, PA: Pennsylvania State University Press, 1996). The book also contains references to the monarchiens, especially Mounier and Malouet.

11. The groups of the Feuillants included Antoine Barnave, Alexandre de Lameth, and Adrien Duport. The political agenda of A. de Lameth is discussed in Doina P. Harshanyi, "The Memoires of Lameth and the Reconciliation of the Nobility and the Revolution," in *The French Nobility in the Eighteenth-Century: Reassessments and New Approaches,* Jay M. Smith, ed. (University Park, PA: Pennsylvania State University Press, 2009), 279–302. Lameth also published an important history of the Constituent Assembly in 1828 (2 vols).

12. The phrase is borrowed from Mme de Staël, *CPE*, 213. On the nobles' hatred of the monarchies, see Griffith, *Le Centre perdu*, 140–41, and the following statement of Mounier in *Exposé de ma conduite*: "Au commencement de cette année, mon zèle était désapprouvé par ceux qui étaient intéressés, en France, au maintien des anciens abus. On calomniat mes intentions; on m'attaquait dans des libelles; on me représentait comme un incendiaire, un ardent novateur. Aujourd'hui, avec les mêmes opinions qui me conciliaient précédemment la faveur du people, je suis détesté par le parti démocratique. Eh bien, je suis précisément placé dans la position où je voulais pour être assuré de la bonté de mes opinions; car *la vérité est toujours entre les deux extrêmes*" (*ORF*, 986; all emphases added).

13. Alexis de Tocqueville, *The Old Regime and the Revolution*, vol. 2, trans. Alan S. Kahan (Chicago: University of Chicago Press, 2011), 89. Tocqueville referred to Mounier and Rabaut Saint-Étienne. See also Pasquino, "La théorie de la 'balance du legislatif' du premier Comité de Constitution," in *Terminer la Révolution*, 81.

14. See Griffiths, *Le Centre perdu*, 34, 41, 90.

15. On Necker, see chapter 4 below.

16. On the dialogue between Mounier, Montesquieu, and Sieyès, see Moro, "La dottrina politica di J. J. Mounier," 464–68. The pre-revolutionary debates on sovereignty are examined in L. Ameline, *L'Idée de souveraineté d'après les écrivains français du XVIIIe siècle* (Paris, 1904). On sovereignty in the revolutionary context, see Lucien Jaume, *Le discours jacobin et la démocratie* (Paris: Fayard, 1989), 263–312; P. Duclos, *La notion de constitution dans l'œuvre de l'Assemblée constituante* (Paris, 1931). In chapter 1 of *Échec au libéralisme: Les Jacobins et l'État* (Paris: Kimé, 1990), Jaume comments on the contradictions of the moderate approach to sovereignty espoused by the monarchiens (21–25). The relationship between sovereignty

and the separation/balance of powers (with references to Rousseau and Montesquieu) is analyzed in Vile, *Constitutionalism*, 193–205.

17. This is Diderot's phrase taken from his *Observations sur l'Instruction de A.M.I. aux Députés* (1774), as quoted in Gabriel Bonno, *La Constitution britannique devant l'opinion française de Montesquieu à Bonaparte* (Paris: Honoré Champion, 1932), 107.

18. Mounier, *RC*, II: 149.

19. For an English translation, see the selections from Mounier's *CSG* in *French Liberalism: 1789–1848*, W. Simon, ed. (New Work: Wiley, 1972), 11–18.

20. Ibid., 14.

21. Ibid., 12.

22. Mounier, "Sur la sanction royale (September 5, 1789)," in *ORF*, 892.

23. Ibid., 891.

24. Mounier, *NO*, 212. A part of the final chapter of Mounier's book was translated into English in *The French Revolution*, Paul H. Beik, ed. (New York: Harper & Row, 1970), 38–44.

25. Mounier, *NO*, 215.

26. Ibid., 217.

27. Interestingly, Mounier then went on to defend Montesquieu against the charge of having fomented anarchy. His work, Mounier insisted, was not a threat to social order since Montesquieu did not propose a "limitless democracy," but was a friend of moderation (Mounier, *DIAP*, 36). Mounier's book on the influence of the *philosophes*, which was conceived as a rejoinder to Abbé Barruel's *Mémoires pour servir à l'histoire du Jacobinisme*, was translated into English as *On the Influence Attributed to Philosophers, Freemasons, and to the Illuminati on the Revolution of France* (London: W. and C. Spilsbury, Snowhill, 1801). A reprint of the English translation was published by Scholars' Facsimiles & Reprints, Inc., Delmar, NY, 1974, with an introduction by Theodore A. Di Padova. On the indictment of the *philosophes* and the proliferation of conspiracy theories during the revolution, see Darrin M. McMahon, *Enemies of the Enlightenment: The French Counter-Enlightenment and the Making of Modernity* (Oxford: Oxford University Press, 2001), chapter 2.

28. The phrase is Michelet's and is taken from his *Historical View of the French Revolution*, trans. G. Cocks (London: George Bell, 1902), 51.

29. Mounier, "Sur la sanction royale," in *ORF*, 904. Also see J. Kent Wright, "National Sovereignty and the General Will: The Political Program of the Declaration of Rights," in *The French Idea of Freedom: The Old Regime and the Declaration of Rights of 1789*, Dale Van Kley, ed. (Stanford, CA: Stanford University Press, 1994), 222.

30. Rabaut as quoted in Keith M. Baker, *Inventing the French Constitution* (Cambridge: Cambridge University Press, 1990), 287.

31. Sieyès, *Political Writings*, Michael Sonnescher, ed. (Indianapolis, IN: Hackett, 2003), 138. The complex relationship between Sieyès and Rousseau as well as the connection between the social contract and the concept of the "constituent power" are discussed in Bronislaw Baczko, "Le contrat social des Français: Sieyès et Rousseau," in *The French Revolution and the Creation of Modern Political Culture*, vol. 1: *The Political Culture of the Old Regime*, Keith M. Baker, ed. (Oxford: Pergamon, 1987), 493–514. On Sieyès' theory of representation, also see Jaume, *Échec au libéralisme*, chapter 2. The ambiguities of Sieyès' doctrine are discussed in Jaume, *Le discours jacobin*, 157–69 and Israel, *Democratic Enlightenment*, 813–14, 911–16.

32. Cf. Article III of the *Declaration of the Rights of Man* (drafted by Mounier). Note that Mounier does not refer here to *la souveraineté du peuple*; on the important differences between the sovereignty of the nation and the sovereignty of the people, see Jaume, *Échec au libéralisme*, 21–22.

33. Mounier in Simon, ed., *French Liberalism*, 16. Also see Mounier, *RC*, II: 132; and Mounier's "Rapport du Comité chargé du travail sur la constitution" (July 9, 1789) in *ORF*, 866. "Comment garantir à son tour le pouvoir exécutif des enterprises des représentants?" Mounier asked. "Sans doute, si les représentants parvenaient dans la suite à s'emparer des prérogatives du trône, le peuple, malgré la liberté des élections, gémirait sous le poids de la tyrannie. Quelle que soit la sagesse de ceux qui gouvernent, quand ils peuvent tout impunément, quand ils ne sont pas asservis à des règles précises, leurs passions les égarent, et l'amour même du bien publique devient la source des erreurs les plus funeste" (*ORF*, 891).

34. Mounier, *NO*, 218–19.

35. Mounier, "Sur la sanction royale," in *ORF*, 894, 904.

36. Ibid., 895.

37. Thomas Paine, *The Rights of Man*, Henry Collins, ed. (Harmondsworth: Penguin, 1969), 93.

38. Paine's critique of the balance of powers and complex government can be found in the conclusion to Part 1 of *The Rights of Man*. Paine argued that the English government arose out of conquest and not out of society, and that the country lacked a constitution in the proper sense of the term (ibid., 94). It is interesting to note that a critique of complex government and the balance of powers can also be found in the writings of the Anti-federalists (see, for example, the first essay by Centinel, written as a refutation of John Adams' theory of balanced government).

39. Thomas Paine, *Common Sense*, Isaac Kramnick, ed. (Harmondsworth: Penguin Books, 1982), 70.

40. Mounier, *RC*, II: 150.

41. Ibid., 156–57. As Jaume remarked (*Échec au libéralisme*, 80), this prudent distinction was not an invention of the monarchiens; it can be traced back to Locke and Bellarmin.

42. Mounier, "Sur la sanction royale," in *ORF*, 896.

43. *Mounier, RC*, II: 249–50. Jaume notes the fragility of Mounier's eclectic approach in *Échec au libéralisme*, 24.

44. "Il est donc indispensable de placer entre ces deux pouvoirs un troisième pouvoir, un corps aristocratique, c'est-à-dire, indépendant, quant à ses fonctions, du roi et du peuple" (Mounier, *RC*, II: 253–54). For Mounier, who believed that no free government had ever existed without a certain aristocracy, the latter term connoted "le pouvoir des grands, des premiers, des meilleurs" (ibid., 254, n. 1).

45. Ibid., 255.

46. See Lally-Tollendal, "Premier discours sur l'organisation du pouvoir législatif et la sanction royale," in *ORF*, 366. For an extensive discussion on the need for a third (moderating) power, see chapter 6 below.

47. Michael Walzer, ed., *Regicide and Revolution: Speeches at the Trial of Louis XVI* (Cambridge: Cambridge University Press, 1974), 169.

48. Ibid., 183. On the skepticism toward moderates during the French Revolution, also see Griffiths, *Le Centre perdu*, 93, 123, 136, 163.

49. *Annales Patriotiques* 627 (June 21, 1791): 1575, as quoted by Halévi, "La modération à l'épreuve de l'absolutisme," 75. The author of a previous article from

276 • Notes to Chapter Three

January 1791 had denounced "les écrivains hypocrites ou prétendus modérateurs" as enemies of the constitution.

50. Robespierre as quoted in Benrekassa, "Modération, Modéré, Modérantisme," 144.

51. Brissot's remark is quoted in Norman Hampson, *Will and Circumstance: Montesquieu, Rousseau, and the French Revolution* (London: Duckworth, 1983), 274.

52. "Les Modérés, les Impartiaux ... se dissent les amis du peuple, se font ses apôtres; je la crains plus sous ce masque que le poignard à la main. Les ecrivains patriotes doivent démasquer cette impartialité, cette modération qui nous perdraient" (quoted in Griffiths, *Le Centre perdu*, 93).

53. "L'esprit de modération tend à arrêter les progrès d'une révolution, dont le dernier résultat tend à être le bonheur des peuples; c'est donc être ennemi de ses semblables que de conserver des sentiments modérés au milieu des orages révolutionnaires; l'homme dont le coeur ne brûle pas sans cesse pour la liberté est coupable envers la patrie. *La modération est un crime contre l'humanité* (quoted in Benrekassa, "Modération, Modéré, Modérantisme," 144; emphases added).

54. Quoted in Griffiths, *Le Centre perdu*, 123.

55. Sieyès, *Political Writings*, 41. Sieyès' political and economic ideas are also discussed in Sonenscher, *Before the Deluge* (Princeton, NJ: Princeton University Press, 2007), 67–94; and William H. Sewell, *A Rhetoric of Bourgeois Revolution: The Abbé Sieyès and 'What Is the Third Estate?'* (Durham, NC: Duke University Press, 1994).

56. Sieyès, *Political Writings*, 41; on the issue of moderation, also see 158–61.

57. Ibid., 116.

58. Ibid., 159; also 160–61.

59. See Griffiths, *Le Centre perdu*, 136.

60. Ibid., 136.

61. Ibid., 142.

62. Ibid., 163.

63. See ibid., 135–36.

64. "Peut-être faudrait-il distinguer entre le modérantisme et la modération: le premier pousse à la faiblesse; mais l'autre est le principe conservateur de la force et de l'énergie; elle se concilie avec la sévérité des measures et la célérité des résultats" (*Annales patriotiques* 413 [February 18, 1794], as quoted in Benrekassa, "Modération, Modéré, Modérantisme," 145).

65. Montlosier, *Des effets de la violence et de la modération dans les affaires de France* (London, 1796), 7.

66. Ibid., 15.

67. Tackett notes that the liberal group of nobles amounted to approximately seventy deputies, a fourth of the Second Estate; for more details, see *Becoming a Revolutionary*, 132–34. The opinions of the Third Estate on the eve of the meeting of the Estates-General in May 1789 are analyzed toward the end of chapter 3 of his book (pp. 100–13).

68. See Egret, *La révolution des notables*, 52–53; Tackett, *Becoming a Revolutionary*, 125–29. Tackett contrast the caucuses of Dauphiné and Brittany, the two most influential ones, noting that the latter (compared by Adrien Duquesnoy to the English Levellers) was much more radical than the former.

69. Such obsolete rules determined the costumes to be worn by the members of the Third Estate and obliged them to kneel when the king entered the hall, unlike the members of the privileged orders.

70. The definitive works on this topic are: Edna H. Lemay, ed., *Dictionnaire des constituants,* 2 vols. (Paris: Universitas, 1991); and Edna H. Lemay, Alison Patrick, Joël Félix, *Revolutionaries at Work: The Constituent Assembly, 1789–1791* (Oxford: Voltaire Foundation, 1991). For recent statements offering two different analyses, see Patrice Gueniffey, *La Politique de la Terreur: Essai sur la violence révolution-naire, 1789–1794* (Paris: Gallimard, 2003), ch. 4; and Tackett, *Becoming a Revolu-tionary,* especially 77–116, 304–306. Tackett noted that at least a fifth of the Third Estate deputies had been mayors or town administrators who must have had at least some managerial and political experience. Gueniffey ascribed the (alleged) "modera-tion of means" displayed by the assembly to the social origin of the deputies, many of whom were of aristocratic extraction. The assembly, he argued, functioned *de facto* as a bicameral legislative body (*sui generis,* of course). Nonetheless, Gueniffey did not imply that a moderate majority existed within the Constituent Assembly; he insisted in fact that the latter was often neither moderate in its principles nor in its actions (*La Politique de la Terreur,* 104). This view updates the classical thesis de-fended by Burke, Tocqueville, and Taine, who emphasized the immoderation of means and principles in an assembly dominated, in their view, by country lawyers who allegedly lacked *any* political experience.

71. See Gueniffey, *La Politique de la Terreur,* 129–32. Tackett also points out that the meetings of the clergy were the most contentious ones.

72. Mme de Staël described the two parties among the deputies of the Third Es-tate in *CPE,* 141. On this issue, see also Gunn, *When the French Tried To Be British,* 11–61.

73. How much influence the galleries had on parliamentary debates and espe-cially on the drafting of the Constitution of 1791 remains an open question. As Gueniffey points out, it is possible that historians of the French Revolution might have overestimated it while underestimating the importance of the committees (Gueniffey, *La Politique de la Terreur,* 118–20).

74. There were also several circumstantial reasons for the increasing radicaliza-tion of the Third Estate in the summer of 1789. As Tackett pointed out, the complex dynamic and interaction among many groups, passions, and interests soon took on a life of its own. For a full account of the radicalization of the Constituent Assembly that pays due attention to the emergence of factions and a culture of intransigence, see Tackett, *Becoming a Revolutionary,* 121–48.

75. Sieyès as quoted in Robert D. Harris, *Necker and the Revolution of 1789* (Lanham, MD: University Press of America, 1986), 486. Also see Tackett, *Becoming a Revolutionary,* 146–48.

76. Keith M. Baker, ed., *The Old Regime and the Revolution* (Chicago: University of Chicago Press, 1987), 201.

77. Lord Acton, *Lectures on the French Revolution* (New York: Noonday Press, 1959), 72.

78. See Malouet, *Mémoires,* I: 284, 318.

79. Ibid., 319.

80. "Notre pretention de constituer le Gouvernement sans son intermediaire," Malouet recognized, "était donc une usurpation manifeste, et c'était de plus une ex-

travagance. En nous astreignant à nos mandats, en ne sortant pas de cette ligne, le choix et la confiance de nos commettants étaient un titre suffisant pour remplir notre mission" (Malouet, *Mémoires*, I: 338). See also Ran Halévi, "La Révolution consti-tuante: les ambiguïtés politiques," in *The French Revolution and the Creation of Modern Political Culture*, vol. 2: *The Political Culture of the French Revolution*, Colin Lucas, ed. (Oxford: Pergamon Press, 1988), 69–85.

81. Carcassonne, *Montesquieu*, 469–580; Marina Valensise, "The French Consti-tution in Pre-revolutionary Debate, *Journal of Modern History* 60 Supplement: "Re-thinking French Politics in 1788" (September 1988): S22–S57; also Valensise, "La Constitution française," in *The Political Culture of the Old Regime*, 441–68; Denis Richet, "L'Esprit de la constitution, 1789–1791," in *The Political Culture of the French Revolution*, 63–68; and Hubert Carrier, *Le Labyrinthe de l'État. Essai sur le débat politique en France au temps de la Fronde* (1648–1653) (Paris: Honoré Cham-pion, 2004), 161–242, 300–327, 343–58.

82. See Pierre Duclos, *La notion de constitution dans l'œuvre de l'Assemblée con-stituante* (Paris, 1923); Baker, "Constitution," in *CDFR*, 479–93. On the formation of the Constituent Assembly, see Lynn Hunt, "The 'National' Assembly," in *The Po-litical Culture of the Old Regime*, 403–15.

83. See Valensise, "La Constitution française," 451–53; and Carcassonne, *Mon-tesquieu*, 478–524; Baker, *Inventing the French Revolution*, 59–85. A few years later, Moreau's traditionalist thesis was restated by Joseph de Maistre, who insisted that the kingdom of France did have an ancient constitution. The monarch, Maistre ar-gued, was bound by the fundamental laws of the kingdom, and these formed its "true" constitution.

84. Valensise, "The French Constitution in Pre-revolutionary Debate," 552. Va-lensise argues that the first prominent thinker to deny the existence of an ancient constitution of France was Necker. In fact, Mounier had made this point before Necker, but it could also be found in Mably's *Observations sur l'histoire de France* (written after 1771). On Mably's political thought, see J. Kent Wright, *A Classical Republican in the Eighteenth Century: The Political Thought of Mably* (Ithaca, NY: Cornell University Press, 1997). For a general account, see Baker, *Inventing the French Revolution*, 252–306.

85. Mounier's "Rapport sur la constitution," can be found in *ORF*, vol. 1, 863–72. On the ideas of *RC*, see Lanzac de Laborie, *Un royaliste liberal en 1789*, 259–80. Laborie is right to point out the importance of Mounier's book. Three years later, Mounier published *Adolphe, ou Principes élémentaires de doctrine et résultats de la plus cruelle des expériences* (London, 1795). Several publications came out during this period that were wrongly attributed to Mounier (such as *Lettre de M. Mounier, député aux États Généraux de 1790, aux Français*, and *Refléxions politiques sur les circonstances actuelles*) and were meant to discredit his name and reputation.

86. Mounier, "Rapport sur la constitution," in *ORF*, 864. This ambiguity in Mounier's position was also highlighted by Jaume, *Échec au libéralisme*, 23–24.

87. Mounier, "Rapport sur la constitution," in *ORF*, 865.

88. Ibid., 867.

89. Ibid., 863. For a slightly different definition, see Mounier, *NO*, 182. He also emphasized the necessity of adopting new rules for future meetings of the Estates-General (Mounier, *RC*, I: 65).

90. *Ibid.*, 63.

91. "En France, avant la révolution, rien n'était réglé d'une manière précise, ni les droits de la couronne, ni ceux du peuple, ni ceux des tribunaux; l'aristocratie avait trop d'influence dans le gouvernement; la liberté personnelle était fréquemment exposée aux atteintes de diverses autorités arbitraries; la liberté politique était presque nulle; la puissance légitime du roi, celle qui était nécessaire au bonheur public, n'était pas assez solidement établie; les remonstrances des parlements, quelle que pût être leur utilité, étant pleines de maxims dangereuses, et souvent écrites sur le ton de la menace, accoutumaient, par degrés, les sujets à perdre tout respect pour le trône, qu'ils voyaient sans cesse accusé d'être l'auteur de leurs maux, et qu'ils ne voyaient jamais obtenir un triomphe durable" (ibid., 25); also see Mounier, *NO*, 184–85.

92. Ibid., 187.

93. Ibid., 185.

94. Ibid., 195.

95. Ibid., 186.

96. Ibid., 193. A similarly skeptical attitude toward the *parlements* can be found in Lally-Tollendal's and Malouet's writings, in which they claimed that these bodies weakened the authority of the king's government, impeding the smooth functioning of the royal administration. See Lally-Tollendal, *Plaidoyer pour Louis XVI* (London, 1793), 43–49; Malouet's words are quoted in Griffiths, *Le Centre perdu*, 236–37.

97. Mounier, "Rapport sur la constitution," in *ORF*, 867.

98. On the drafting of the *Declaration*, three volumes stand out: *La Déclaration des droits de l'homme et du citoyen*, Stéphane Rials, ed. (Paris: Hachette, 1988); *Les Déclarations des droits de l'homme*, Lucien Jaume, ed. (Paris: Flammarion, 1989); and Marcel Gauchet, *La Révolution des droits de l'homme* (Paris, Gallimard, 1989). Also useful is Keith Baker's "The Idea of a Declaration of Rights," in *The French Idea of Freedom*, Van Kley, ed., 154–96. The political philosophy of the Declaration is discussed in Wright, "National Sovereignty and the General Will," *ibid.*, 199–233; Philippe Raynaud, "La Déclaration des droits de l'homme," in *The Political Culture of the French Revolution*, 139–49; and Gauchet, *La Révolution des droits de l'homme* (especially Part I), along with Gauchet's entry "Rights of Man," in *CDFR*, 818–28.

99. Mounier, "Rapport sur la constitution," in *ORF*, 869.

100. Ibid., 869–70.

101. *AP*, VIII: 221.

102. Lally-Tollendal, "Premier discours sur la Déclaration des droits de l'homme" (July 11, 1789), in *ORF*, 353–54. Also see Gauchet, *La Révolution des droits de l'homme*, 36–59; Thompson, "The American Founding and the French Revolution," 122–28.

103. The full text of Sieyès' declaration can be found in *ORF*, 1004–18. On the complex relationship between Sieyès and Rousseau, see Gauchet, *La Révolution des droits de l'homme*, 77–84; Baczko, "Le contrat social des Français."

104. See Egret, *La Révolution des notables*, 114.

105. See *Journal d'Adrien Duquesnoy*, Robert de Crèvecœur, ed. (Paris: Alphonse Picard et Fils, 1894), I: 302.

106. See *AP*, VIII: 286–87. Art. I of the "Declaration of the Principles of the French Government" stipulated: "Il n'y a point d'autorité supérieure à la loi. Le Roi ne règne que par elle" (ibid., 286).

107. See Art XV of Sieyès' declaration in Rials, ed., *La Déclaration des droits de l'homme,* 604.

108. See ibid., 614–21. Sieyès offered a revised version of his draft in early August, the new one comprising forty-two articles.

109. *Journal d'Adrien Duquesnoy,* I: 240.

110. "Il n'est aucun des droits naturels qui ne se trouve modifié par le droit positif," he argued. "Pourquoi présenter aux hommes, dans toute leur plénitude, des droits dont ils ne doivent user qu'avec de justes limites?" (Malouet, *Mémoires,* I: 338–39). Malouet intervened in the debates after Barnave, who thought that the new constitution must be preceded by the declaration of rights. "Il faut qu'elle soit simple, à portée de tous les esprits, et qu'elle devienne le *catéchisme national,*" Barnave argued (*AP,* VIII: 322). For Malouet's position, see ibid., 322–23.

111. Malouet's discourse can be found in Rials, ed., *La Déclaration des droits de l'homme,* 158, and *AP,* VIII: 322ff. Malouet's views were echoed by the comte de La Blanche (as quoted by Egret, *La Révolution des notables,* 113).

112. Clermont-Tonnerre, *ARCF,* 29.

113. Ibid., 36–37.

114. Ibid., 35–36.

115. Ibid., 36.

116. Ibid., 51.

117. Ibid., 68.

118. Ibid., 70.

119. Mounier, *RC,* II: 23, n. 1.

120. See Acton, *Lectures on the French Revolution,* 111.

121. *ORF,* 1510.

122. See Pasquale Pasquino, "La théorie de la 'balance du législatif'," in *Terminer la Révolution,* 67–89; Thompson, "The American Founding and the French Revolution," 122–28, 139–43. The complexity of the monarchiens' position on royal veto and balance of powers is highlighted in Guillaume Glénard, *L'Exécutif et la Constitution de 1791* (Paris: PUF, 2010), 111–41.

123. Lally-Tollendal, "Premier discours sur l'organisation du pouvoir législatif et la sanction royale" (August 31, 1789), in *ORF,* 370.

124. Mounier, "Discours sur la sanction royale," in *ORF,* 882–83.

125. Mounier, *NO,* 273–75.

126. Mounier, *CSG,* 43–44.

127. As late as 1792, Mallet du Pan remained convinced that the nobility must have an institutionalized political role and occupy a second aristocratic chamber.

128. Mounier, *CSG,* 50–51.

129. Lally-Tollendal, "Premier discours sur l'organisation du pouvoir législatif," in *ORF,* 365.

130. The phrase is Mallet du Pan's and is quoted in Boudon, "La voie royale de Mallet du Pan," 22.

131. Lally-Tollendal, "Premier discours sur l'organisation du pouvoir législatif," in *ORF,* 364. Also see Jean Louis De Lolme, *The Constitution of England,* David Lieberman, ed., trans. Thomas Nugent (Indianapolis, IN: Liberty Fund, 2007), 57–63, 271–74. De Lolme notes that in England, "the King is the third constitutive part of Parliament" (57). For an interpretation emphasizing that the Constitution of 1791 did, in fact, underscore the co-legislative function of the executive power, see Glénard, *L'Exécutif et la Constitution de 1791,* 9–13, 132–79.

132. This is one of the main claims made by Mirabeau in his September 1, 1789 speech on the veto (reprinted in *ORF*, 674–86).

133. Sieyès' important discourse on the organization of the legislative power and the royal sanction from September 7, 1789 can be found in *ORF*, vol. 1, 1019–35. For a commentary, see Bredin, *Sieyès. La clé de la Révolution française*, 147–51.

134. See Lally-Tollendal, "Premier discours sur l'organisation du pouvoir législatif," in *ORF*, 366.

135. Mounier, *RC*, II: 125.

136. Lally-Tollendal, "Premier discours sur l'organisation du pouvoir législatif," in *ORF*, 365.

137. Malouet, "Discours sur la sanction royale" (September 1, 1789), in *ORF*, vol. 1, 458.

138. Mounier, "Discours sur la sanction royale" (September 5, 1789), in *ORF*, 898; 890. The similarity with Adams' theory of the balance of powers is discussed in Thompson, "The American Founding and the French Revolution," 125–27.

139. Mounier, *RC*, II: 135.

140. These concepts are discussed in detail in chapters 4 and 6 below.

141. Lally's reference to Adams is quoted in Thompson, "The American Founding and the French Revolution," 127.

142. Lally-Tollendal, "Premier discours sur l'organisation du pouvoir législatif," in *ORF*, 368.

143. Ibid., 368; all emphases added.

144. Ibid., 368.

145. *AP*, VIII: 574. Also see Pasquino, "La théorie de la 'balance du législatif,'" 67–89.

146. Clermont-Tonnerre, *ARCF*, 133–35. "Si elle [la nation] donne à un pouvoir toute autorité sur les autres, la vie de ce pouvoir est substituée à la vie constitutionnelle de la nation, et la nation est esclave de ce pouvoir; si elle balance tellement les pouvoirs, qu'aucun d'eux n'absorbe les autres, sa vie constitutionnelle étant composée de leur juste combinaison, est aussi pure, aussi libre, aussi bien ordonnée que possible" (132–33). The language of separation of powers appears in the following passage: "Aucun pouvoir ne doit réunir ces deux facultés (agir et vouloir); car il serait souverain et la nation serait esclave. . . . De ce principe naissent le pouvoir législatif et le pouvoir exécutif. Il doivent être indépendants; leur perfection consiste donc à ce que le pouvoir législatif ne puisse jamais produire une action, et à ce que le pouvoir exécutif ne puisse jamais produire une volonté. De ce principe bien réfléchi, bien approfondi, doit naître l'unité du pouvoir exécutif, et la division du pouvoir législatif. . . . Alors la séparation et l'indépendance des pouvoirs deviennent possible, et la nation n'est plus esclave" (133–35).

147. Lally-Tollendal, "Premier discours sur l'organisation du pouvoir législatif," in *ORF*, 369.

148. See ibid., 373.

149. Malouet presented his views on the Constitution of 1791 in his "Opinion sur l'acte constitutionnel," on August 8, 1791 (reprinted in *ORF*, 501–10). Mallet du Pan also rejected the "democratic monarchy" created by the new constitution, which in his view relied upon the "confusion" of powers. Instead, he preferred a "free and tempered" monarchy based upon an effective balance of powers. Another seminal reflection on the Constituent Assembly and the Constitution of 1791 came from the pen of Antoine Barnave, author of *De la Révolution et de la constitution*. The full

text (originally drafted in prison, before the execution of Barnave in November 1793) was edited by Patrice Gueniffey (Grenoble: Presses Universitaires de Grenoble, 1988), with an important preface by François Furet (9–29).

150. See Burke, *Further Reflections on the Revolution in France*, 60–61.

151. Ibid., 60.

152. Burke, as quoted in Griffiths, *Le Centre perdu*, 164, n. 5.

153. Burke, *Further Reflections on the Revolution in France*, 60.

154. Ibid., 60–61.

155. Ibid., 61.

156. Ibid., 61.

157. Ibid., 61.

158. *Seconde lettre de M. de Lally-Tollendal à M. Burke* (London, 1792), 6.

159. "Des citoyens modérés posent l'ancre auquel devait se rattacher le vaisseau de l'état" (ibid., 7). Also: "Je ne combats ni pour la liberté qui attaquerait le trône, ni pour le trône qui ménacerait la liberté," Lally-Tollendal wrote in a Burkean vein. "Je ne sépare plus le Roi de la Nation, la prérogative royale du droit des peuples, le trône de la liberté" (27).

160. Ibid., 37.

161. Ibid., 14.

162. Mounier, *RC*, II: 42–56.

163. Mounier, *DIAP*, 89.

164. Malouet, *Mémoires*, I: 335.

165. Malouet, *Mémoires*, II: 190–92.

166. *The Correspondence of Edmund Burke,* vol. 7 (January 1792–August 1794), Alfred Cobban and Robert A. Smyth, eds. (Cambridge: Cambridge University Press, 1968), 166–67.

167. See Acomb, *Mallet du Pan*, 236–237. Acomb notes that in 1791 Mallet du Pan came to express a more positive view of Burke.

168. Burke, *Further Reflections on the Revolution in France*, 16.

169. Mounier, *DIAP*, iii–iv.

170. On Mounier's moderation, see *CSG*, 39, 60–61. In spite of his moderate tone, Mounier did not mince his words when summarizing the work of the Constituent Assembly: "Jamais le plus long règne du despote le plus absolu ne ravagea le pays soumis à son gouvernement comme la France, en trois ans, a été ravagée par l'Assemblée nationale de 1789 ou par les factieux qui la faisaient agir. Il faudrait réunir dans l'histoire les actions d'un grand nombre de tyrans pour retrouver autant de démence et d'injustice" (Mounier, *RC*, II: 41).

171. Mounier, *CSG*, 63.

172. Ibid., 64.

173. Here is Malouet's moving plea for moderation: "Combien, dans ces dissentiments politiques, dans les troubles civiles, il est nécessaire de laisser une porte ouverte aux rapprochements, à la conciliation; de ne pas croire trop à ses propres lumières er d'être indulgent pour les erreurs, pour les passions des autres" (Malouet, *Mémoires*, I: 317).

174. Ibid., 428.

175. It might be useful to examine the similarities and differences between the monarchiens' agenda and attempts to reform the Old Regime prior to 1789, with a view to creating a more effective centralized administration.

176. See Griffiths, "Le 'monarchienisme' et la 'monarchie limitée,'" 63–64.

177. This is a point made by Mounier in *RC*, II: 52.

178. The full quote from Mallet du Pan can be found in Griffiths, *Le Centre perdu*, 170.

179. Staël, *CPE,* 200–201.

180. Tocqueville, *The Old Regime and the Revolution*, vol. 2, 110.

181. Tocqueville noted an important affinity between the monarchiens and other revolutionary leaders, and regarded Mounier as defending a set of ideas fundamentally opposed to Montesquieu's theory of intermediary powers (ibid., 108–109).

182. "[Mounier] does not exactly want centralization, but what leads to it," Tocqueville noted. "It is true that in his opinion about local government he wants to leave great power to localities . . . but by destroying everything which could facilitate resistance and even life in the old provincial institutions, he unknowingly prepared not the destruction of provincial privileges, but the extinction of all local life. What he asked from within the limits that he asked for, was just: it seems he only wanted to take away from the provinces some rights which belonged to sovereignty, like voting taxes . . . and he was right. But for lack of knowing exactly what they wanted and what was possible, men, even the most prudent men of the times, through logic always went far beyond the goal they intended to reach" (ibid., 107).

183. Ibid., 109–110.

184. Lord Acton, *Lectures on the French Revolution*, 113.

185. Ibid., 59–60.

186. Ibid., 60.

187. Ibid.

188. Sieyès, *Political Writings*, 83; for Mounier's position, see his "Rapport sur la constitution," in *ORF*, 865. In *Considérations sur les intérêts du Tiers État* (1789), Rabaut Saint-Étienne argued that intermediary powers do not belong to the natural order of a free society and hence have no role in a sound constitution.

189. Denouncing the *Club monarchique* on January 25, 1791, Barnave argued: "Une autre secte s'élève; elle invoque la constitution monarchique, et sous cette astucieuse égide, quelque factieux cherchent à attirer les citoyens dans des pièges, en donnant au people un pain empoisonné" (apud Malouet, *Mémoires*, II: 400). For Malouet's response, see "Reponse à la denunciation du Club de la Constitution Monarchique, par Monsieur Barnave," in Malouet, *Collection des opinions de M. Malouet* (Paris: 1791), II: 195–202.

190. *Journal d'Adrien Duquesnoy*, I: 254.

191. Malouet, *Mémoires*, I: 382.

192. As Malouet himself acknowledged, the monarchiens "parlaient au people de ses intérêts, de ses droits légitimes: ce n'était pas assez pour obtenir sa confiance. Moi aussi j'ai parlé raison, et je n'ai pas manqué de courage: ma persévérance n'a abouti qu'aux honneurs de la proscription" (*Mémoires*, II: 32). Malouet restated his political views in "Lettre de M. Malouet, député d'Auvergne, à ses commettants" (May 13, 1790), reprinted in *Collection des opinions de M. Malouet*, II: 7–51.

193. The monarchiens, Duquesnoy argued, were "gens faibles et lâches."

194. On the relationship between Necker and the monarchiens, see Mounier, *RC*, II: 27, 96–98; Mounier, *DIAP*, 91; Malouet, *Mémoires*, I: 287ff. Necker pointed to the monarchiens' lack of confidence in their mission: "Il ne leur a manqué peut-être qu'une voix plus sonore ou une confiance plus grande dans leurs intentions et dans leurs moyens" (quoted in Egret, *La Révolution des notables*, 133).

195. See Doyle, "La pensée politique de Mounier," 25.

196. Quoted in Lanzac de Laborie, *Un royaliste liberal en 1789*, 334.

197. Mounier, *CSG*, 4. Mounier insisted on the continuity of his thought and his commitment to moderation in *Exposé de ma conduite* (*ORF*, 986). See also Mounier, *RC*, I: xii, and the account given by Virieu of "l'honnête Mounier . . . ferme comme un rocher dans tous ses principes" (quoted in Egret, *La Révolution des notables*, 124–25).

198. Malouet, *Mémoires*, I: 317; see also 402–403, 428.

199. "Lettre de M. Malouet, député d'Auvergne, à ses commettants," 22–23. For Malouet's principles, see ibid., 30; and *Collection des opinions de M. Malouet*, I (Paris: 1791): 54–69.

200. Moro, "La dottrina politica di J. J. Mounier," 472.

201. Referring to the agenda pursued by Mounier and his colleagues, Périsse de Luc argued: "Ils s'étaient flattés d'être nos législateurs, mais ils n'ont pas été sur la ligne de l'esprit public et des connaissances de notre siècle" (quoted in Egret, *La Révolution des notables*, 130).

202. This was a point made by Malouet in a letter from December 1791, reprinted in his *Mémoires*, II: 185–90.

203. See Gunn, *When the French Tried to Be British*, 23–40.

204. See Mounier, *NO*, 190, 231; and Moro, "La dottrina politica di J. J. Mounier," 469–70.

205. A. P. Barnave, *Œuvres*, I (Paris: 1842): 102–103.

206. "M. Mounier ne sentit pas que changer avec les circonstances, ce n'est pas réellement changer; qu'il faut pour les hommes publics une attention scrupuleuse à demeurer au niveau des lumières des autres hommes, et l'opinion générale; et qu'une constance infléxible au milieu des révolutions, peut n'être qu'une vicissitude perpétuelle" (Boissy d'Anglas, as quoted in Christine Le Bozec, "Les idées politiques de Boissy d'Anglas," in *La Constitution de l'an III: Boissy d'Anglas et la naissance du libéralisme constitutionnel*, Gérard Conac and Jean-Pierre Machelon, eds. [Paris: PUF, 1999], 147–48).

207. "C'est le mélange d'intérêts et passions contraires qui a tout perdu, qui a discredité la modération, la saine raison" (Malouet, *Mémoires*, II: 27).

208. In December 1831, a critic of the monarchiens, P-M. Laurent, offered an interesting account of the enduring influence of the monarchiens' moderation in "De la modération politique," *Revue encyclopedique*, LII: (1831): 571–72.

209. Mounier, *CSG*, 23.

Chapter Four: Moderation and the "Intertwining of Powers"

1. Necker, *FR*, I: 292; I have slightly amended the existing English translation.

2. Marcel Gauchet, "Necker," in *CDFR*, 287.

3. Boissy d'Anglas as quoted in Robert D. Harris, *Necker: Reform Statesman of the Ancien Régime* (Berkeley: University of California Press, 1979), 241. Two sympathetic portraits of Necker can be found in Mme de Staël's "Du caractère de M. Necker et de sa vie privée" (*OCS*, II: 261–90) and *Considérations*, as well as in Auguste de Staël's "Notice sur M. Necker," published as the second volume of *Œuvres diverses de M. le Baron Auguste de Staël* (Paris: Treuttel et Würtz, 1829). Mme de Staël's portrait of Necker in *Considérations* was criticized for its excessive praise which, according to some of her readers, bordered on idolatry (see Talleyrand's caus-

tic remark to this effect quoted in Diesbach, *Necker*, 464–65). She also took her father's ideas and actions as a point of departure for her own discussion of events and ideas. Yet, it would be an exaggeration to claim that Necker as presented in her book was a mere figment of imagination, as Charlotte Hogsett argued ("Generative Factors in *Considerations on the French Revolution*," in *Germaine de Staël: Crossing the Borders*, Madelyn Gutwirth, Avriel Goldberger, and Karyna Szmurlo, eds. [New Brunswick, NJ: Rutgers University Press, 1991], 39).

4. For a comprehensive analysis of Necker's ideas, see Henri Grange, *Les idées de Necker* (Paris: Klinksieck, 1974), which also has a bibliography of Necker's works. A good overview is Gauchet's entry on Necker in *CDFR*, 287–97. With several exceptions, Necker has been underestimated by historians in the English-speaking world. One such exception was Robert D. Harris, author of *Necker: Reform Statesman of the Ancien Régime*, and *Necker and the Revolution of 1789* (Lanham, MD: University Press of America, 1986). At the time of his death in 2007, Harris completed the third part of his trilogy, examining Necker's career and trajectory after 1789. His manuscript is entitled *Necker and the Revolutionary Decade* (Moscow, ID: Special Collections & Archives, University of Idaho Library, Collection: ma. 2007–031). Jean Egret's *Necker, ministre de Louis XVI: 1776–1790* (Paris: Honoré Champion, 1975), Ghislain de Diesbach's *Necker, ou la faillite de la vertu* (Paris, 1987), and Jean-Denis Bredin's *Une singulière famille: Jacques Necker, Suzanne Necker et Germaine de Staël* (Paris: Fayard, 1999) are also useful sources of information.

5. Jacques Necker, *Sur l'administration de M. Necker par lui-même* (Paris, 1791), 1.

6. The phrase belongs to Eugène Lavaquery, author of *Necker: Fourrier de la révolution, 1732–1804* (Paris: Plon, 1933), as quoted in Harris, *Necker: Reform Statesman of the Ancien Régime*, vii.

7. Rivarol, *Pensées, répliques et portraits* (Paris: Le cherche midi éditeur, 2001), 143.

8. Harris, *Necker and the Revolution of 1789*, 446.

9. Bredin, *Une singulière famille*, 15.

10. See Alexis de Tocqueville, *Œuvres Complètes*, II: 2, André Jardin, ed. (Paris: Gallimard, 1953), 113; Jules Michelet, *Histoire de la Révolution française*, Claude Mettra, ed. (Paris: Robert Laffont, 1979), 126.

11. Jacques Necker, *Compte rendu* (Paris, 1781), 1–2. For more information, see Egret, *Necker*, 201–15.

12. See Harris, *Necker: Reform Statesman of the Ancien Régime*, 217–35. The libels attacked Necker's religion (Protestantism) and accused him of not being French (he was born in Switzerland).

13. Quoted in Harris, *Necker: Reform Statesman of the Ancien Régime*, 240.

14. The fascinating story of Necker's loan is recounted in Othénin d'Haussonville, "La liquidation du 'dépôt' de Necker: entre concept et idée-force," *Cahiers staëliens* 55 (2004): 153–206.

15. Staël, *CGIII*: 2, 137.

16. Mme de Staël referred to Necker's *Du pouvoir exécutif* as "the best guide that can be followed by men called on to make or to modify a constitution of any kind" and "the political chart in which all the dangers that are found in the track of liberty are pointed out" (*CPE*, 298).

17. Necker's *De la Révolution française* was widely read upon its publication. Of

the many reviews of the book, I would like to point out two. The first came from the pen of Pierre-Louis Ginguené (1748–1816) whose long and critical account of Necker's history was printed in 1797 as a book entitled *De M. Necker et de son livre intitulé: De la Révolution française*. It was originally a compilation of articles from the *La Décade philosophique, littéraire et politique*, nos. 23, 24, 26, 28 (Year V [1797]). Ginguené denounced Necker's alleged inaccuracies, omissions, and partiality in his account of the revolution. He pointed to his inadequate account of the Vendée episode and his biased analysis of the faults of the Constitution of 1795, and took him to task for glossing over the names of many revolutionary actors. (Ginguené also criticized Necker's writing style which he found occasionally pompous and trivial). The second, much more sympathetic review was written by Roederer and was reprinted in *Œuvres du Comte P. L. Roederer*, IV, A. M. Roederer, ed. (Paris: Firmin Didot, 1856), 559–90.

18. *OCN*, XI: 7.

19. Staël, *CPE*, 475.

20. Necker, *FR*, II: 273–74. The same conclusion was reached by Mme de Staël in *CPE*, Book I, Chapter XI. For more information, see chapter 5 below.

21. Necker, *FR*, II: 267–68.

22. Necker, *FR*, I: 41; also see *OCN*, X: 278–79. For a general account, see William Doyle, "The Parlements," in Baker, ed., *The Political Culture of the Old Regime*, 157–58.

23. Also see Harris, *Necker: Reform Statesman of the Ancien Régime*, 181–94.

24. As quoted in ibid., 184.

25. Necker's account of the Assembly of the Notables of 1787 can be found in *FR*, I: 59–63. For more information on general background, see Furet, *Revolutionary France*, 41–45; Baker, ed., *The Old Regime and the French Revolution*, 124–35.

26. The *pays d'état* were newly acquired provinces, permitted to maintain their assemblies of estates, unlike the so-called *pays d'élections*, which were geographical areas administered by delegates of the intendants. A *generality* designated the area administered by an intendant.

27. For Necker's views on public opinion, see Léonard Burnand, *Necker et l'opinion publique* (Paris: Honoré Champion, 2004). On the growth of public opinion in pre-revolutionary France, see Baker, *Inventing the French Revolution*, 167–99; and Mona Ozouf, "L'opinion publique," in *The Political Culture of the Old Regime*, 420–34.

28. Necker, *FR*, I: 12.

29. Necker, *De l'Administration des finances de la France* (Paris, 1784), lxi–lxii. Also see Burnand, *Necker et l'opinion publique*, 51.

30. *OCN*, VI: 613–14.

31. Necker, *FR*, II: 272.

32. Ibid. See also Tackett, *Becoming a Revolutionary*, 100–13.

33. Staël, *CPE*, 132.

34. As Mme de Staël pointed out, "in this, as in almost every other point, [Necker] observed a medium; for he would not go the length of saying to the representatives of the people, 'Employ yourselves only on a constitution;' and still less would he consent to relapse into the arbitrary system, by contenting himself with momentary resources, that would neither have given a stable assurance to the public creditors, not have satisfied the people in regard to the appropriation of its sacrifices" (*CPE*, 133). Necker's important speech of May 5, 1789 is also analyzed in Grange, *Les idées de Necker*, 408–16.

35. See Necker, *FR*, I: 107–113.

36. Ibid., 200. For a slightly different account, see Tackett, *Becoming a Revolutionary*, 94–100. He remarked that many of the future deputies of the Third Estate had acquired valuable experience in municipal and provincial assemblies so that, by early May 1789, "the deputies were already prepared for the *forms* of revolutionary politics" (ibid., 100).

37. Necker, *FR*, I: 122.

38. Ibid., 193–94.

39. Ibid.

40. Ibid., 195.

41. See *OCN*, VI: 559–61 and Harris, *Necker and the Revolution of 1789*, 425.

42. *OCN*, VI: 603, 612.

43. Ibid., 605–606. I use here Harris' translation from *Necker and the Revolution of 1789*, 433–34. See also Egret, *Necker*, 272–87.

44. Necker, *FR*, I: 123.

45. Ibid., 308–309.

46. Ibid., 128–29.

47. Ibid., 59–63. See Egret, *Necker*, 233–48; William Doyle, *The Oxford History of the French Revolution* (Oxford: Oxford University Press, 2003 [1989]), 96–11; Roland Mousnier, *Les institutions de la France sous la monarchie absolue, 1598–1789* (Paris: PUF, 2005).

48. *OCN*, VI: 609; see also 610–11.

49. See Mme de Staël, *CPE*, 148–50. As she pointed out, Necker's declaration was "almost word for word" similar to the declaration issued in 1814 by Louis XVI's brother, the future Louis XVIII, at St. Ouen, on May 2, 1814, on the occasion of his return to the throne of France.

50. Necker, *FR*, I: 123.

51. As quoted in Harris, *Necker and the Revolution of 1789*, 482.

52. Ibid., 520.

53. *Necker, FR*, I: 160.

54. Staël, *CPE*, 151.

55. Grange comments on the similarities and differences between Necker and Mounier in *Les idées de Necker*, 344–49.

56. *Necker, FR*, I: 166–205.

57. Ibid., 164.

58. See ibid., 177, 209–210, 221–22; Harris, *Necker and the Revolution of 1789*, 506–507.

59. Ibid., 180.

60. See ibid., 164.

61. Quoted in Harris, *Necker and the Revolution of 1789*, 521–22.

62. This passage from Duquesnoy's diary is quoted in Harris, *Necker and the Revolution of 1789*, 525.

63. See the declaration of Necker's First-Secretary, Joseph-François Coster, quoted in ibid., 498.

64. *Necker, FR*, I: 160.

65. Ibid., 306.

66. Necker commented on the lack of moderation of all three orders as follows: "Neither party chose to conduct themselves with moderation; and they were led astray, like all other men, by the seductions of the passions, and their triumph over the suggestions of reason" (ibid., 238, 240).

67. Ibid., 242.

68. Ibid., 231.

69. Necker, *FR*, II: 25.

70. See ibid., 24–29.

71. The spirit of abstraction, Necker argued, was in good part due to the influence of the *philosophes*; see ibid., 332, 421–22; Necker, *ETPEP*, II: 243–44.

72. Necker, *ETPEP*, II: 260.

73. Necker, *FR*, I: 248–49. On the promise and dangers of equality, see ibid., I: 252.

74. Necker, *ETPEP*, II: 194–95.

75. Ibid., 195.

76. Necker, *FR*, II: 31.

77. Ibid., 350.

78. Ibid.

79. Ibid., 349.

80. Ibid., 372.

81. Necker, *ETPEP*, II: 121.

82. Necker, *FR*, II: 336.

83. Necker, *FR*, I: 245.

84. Necker, *ETPEP*, II: 248.

85. Ibid.

86. Necker, *ETPEP*, II: 312.

87. Ibid., 121. For a recent reassessment of the work of the Constituent Assembly, see Gueniffey, *La Politique de la Terreur*, 81–122.

88. Necker, *ETPEP*, II: 245.

89. Ibid., 244; also Necker, *FR*, I: 279.

90. Necker, *FR*, I: 248.

91. Ibid., 272–73.

92. Ibid., 275.

93. *Necker, ETPEP*, II: 196.

94. *Necker, FR*, I: 249–50; 279–80.

95. Necker, *ETPEP*, I: 342.

96. Ibid., 341.

97. Ibid., 344.

98. Necker, *FR*, I: 250.

99. Necker, *ETPEP*, I: 4.

100. Ibid., 5; emphases added.

101. Necker, *FR*, I: 281.

102. Mme de Staël explained Necker's endorsement of the suspensive veto (valid for two legislatures) in a letter to her husband of September 10, 1789, quoted in Egret, *La Révolution des notables*, 153–54. See also Grange, *Les idées de Necker*, 421.

103. Necker, *FR*, I: 286.

104. For a different view, see Glénard, *L'Exécutif et la Constitution de 1791*.

105. Necker, *ETPEP*, II: 174; also *OCN*, VIII: 2, 464–65, 468–70, 502–505.

106. See Bronislaw Baczko, *Comment sortir de la Terreur? Thermidor et la Révolution* (Paris: Gallimard, 1989). Necker's views on this period are analyzed in Harris, *Necker and the Revolutionary Decade*, 264–78.

107. See Michel Troper, *Terminer la Révolution. La Constitution de 1795* (Paris:

Fayard, 2006); Marc Lahmer, *La Constitution américaine dans le débat français, 1795–1848* (Paris: L'Harmattan, 2001); Andrew Jainchill, *Reimagining Politics after the Terror* (Ithaca, NY: Cornell University Press, 2008), 26–61; François Luchaire, "Boissy d'Anglas et la Constitution de l'an III," in *La Constitution de l'an III. Boissy d'Anglas et la naissance du libéralisme constitutionnel*, 49–50 ; Stefano Mannoni, *Une et indivisible. Storia dell'accentramento amministrativo in Francia*, 2 vols. (Milan: Giuffrè, 1994).

108. To give only two examples, all the members of the upper chamber—the Council of the Ancients—had to be either married or widowers, and no one was considered to be a good citizen if he was not also a "good" son, father, friend, or husband.

109. Quoted in Troper, *Terminer la Révolution*, 27; see also 28–30.

110. Quoted in Jainchill, *Reimagining Politics*, 37.

111. These ideas can be found in Francis d'Ivernois' *Des révolutions de France et de Genève* (1795). He referred to the English monarch as the supreme mediator among powers, "le balancier destiné à empêcher les oscillations des deux bassins [du corps législatif], et à les tenir invariablement en équilibre." He explained : "La prérogative royale de dissoudre ce corps, et de rejeter ses projets de bills, voilà le vrai balancier qui empêche en Angleterre l'un des bassins de la balance de renverser l'autre. Voilà le véritable sceptre, et le sceptre tutélaire avec lequel le Modérateur suprême trace à chacune des deux chambres le cercle qu'elles parcouront, et dont elles savent fort bien qu'il pourra les empêcher d'en sortir" (as quoted in Lahmer, *La Constitution américaine*, 181).

112. From an article published in *La Gazette française* (June 24, 1795), quoted in Lahmer, *La Constitution américaine*, 177.

113. Quoted in ibid., 167.

114. See ibid., 158, 173. Lahmer quotes from *Opinion de J.C.G. Delahaye, représentant du peuple, sur la nouvelle constitution proposée par la commission des Onze* (Paris: Imprimerie Nationale, 1795), 2–6.

115. See Lahmer, *La Constitution américaine*, 167.

116. Ibid., 169.

117. Vaublanc argued: "Point de balance, si les pouvoirs ne peuvent s'arrêter réciproquement; et vous avez dit vous-même que sans la balance des pouvoirs, il n'y avait point de vrai gouvernement" (ibid., 172).

118. Marc Lahmer rightly points out that the five directors were given, however, two new important prerogatives. According to Article 131, they could initiate a formal assessment of the constitutionality of the laws. According to Article 144, the executive power received "le pouvoir réglementaire dérivé," which granted it the right "de faire des proclamations conformes aux lois et pour leur exécution" (ibid.,164–65).

119. See ibid., 135–64.

120. For more information, see the brief analysis of Sieyès' proposals in chapter 6 below.

121. See Jean-Pierre Machelon, "La Constitution du 5 fructidor an III (22 août 1795): archaïsme ou modernité?" in *La Constitution de l'an III*, 36.

122. See Lahmer, *La Constitution américaine*, 178.

123. For more details, see Machelon, "La Constitution du 5 fructidor an III," 32–34; Lahmer, *La Constitution américaine*, 216, n. 43. One in five articles of the new constitution dealt with questions regarding the government and administration,

which shows that the Thermidorians did not entirely overlook the executive power. It is revealing that the Directory drew its name from the executive and the constitution distinguished between governmental and administrative functions. It made clear that the government was entrusted to the five directors who governed but did not administer the country, while the proper administration was the domain of the ministers (as administrators who did not govern). The five directors were granted considerable authority in the application of the laws, such as the right to dispose of the army and make senior appointments (Art. 144 and 148), the right to issue mandates of arrest (Art. 145), and the right to dismiss generals and to receive taxes from each department (Art. 153). According to Article 147, they were also granted the right to nominate agents to survey and ensure the execution of the laws in administration and tribunals. Nonetheless, the directors had neither the right to initiate laws nor the right to veto them, and they possessed no means of delaying or blocking the laws voted by the two chambers.

124. See Joseph Barthélemy and Paul Duez, *Traité de droit constitutionnel* (Paris: Dalloz, 1933), 142; A. Esmein, *Éléments de droit constitutionnel français et comparé*, 3rd ed. (Paris: Librairie de la Société du recueil général des lois et des arrêts, 1903), 300–76 ; also Michel Troper, "La séparation des pouvoirs dans la Constitution de l'an III," in *La Constitution de l'an III*, 51–71.

125. See Troper, "La séparation des pouvoirs," 59–61.

126. *FR,* II: 130–31. Roederer commented on Necker's critique of the Constitution of 1795 in his review of *De la Révolution française* published in Roederer, *Œuvres*, IV: 578–85. In turn, Ginguené criticized Necker's account of the 1795 constitution in the third part of his long review of Necker's book published in *La Décade philosophique, littéraire et politique* 26 (June 8, 1797): 468–74.

127. *Necker, FR,* II: 235.

128. Ibid., 247.

129. Ibid., 127.

130. Ibid., 116.

131. Ibid., 137–38.

132. Ibid., 117.

133. Ibid., 118. Also see Lucien Jaume, "Necker: examen critique de la Constitution de l'an III," in *La constitution de l'an III*, 170–73.

134. Necker, *FR,* II: 119.

135. Ibid., 122.

136. Ibid., 141.

137. "It will be a witness of injuries done to the public liberty, or to the rights of individuals," Necker predicted; "it will hear lawful demands, or affecting complaints, and it will not be able to say a word; it will have neither the right of representation nor the right of counseling" (ibid., 146).

138. Ibid., 145.

139. Ibid., 142.

140. Ibid., 146.

141. See ibid., 124, and Jaume, "Necker: examen critique," 173–78.

142. See Necker, *FR,* II: 125. Necker also took issue with the constitutional article that recalled to the administration a director who had been acquitted by the national high court. He praised the Americans for setting the end of the term of the head of state at the moment when the Senate, upon the recommendation of the House of Representatives, had pronounced his impeachment (ibid., 132–33).

143. Ibid., 155–56.

144. Ibid., 183–85; also see Jaume, "Necker: examen critique," 179–82.

145. Necker, *FR,* II: 149.

146. Ibid.

147. Ibid., 198–99.

148. Ibid., 201.

149. Ibid., 236.

150. See ibid., 204–207.

151. Ibid., 234. I have slightly amended the old English translation; see also ibid., 236–37. Necker also analyzed the right of petition, freedom of the press, and exceptional circumstances.

152. *OCN,* XI: 8. For a brief analysis of Necker's last book, see Grange, *Les idées de Necker,* 71–80, 477–89.

153. See Constant's remark in Étienne Hofmann, "Necker, Constant, et la question constitutionnelle (1800–1802)," *CS,* 36 (1985): 76.

154. *OCN,* XI: 7. For Necker's views on the Directory and the Consulate, see Harris, *Necker and the Revolutionary Decade,* 279–308.

155. *OCN,* XI: 10.

156. Ibid., 20.

157. Ibid., 13.

158. Ibid., 71–72.

159. Ibid., 34, 45; see also 68–69, 41–43.

160. Ibid., 48, 50.

161. On Rousseau's legacy in France, see Roussel, *Jean-Jacques Rousseau en France après la Révolution, 1795–1830.* Constant's and Staël's interpretations of Rousseau are discussed also discussed in Roussel's book (315–58, 489–524) as well as in Paulet-Grandguillot's *Libéralisme et démocratie,* especially 215–302, 339–416. Also see Vile, *Constitutionalism,* 193–99.

162. To this list, two other concepts ought to be added: ministerial (political) responsibility and bicameralism.

163. Necker was accused by one of his reviewers of pursuing an imaginary enemy—absolute equality—which, in Ginguené's opinion, almost no one defended in France after 1795 (see the fourth part of Ginguené's review of Necker's *De la Révolution française,* in *La Décade philosophique, littéraire et politique* 28 [June 28, 1797]: 34).

164. Necker, *Philosophical Reflections on Equality* in *FR,* II: 398.

165. Ibid., 393.

166. Education, Necker argued, promotes moderation, "that virtue of the heart and of the understanding [which] will never be united with ignorance" (ibid., 355).

167. Ibid., 421.

168. Ibid., 398.

169. Ibid., 395.

170. Ibid.

171. Ibid., 399.

172. Ibid., 398.

173. Ibid., 356.

174. Ibid., 404.

175. Ibid., 402. On this issue, see also Marcel Morabito, "Necker et la question du chef de l'État," in *Coppet, creuset de l'esprit liberal: les idées politiques et consti-*

tutionnelles du group de Madame de Staël, Lucien Jaume, ed. (Marseille and Paris: Presses Universitaires d'Aix-Marseille & Economica, 2000), 41–51.

176. Necker, *ETPEP*, II: 136–37.

177. Necker, *FR*, II: 403.

178. Ibid., 422–23.

179. Ibid.

180. See chapter 2 above; also Troper, *La Séparation des pouvoirs et l'histoire constitutionnelle française*.

181. In this regard, Montesquieu's heirs such as De Lolme and the French monarchiens offered a different interpretation of the workings of the English constitution than Necker and Mme de Staël. For more details, see Luigi Lacchè, "Coppet et la percée de l'Etat libéral constitutionnel," in *Coppet, creuset de l'esprit libéral*, 135–55.

182. Necker, *ETPEP*, I: 2.

183. Ibid., 4.

184. Ibid., 5.

185. Ibid.

186. Henri Grange, "De l'originalité des idées politiques de Necker," in *Cahiers staëliens* 36 (1985): 54–55.

187. Necker, *ETPEP*, I: 194.

188. Ibid., 68; all emphases added.

189. Ibid., 68–69; emphases added. On the right of legislative initiative, see Grange, *Les idées de Necker*, 291–92, 295.

190. Necker, *ETPEP*, I: 194, 196; I have silently amended the old English translation to bring it closer to the original text.

191. *OCN*, XI : 125–26; see also Grange, *Les idées de Necker*, 272ff.

192. Necker, *ETPEP*, II: 170.

193. Necker, *FR*, II: 127; all emphases added. Here is the original French text: "On doit chercher à établir une liaison constitutionnelle entre le pouvoir exécutif et le pouvoir législatif; on doit songer que leur prudente association, leur ingénieux entrelacement seront toujours la meilleure caution d'une circonspection mutuelle et d'une surveillance efficace" (*OCN*, X: 133).

194. J.C.L. Simonde de Sismondi, *Études sur les constitutions des peuples libres* (Brussels: Société typographique belge, 1839), 30. Sismondi's views on Montesquieu and Necker are discussed in the seventh essay in Part III. On Sismondi's political thought, his theory of sovereignty, and his dialogue with Rousseau and Constant, see Paulet-Grandguillot, *Libéralisme et démocratie*, 289–337; Lucien Jaume, "La conception sismondienne du gouvernement libre comparée à la version française," in *Sismondi e la civiltà toscana*, Francesca Sofia, ed. (Milan: Leo S. Olschki, 2001), 213–30; and Francesca Sofia, "Formes constitutionnelles et organisation de la société chez Sismondi" in *Coppet, creuset de l'esprit libéral*, 54–73.

195. Wrote Mme de Staël: "Il a toujours soutenu ces idées modérées qui irritent si vivement les hommes dont les idées extrêmes sont les armes et l'étendard" (*OCS*, II: 270); see also *CPE*, 480–81.

196. Necker, *Sur l'administration de M. Necker*, 3.

197. *OCS*, II: 263; *Œuvres diverses de M. le Baron Auguste de Staël*, 308–309.

198. *OCS*, II: 285. The excessive praise lavished upon Necker by her daughter bordered on idolatry in the eyes of some like Talleyrand (see Diesbach, *Necker*, 464–65).

199. In 1800, Necker published another important book, *Cours de morale religieuse*. Necker's religious views and policy are discussed in detail in Grange, *Les idées de Necker*, 517–614.

200. *OCN*, XII: 16.

201. Ibid., 10; see also 28–29, 42–44 (religion and justice), and 426–38 (the conclusion).

202. Ibid., 44.

203. Ibid., 43.

204. Sieyès' remark was quoted by Louis de Bonald in his critique of Mme de Staël; see Bonald, *La vraie Révolution. Réponse à Madame de Staël*, Michel Toda, ed. (Étampes: Clovis, 1997), 84, fn (a).

205. Roederer's letter in Staël, *CGIII*: 2, 244, fn. 7. Also see Roederer, *Œuvres*, IV: 590.

206. Hume, *Essays*, 27.

207. Gauchet, "Necker," 289.

208. Staël, *CPE*, 113–14. The same point was made by Auguste de Staël a few decades later in his portrait of his grandfather.

209. Necker, *FR*, I: 294–95.

210. Ibid., 296.

211. Gauchet, "Necker," 287.

212. The expression belongs to Ségur as quoted in Diesbach, *Necker*, 467.

213. Roederer, *Œuvres*, IV: 569.

214. *OCS*, II: 273 and Staël, *CPE*, 56; also Mounier, *DIAP*, 97.

215. Gauchet, "Necker," 291.

216. Necker, *FR*, I: 297. A similar point was made by Roederer (*Œuvres*, IV: 572).

217. Necker, *FR*, II: 355.

218. Necker, *FR*, I: 308.

219. Ibid.

Chapter Five: Moderation after the Terror

1. Staël, *DCA*, 313.

2. *OCS*, I: 54.

3. The *Cahiers staëliens* published by the Société des études staëliennes (http://www.stael.org/) and Éditions Honoré Champion are an indispensable source for any student of Mme de Staël; to date, sixty-one volumes have appeared in print. Mme de Staël's complete works were originally edited by her son, Auguste, in seventeen volumes at Treuttel and Würtz in Paris in 1821 (henceforth abbreviated as *OCS*, followed by the volume number). A new series of *Œuvres Complètes* was initiated in 2000, (henceforth abbreviated as *OCS(NS)*). Of special interest to students of Mme de Staël's political thought is Série III: *Œuvres historiques*, Tome I, *Des circonstances actuelles et autres essais politiques sous la Révolution*, Lucia Omacini, ed. (Paris: Honoré Champion, 2009) which contains an updated and enlarged version of *DCA*. I reviewed this important volume in my essay "Flirting with Republicanism: Mme de Staël's Writings from the 1790s," *History of European Ideas* 36-3 (2010): 343–46. In this chapter, references are made to the edition of *DCA* published by Lucia Omacini at Slatkine in 1979. For a selection from Mme de Staël's rich correspondence, see *Mme de Staël, ses amis, ses correspondants. Choix de lettres* (1778–1817), Georges

Solovieff, ed. (Paris: Klinksieck, 1970). The complete correspondence was edited by the late Béatrice Jasinski who, unfortunately, passed away before completing her monumental work. With the exception of *Considérations*, the other political works of Mme de Staël have not yet been translated into English. Where available, I have used and referred to the existing English editions; otherwise, all translations are my own.

4. The remark is attributed to Baron du Montet, an Austrian of French origin, who met Mme de Staël in 1813 and recorded his impressions in his memoirs. For more details, see Gieslain de Diesbach, *Madame de Staël* (Paris: Perrin, 1983), 485–86; Maria Fairweather, *Mme de Staël* (London: Carroll and Graf, 2005), 3. See also the account given by one of Mme de Staël's critics, Fontanes, as quoted in Bronislaw Baczko, *Politiques de la Révolution française* (Paris: Gallimard, 2008), 453. Among the interpreters of Mme de Staël, Simone Balayé's books occupy a prominent place: *Madame de Staël, Lumière et liberté* (Paris: Klincksieck, 1979); *Madame de Staël: écrire, lutter, vivre* (Geneva: Droz, 1994). An useful overview of the secondary literature can be found in Stéphanie Tribouillard, *Le Tombeau de Madame de Staël. Les discours de la posterité staëlienne en France (1817–1850)* (Geneva: Slatkine, 2007), 19–40. For an overview of Mme de Staël's political thought, see Marcel Gauchet, "Staël" in *CDFR*, 1003–10 and my introduction ("A Thinker for Our Times: Madame de Staël, Her Life and Works") to the recent English edition of *CPE* (pp. vii–xxiv). A shorter account can be found in Ruth Scurr, "For Liberty: Madame de Staël as a Political Thinker," *TLS* (December 10, 2010): 14–15. The place of Mme de Staël in modern French thought is analyzed in Lucien Jaume, *L'Individu effacé ou le paradoxe du libéralisme français* (Paris: Fayard, 1997), 25–62; and Chinatsu Takeda, "Madame de Staël's Contribution to Liberalism in France (1788–1820s)," unpublished Ph.D. dissertation, University of London, 2001. In addition to the works of Diesbach and Fairweather cited above, there are several other important biographies of Mme de Staël: Lady Blennerhassett, *Mme de Staël. Her Friends, and Her Influence in Politics and Literature*, 3 vols. (London: Chapman and Hall, 1889); Christopher J. Herold, *Mistress to an Age: A Life of Mme de Staël* (Indianapolis, IN: Bobbs Merrill, 1958); Francine Du Plessix Gray, *Madame de Staël: The First Modern Woman* (New York: Atlas, 2008); Angelica Gooden, *Madame de Staël: The Dangerous Exile* (New York: Oxford University Press, 2008); Renée Weingarten, *Germaine de Staël and Benjamin Constant: A Dual Biography* (New Haven, CT: Yale University Press, 2008).

5. "Lettre sur l'ouvrage de Mme de Staël," in *Rivarol*, Jean Dutourd, ed. (Paris: Mercure de France, 1963), 119–23.

6. As quoted in Fairweather, *Mme de Staël*, 426.

7. Ibid., 112.

8. Quoted in Mona Ozouf, *Women's Words: Essay on the French Singularity*, trans. Jane Marie Todd (Chicago: University of Chicago Press, 1997), 68.

9. *MWGS*, 170. See also Madame Necker de Saussure, "Notice sur le caractère et les écrits de Madame de Staël," in *OCS*, I.

10. Baczko, *Politiques*, 464. On this issue, see Benedetta Craveri, *The Age of Conversation*, trans. Teresa Waugh (New York: New York Review Books, 2006). Mme de Staël, "Du talent d'être aimable en conversation," *CS*, 52 (2001): 25–31. The issue of the art of conversation in Mme de Staël's works has been the subject of many commentaries: Brunhilde Wehinger, *Conversation um 1800: Salonkultur und liter-*

arische Autorschaft bei Germaine de Staël (Berlin: Walter Frey Verlag, 2002), 61–216 ; Aurelio Principato, "Mme de Staël: la conversation et son miroir," *CS*, 52 (2001): 53–74; Jean-Paul Sermain, "Conversation et écriture chez Mme de Staël," *CS*, 52 (2001): 75–94. For a representative view of what a good conversation entails, see Germaine de Staël, *On Politics, Literature, and National Character*, Morroe Berger, ed. (New York, Doubleday, 1964), 287.

11. Quoted in Baczko, *Politiques*, 480, 490; see also Blennerhassett, *Madame de Staël*, vol. 3, 507.

12. See Balayé, *Madame de Staël*. Among the numerous feminist interpretations of Mme de Staël, worth noting are: Madelyn Gutwith, *Madame de Staël, Novelist: The Emergence of the Artist as Woman* (Urbana: University of Illinois Press, 1978) and the collection of essays *Germaine de Staël: Crossing the Borders*, Madelyn Gutwirth, Avriel Goldberger, and Karyna Szmurlo, eds. (New Brunswick, NJ: Rutgers University Press, 1991). The connection between contemporary feminism and Mme de Staël's political theory is analyzed in Susan Tenenbaum, "Montesquieu and Mme de Staël: The Woman as a Factor in Political Analysis," *Political Theory* 1 (1973): 92–103.

13. Quoted in Solovieff's introduction to *Mme de Staël, ses amis, ses correspondants*, 16.

14. See "Lettres inédites de Sismondi sur la mort de Madame de Staël," *CS*, 8 (1969): 29–30.

15. See Takeda, "Madame de Staël's Contribution to Liberalism in France," chapter 3; also Florence Lotterie's introduction to "À quels signes peut-on connaître quelle est l'opinion de la majorité de la nation?" in Staël, *OCS(NS)* III: 1, 557, n. 8. Compare with Andreas Kaylvas and Ira Katznelson, *Liberal Beginnings: Making a Republic for the Moderns* (Cambridge: Cambridge University Press, 2008), 142.

16. *MWGS*, 154. This definition appears in *De l'influence des passions sur le bonheur des individus et des nations* (1796), in which Mme de Staël analyzed the connection between happiness and passions (unfortunately, the political part of the book was never written). By emphasizing the importance of political passions and distinguishing between destructive and moderate passions, she suggested that a sound political system could not appear and maintain itself without properly cultivating passions such as generosity, pity, sympathy which serve as guarantees of social order. In a letter to Roederer dated October 1, 1796, Mme de Staël referred to this book as "the testament of my thought" (*CGIII: 2, 247*). For more information, see Biancamaria Fontana, "Mme de Staël, le gouvernement des passions et la Révolution française," *ABC* 8–9 (Lausanne & Paris: Institut Benjamin Constant & Jean Touzot, 1988), 175–81; and Takeda, "Madame de Staël's Contribution to Liberalism in France," chapter 3, section 3.

17. Mme de Staël regarded the love of glory as "the most commanding of all the passions to which the human heart is susceptible" (*MWGS*, 156).

18. Susan Tenenbaum, "The Politics of History," *ABC*, 8–9 (Lausanne & Paris: Institut Benjamin Constant & Jean Touzot, 1988), 103.

19. Staël, *DCA*, 273.

20. *MWGS*, 155.

21. Staël, *CPE*, 17.

22. Benjamin Constant, *Mélanges de politique et d'histoire* (Paris: Pichon et Didier, 1829), 163–210.

23. Ibid., 195.

24. This idea was also at the heart of Guizot's *History of Civilization in Europe* and *History of Civilization in France*.

25. Staël, *CPE*, 14.

26. In a surprisingly short (four-page) chapter of his own book, Bailleul pointed out the contradictions in Mme de Staël's analysis (Part I, chapter XI). He noted (*Examen critique*, I, 146–47) that, by concluding that France had no genuine constitution under the Old Regime, Mme de Staël ended up contradicting some of her earlier statements such as the existence of a forceful opposition to royal power coming from local privileges and intermediary bodies. For an overview of the debates on amending the French constitution, see chapter 3 above.

27. Staël, *CPE*, 96.

28. Ibid., 105.

29. Ibid., 143.

30. Ibid., 155.

31. Ibid., 152.

32. Staël, *DCA*, 34–36; *CPE,* 145.

33. Staël, *CPE*, 252.

34. Ibid., 282; see also 180–81, 186–93, 199–203, 211–18. More recently, Patrice Gueniffey has made a similar point, calling our attention to the (generally overlooked) self-restraint and "moderation of means" displayed by the Constituent Assembly (Gueniffey, *La Politique de la Terreur*, 100–10).

35. According to Ch. IV, Section 2 of the Constitution of 1791, the administrators of every department enjoyed a certain independence from the central power. They were "elected at stated times by the people to perform administrative duties under the supervision and authority of the King" (*A Documentary Survey of the French Revolution*, John Hall Stewart, ed. [New York: Macmillan, 1952], 252).

36. It is worth pointing out the similarity between Mme de Staël's and Tocqueville's interpretations of the initial phase of the revolution as "a time of inexperience doubtless, but of generosity, of enthusiasm, of virility, and of greatness, a time of immortal memory" (Tocqueville, *The Old Regime and the Revolution,* vol. 1, 244).

37. Staël, *CPE*, 180.

38. Ibid., 315.

39. OCS(NS), III: 1, 563–64.

40. Staël, *CPE*, 201; see also 200.

41. Ibid., 203.

42. Ibid., 202.

43. Ibid., 214.

44. Ibid., 203.

45. To all this we should add the tragic figure of Louis XVI, the monarch placed by history at the center of a revolutionary drama whose magnitude he never fully grasped until it was too late to avoid the scaffold.

46. The Constituent Assembly was dissolved on September 30, 1791, after having decreed that none of its members was eligible for the next legislature (Robespierre had been one of the most vocal defenders of this measure).

47. The first emigrants left France immediately after July 14, 1789; others after 1791 or shortly after the beginning of the Reign of Terror; their total number was between 150,000 and 160,000. For more details, see Massimo Boffa's entry in

CDFR, 324–36 and Ernest Daudet's *Histoire de l'émigration pendant la Révolution française*, 3 vols. (Paris, 1904–1907).

48. Officially established on April 6, 1793, the Committee of Public Safety gave official acknowledgment to the doctrine of the reason of state and ruled according to the belief that extraordinary circumstances call for exceptional methods. As Marat claimed, "it is through violence that liberty must be established, and the time has come to arrange for a temporary despotism of liberty in order to crush the despotism of kings" (*CDFR*, 476). For more information, see R. R. Palmer, *Twelve Who Ruled* (Princeton, NJ: Princeton University Press, 1969); Doyle, *The Oxford History of the French Revolution*, 247–72; *CDFR*, 137–51; Gueniffey, *La politique de la Terreur*; Donald Greer, *The Incidence of the Terror during the French Revolution: A Statistical Interpretation* (Cambridge, MA: Harvard University Press, 1935).

49. Staël, *CPE*, 120.

50. As Lucien Jaume noted (*L'individu effacé*, 58–59), this distinction between fanaticism and enthusiasm allowed Mme de Staël to condemn the Terror for having unleashed the worst forms of enthusiasm while also praising the noble ideals of 1789, in which she saw a reflection of the best form of enthusiasm. On the place of enthusiasm in Mme de Staël's works, see Jaume, ibid., 54–59; Louis Moreau de Bellaing, *L'enthousiasme de Mme de Staël* (Paris: L'Harmattan, 2005); John Isbell, *The Birth of European Romanticism: Truth and Propaganda in Staël's De l'Allemagne* (Cambridge: Cambridge University Press, 1994), 199–202; Paul Gautier, *Mme de Staël et Napoléon* (Paris: Plon, 1902), 271–74. For a general discussion of the various usages of "enthusiasm" during the Enlightenment, see Klein and La Vopa, eds., *Enthusiasm and Enlightenment in Europe, 1650–1850*.

51. Staël, *CPE*, 357.

52. Ibid., 113.

53. See Part I, chapter VII ("De l'esprit de parti") of *De l'influence des passions*, in *OCS*, I: 146. This interpretation provoked a trenchant critique from Fontanes; for more details, see Baczko, "Opinions des vainqueurs, sentiments des vaincus," in *OCS*(NS) III: 1, 194.

54. Staël, *CPE*, 361.

55. Ibid., 359.

56. Ibid., 357.

57. *OCS*, I: 33.

58. Ibid., 54.

59. The fanatic, Mme de Staël wrote, "ne se croit pas culpable; il se sent determiné à se dévouer lui-même, et cette idée l'aveugle sur l'atrocité de sacrifier les autres. Il sait que l'immoralité consiste à tout immoler à son intérêt personnel; et, voulant se livrer lui même pour la cause qu'il soutient, il pourrait encore conserver le sentiment de la vertu, en commettant de véritable crimes" (ibid., 55). It might be interesting to compare Mme de Staël's views on fanaticism with those of Jean François de la Harpe, author of *Du fanatisme dans la langue révolutionnaire ou de la persécution suscitée par les Barbares du dix-huitième siècle contre la religion chrétienne et ses Ministres* (Paris, 1797).

60. *OCS*, I: 146.

61. Ibid., 144. Mme de Staël's critique of fanaticism in this text ought to be compared and contrasted with her praise of enthusiasm in the last chapter of *De l'Allemagne*. On this issue, see Eric Gidal, "Melancholy, Trauma, and National Char-

acter: Mme de Staël's *Considérations sur les principaux événements de la Révolution française*," *Studies in Romanticism* 49-2 (2010): 261–92.

62. Staël, *DCA*, 42.

63. Ibid., 258.

64. She argued that justice and humanity would never be respected in countries where the supreme law is *salus populi* (ibid., 261).

65. "Ils ne voient qu'une idée, ils rattachent tout à elle, la séparent de ses connections et font ainsi, toujours, une erreur d'une idée juste" (ibid., 257). Also: "Ce qu'il faut, c'est marcher au but. L'homme le plus propre aux emplois publics, ce n'est pas le plus instruit, c'est le plus enthousiaste. Tous les fanatiques ne vous demandent qu'une chose: croire et vouloir, et la plupart des hommes peuvent bien aisément paraître l'un et l'autre, si l'ambition les y excite" (ibid., 260).

66. "Rien, dans le monde moral, n'est vrai que rélativement, qu'à son dégré, qu'à sa place, qu'avec ses environnants, et chaque idée tient à toutes" (ibid., 258).

67. Staël, *CGIII*:1, 231.

68. In *De la littérature*, II: XX, Mme de Staël had harsh words for Voltaire and took the *philosophes* to task for having promoted a lax moral code which encouraged political irresponsibility.

69. At war against European powers, France was confronted with an acute depreciation of paper money, and peace with England seemed a distant and unlikely prospect as leading British intellectuals and politicians (like Burke) questioned or opposed making peace with a regicide government. For more information about the reception of Staël's book in England, see Staël, *CGIII*: I, 323–34. For an analysis placing Mme de Staël's writings in the Thermidorian context, see Biancamaria Fontana, "The Thermidorian Republic and Its Principles," in Biancamaria Fontana, ed., *The Invention of the Modern Republic* (Cambridge: Cambridge University Press, 1994), 118–38.

70. Staël, *CPE*, 376.

71. Ibid., 377–78. For more details on this period, see Baczko, *Comment sortir de la Terreur* (Paris: Gallimard, 1989); Jainchill, *Reimagining Politics*; Isser Wolloch, *The New Regime: Transformations of the French Civic Order, 1789–1820s* (New York: Norton, 1995); George Lefebvre, *The Thermidorians and the Directory: Two Phases of the French Revolution*, trans. Robert Baldick (New York: Random House, 1964), especially Part I ("The Thermidorians"). Also useful is Claude Nicolet, *L'idée républicaine en France (1789–1924): Essai d'histoire critique* (Paris: Gallimard, 1982), Part 1.

72. Staël, *DCA*, 33, 39–40, 42.

73. Ibid., 34–35, 40. Compare this explanation with the slightly different account given in *CPE*, book 3, chapters XVI, XVIII.

74. Lahmer, *La Constitution américaine*, 170–71.

75. On the composition of Mme de Staël's *RPI*, see Lucien Jaume's introduction in *OCS*(NS), III: 1, 123–32; also Staël, *CGIII*: 2, 73, fn. 5.

76. Staël, *CGIII*: 2, 7. Roederer published a very favorable review of *RPI* in which he praised Mme de Staël's republicanism.

77. Ibid., 8.

78. A former member of the Mountain and convinced republican, Thibaudeau, also dreamt of establishing a republic of the center. See Pierre Serna, *La République des girouettes (1789–1815 . . . et au-delà). Une anomalie politique: La France de l'extrême centre* (Paris: Champ Vallon, 2005), 477–85.

79. In October 1796, Mme de Staël asked Roederer to refer to her, in his review of her work on the influence of passions, as a "French" patriot and French citizen by birth and residence; see Staël, *CGIII: 2*, 249; *CGIII: 1*, 322–23.

80. For a few passages from Legendre's speech, see Staël, *CGIII: 2*, 43. Legendre's denunciation was followed by the publication of a moving *éloge* of Mme de Staël in *Nouvelles politiques nationales et etrangères* on August 26, 1795. On October 25, the Convention voted a harsh law against the émigrés, excluding them from all public functions, along with their relatives.

81. In May 1796, the minister of the police, Cochon de Lapparent, fearing a secret alliance between Mme de Staël and the émigrés, sent an emissary to Coppet to follow and arrest her if she tried to cross the border into France. For more information, see Staël, *CGIII: 2*, 165–66, 190–91. As Jasinski pointed out, it is likely that the characterization of Mme de Staël as *persona non grata* in France was due to a transcription error on the part of the officer of the department of Ain (ibid., 204)

82. For an extract from Monachon's secret report about Mme de Staël that called into question her republican credentials and accused her of opportunism, see ibid., 194.

83. "Dans un temps de révolution, il faut du fanatisme pour triompher, et jamais un parti mixte n'inspira du fanatisme. Les Vendéens et les républicains peuvent se battre, et la chance du combat rester incertaine. Mais toutes les opinions placées entre les deux partis éxigent une sorte de raisonnement dont un esprit enthousiaste est incapable" (*OCS*, I: 54). During a private dinner with a few friends who belonged to the camp of moderate constitutionalists, Mme de Staël said: "Dans un état de fermentation, toutes les opinions extrêmes tendent à prévaloir, et vous, constitutionnels modérés, après avoir été victimes sous le règne d'une faction sanguinaire, vous le serez encore sous le règne d'une faction violente" (Staël, *CGIII: 2*, 48). See also the following fragment: "L'impulsion, le choc d'une révolution fait aller les opinions aux deux extrêmes opposés; non-seulement un troisième parti est difficile à faire triompher, mais il faudrait que les constitutionnels en soutinssent un quatrième; et un tel équilibre, à travers tant d'écueils, paraît tout à fait impossible" (*OCS*, I: 48).

84. "Nous avons tous transigé pour le bien avec le mal: ce joug des circonstances a pèsé sur les cœurs les plus purs . . . rien aujourd'hui n'est vrai, rien n'est équitable, que d'une manière rélative" (ibid., 59).

85. "Vous avez à choisir entre la dictature des institutions et celles des persécutions, et je préfère de beaucoup la première. . . . S'il faut une dictature, c'est-à-dire une suspension de l'exercice de la volonté de tous, comment ne pas la chercher dans des institutions légales, au lieu de l'abandonner à des violences arbitraires?" (Staël, *DCA*, 177).

86. *OCS*, I: 46. Also: "Cette fermentation brûlante produit un monde nouveau; un jour peut rendre impossible le plan de la veille; et c'est pour qui tend toujours au même but, la liberté, que les moyens changent sans cesse" (ibid., 50). The standard reference remains Basil Munteano, *Les idées politiques de Mme de Staël et la Constitution de l'an III* (Paris: Les Belles Lettres, 1931), 17. To Roederer, Staël wrote on July 17, 1796: "La république de 1795 est la moralité de tous les temps" (Staël, *CGIII: 2*, 9). On August 20, she remarked: "Que la Constitution soit entre les mains des honnêtes gens, et cette Constitution sera reconnue ce qu'elle est, la plus raisonnable de l'univers" (ibid., 230).

87. "Les hommes ignorants veulent être libres; les esprits éclairés savent seuls comment on peut l'être" (*OCS*, I: 46).

88. Staël, *DCA*, 313.

89. Ibid., 49. As Lucien Jaume has noted (in OCS[NS] III: 1, 173, n. 42), this view seems to contradict Mme de Staël's later skepticism toward invoking circumstantial justifications in *De l'Allemagne* (Part III, Ch. XIII).

90. See Jasinski's note in Staël, *CGIII*: 2, 23.

91. *OCS*, I: 46.

92. Ibid., 53.

93. Ibid., 58.

94. To Roederer's reservations about Constant's *Des réactions politiques*, she replied: "Vous vous amusez à combattre des ombres, tandis que l'ennemi le plus rédoubtable, l'ennemi sans appel, est à vos portes. . . . Les républicains ne sont pas si aimables, j'en conviens, mais qu'importe ce qu'ils sont lorsque la liberté périt de toutes parts? Vous rassemblez aux girondins qui, ménacés par les jacobins, criaient sans cesse au royalisme. Il n'y a de danger que du côté de l'aristocratie, et là est la haine éternelle" (quoted in Henri Grange, *Benjamin Constant amoreux et républicain. 1795–1799* [Paris : Les Belles Lettres, 2004], 163–64).

95. The distinction between "legal" and "real" majority can also be found in the writings of Roederer, most notably: "De la majorité nationale de la manière dont elle se forme et des signes auxquels on peut la reconnaître, ou théorie de l'opinion publique" (1795), republished in *Mémoires d'économie publique, de morale et de politique* (Paris: Imprimerie du Journal de Paris, 1799), I: 75–88 (as well as in Jaume, *Échec au libéralisme*, 98–105).

96. Staël, *DCA*, 132.

97. Mallet du Pan denounced the latter as follows: "Cette modération qui a le cachet de la *peur* et que fort peu de gens croient utile et systématique, enfin cette *indifférence* affectée sur des dangers qu'on n'a l'air ni de prévoir ni de vouloir prévenir, font perdre aux Conseils ces avantages moraux et politiques qui feraient triompher leur cause, sans aucun doute, s'ils osaient en faire usage" (quoted in Staël, *DCA*, 138–39, n. 4).

98. A. C. Thibaudeau, *Mémoires sur la Convention et le Directoire*, (Paris: Baudoin Frères, 1824), II: 211. In a letter sent to Thibaudeau after 18th Fructidor, Mme de Staël expressed her admiration for his republican commitment (see Blennerhassett, *Madame de Staël*, II: 345).

99. I borrow the term from Serna, *La République des girouettes*.

100. Necker's letter to Meister is quoted in Grange, *Les idées de Necker*, 462.

101. Quoted in G. E. Gwynne, *Mme de Staël et la Révolution française* (Paris: A.-G. Nizet, 1969), 29. Gwynne's is one of the best analyses of Mme de Staël's *political* thought.

102. Staël, *CGIII*: 2, 275.

103. *OCS*, I: 61.

104. Staël, *DCA*, 48.

105. Ibid., 152.

106. See ibid., 143–52.

107. See Gerard Gengembre and Jean Goldzink, "Une femme révolutionnée: le Thermidor de Mme de Staël," *ABC*, 8–9 (1988): 275–91. See also Henri Grange, "Mme de Staël et la Constitution de l'an III: avant et après," in Gérard Conac and Jean-Pierre Machelon, eds., *La Constitution de l'an III*, 183–99. Pierre Rosanvallon demonstrated why democracy had so few defenders in the aftermath of the Terror

(Rosanvallon, "The History of the Word 'Democracy' in France," *Journal of Democracy*, 6-4 [1995]: 140–54).

108. On Mme de Staël's elitist form of republicanism, see the following fragment from her letter to Lameth of November 24, 1796: "Le gouvernement ne peut aller que par l'aristocratie des meilleurs, mais ce qui m'attache à la constitution actuelle, c'est la répugnance que j'aurais au rétablissement de l'hérédité, sous quelque forme que ce soit" (Staël, *CGIII*: 2, 275).

109. Staël, *DCA*, 188. Also: "C'est par l'élection libre et sagement combinée que vous consacrerez l'inégalité naturelle, seule remède aux suites funestes de l'inégalité factice" (ibid., 40).

110. "Mettez le pouvoir et la fortune ensemble: vous n'aurez pas encore tout fait, si vous n'y joignez les vertus et les lumières" (ibid., 169).

111. Ibid., 169–70.

112. Ibid., 111.

113. *OCS*, I: 58.

114. Staël, *DCA*, 19.

115. See the analysis of Paulet-Grandguillot in *Libéralisme et démocratie*, 206–209.

116. Staël, *CPE*, 379; she also included Daunou on this list. The contribution of these thinkers to the development of French liberalism is analyzed in Jean-Paul Clément, *Aux sources du libéralisme français: Boissy d'Anglas, Daunou, Lanjuinais* (Paris: Librairie Générale de Droit et de Jurisprudence, 2000).

117. See also Jainchill, *Reimagining Politics*, 26–61; Lahmer, *La constitution américaine*, 135–64; and Stefano Mannoni, *Une et indivisible. Storia dell'accentramento amministrativo in Francia* (Milan: Giuffrè, 1994).

118. *OCS*, I: 5.

119. Ibid., 51.

120. Ibid., 52.

121. Staël, *DCA*, 186.

122. Ibid., 181–82, 191.

123. Ibid., 171. The "eloquent thinker" invoked by Mme de Staël was, most likely, Necker. Lahmer also suggested the name of Sieyès.

124. Ibid., 181.

125. Staël, *CGIII*: 2, 15–17; emphases added. It is interesting to note that, in Roederer's view, it was the composition of the Directory that contained the seeds of factions and disunion. "Le Directoire exécutif," he wrote on July 18, 1795 in the *Journal de Paris*, "tel que le projet l'annonce est un berceau, qu'on nous passe ce mot, *un nid* de factions ennemies" (ibid., 16, fn. 6). See also Henri Grange, "Mme de Staël et la Constitution de l'an III: avant et après," 186–87.

126. Staël, *DCA*, 181.

127. On Sieyès' proposals for a *jury constitutionnaire*, see chapter 6 below. Here is what Mme de Staël wrote: "Je voudrais que les attributs de ce Jury constitutionnaire fussent réunis à la puissance du Conseil des Anciens, parce qu'il serait à craindre qu'un corps dont on n'aurait besoin que pour décider les querelles entre les pouvoirs et qui resterait pendant les intervalles constamment étranger à l'exercise du pouvoir, aux intérêts habituels des hommes, fût bientôt oublié et ne possédât pas cette considération qui se compose des lumières, de la fortune et surtout du crédit" (*DCA*, 163)

128. I commented on this issue in Craiutu, "Tocqueville's Paradoxical Moderation," *Review of Politics*, 67: 4 (2005): 599–629. Anticipating Tocqueville, Mme de Staël wrote that democratic principles must be placed "sous la sauvegarde des formes aristocratiques," adding that "la démocratie ne se détruit qu'avec les principes de la démocratie" (*DCA*, 164, 174).

129. See Olivier Passelecq, "Actualité de la Constitution de l'an III," in Conac and Machelon, eds., *La Constitution de l'an III*, 94.

130. Staël, *CPE*, 201.

131. Thibaudeau, *Mémoires*, II: 20.

132. See Staël, *CPE*, 412.

133. Ibid., 402.

134. Quoted in Fairweather, *Mme de Staël*, 236.

135. Staël, *CPE*, 396, 399. She came to view the second half of the Directory as dominated by an intolerant and inhuman oligarchy, which created a regime nourished on corruption (see Blennerhassett, *Madame de Staël*, vol. 2, 337–47).

136. Mauro Barberis, "Constant, Mme de Staël et la constitution républicaine: un essai d'interprétation," in *Le groupe de Coppet et le monde moderne: conceptions-images-débats*, Francoise Tilkin, ed. (Geneva: Droz, 1998), 193.

137. Gengembre and Goldzink, "Une femme révolutionnée," 275. See also Roland Mortier, "Comment terminer la Révolution et fonder la République," *ABC* 8–9 (1988): 293–307.

138. Staël, *DCA*, 4–5.

139. A similar concern can be found in Benjamin Constant's lecture, "The Liberty of the Moderns Compared to the Liberty of the Ancients," which drew inspiration from Mme de Staël's writings.

140. "Les passions des hommes sont aussi susceptible de calcul que les frottements dans les machines. . . . Le dernier dégré de la perfectibilité de l'esprit humain, c'est l'application du calcul à toutes les branches du système moral. Il y a donc un grand avantage à fonder son gouvernement sur des principes géometriquement vrais" (Staël, *DCA*, 27).

141. Ibid., 44. This point must be linked to her apology of writers and philosophers later in the book. For a general view on the role of intellectuals during this period, see *Tropes of Revolution: Writers' Reaction to Real and Imagined Revolutions, 1789–1989*, C. C. Barfoot and Theo D'haen, eds. (Amsterdam: Rodopi, 1991).

142. See chapter V of *DCA*. The naiveté of Mme de Staël's views on the Directory a year after 18th Fructidor and shortly before its demise in November 1799 has not passed unnoticed among her interpreters and remains an object of speculation and controversy. See, for example, Gengembre and Goldzink, "Une femme révolutionnée," 280–89.

143. Staël, *DCA*, 119–20.

144. Why Mme de Staël chose not to send this manuscript to press (a similar fate befell her *RPI*) remains unclear. Benjamin Constant had read the entire manuscript and made numerous comments in the margin.

145. For a comprehensive analysis, see Patrice Gueniffey, *Le Dix-huit Brumaire: L'épilogue de la Révolution française* (Paris: Gallimard, 2008).

146. See chapter 4 above.

147. "I felt in my soul a cold sharp-edged sword, which froze the wound that it inflicted" (Staël, *CPE*, 199).

148. Quoted in Fairweather, *Mme de Staël*, 275.

149. Ibid., 293.

150. See Mme de Staël, *Ten Years of Exile*, trans. Doris Beik (New York: Saturday Review Press, 1972), 4.

151. Staël, *CPE*, 535–36.

152. Ibid., 197.

153. Ibid., 517.

154. Ibid., 521.

155. Ibid., 516.

156. Ibid., 536.

157. Ibid., 586.

158. Ibid., 619.

159. Ibid., 566. Mme de Staël reopened her salon at the Hôtel Lamoignon, where she began to receive her guests again; see Blenerhassett, *Madame de Staël*, III: 493–518.

160. See the description given by Charles de Rémusat in *Mémoires de ma vie*, (Paris: Plon, 1958), I: 202–203.

161. For more details, see Herold, *Mistress to an Age*, 544–49, 562–78.

162. Although Mme de Staël worked on the book for a few years, at the time of her death she managed to revise only the first two volumes and a part of the third. The task of preparing the final manuscript fell to her son and son-in-law, Auguste de Staël and Victor de Broglie, assisted by her friend, August Wilhelm von Schlegel, who published the French text of the *Considérations* in 1818, after editing the last part of the book. A French critical edition of this important book has yet to be published. For more information, see my introduction ("A Thinker for Our Times: Madame de Staël, Her Life and Works") to Staël, *CPE*, vii–xxiv.

163. Staël, *CPE*, 17.

164. On the polemic triggered by the publication of *Considérations*, see Tribouillard, *Le Tombeau de Madame de Staël*; Frank P. Bowman, "La polemique sur les *Considérations sur la Révolution française*," *ABC* 8–9 (1988): 225–41; Blennerhassett, *Madame de Staël*, III: 578–86; Michael Delon, "Germaine de Staël and Other Possible Scenarios of the Revolution," in *Crossing the Borders*, 24–26.

165. From a review published in *Les Lettres normandes*, quoted in Ezio Cappadocia, "The Liberals and Mme de Staël in 1818" in *Ideas in History: Essays presented to Louis Gottschalk*, Richard Herr and Harold T. Parker, eds. (Durham, NC: Duke University Press, 1965), 193.

166. Rémusat's article appeared in *Archives politiques, philosophiques et littéraires*, V (1818).

167. Mme de Staël's book, Bonald dismissively remarked, is nothing but "a novel on politics and society, written under the influence of domestic affections and political passions which have occupied or agitated the author; it is still *Delphine* and *Corinne*, who make politics as if they were making love" (Bonald, *La vraie Révolution*, 83).

168. See ibid., 92–108. France, Bonald wrote, did have a constitution formed by "la royauté, la religion, et la justice" (ibid., 106).

169. For more details, see Pierre Rosanvallon, *La monarchie impossible. Les Chartes de 1814 et de 1830* (Paris: Fayard, 1994).

170. Staël, *CPE*, 559, 604.

171. Ibid., 558.

172. Ibid., 577.

173. Ibid., 602.

174. Ibid., 604.

175. Mme de Staël also referred in favorable terms to the principles of American democracy, and admired its constitution for its sound balance of power. She praised the Americans' dedication to political liberty and predicted the rise of the United States to the status of a superpower. "There is a people who will one day be very great," she wrote in the *Considérations*, "I mean the Americans. . . . What is there more honorable for mankind than this new world which has established itself without the prejudices of the old; this new world where religion is in all its fervor without needing the support of the state to maintain it, where the law commands by the respect it inspires, without being enforced by any military power?" (ibid., 707).

176. "The great problem that ministers had to solve in 1814 could have been studied in the history of England," Mme de Staël claimed. "They ought to have taken as a model the conduct of the House of Hanover, not that of the House of Stuart" (ibid., 601). She criticized, however, the attempt to create a peerage modeled upon the English upper class. On the image of England in her works, see Robert Escarpit, *L'Angleterre dans l'œuvre de Madame de Staël* (Paris: Didier, 1954).

177. Staël, *CPE*, 633.

178. Ibid., 607.

179. Ibid., 125.

180. Ibid., 237.

181. Ibid., 632.

182. Ibid., 602.

183. This system was developed in England and Germany and was linked to Protestantism.

184. Staël, *CPE*, 603.

185. Ibid., 664.

186. Ibid., 667.

187. See Gunn, *When the French Tried To Be British*, 3–10, 463–69.

188. Staël, *CPE*, 243.

189. Ibid., 244.

190. Ibid., 687.

191. Ibid., 678.

192. Constant as quoted on the back cover of Diesbach's *Madame de Staël*.

193. *MWGS*, 152.

194. Ibid., 322.

195. *OCS*, I: 147.

196. "Il faut de l'esprit de parti pour lutter efficacement avec un autre esprit de parti contraire, et tout ce que la raison trouve absurde est précisément ce qui doit réussir contre un ennemi qui prendra aussi des mésures absurdes; ce qui est au dernier terme de l'exagération transporté sur le terrain où il faut combattre, et donne des armes égales à celles de ses adversaries" (ibid., 147).

197. Staël, *DCA*, 284–85.

198. Ibid., 285.

199. Kaylvas and Katznelson, *Liberal Beginnings*, 137–40.

200. Gwynne, *Mme de Staël et la Révolution française*, 76.

201. For a similar view, see Baczko, "Opinions des vainqueurs," 199; Gwynne, *Mme de Staël et la Révolution française*, 56.

202. *MWGS*, 154.

Chapter Six: Moderation and "Neutral Power"

1. Benjamin Constant, *De la liberté chez les modernes*, Marcel Gauchet, ed. (Paris: Hachette, 1980), 519.

2. For an overview of Constant's reception, see Helena Rosenblatt, "Eclipses and Revivals: Constant's Reception in France and America, 1830–2007," in *The Cambridge Companion to Constant*, Helena Rosenblatt, ed. (New York: Cambridge University Press, 2009), 351–78. The *Companion* also contains a primary and secondary bibliography. On the place of Constant's individualist liberalism in modern French thought, see Laboulaye's preface to Benjamin Constant, *Cours de politique constitutionnelle ou collection des ouvrages publiés sur le gouvernement représentatif*, Édouard Laboulaye, ed., 2 vols. (Paris: Guillaumin, 1861); Jaume, *L'individu effacé*, 63–117; *Coppet, creuset de l'esprit libéral. Les idées politiques et constitutionnelles du groupe de Madame de Staël*, Lucien Jaume, ed. (Marseille and Paris: Presses Universitaires d'Aix-Marseille and Economica, 2000); and George Armstrong Kelly, *The Humane Comedy: Constant, Tocqueville, and French Liberalism* (Cambridge: Cambridge University Press, 1992). For a comprehensive analysis of Constant's political thought, see Paul Bastid, *Benjamin Constant et sa doctrine*, 2 vols. (Paris: Armand Colin, 1966). On Constant's liberalism and his intellectual dialogue with Rousseau, see Stephen T. Holmes, *Benjamin Constant and the Making of Modern Liberalism* (New Haven, CT: Yale University Press, 1984); on Constant as political thinker, see Armstrong Kelly, *The Humane Comedy*, chapter 2, and K. Steven Vincent, *Benjamin Constant and the Birth of French Liberalism* (Basingstoke: Palgrave Macmillan, 2011). On Constant's life, see Kurt Kloocke, *Benjamin Constant: Une biographie intellectuelle* (Geneva: Droz, 1984); and Dennis Wood, *Benjamin Constant: A Biography* (London: Routledge, 1993). A rich secondary literature on Constant can be found in *ABC*.

3. Three of Constant's most important texts during the Directory were edited by Philippe Raynaud and published in a single volume in 1988 (henceforth *DFGA*, *DRP*, *DET*); a critical edition of these texts can be found in *OCC*, IV. Constant's *De la force du gouvernement actuel* was translated into English as *Observations on the Strength of the Present Government of France and upon the Necessity of Rallying Round It*, trans. James Losh (Bath: R. Crittwell, 1797). The two editions of *Principes de politique* (1810–1810 and 1815) were translated into English as *Principles of Politics Applicable to All Governments*, trans. Dennis O'Keeffe (Indianapolis, IN: Liberty Fund, 2003) and *Principles of Politics* in *Political Writings*, trans. Biancamaria Fontana (Cambridge: Cambridge University Press, 1988). The first French edition of Constant's *Principes* (1806–1810) was published with an introduction and commentary by Étienne Hofmann in *"Les 'Principes de politique' de Benjamin Constant. La genèse d'une œuvre et l'evolution de la pensée de leur auteur* (1789–1806), 2, vols. (Geneva: Droz, 1980). The French text was republished in *OCC*, IX, 2, *Principes de politiques et autres écrits (juin 1814–juillet 1815)*, Olivier Devaux and Kurt Kloocke, eds. (Tübingen: Niemeyer Verlag, 2001), 653–858. One of Constant's most important works, *Fragments d'un ouvrage abandonné sur la possibilité d'une constitution républicaine dans un grand pays*, was never published during the author's life; the first edition (by Henri Grange) appeared at Aubier in 1991. A critical edition of the text has recently been published in *OCC*, IV. *Discours au Tribunat. De la possibilité d'une constitution républicaine dans un grand pays (1799–1803)*,

María Luisa Sánchez-Mejía and Kurt Kloocke, eds. (Tübingen: Niemeyer Verlag, 2005), 355–761. An edition of Constant's works (including some of his political writings) was also published in the prestigious Pléiade series (*Œuvres*, Alfred Roulin, ed. [Paris: Gallimard, 1957]).

4. This fragment is taken from a letter to Constant's cousin Rosalie, as quoted in Wood, *Benjamin Constant*, 243.

5. Much like Madame de Staël's husband, Constant was an avid gambler and shortly before his death, King Louis-Philippe gave him "in the name of liberty" a gift of 200,000 francs to pay off his gambling debts (ibid., 247).

6. See K. Steven Vincent, "Constant and Women," in *The Cambridge Companion to Constant*, 173–205.

7. Sainte-Beuve, *Portraits littéraires*, III (Paris: Garnier, 1878), 280.

8. See Benjamin Constant, *Mémoires sur les Cent-Jours* in OCC, IV, Kurt Kloocke, ed. (Tübingen: Max Niemeyer Verlag, 1993).

9. For a recent edition, see Benjamin Constant, *Commentaire sur l'ouvrage de Filangieri* (Paris: Les belles letters, 2004).

10. The importance of Constant's early years is discussed in Béatrice Jasinski, *L'engagement de Benjamin Constant. Amour et politique, 1794–1796*, (Paris: Minard, 1971).

11. The genesis of the original edition of *POP* (1806–1810) is explored in Hoffmann, *Les 'Principes de politique' de Benjamin Constant*.

12. In addition to Constant's *Fragments*, two other seminal political works belonging to other members of the Coppet group and written roughly during the same period were never published: Staël's *Des circonstances actuelles* and Sismondi's *Recherches sur les constitutions des peuples libres*, Marco Minerbi, ed. (Geneva: Droz, 1965).

13. See Helena Rosenblatt, *Liberal Values: Benjamin Constant and the Politics of Religion* (Cambridge: Cambridge University Press, 2008). Constant's views on religion were unconventional and some critics accused him of espousing a purely sentimental and individualist form of religion, drawing a fallacious distinction between religious sentiment and religious forms.

14. See Grange, *Les idées de Necker*, 495–502; "De l'influence de Necker sur les idées politiques de Benjamin Constant," *ABC*, 2 (1982): 73–80; Jaume, *L'individu effacé*, 108.

15. Most recently by Winegarten, *Germaine de Staël and Benjamin Constant*; also see Jasinski, *L'engagement de Benjamin Constant*, 9–70. Jasinski also pointed out the differences between Constant and Mme de Staël. Henri Guillemin suggested that Constant might have been attracted not so much by Madame de Staël's intellect or beauty as by Necker's fabulous wealth (Guillemin, *Benjamin Constant muscadin, 1795–1799* [Paris: Gallimard, 1958]).

16. Here is how Constant described his relationship with Mme de Staël in his diary (January 26, 1803): "Depuis huit ans, Germaine me fait vivre dans un orage perpétuel, ou plutôt dans une complication d'orages. . . . Je n'ai pas passé un jour sans être en fureur et contre elle et contre moi" (Constant, *Œuvres*, 199–200). In a letter of January 23, 1796 to her former lover Ribbing, Madame de Staël described Constant's character in unflattering words: "C'est un homme d'un esprit très supérieur, quoi que l'on puisse vous dire, et il en est peu qui, comme société, convienent autant à mes goûts de conversation et surtout de littérature. . . . Du caractère et de la figure lui manquent absolument" (*CGIII*: II, 120). In a previous letter to the same Ribbing from

March 3, 1795, Madame de Staël had this to say about Constant: "C'est un fou de beaucoup d'esprit, et singulierement laid, mais c'est un fou" (Staël, *CGIII*: I, 264).

17. Kalyvas and Katznelson, *Liberal Beginnings*, 146. For a different view, see Gérard Gengembre, "Le Cercle constitutionnel: un laboratoire du libéralisme," 147, fn. 39.

18. All of them were collected in OCC, I.

19. Mauro Barberis, *Sette studi sur liberalismo rivoluzionario* (Torino: Il Mulino, 1989); *Benjamin Constant: Rivoluzione, costituzione, progresso* (Torino: Il Mulino,1988); Stefano de Luca, *Alle origini del liberalismo contemporaneo: il pensiero di Benjamin Constant tra il Termidoro e l'impero* (Lungro Cosenza: Marco, 2003); Vincent, *Benjamin Constant and the Birth of French Liberalism*; and Hofmann, *"Les 'Principes de politique' de Benjamin Constant."*

20. Constant, "De Madame de Staël et de ses ouvrages," in *Œuvres*, 843–44.

21. See de Luca, *Alle origini del liberalismo contemporaneo*, 17.

22. Constant, *DFGA, DRP, DET*, 96. I also recommend Philippe Raynaud's excellent introduction to this edition; it was reprinted as "Comment terminer la Révolution" in Raynaud, *Trois révolutions de la liberté: Angleterre, Amérique, France* (Paris: PUF, 2009), 255–69.

23. "Tous les freins se brisent, tous les parties deviennent également coupables, toutes les bornes sont depasées; les forfaits sont punis par des forfaits; le sentiment de l'innocence . . . n'existe nulle part, et toute une génération pervertie par l'arbitraire, est poussée loin des lois par tous les motifs, par la crainte et par la vengeance, par la fureur et par le remords" (Constant, *DFGA, DRP, DET,* 97).

24. The partial renewal of the Convention was also defended by moderates like Boissy d'Anglas. The two decrees were submitted to popular referendum at the same time as the final text of the Constitution of Year III. Only 200,000 votes in favor were counted (100,000 votes against). For more information, see OCC, I: 283, fn 1. The decision to invoke the *salus populi* was criticized later by Mme de Staël in *DCA*, 242–68, 314–15.

25. See Vincent, *Benjamin Constant and the Birth of French Liberalism*, 39–80; de Luca, "Benjamin Constant and the Terror," 92–114; *The French Revolution and the Creation of Modern Political Culture*, 4: *The Terror*, Keith M. Baker, ed. (Oxford: Pergamon Press, 1994), 3–54, 327–46.

26. Constant's letters were republished in *OCC*, I: 277–88. They triggered a powerful response from Jean-Baptiste Louvet, an ex-Girondist with whom Constant later co-authored three important discourses that expressed support for the renewal of two-thirds of the Convention (ibid., 309–18).

27. Ibid., 281.

28. Ibid., 284.

29. In Mauro Barberis's view, Constant's change was neither a mere strategic adjustment nor an expression of opportunism; it was in accord with his overall attitude during Thermidor and the Directory. Barberis also saw in Constant's change a move to the left and a departure from the centrist position held by Mme de Staël during this period.

30. *OCC,* I: 305.

31. Vincent, *Benjamin Constant and the Birth of French Liberalism*, 90.

32. On this issue, see Grange, *Benjamin Constant amoureux et republicain, 1795–1799* (Paris: Les Belles Lettres, 2004). Grange's book is highly critical of Constant and must be taken with a grain of salt.

33. Constant, *POP (1806–1810)*, 415.

34. Ibid., 420.

35. Ibid., 419. "Everything is only mire and blood and dust," writes Constant (ibid., 420).

36. Ibid., 420.

37. Constant, *OSPG*, 99.

38. Ibid., 99.

39. Constant, *DFGA, DRP, DET,* 127.

40. Madame de Staël had this to say about Constant's "brochure" in a letter to Roederer on July 17, 1796: "Séparez de ce livre ce qui peut être blamé dans quelques endroits, et voyez s'il est possible de mettre plus d'idées et de style dans une brochure. . . . Enfin, il y a des pages dans cette brochure que je crois à l'égal de ce que nous admirons le plus dans la langue française" (Staël, *CGIII*: 2, 217–18). Roederer commented on Constant's book in *Journal de Paris* (June 11, 1796). Among other things, he was displeased by Constant's highly polemical comments about journalists (like himself) who had remained skeptical toward the Directory. Two decades later, when Constant himself published a four-volume edition of his writings on representative government (1819–20), he did *not* include *De la force du gouvernement actuel.* For an analysis of the latter, see Vincent, *Benjamin Constant and the Birth of French Liberalism*, 52–63.

41. Constant, *OSPG*, 21.

42. Ibid., 21.

43. Ibid., 31.

44. Ibid., 9.

45. Ibid., 10.

46. Ibid., 30.

47. Ibid., 29.

48. Ibid., 27–28.

49. Ibid., 62.

50. See ibid., 62–63. On the evolution of public opinion during this period, see Grange, *Benjamin Constant,* 100–102.

51. A similar position can be found in Constant's speeches at the Constitutional Circle in 1797 collected in *OCC,* I. Also see Vincent, *Benjamin Constant and the Birth of French Liberalism*, 63–67, 76–90.

52. Constant, *DFGA, DRP, DET,* 138, 141. "Je ne méconnais point l'empire des circonstances," Constant wrote. "Mais on ne doit pas oublier combien dans ce genre l'abus est facile. Si l'on n'y prend garde, il y aura toujours des circonstances à invoquer contre les principes. Les factions marcheront de circonstances en circonstances, sans cesse en dehors de la loi, tantôt avec des intentions pures, tantôt avec des projects perfides, demandant éternellement de grandes mésures, au nom du Peuple, de la liberté, de la patrie. . . . Dans tout ce que le salut public éxige, il y a deux manières de procéder, l'une légale, l'autre arbitraire" (ibid., 85).

53. Ibid., 104.

54. "Ceux-là enfin sont partisans de l'arbitraire qui, prétendant avec Burke, que des axioms, métaphysiquement vrais, peuvent être politiquement faux, préferent à ces axioms des considérations, des préjugés, des souvenirs, des faiblesses, toutes choses vagues, indéfinissables, ondoyantes, rentrant par conséquent dans le domaine de l'arbitraire" (ibid., 142). Also see Raynaud's preface to Constant, *DFGA, DRP, DET,*

22–26, and Vincent, *Benjamin Constant and the Birth of French Liberalism*, 120–24.

55. Serna, *La République des girouettes*, 420.

56. See P.-L. Roederer, *The Spirit of the Revolution of 1789 and Other Writings of the Revolutionary Epoch* (1789–1815), M. Forsyth, ed. (Aldershot: Scholar Press, 1989); also Ruth Scurr, "Pierre-Louis Roederer and the Debate on Forms of Government in Revolutionary France," *Political Studies* 52 (2004): 251–68; and Thierry Lentz, "La presse républicaine modérée sous la Convention thermidorienne et le Directoire: Pierre-Louis Roederer, animateur et propriétaire du 'Journal de Paris,' et du 'Journal d'économie publique,'" *Revue historique* 292-2 (1994): 297–313.

57. Edgar Quinet wryly noted: "Les Jacobins ont pu, en d'autres temps, rêver de la dictature; mais bien certainement, ce sont les modérés qui l'ont faite" (quoted in Serna, *La République des girouettes*, 414).

58. Serna, *La République des girouettes*, 417.

59. See François Furet and Denis Richet, *French Revolution* (New York: Macmillan, 1970). Also see *OCC*, I: 305, fn. 4.

60. See chapter VIII of Constant's *Des réactions politiques*.

61. Hofmann, *Les 'Principes de politique' de Benjamin Constant*, 156. Also see Gérard Gengembre, "Le Cercle constitutionnel: un laboratoire du libéralisme," in *Benjamin Constant et la Révolution française, 1790–1799*, Dominique Verrey and Anne-Lise Delacrétaz, eds. [Geneva: Droz, 1989], 149).

62. Constant, *DFGA, DRP, DET*, 130.

63. Ibid., 130.

64. Ibid. In a June 1794 letter to Isabelle de Charrière, Constant had previosuly expressed skepticism toward the possibility of a center: "To occupy the middle ground is to take up a worthless position, at this juncture it is more worthless than ever. That is my profession of faith" (quoted in Vincent, *Benjamin Constant and the Birth of French Liberalism*, 34).

65. Grange, *Benjamin Constant*, 11.

66. For more details, see Egon Graf von Westerholt, *Lezay-Marnésia, Sohn der Aufklärung and Präfekt Napoleons (1769–1814)* (Meisenheim am Glan: Anton Hain Verlag, 1958), 39–62. On the intellectual dialogue between Constant and Lezay-Marnésia, see de Luca, "Benjamin Constant and the Terror;" and Raynaud's introduction to Constant, *DFGA, DRP, DET*, 8–20; Vincent, *Benjamin Constant and the Birth of French Liberalism*, 65–66.

67. Adrien Lezay-Marnésia, *De la faiblesse d'un gouvernement qui commence, et de la nécessité où il est de se rallier á la majorité nationale* (Paris: Mathey, Desenne, Maret, 1796), 60.

68. Ibid., 60.

69. Ibid., 61.

70. Ibid., 58–59.

71. Ibid., 14–15. The distinction between "legal" and "real" majority can also be found in the writings of Roederer of that period. Therefore, it is possible that Lezay might have borrowed it from Roederer's "De la majorité nationale de la manière dont elle se forme et des signes auxquels on peut la reconnaître, ou théorie de l'opinion publique" (1795).

72. Lezay-Marnésia, *De la faiblesse d'un gouvernement*, 61.

73. On Say's contributions to *La Décade philosophique, littéraire et politique*, see

Richard Whatmore, *Republicanism and the French Revolution: An Intellectual History of Jean-Baptiste Say's Political Economy* (Oxford: Oxford University Press, 2000), 117–20.

74. Quoted in Serna, *La République des girouettes*, 441.

75. Ibid., 442.

76. For more details, see Grange, *Benjamin Constant*, 175–83; Gengembre, "Le Cercle constitutionnel," 149. As already mentioned, the Constitution of 1795 did not provide for effective means of resolving the tensions between the executive and legislative powers.

77. *La Décade philosophique, littéraire et politique*, 24 (May 19, 1798): 377–80; also quoted in Serna, *La République des girouettes*, 447–48. Thanks to Michael Sonenscher for sending a copy of Say's original article.

78. Serna, *La République des girouettes*, 447.

79. See *OCC*, I: 594.

80. The words belong to a contemporary of Constant, the deputy Jean de Bry, as quoted in Jasinski, "Constant et le Cercle constitutonnel," 120. De Bry was allegedly among the founding members of the circle, along with Talleyrand, Réal, Garat, and Constant.

81. Constant praised Barras for his service to the Republic and claimed that, in spite of his flaws, Barat was "le point de force du Directoire"; see Béatrice Jasinski, "Constant et le Cercle constitutionnel," in *Benjamin Constant et la Révolution française*, 123.

82. See Jasinski, "Constant et le Cercle constitutionnel," 119–40; Gengembre, "Le Cercle constitutionnel," 141–49.

83. "Discours prononcé au Cercle constitutionnel pour la plantation de l'arbre de la liberté" (*OCC*, I: 551–62). Equally important is the speech given on 9th Ventose Year VI (27 February 1798), also at the Constitutional Circle, in which Constant launched a formidable attack on the neo-Jacobins (ibid., 585–601).

84. Ibid., 555; see also ibid., 553–54; Gengembre, "Le Cercle constitutionnel," 144–47.

85. On the one hand, Constant argued that "rien ne peut suppléer à l'arbitraire que la force morale des institutions" (*OCC*, I: 555). On the other hand, he claimed: "Il ne faut pas que sur toute l'étendue de la République, il se trouve dans une fonction quelconque, depuis l'administrateur municipal de la plus petite jusqu'aux dépositaires suprêmes de l'autorité exécutive . . . un seul homme qui ne soit solidaire de la liberté républicaine" (ibid.).

86. Ibid., 590–91.

87. Ibid., 594–96.

88. Ibid., 559.

89. "Il ne faut jamais supposer que, dans aucune circonstance, une puissance illimitée puisse être admissible, et, dans la realité, jamais elle n'est nécessaire" (Constant, *DFGA, DRP, DET*, 166).

90. De Luca, "Benjamin Constant and the Terror," 114. Also see Léonard Burnand, "Benjamin Constant et l'interprétation de la Terreur," *ABC*, 35 (2010): 43–56; Patrice Thompson, "La Terreur de Benjamin Constant," in *Benjamin Constant et la Révolution française*, 61–72; François Furet, "La Terreur sous le Directoire," in *The French Revolution and the Creation of Modern Political Culture, 3: The Transformation of Political Culture 1789–1848*, François Furet and Mona Ozouf, eds. (Oxford: Pergamon Press, 1990), 173–86.

91. Joseph de Maistre also argued that violence had played an essential role during the revolution (see chapter 2 of *Considérations sur la France*). See also Susan Tenenbaum, "The Politics of History," *ABC*, (8–9): 96–99.

92. The importance of this text is illustrated by the fact that Constant chose to include it in his last published book, *Mélanges de littérature et politique* (1829), his political testament. For more details, see Burnand, "Benjamin Constant et l'interprétation de la Terreur," 51–54.

93. A favorable review of Lezay-Marnésia's book was published in *La Décade philosophique, littéraire et politique*, 23 (May 9, 1797): 273–79.

94. Lezay-Marnésia, *Des causes de la révolution*, 12–13.

95. "Il restera de la révolution un esprit de liberté qui s'opposera desormais à toute tyrannie durable.... Ce résultat est le plus solide de tous; mais c'est aussi le moins brillant" (ibid., 44).

96. Ibid., 14, 20.

97. Benjamin Constant, "Histoire abrégée de l'égalité" in Beatrice Fink, "Un inédit de Benjamin Constant," *Dix-huitiéme siècle* 14 (1982): 199–218. This text was most likely written during the second half of the Directory.

98. Constant, *DFGA, DRP, DET*, 167.

99. Ibid., 172–73.

100. On the influence of Rousseau in France, see Roussel, *Jean-Jacques Rousseau en France après la Révolution*. On the dialogue between Constant and Rousseau, see Holmes, *Benjamin Constant and the Making of Modern Liberalism*, 79–103; Bertrand de Jouvenel, *On Power: Its Nature and the History of Its Growth*, trans. J. F. Huntington (New York: Viking, 1949), chapters 2, 14–16.

101. It is worth noting that Sismondi took a different route, as Paulet-Grandguillot demonstrated in *Libéralisme et démocratie*, 394–95. As a result, she wrote, "Le Rousseau de Sismondi s'en trouve plus complexe et beaucoup moins caricatural que celui de Constant" (395).

102. "Le besoin constant de l'espèce humaine," Constant wrote, "c'est l'égalité. Quelques tentatives qu'on ait faites pour obscurcir cette vérité, les hommes naissent égaux, c'est-à-dire, la différence des forces physiques et des facultés morales ne serait jamais de nature à fonder une inégalité permanente, si des institutions crées pas ceux qui sont les plus forts momentanément, ne venaient à l'appui de ces disproportions passagères. Suspendez l'action de ces institutions, les faibles se reuniront contre le fort qui les opprime, et leur réunion rétablira l'équilibre" ("Histoire abrégée de l'égalité," 205–206). Also: "L'amour de l'égalité est une passion, allumée au fond de nos cœurs par la nature" (ibid., 208–209). Constant's text remained incomplete. In the plan he made for the rest of this work, he indicated his intention to examine, in Rousseau's footsteps, how inequality developed from this natural desire for equality. It is likely that the development of Constant's plan examining the factors that prevented equality from existing in all human societies would have required a sustained engagement with Rousseau's ideas on this topic.

103. Constant, *POP (1806–1810)*, 20.

104. "Le principe sur lequel repose le besoin d'unité du corps electoral est donc complètement erroné" (Constant, *Fragments*, 309). Constant's emphasis on the importance of limiting sovereignty was highlighted by Jouvenel in *On Power*, 26–42.

105. Constant, *Fragments*, 408.

106. See Constant, *POP (1815)*, 177. Also see the following claim: "Ce sont les individus, ce sont les sections qui composent le corps politique. Ce sont par con-

séquent les intérêts de ces individus et de ces sections qui doivent être protégés" (Constant, *Fragments,* 309).

107. Constant, *POP (1806–1810),* 33.

108. Ibid., 21.

109. Ibid., 36.

110. Ibid., 19.

111. Selections from Constant's writings in *French Liberalism, 1789–1848,* Walter Simon, ed. (New York: John Wiley and Sons, 1972), 67.

112. Ibid., 67.

113. Constant, *POP (1806–1810),* 31.

114. Constant, *POP (1815),* 182.

115. The same idea appeared in Constant, *POP (1806–1810),* 37.

116. Simon, ed., *French Liberalism,* 68. This idea underscored Constant's belief that "the boundaries within which the authority must be kept are fixed by justice. and by the rights of individuals" (ibid., 67).

117. J.C.L. Simonde de Sismondi, *Political Economy and the Philosophy of Government* (London: John Chapman, 1847), reprinted with the same title (New York: Augustus M. Kelley, 1966). See also ibid., 411–13; and Sismondi, *Recherches sur les constitutions,* 162.

118. See Constant, *POP (1815),* 175–82; Paulet-Grandguillot, *Libéralisme et démocratie,* 208–13, 359–62.

119. See Constant, *Principes de politique* (Hoffman, ed.), 115. As Luigi Lacchè argued, it is this form of *garantisme* that, along with other things, made French constitutionalism different from its Anglo-American counterpart (Lacchè, "Coppet et la percée de l'État libéral constitutionnel," in *Coppet, creuset de l'esprit libéral,* 135–55).

120. Constant, *POP (1806–1810),* 385, 393.

121. Constant, *Fragments,* 278–79.

122. Ibid., 287.

123. Ibid., 288. Note Constant's affinity with Necker on this issue. The emphasis on accommodation and moderation is particularly important and can also be found in chapter 8 of Constant's *POP* (1815).

124. "Aucune de nos constitutions libres n'avait assigné de limites au pouvoir législatif. Or, lorsque le pouvoir législatif n'a point de limites, lorsque les représentants de la nation se croient investis d'une souveraineté sans bornes, lorsqu'il n'existe de contrepoids à leurs décrets, ni dans le pouvoir exécutif, ni dans le pouvoir judiciaire, alors la tyrannie des élus du peuple est aussi desastreuse que toute autre tyrannie, quelque dénomination qu'elle porte " (Constant, *Fragments,* 295).

125. *"Elle n'établissait contre ses excès aucun contrepoids,* elle ne consacrait ni l'indispensable veto du pouvoir exécutif, ni la possibilité non moins indispensable de la dissolution des assemblées représentatives, elle ne garantissait pas même, comme certaines constitutions américaines, les droits les plus sacrés des individus contre les empiètements des législateurs. . . . Il n'en fallait point accuser le mode de nomination des législateurs despotes, mais la nature de leur autorité: la faute n'en était pas au choix fait par les représentes, mais aux pouvoirs sans frein des représentants. . . . Ce mal tenait à ce que *leur volonté décorée du nom de loi n'était contrebalancée, reprimée, arrêtée par rien*" (ibid., 295–96; all emphases added).

126. "La faiblesse d'une partie quelconque du gouvernement est un mal" (ibid., 152).

127. Ibid., 235–36.

128. "Toutes les erreurs du Directoire sont venues, non de sa complexité, mais de ce que la constitution l'avait organisé faiblement, et l'absence des prérogatives les plus ncessaries a été la cause de ce qu'il a saisi des pouvoirs arbitraires et illimités" (ibid., 248); see also 245–46.

129. Constant, *POP (1806–1810)*, 47. On the differences between Necker and Constant, see Étienne Hofmann, "Necker, Constant, et la question constitutionnelle (1800–1802)," *CS* 36 (1985): 78–79, 83–84.

130. As quoted in Constant, *POP (1806–1810)*, 47.

131. Ibid., 54.

132. Ibid., 56.

133. For Necker's position, see *OCN*, XI: 155. Constant's ideas on political responsibility are analyzed in Lucien Jaume, "Le concept de 'responsabilité des ministres' chez Benjamin Constant," *Revue francaise de droit constitutionnel* 42 (2000): 227–43; Mart Hartman, "Benjamin Constant and the Question of Ministerial Responsibility in France, 1814–1815," *Journal of European Studies* 6 (1976): 248–61; Gunn, *When the French Tried to Be British,* 301–10.

134. Necker, *OCN*, XI: 155.

135. Constant, *Fragments,* 287–88.

136. A first edition of *De la responsabilité des ministres* appeared on February 1, 1815; a second revised edition was included in the 1818 edition of *Collection complète des ouvrages publiés sur le gouvernement représentatif . . . formant une espèce de cours de politique constitutionnelle,* II (Paris: Plancher, 1818).

137. Constant's book ended with an appeal to all friends of liberty, inviting them to acknowledge that "without a constitutional monarchy, there will be no secure liberty in France" (*De la responsabilité,* 98). This claim was surprising, given his belief that forms of government were less important than liberty.

138. Ibid., 1.

139. Ibid., 91.

140. On this topic, see Alain Laquièze, "Benjamin Constant et l'Acte Additionnel aux Constitutions de l'Empire du 22 Avril 1815," *Historia constitutional* 4 (2003): 197–234, http://www.historiaconstitucional.com/index.php/historiaconstitucional/article/view/197/175 (accessed July 1, 2010). Constant's change occurred soon after he declared in strong terms his distrust of Napoleon and support for the Bourbons in an article published in *Journal des débats* on March 19. Constant wrote: "Nous subirions sous Bonaparte un gouvernement de mamelouks, son glaive seul nous gouvernerait (. . .) C'est Attila, c'est Gengis Khan, plus terrible et plus odieux, parce que les ressources de la civilisation sont à son usage" (quoted in ibid., 201–202). For a general history of *l'Acte additionnel,* see K. Kloocke, "Historique du texte de l'Acte additionnel," in *OCC*, IX: 2, 565–67. Constant explained his position in *Mémoires sur les Cent-Jours.*

141. On the relation between trial by jury and political responsibility, see Constant, *POP (1815),* 247–49.

142. Ibid., 239.

143. Ibid., 228–29.

144. I follow here Jaume's argument in "Le concept de responsabilité des ministres," 232. See also Alain Laquièze, "Le modèle anglais et la responsabilité ministerielle selon le groupe de Coppet," in *Coppet, creuset de l'esprit libéral,* 157–74.

145. Constant, *POP (1815),* 227.

146. Ibid., 229.

147. Ibid., 239.

148. Constant, *Fragments*, 390.

149. This concept is discussed, among others, by Henri Grange in his introduction to Constant, *Fragments*, 44–56; Marcel Gauchet's introduction to Constant, *De la liberté chez les modernes* (Paris: Hachette, 1980), 82–91; Paul Bastid, *Benjamin Constant et sa doctrine*, vol. 2 (Paris: Armand Colin, 1966), 917–27.

150. See Carl Schmitt, *Constitutional Theory* (Durham, NC: Duke University Press, 2008), 312.

151. Thomaz Diniz Guedes, "Le pouvoir neutre et le pouvoir modérateur dans la Constitution brésilienne de 1824," in *Benjamin Constant en l'an 2000: nouveaux regards*, Alain Dubois, Anne Hofmann, and François Rosset, eds. (Paris and Geneva: Honoré Champion and Slatkine, 2000), 245. It is revealing that the constitutional text refers to the equilibrium and harmony of powers. On this topic, see Silvana Mota Barbosa, "L'influence de l'oeuvre de Constant sur la pratique politique brésilienne: présentation d'un inédit" (ibid., 217–34).

152. Among them, Rousseau's *Social Contract*. It will be recalled that in book IV, chapter 5, Rousseau justified the creation of a Tribunate whose main function was to serve as a link between the prince and the people and to block anything that might threaten the liberties of the people. For an excellent account, see Marcel Gauchet, *La Révolution des pouvoirs. La souveraineté, le peuple et la représentation, 1789–1799* (Paris : Gallimard, 1995), 66–77.

153. See ibid., 77, 88–89.

154. Ibid., 117.

155. Ibid., 97.

156. See ibid., 133. Gauchet also analyzes four other important writings on the balance of powers published in 1795 (ibid., 137–58). The first came from the pen of Lamare and was entitled *Équipondérateur*; the second was an anonymous brochure, *De l'équilibre des trois pouvoirs politiques*. The third belonged to Delahaye, the fourth to Roederer.

157. *Les Discours de Sieyès*, Paul Bastid, ed. (Paris: Hachette, 1939), 14–15; see also Bastid, *Sieyès et sa pensée* (Paris: Hachette, 1939), 416–33, 597–605. Gauchet examines Sieyès' proposals in *La Révolution des pouvoirs*, 159–86. See also Pasquale Pasquino, *Sieyès et l'invention de la constitution en France* (Paris: Odille Jacob, 1998), 147–56; Michel Troper, "Sieyès et le jury constitutionnaire," in *Mélanges en l'honneur de Pierre Avril: La République* (Paris: Montchretien, 2001), 265–82. As Troper and Jaume pointed out, among the first to have raised the issue of the control of the constitutionality of laws in France was Kersaint, a deputy to the Convention.

158. See Michel Troper, "Sieyès et le jury constitutionnaire," 272–77.

159. Eschassériaux endorsed the idea of creating within the regular system of power "un élément politique qui, en conjurant les grandes révolutions, maintient tous les pouvoirs d'une constitution dans l'harmonie, sans nuire à leur marche, à leur activité, à leur fonctions naturelles; qui surveille l'exécution des lois comme la censure surveillait les moeurs, qui n'a de puissance que pour ramener toujours à la loi constitutionnelle et n'en a aucune pour la renverser" (quoted in Gauchet, *La Révolution des pouvoirs*, 182).

160. In the opening pages of *Réflexions sur les constitutions*, Constant credited Clermont-Tonnerre with being the first to make this distinction between executive and royal power.

161. See Staël, *DCA*, 162–63. Also Lacchè, "Coppet et la percée de l'Etat libéral

constitutionnel," 153–55; Laquièze, "Le modèle anglais et la responsabilité ministe-rielle selon le groupe de Coppet," 173–74.

162. For more information, see Grange's introductory study to Constant, *Fragments*, 27–30.

163. Constant, *Fragments*, 438.

164. "Il faudrait créer un pouvoir dont l'intérêt fût distinct à la fois de celui du pouvoir législatif et de celui du pouvoir exécutif, et combiné de manière à ce qu'il eût besoin pour lui-même, non de nuire à ces deux rivaux éternels, mais de maintenir entre eux l'équilibre et la concorde" (ibid., 375–76).

165. Ibid., 384.

166. Constant, *Réflexions*, 3.

167. Constant, *POP (1815)*, 189.

168. Ibid., 190.

169. Ibid., 190.

170. Ibid., 190–91.

171. Ibid., 184.

172. Constant, *Fragments*, 451.

173. "Il est donc clair que si tous les freins que nous avons essayés contre les divers pouvoirs sont insufffisants, et si pour empêcher ces pouvoirs de lutter ensemble, sans que rien modére cette lutte, ou y mette un terme, il faut créer une autorite in-dépendante du people, comme du pouvoir exécutif" (ibid., 377). Also: "Le vice de la plupart des constitutions a été de ne pas créer un pouvoir neutre, mais de placer la somme d'autorité dont il doit être investi, tantôt dans les mêmes mains que le pouvoir exécutif, tantôt dans les mêmes mains que le pouvoir législatif" (ibid., 373).

174. "C'est cette lacune qu'il faut remplir; et pour la remplir il faut créer un troisième pouvoir qui soit neutre entre le pouvoir législatif et le pouvoir exécutif" (ibid., 373).

175. "Lorsque les pouvoirs publics se divisent, et sont prêts à se nuire, il faut une autorité neutre qui fasse à leur égard ce que le pouvoir judiciaire fait à l'égard des individus. Le pouvoir préservateur est, pour ainsi dire, le pouvoir judiciaire des au-tres pouvoirs" (ibid., 390).

176. Constant, *POP (1815)*, 187; see also 183–84, 191.

177. Ibid., 189.

178. Constant, *Fragments*, 391. No other punishment may be allowed to follow dismissal by the neutral power.

179. Ibid., 398. The same distinction was made in Constant, *Réflexions*, 2.

180. Constant, *Fragments*, 451.

181. Constant, *POP (1815)*, 184–85.

182. Ibid., 185.

183. Ibid., 237.

184. Ibid., 244; all emphases added. Royal power can restore the three powers to their proper places when their interests clash. This restoring force must be external to all three powers, "so that its action might be necessarily applied whenever it is genuinely needed, so that it may preserve and restore without being hostile" (ibid., 184). See also Schmitt, *Constitutional Theory*, 312.

185. See Constant, *POP (1815)*, 188.

186. Ibid., 187.

187. Constant, *Fragments*, 451–52.

188. Ibid., 399.

189. Ibid., 398.

190. See ibid., 401, 417, 451.

191. For a summary of Constant's constitutional provisions and recommendations, see ibid., 447–48.

192. Constant, *POP (1815)*, 191.

193. Jaume, *L'individu effacé*, 63.

194. *The Marx-Engels Reader*, Robert C. Tucker, ed. (New York: Norton, 1978), 595.

195. Faguet as quoted in Rosenblatt, *Liberal Values*, 247. On Constant's reputation, see also Armstrong Kelly, *The Humane Comedy*, 12–13.

196. Quoted in Rosenblatt, *Liberal Values*, ibid., 244.

197. Ibid., 243.

198. Ibid., 240.

199. Bastid, *Benjamin Constant et sa doctrine*, II: 727. On the complex relation between Constant's political principles and his life, see Wood, *Benjamin Constant,* and Kloocke, *Benjamin Constant. Une biographie intellectuelle.*

200. Bernard Manin, "Les deux libéralismes: la règle et la balance," in *La famille, la loi, l'État* (Paris: Imprimerie Nationale, Centre Georges Pompidou, 1989), 376–77.

201. In Vincent's view, Constant's liberalism was "a balance of competing principles" (*Benjamin Constant and the Birth of French Liberalism*, 89).

202. On this concept (borrowed from Walter Bagehot), see the epilogue.

203. On the connection between moderation and pluralism in Constant, see Vincent, *Benjamin Constant and the Birth of French Liberalism*, 208-211.

204. Constant, *Commentaire sur l'ouvrage de Filangieri*, 45.

205. Ibid., 51.

206. Ibid., 54.

207. Constant, *POP (1806–1810)*, 420.

208. Constant elaborated on this concept in *Des réactions politiques.*

209. Constant, *POP (1806–1810)*, 421.

Epilogue: Moderation, "the silken string. . ."

1. As quoted in Blennerhassett, *Mme de Staël*, vol. III, 488–90.

2. I borrow Camus' phrase from *The Plague* (New York: Modern Library, 1974), 121.

3. For a similar view, see Clor's *On Moderation*. The affinities between moderation, courage, and self-control were highlighted in Aleksandr Solzhenitsyn's speech "We have ceased to see the Purpose: Address to the International Academy of Philosophy, Lichtenstein, September 14, 1993," reprinted in *The Solzhenitsyn Reader*, Edward E. Ericson and Daniel J. Mahoney, eds. (Wilmington, DE: ISI Books, 2006), 591–601.

4. Walter Bagehot, *Physics and Politics* (London: King & Co., 1872), 201.

5. Ibid., 202–203.

6. On "civil" politics, see Edward Shils, *The Virtue of Civility* (Indianapolis, IN: Liberty Fund, 1997), 48–53. On the art of conversation, see Benedetta Craveri, *The Age of Conversation*, xiii.

7. Thomas Fuller's phrase as quoted in Robert C. Calhoon, "On Political Moderation," *Journal of the Historical Society,* VI-2 (2006): 275–95.

8. Montlosier, *Des effets de la violence et de la modération*, 3.

9. Burke, *Further Reflections*, 16.

10. Bobbio, *In Praise of Meekness*, 19–36. In his view, meekness must not be confounded with passivity or submissiveness and is *not* meant to be a political virtue.

11. Hence the difference between our "animated moderation" and the "Parnassian liberalism" described by G. A. Kelly in *The Humane Comedy*, chapter 6. Burke's defense of a bold form of moderation (used as an epigraph of this book) can be found in *Further Reflections*, 16. Also see the following claim of Bastiat: "La modération ne consiste pas à dire qu'on a une demi-conviction, quand on a une conviction entière. Elle consiste à respecter les opinions contraires, à les combattre sans emportement, à ne pas attaquer les personnes, à ne pas provoquer des proscriptions ou des destitutions, à ne pas soulever les ouvriers égarés, à ne pas menacer le gouvernement de l'émeute" (Frédéric Bastiat, *Œuvres Complètes, II* [Paris: Guillemin, 1854], 348).

12. I borrow the concept of the "complex center" from Karol Soltan's essay, "Liberal Conservative Socialism and the Politics of a Complex Center," *The Good Society* 11-1 (2002): 19–22.

13. Burke, *Reflections*, 153.

14. This was Constant's definition of fanaticism in *POP (1806–1810)*, 415.

15. Nancy Rosenblum, *On the Side of Angels: An Appreciation of Parties and Partisanship* (Princeton, NJ: Princeton University Press, 2008), 405.

16. Joseph Hall, *Of Christian Moderation* (London, 1640), 6, as quoted in McCluer Calhoon, *Political Moderation in America's First Two Centuries*, 274.

17. See Martin Luther King Jr.'s sermon with this title in *Strength to Love* (Minneapolis, MN: Fortress Press, 2010), 1–10.

18. See for example, the following claim recently made by David Brooks in a conversation with Gail Collins: "Moderation is a disposition rather than an agenda. It means calibrating your opinions to the strength of the evidence. It means pausing to look at any event from alternate perspectives." (Does Moderation Work?" *The New York Times*, January 12, 2011; http://opinionator.blogs.nytimes.com/2011/01/12/does-moderation-work/)

19. I borrow again Bernard Manin's distinction (see chapter 6 above).

20. Hansen, "The Mixed Constitution versus the Separation of Powers," 509. It is interesting to note that the concept of mixed government also played a key role in Sismondi's analysis of representative government in *Recherches sur les constitutions des peuples libres* and *Études sur les constitutions des peuples libres*. For an analysis of Sismondi's approach on sovereignty and mixed government, see Paulet-Grandguillot, *Libéralisme et démocratie*, 181–213 and Francesca Sofia, "Formes constitutionnelles et organisation de la société chez Sismondi," in *Coppet, creuset de l'esprit libéral*, 54–73.

21. A similar point can be found in Backes, *Political Extremes*, 181–84.

22. For a spirited defense of moderation, see Soltan, "Liberal Conservative Socialism and the Politics of a Complex Center" as well as his "Constitutional Patriotism and Militant Moderation," *International Journal of Constitutional Law* 6-1 (2008): 96–116.

23. Starzinger, *Middlingness*, 16. Starzinger also argued that "middlingness does seem to prove least realistic where it is most relevant, and least relevant where it is most realistic" (ibid., 145). The complexity of the center is analyzed in Rosenblum, *On the Side of Angels*, 369–411.

318 • Notes to Epilogue

24. See, for example, Lezay-Marnésia's critique of Constant in chapter 6 above. For a critique of the center as the mentality of the herd, see Friedrich Nietzsche, *The Will to Power*, trans. Walter Kaufmann (New York: Vintage, 1967), 159. On Nietzsche's critique of moderation, see Clor, *On Moderation*, 90–95.

25. See Eugene Goodheart, "In Defense of Trimming," *Philosophy and Literature* 25 (2001): 49. Goodheart also points out that "A trimmer's party is something of an oxymoron" (ibid.). He adds: "He must choose and act, but his choices and actions have a provisional and skeptical cast" (ibid., 50).

26. Rosenblum, *On the Side of Angels*, 395.

27. See, for example, the following portrait of the trimmer at the end of Burke's *Reflections*: "When the equipoise of the vessel in which he sails, may be endangered by overloading it upon one side, [he] is desirous of carrying the small weight of his reasons to that which may preserve its equipoise" (Burke, *Reflections*, 377).

28. David Brooks and Gail Collins, "Does Moderation Work?"

29. Joseph Hamburger, *Macaulay and the Whig Tradition* (New Haven, CT: Yale University Press, 1976), 188. Also see the brief discussion of Halifax in chapter 1 above.

30. Starzinger, *Middlingness*, 146.

31. Backes, *Political Extremes*, 192. Also see Toscano, *Fanaticism*, 10–12; Joel Olson, "The Freshness of Fanaticism: The Abolitionist Defense of Zealotry," *Perspectives on Politics* 5-4 (2007): 685–701. Sometimes, as Olson remarks, fanaticism is nothing but "the political mobilization of the refusal to compromise" on issues on which there can be no reasonable compromise in the long-run (Olson, "Friends and Enemies, Slaves and Masters: Fanaticism, Wendell Phillips, and the Limits of Democratic Politics," *Journal of Politics* 71-1 [2009]: 93).

32. On this distinction, see Toscano, *Fanaticism*, 8–31.

33. Martin Luther King Jr., "Letter from Birmingham Jail," in *Ideals and Ideologies: A Reader*, 5th edition, Terence Ball and Richard Dagger, eds. (New York: Pearson Longman, 2004), 344–45. One is also reminded of Barry Goldwater's witty aphorism: "Extremism in the pursuit of liberty is no vice, moderation in the pursuit of justice is no virtue."

34. The question remains: are there situations when moderation *is* cowardice and weakness and might promote "rotten" compromises? The answer is, of course, yes. To properly answer these questions one must examine the complex relationship between moderation and compromise. One can be a radical or extremist and still engage in compromises without becoming a moderate or adopting a moderate tone. At the same time, it is true that moderates often (though not always) recommend and justify what they take to be reasonable compromises. For a recent approach, see Avishai Margalit, *Compromises and Rotten Compromises* (Princeton, NJ: Princeton University Press, 2009).

35. Hume, *Essays*, 494; also see chapter 1 above.

36. "Nous sommes dans un temps où il faut se jeter dans un des partis extrêmes si l'on veut réussir. Quiconque voit d'un œil froid les exagérations des partis et les combat, reste délaissé et écrasé au milieu" (Frédéric Bastiat, *Œuvres complètes mises en ordre, revues et annotées d'après les manuscrits de l'auteur*, 2nd ed., [Paris: Guillaumin, 1862], I: 97).

37. Hume, *The History of England*, VI: 533–34.

Index

liberty, 2, 7, 24, 26, 28–29, 31, 33, 37, 40–
41, 47, 51, 53–54, 56, 87, 93, 130, 149,
164, 173, 198, 214, 220, 233, 253n21,
257n50, 297n48, 318n33; distinction between civil and natural, 87; distinction between the liberty of the ancients and the
liberty of the moderns, 178–79, 199, 201;
distinction between political and philosophical, 41; in England, 49, 65–66, 190–
94, 270n135; and moderate governments,
8, 33, 40–42, 45–46, 49–50, 61, 265n41;
and neutral power, 232–33; of the press,
80, 126; social, 41; of speech, 163; of suffrage, 202; suspension of, 59–60, 184,
226. See also freedom
lits de justice, 124, 162
Locke, John, 42, 48, 55, 67, 103, 256n40,
262n5
Louis XVI, 69, 78, 97–98, 113, 115, 124,
133, 162, 275n47, 279n96, 296n45; and
the Royal Council of June 23, 126–27,
296n45
Louis XVIII, 170, 189, 287n49
Louis-Philippe, 306n5
Louvet, Jean-Baptiste, 203, 307n26
love, 158, 198; of country, 40, 44, 59; of
equality, 38, 40; of glory, 295n17; of justice, 107; of liberty, 38, 49, 66, 172–73,
193, 217
lumières, 35, 178, 217, 282n173, 284n206,
301n110, 301n127
luxury, 64, 204, 236
Lycurgus, 23, 135, 257n45

Mably, Gabriel Bonnot de, 278n84
Macaulay, Thomas Babington, 2, 246,
318n29; on Halifax, 260n95
Machiavelli, Niccolò, 1, 15, 26, 269n113,
270n123; and Montesquieu, 55, 59, 63,
269n113, 270n123
Machiavellianism, 187
Madison, James, 15, 67–68
magnanimity, 257n48
Maistre, Joseph de, 190, 201, 216, 278n83,
311n91
majority, 19, 52, 72, 175, 180, 206, 218–19,
255n23; distinction between real and
legal, 175, 210–11, 300n95, 309n71
Mallet du Pan, Jacques, 69, 93, 101,
280n127, 280n130, 281n149, 282n167,
283n178; on moderation, 300n97; on the
monarchiens, 103, 272n4
Malouet, Pierre Victor, 8, 69–71, 79–81, 98,

101–4, 106–8, 156, 241, 273n8, 277n80,
283n189, 283n192; on compromise (and
prudence), 82, 102, 107; on the Declaration of the Rights of Man and of the Citizen, 280n110; on moderation, 107,
282n173, 284n207; on rights, 89,
280n110; on the Tennis Court Oath, 81–
82; on veto, 95
Malouet, Pierre Victor, works of: Mémoires
(2 vols.), 273n8, 278n80, 280n110,
282n173, 283n189
mandates, 82, 100, 290n123
Manent, Pierre, 261n5, 270n131, 271n142
Manichaeism, 9
Manin, Bernard, 235, 263n21, 270n128,
316n200, 317n19
manners, 36, 42, 55, 58–59, 64, 121, 130,
145
Marat, Jean-Paul, 297n48.
Margalit, Avishai, 318n34
Marx, Karl, 4, 16–17, 63, 254n13; on Constant, 234
Mazarin, Cardinal, 161, 201
McCloskey, Deirdre, 16
mean, 5, 19–22, 62, 241, 247, 255n23. See
also middle
meekness, 239, 254n16, 317n10
Meillet, Antoine, 253n22
Meister, Henri, 176, 300n100
mesotes, 18. See also middle; mean
Michelet, Jules, 73, 114, 274n28
middle, 9, 13, 15, 18–19, 21–22, 28, 44, 54,
63–64, 67, 69, 85–86, 100–101, 103, 105,
107, 109, 120–21, 157, 174, 200, 205,
209, 238, 248–49, 255n23, 256n33,
259n71, 309n64; difference between the
mean and the, 21; excluded, 13. See also
mean; mesotes
middle class, 7, 22–24, 256n33
middling mind, 17, 239, 244. See also
middlingness
middlingness, 77, 241, 253n23, 317n23. See
also middling mind
military, 86, 186; dictatorship, 190; government, 177, 184, 215, 267n79
Mirabeau, Honoré Gabriel Riqueti, comte
de, 2, 7, 70, 80, 94–95, 114, 124–25, 129,
156, 270n126, 281n132
mixed government (regime). See government;
mixture
mixture, 22–23, 32, 37–38, 49, 76, 97, 103,
167, 245. See also mixed government
mobocracy, 178